Islamic Law and

This book places context at the core of the Islamic mechanism of *iftā'* to better understand the process of issuing *fatwās* in Muslim and non-Muslim countries, thus highlighting the connection between context and contemporaneity, on one hand, and the adaptable perception of Islamic law, on the other.

The practice of *iftā'* is one of the most important mechanisms of Islamic law that keeps Islamic thought about ethical and legal issues in harmony with the demands, exigencies and developments of time. This book builds upon the existing body of work related to the practice of *iftā'*, but takes the discussion beyond the current debates with the intent of unveiling the interaction between Islamic legal methodologies and different environmental contexts. The book specifically addresses the three institutions (Saudi Arabia's Dār al-Iftā', Turkey's Diyanet and America's FCNA) and their Islamic legal opinions (*fatwās*) in a comparative framework. This demonstrates the existence of complex and diverse ideas around similar issues within contemporary Islamic legal opinions that is further complicated by the influence of international, social, political, cultural and ideological contexts. The book thus unveils a more complicated range of interactive constituents in the process of the practice of *iftā'* and its outputs, *fatwās*.

The work will be of interest to academics and researchers working in the areas of Islamic law, Middle Eastern studies, religion and politics.

Emine Enise Yakar completed her BA in the Faculty of Theology, Ankara University, Turkey, in 2010. She received her MA and PhD from the Institute of Arab and Islamic Studies, the University of Exeter, UK, in 2014 and 2018, respectively. She is specifically interested in the interaction between Islamic legal methodologies and social context to provide insight into the flexible, practicable and applicable dimensions of Islamic law in both Muslim and non-Muslim countries. Currently, she is Assistant Professor of Islamic law at Recep Tayyip Erdogan University, Turkey.

Islamic Law in Context

The Islamic Law in Context series addresses key contemporary issues and theoretical debates related to the Sharia and Islamic law. The series focuses on research into the theory and practice of the law, and draws attention to the ways in which the law is operational within modern State practices. The volumes in this series are written for an international academic audience and are sensitive to the diversity of contexts in which Islamic law is taught and researched across various jurisdictions as well as to the ways it is perceived and applied within general international law.

Series Editor:
Javaid Rehman, Brunel University, UK

Woman's Identity and Rethinking the Hadith
Nimat Hafez Barazangi

Changing God's Law
The dynamics of Middle Eastern family law
Edited by Nadjma Yassari

Applied Family Law in Islamic Courts
Shari'a courts in Gaza
Nahda Shehada

Islamic Law and International Commercial Arbitration
Maria Bhatti

Islamic Law and Society
The Practice of *Iftā'* and Religious Institutions
Emine Enise Yakar

For more information about this series, please visit:
www.routledge.com/Islamic-Law-in-Context/book-series/ISLAMLAWCXT

Islamic Law and Society

The Practice of *Iftā'* and Religious Institutions

Emine Enise Yakar

Routledge
Taylor & Francis Group
LONDON AND NEW YORK

First published 2022
by Routledge
2 Park Square, Milton Park, Abingdon, Oxon OX14 4RN

and by Routledge
605 Third Avenue, New York, NY 10158

Routledge is an imprint of the Taylor & Francis Group, an informa business

British Library Cataloguing-in-Publication Data
A catalogue record for this book is available from the British Library

Library of Congress Cataloging-in-Publication Data
Names: Yakar, Emine Enise, author.
Title: Islamic law and society: the practice of Iftā' and religious institutions/ Emine Enise Yakar.
Description: Abingdon, Oxon; New York, NY: Routledge, 2022. |
Series: Islamic law in context | Includes bibliographical references and index.
Identifiers: LCCN 2021017257 (print) | LCCN 2021017258 (ebook) |
ISBN 9780367480172 (hardback) | ISBN 9781032103808 (paperback) |
ISBN 9781003037637 (ebook)
Subjects: LCSH: Fatwas. | Advisory opinions (Islamic law)–Saudi Arabia. | Advisory opinions (Islamic law)–Turkey. | Advisory opinions (Islamic law)–United States. | Dār al-Iftā' al-'Āmmah (Saudi Arabia) | Turkey. Diyanet İşleri Başkanlığı | Fiqh Council of North America.
Classification: LCC KBP491 .Y25 2022 (print) | LCC KBP491 (ebook) |
DDC 340.5/922–dc23
LC record available at https://lccn.loc.gov/2021017257
LC ebook record available at https://lccn.loc.gov/2021017258

ISBN: 978-0-367-48017-2 (hbk)
ISBN: 978-1-032-10380-8 (pbk)
ISBN: 978-1-003-03763-7 (ebk)

DOI: 10.4324/9781003037637

Typeset in Times New Roman
by Deanta Global Publishing Services, Chennai, India

Contents

Tables

Acknowledgements

I owe a great depth of gratitude to the many people and institutions that have contributed to the completion of this book. Without their promotive assistance and support, this book could not have been completed. My deep appreciation goes to Professor Robert Gleave, whose encouragement and support contributed greatly to the research phase of this book. His continuous guidance and support advanced this work beyond its initial limitations. I am also grateful to my professors and colleagues at the University of Exeter for their guidance, reviews and suggestions during the research process of this book.

In the course of writing this book, I have accumulated a huge debt to various members of the Diyanet, the Dār Al-Iftā and the FCNA. I would like to specifically acknowledge Professor Mehmet Gormez, who was formerly the Diyanet's President, and also Abdurezzak Ateş, Mustafa Bülent Dadaş and Ekrem Keleş. Their continual support and essential assistance in accessing rare materials enabled me to complete the research phase of this book. I am indebted to Doctor Saud Al-Sarhan, who is currently the Secretary-General of the King Faisal Center for Research and Islamic Studies in Riyadh. Without his assistance and the guidance of members at the research centre, this work could not have been completed. I would like to kindly thank the staff of the Dār Al-Iftā, specifically Shaykh 'Abd Allāh ibn Muḥammad al-Muṭlaq and Shaykh 'Abd Allāh ibn 'Abd al-Rahman al-Tuwayjirī who volunteered to be interviewed. I also owe a huge debt to the members of the FCNA, who kindly answered my questions through e-mail, especially Doctor Muzammil Siddiqi and Doctor Zainab al- Alwani.

I record also my gratitude to my warmly supportive publisher, Routledge, Taylor & Francis Group, for its admirable patience and assistance in the formation process of this book. Last but not least, I would like to send my special thanks and appreciation to my sister and colleague, Doctor Sumeyra Yakar, whose vulnerable assistance, kindness and support cannot be expressed in words. My deep gratitude also goes to all my family whose unconditional love and support have been a constant source of inspiration. Words can never repay them, and it is to them with sincerity I dedicate this work.

Preface

The non-binding Islamic legal opinions (*fatwās*) which are issued by Muslim scholars or modern religious institutions in response to questions asked by Muslim individuals represent the most dynamic genre of (past or present) Islamic legal literature. It was traditionally the case that the practice of *iftā'* resided in the individual authority and effort of Muslim scholars. However, after national and international religious institutions were established at the beginning of the twentieth century, this practice has largely become the responsibility of specific bodies tasked with issuing *fatwās*. Saudi Arabia's Dār al-Iftā' (the General Presidency of Scholarly Research and Iftā'), Turkey's Diyanet (the Presidency of Religious Affairs) and the Fiqh Council of North America (FCNA) in America are concrete products of the twentieth century. All three institutions provide an idiosyncratic insight into the practice of *iftā'* and more specifically its development and application within three very different societies. One of the primary concerns of this book therefore is to identify the authority, function and role of the three institutions and their official *fatwās* in their respective environments.

The book compares the *fatwās* issued by the three institutions with the intention of determining which Islamic legal concepts and methodologies are applied within different contexts. In addition, the discussion also assesses how the institutions interpreted the authoritative sources of Islamic law and the process through which they came to arrive at divergent, and even opposed, *fatwās*. The book provides insight into the dynamic interconnection and interaction between Islamic legal methodologies and societal realities by examining these three religious institutions and focusing on their *fatwās*. The active dimension of Islamic law is visibly rendered within the cultural, legal, political and social context in which the *fatwā* mechanism provides new regulations and opinions. The analysis converges upon the proposition that differences of opinion do not derive from the fundamental Islamic legal sources, the Qur'an and Sunna, but can instead be traced back to the different contextual environments in which *fatwās* emerged, thus illustrating the strong connection between contextual elements and Islamic legal methodologies. In analysing *fatwās* issued by the three institutions on similar subjects within a comparative framework, this book seeks to explore the interaction between Islamic legal methodologies and the contexts in which they are applied. The book therefore provides a contextual and methodological analysis of contemporary *fatwās* issued by the three institutions.

After identifying four thematic criteria (the predominant *madhhab* affiliation, social presumptions and cultural practices, legal systems and political structures), the book then proceeds to identify the points at which the three institutions converge and diverge in each of these respects. *Fatwās* are also used to demonstrate how the three institutions employ different Islamic legal concepts and principles when addressing identical issues. Finally, the book seeks to introduce an advanced comparative model for the study of *fatwās* that encompasses institutions (as social and religious interpreters), Islamic legal theories and methodologies (as an essential source of the law) and the social context from which *fatwās* emerge.

Institutionalised *fatwās* are important elemental materials that provide considerable insight into the points at which Islamic law encounters rapidly changing socio-cultural, socio-legal and socio-political circumstances. The book therefore envisages a comparative analysis of the Dār al-Iftā', the Diyanet and the FCNA to investigate the institutionalised *iftā'* practice and to explore differences of opinion in the modern world.

Introduction

Islamic law and its contemporary implementation have been engaged with in a broad range of recent studies. A number of contemporary scholars maintain that in the aftermath of the formative period (from the time of the Prophet until the Abbāsid period), Islamic law has become increasingly immutable and rigid, in large part because it has been cut off from wider economic, political and social developments. Schacht argues:

> Islamic law, which until the early 'Abbāsid period had been adaptable and growing, from then onwards became increasingly rigid and set in its final mould ... Taken as a whole, Islamic law reflects and fits the social and economic conditions of the early 'Abbāsid period but has grown more and more out of touch with later development of state and society.[1]

For Schacht, the transition from a system of *ijtihād* (independent legal reasoning) to one of *taqlīd* (imitation) accounts for the increasing rigidity of Islamic law which prevents it from keeping pace with actual practice.[2] From this perspective, contemporary Islamic law is viewed as a legal system or set of rulings which does not have a sufficiently flexible epistemology which enables it to productively engage with contemporary challenges and needs. Islamic law may be mistakenly represented or delineated as an immutable, inflexible and speculative system of religious thought, fully imbued with idealistic norms.[3] This view

1 Joseph Schacht, *An Introduction to Islamic Law* (The Clarendon Press 1964) 75.

2 ibid 69–71.

3 Some scholars and academicians stringently argue that Islamic law represents a speculative product of Muslim jurists and scholars. According to this view, Islamic law consists utterly of idealistic norms disconnected from the worldly affairs of Muslim societies. One of the prominent authorities in the area of Islamic law, N.J. Coulson, is among these scholars. Arguably, he claims: "The elaboration of *Sharī'a* doctrine was the result of a speculative attempt by pious scholars, working during the first three centuries of Islam, to define the will of Allāh. In self-imposed isolation from practical need and circumstances they produced a comprehensive system of rules, largely in opposition to existing legal practice, which expressed religious ideal." See N.J. Coulson, 'The State and the Individual in Islamic Law' (1957) 6 (1) *The International and Comparative Law Quarterly* 57 <http://www.jstor.org/stable/pdf/755895.pdf?refreqid=excelsior:7b063c56d7ca6c74f4e095f793b995b1> accessed 13 March 2018.

DOI: 10.4324/9781003037637-101

continues to exert influence despite the fact that the *fatwā* mechanism has demonstrated its ability to adjust to the challenges of modernity. The significant impact that the *fatwā* mechanism has had upon the development of Islamic law appears to have been overlooked. The contribution of *fatwās* (Islamic legal interpretations or opinions) to the emergence of a system that is adjusted to the changing needs of Muslim communities is obscured by a line of argument that has a very specific interpretation of Islamic legal doctrines and the feasibility of Islamic law. However, the dynamic character of Islamic law is revealed in the social context. Crucially then, the *fatwā* mechanism arrives at new regulations and opinions by evaluating contextual realities and utilising the legal methodologies of Islamic law. Muhamad observes:

> A *fatwa* declaration is a mechanism that allows new rulings to be introduced into *sharia* law. It is a product of Islamic scholars' (*ulama*) interpretation and adaptation of Qur'anic verses and *hadith* on contemporary issues, rather than an explicit doctrine from the Qur'an and *hadith*.[4]

The *fatwā* mechanism clearly demonstrates that the connection between Islamic law and the authoritative sources (Qur'an and Sunna) has never ceased to exist. This mechanism can also function as a form of *ijtihād* which enables Muslim scholars and religious institutions to apply, utilise and interpret Islamic legal doctrines, methods and sources while pursuing contemporary goals and objectives.

Etymologically, the term "*fatwā*" can be traced back to the Arabic "*fatā*," which means young (also adolescent and juvenile) or opinion.[5] At the level of terminology, "*fatwā*" refers to an Islamic legal interpretation or opinion that is issued by a qualified and authoritative Muslim scholar (generally known as "*muftī*").[6] It is an Islamic legal tool that is used by efficient and proficient Muslim scholars to clarify any issues that arise among Muslims or in Muslim societies. In being applied as a traditional Islamic legal instrument, the practice of *iftā'* can be acknowledged as an ethical legal formulation that is produced during the consultation process between a lay Muslim and a Muslim scholar. To put it more succinctly, the term *fatwā*, when applied in Islamic legal terminology, entails an answer, opinion or interpretation that has been given by authoritative and qualified Muslim scholars in response to questions pertaining to religious affairs or matters that have been presented by Muslims.

4 Nazlida Muhamad, '*Fatwa* Rulings in Islam: A Malaysian Perspective on Their Role in Muslim Consumer Behaviour' in Özlem Sandıkcı and Gillian Rice (eds), *Handbook of Islamic Marketing* (Edward Elgar Publishing 2011) 35.

5 Hans Wehr, *Arabic-English Dictionary* (Milton Cowan ed, 4th edn, Otto Harrassowitz) 696.

6 'Fatwa' in the Oxford Dictionary of Islam, John L. Esposito (eds), Oxford Islamic Studies Online <http://www.oxfordislamicstudies.com/article/opr/t125/e646> accessed 16 March 2018.

The practice of *iftā'* is a process that consists of certain components. Hallaq approaches the practice of *iftā'* and its components through the prism of classical Islamic law. He observes:

> In its basic form, a *fatwā* consists of a question (*su'āl, istiftā'*) addressed to a jurisconsult (*muftī*), together with an answer (*jawāb*) provided by that jurisconsult. When the question is drafted on a piece of paper – as was the general practice – the paper becomes known as *ruq'at al-istiftā'* or *kitāb al-istiftā'*, and once an answer is given on the same sheet of paper, the document becomes known as *ruq'at al-fatwā*.[7]

Within the parameters of this process, the applicant is known as *mustaftī*; the Muslim scholar who answers the question is referred to as *muftī*, the question is termed *istiftā'* while the answer of the Muslim scholar is designated as a *fatwā*. The interlude between the asking of a question and the obtaining of an Islamic legal answer (between *mustaftī* and *muftī*) falls under the heading of the practice of *iftā'*. Every component of this practice has its own specific function. *Istiftā'*, for example, determines the scope of a particular *fatwā* – the *fatwā* is therefore restricted to the issue or matter which is indicated in the *istiftā'*.[8] The *istiftā'* is also a medium that helps to convey new issues which have arisen in a society, which are then conveyed to the *muftī* or religious authorities – in this specific instance, it appears as an informative communication tool that keeps *muftīs* informed of specific exigencies within society. The *muftī* is a qualified authority who conveys the Islamic legal solution to the applicant and his/her activity during the *fatwā* process is a key component of the practice of *iftā'* – this applies because he/she is a scholar capable of exercising *ijtihād* and deriving an Islamic legal opinion from the authoritative sources of Islamic law. During the *iftā'* process, the *mustaftī* both initiates and concludes the interaction: he/she addresses his/her question to a *muftī*, and he/she is ultimately responsible for deciding whether to pursue the *muftī*'s advice. The interaction between the *muftī* and the *mustaftī* can be broadly characterised as a negotiation in which the *mustaftī* presents his/her problem while expending considerable effort in the process of explaining it; meanwhile, the *muftī* commits his/her energy to find a clear and practicable solution.[9] The practice of *iftā'* is a bargain between the two agents, that is, the *muftī* and *mustaftī* find their way in combination. In fulfilling this function, the *fatwā* appears as a compass that

7 Wael B. Hallaq, 'From Fatwās to Furū': Growth and Change in Islamic Substantive Law' (1994) 1 (1) *Islamic Law and Society* 31 <http://www.jstor.org/stable/pdf/3399430.pdf?refreqid=excelsior%3A14bb4b8f98321893630d4f36943c4716> accessed 03 March 2015.

8 Muhammad Khalid, Masud, Brinkley Messick and David S. Powers, *Islamic Legal Interpretation: Muftis and Their Fatwas* (Harvard University Press 1996) 22.

9 Hussein Ali Agrama, 'Ethics, Tradition, Authority: Toward an Anthropology of the Fatwa' (2010) 37 (1) *American Ethnologist* 13 <http://onlinelibrary.wiley.com/doi/10.1111/j.1548-1425.2010.01238.x/epdf> accessed 17 March 2018.

enables Muslim individuals, and in particular lay Muslims, to advance towards a Muslim prototype that has been set out by God.[10]

After attaining a *fatwā*, the questioner has two options which refer to his/her satisfaction with the *fatwā*.[11] If the questioner is content and is mentally and spiritually satisfied with the *fatwā*, he/she ought to follow the *fatwā* outlined by the *muftī*. If this is not the case, he/she should find another Muslim scholar and solicit a *fatwā* as a second answer to his/her question.[12] After obtaining Islamic legal advice from a *muftī*, the questioner is free to choose whether or not to follow the issued *fatwā* – here the *fatwā* presents itself as a non-binding Islamic ruling that is given to the questioner.[13] The religiosity of the individual questioner – whose pious conscience and creed purely seek to know and then obey the intended law of God – is the root principle of obedience to the *fatwā* or the Islamic legal advice issued by a Muslim scholar.

It is likely that the practice of *iftā'* can be traced back to the time of first Muslims who asked direct questions to the Prophet Muḥammad and received answers during his lifetime.[14] It should be noted that the use of the term *istiftā'* and its derivate forms, along with the term *yas'alūnaka* (they ask you), within the Qur'an is not only intended to signify the existence of a *fatwā* prototype; to the same extent, it also demonstrates that the practice of *iftā'* was applied during the time of the Prophet.[15] Hallaq has therefore argued that the Prophet Muḥammad and his Companions were the first practitioners of *iftā'*.[16] The practice was preserved by the Muslim scholars in succeeding generations. In early Islamic history, the process of *iftā'* (formulating a *fatwā*) and the issuance of *fatwā* were practiced by individual and independent Muslim scholars.[17] However, subsequent to the late nineteenth century, this individual and non-governmental legal practice began to be superseded by institutional religious bodies or establishments.[18] Especially during the modern period, many Muslim states have sought to control the mechanism of *fatwā* by instituting national religious organisations that conduct religious affairs and issue *fatwās*. The Muslim world witnessed a rapid proliferation of modern religious institutions which dispense *fatwās*, whose interventions greatly contribute to the dynamism of Islamic law and, to a more limited extent, to the regulation of local and regional practices.

10 ibid 14.
11 Masud, Messick and Powers (n 8) 26.
12 B. Ibrahim, M. Arifin and S.Z. Abd Rashid, 'The Role of *Fatwa* and *Mufti* in Contemporary Muslim Society' (2015) 23 *Pertanika Social Sciences & Humanities* 322.
13 Muhammad Khalid Masud, 'The Significance of *Istiftā'* in the *Fatwā* Discourse' (2009) 48 (3) *Islamic Studies* 358.
14 Masud, Messick and Powers (n 8) 5–6.
15 For a more detailed explanation concerning the existence of the practice of *iftā* during the time of the Prophet and after his demise among the Companions, refer to Masud, Messick and Powers (n 8) 3, 5–8; Hallaq (n 7) 63–65.
16 Hallaq (n 7) 63.
17 Masud, Messick and Powers (n 8) 5, 7–10.
18 ibid 27.

From the twentieth century onwards, the establishment of religious institutions has substantially contributed to the institutionalisation and standardisation of Islamic knowledge. Despite the restrictions imposed on the autonomy of Muslim scholars (*'ulamā'*) by modern states, individual governments have significantly expedited the installation of their own institutions and tasked them with the production of Islamic knowledge. In many cases, this has resulted in the institutionalisation and standardisation of Islamic knowledge and practices, in which the collective resources of the schools of law (*madhhab*s) have been privileged over any particular *madhhab*.[19] In decreasing the comprehensive authority of the schools of law, institutionalisation has given rise to alternative forms of authority within the sphere of Islamic law. Zaman observes:

> The schools of law carry less overarching authority than they did a century ago, even in regions whose inhabitants continue to adhere to them, with the consequence that the 'ulama' whose authority was long tied to the *madhhab*, have been forced to look for alternative loci of authority. These alternatives have assumed many forms, but they are unified by a shared tendency toward a new institutionalisation of authority.[20]

The institutionalisation process established the grounds for the adoption of the collective *fatwā* issuances through organisational bodies, although some individual scholars continued to offer *fatwās* rooted within their own learned authority. More recently, the scope of these institutions has widened to provide forums for collective legal deliberations and explanations of issues pertaining to Islamic law.[21] Their scholarly explanations of the different problems of believers have commanded substantial attention on the grounds that they are believed to indicate a form of collective *fatwā*. Egypt's Dār al-Iftā' (the Egyptian Organisation for Granting Legal Opinions) is a recognised example of institutionalised authority. It was originally established in 1895 with the intention of standardising the issuance of legal opinions and stamping them with an official imprimatur.[22] In 1924, the Turkish Republic founded the Presidency of Religious Affairs (Diyanet), with the intention of drawing upon the political and social potential of religion.[23] Although the Diyanet continues to be subject to various legislative constraints, it has assumed an active role in educating and informing Turkish Muslims about their religion and Islamic law, with collective *fatwās* making an important contribution

19 Muhammad Qasim Zaman, "Ulama" in Gerhard Bowering (ed), *Islamic Political Thought: An Introduction* (Princeton University Press 2015), 259.

20 ibid 259–260.

21 ibid 260.

22 Muhammad Qasim Zaman, *Modern Islamic Thought in a Radical Age: Religious Authority and Internal Criticism* (Cambridge University Press 2012) 93; Zaman, "Ulama" (n 19) 260.

23 Berna Zengin Arslan, 'State and Turkish Secularism: The Case of the Diyanet' in Bryan S. Turner (ed), *The Religious and the Political: A Comparative Sociology of Religion* (Cambridge University Press 2013) 208.

in this respect. Saudi Arabia's Dār al-Iftā' (the General Presidency of Scholarly Research and Iftā'), which was established by a royal decree of King Sa'ūd Ibn 'Abd al-'Azīz Āl Sa'ūd in 1953,[24] is another institution that can assert a claim to collective *fatwās* and *ijtihād.* Asia's *fatwā* boards include Pakistan's Council of Islamic Ideology and Malaysia's Islamic Religious Council (Majlis Agama Islam) and National Fatwa Committee.[25] Similar bodies have also been established in Jordan, Kuwait, Lebanon, Sudan and other countries.

At the international level, the two *fiqh* academies, both of which are sponsored by Saudi Arabia, are also worth mentioning as forums for collective *fatwās* and collective *ijtihād* and have important contributions to make in both respects. The Fiqh Academy of the Muslim World League, whose headquarters is based in Mecca, was established with the intention of bringing together leading Muslim scholars from across the world to examine various legal issues and promulgate Islamic legal decisions upon the basis of their collective deliberation.[26] The International Islamic Fiqh Academy, which was established in 1983, was founded under the auspices of the Organisation of Islamic Conference (OIC) to address challenging issues related to humanity with the intention of providing reliable knowledge in accordance with Islamic law and ethics.[27] More recent institutional innovations include the Fiqh Council of North America (FCNA), which was established in 1986 with the intention of providing legal guidance to the continent's growing number of Muslims,[28] and the European Council for Fatwā and Research (ECFR), which was founded in 1997 to issue collective *fatwās* for problems that European Muslims face.[29]

These institutions embody a wider trend in which religious norms are becoming increasingly standardised, and there is a growing interest in collective *fatwās* and collective *ijtihād* that are practiced by them.[30] Zaman observes:

> While ijtihād has long been viewed as the exercise of an individual jurist's mental faculties and legal acumen to arrive at new rulings on matters not

24 Muhammad al-Atawneh, *Wahhābī Islam Facing the Challenges of Modernity: Dār al-Iftā in the Modern Saudi State* (Brill 2010) 8.

25 For further insight into the collective *fatwā* and collective *fatwā* institutions, see Mohammad Abdalla, 'Do Australian Muslims Need a Mufti? Analyzing the Institution of *Ifta* in the Australian Context' in Nadirsyah Hossen and Richard Mohr (eds), *Law and Religion in Public Life the Contemporary Debate* (Routledge 2011) 219–220; Zaman, *Modern Islamic Thought* (n 22) 92–107; Jakob Skovgaard-Petersen, *Defining Islam for the Egyptian State: Muftis and Fatwas of the Dār al-Iftā* (Brill 1997) 284–286; Masud, Messick and Powers (n 8) 8–15, 26–32.

26 Zaman, *Modern Islamic Thought* (n 22) 93.

27 ibid 93.

28 Yusuf Talal DeLorenzo, 'The Fiqh Councilor of North America' in Yvonne Y. Haddad and John L. Esposito (eds), *Muslims on the Americanization Path?* (Oxford University Press 2000) 69.

29 Alexandre Caeiro, 'Transnational Ulama, European Fatwas, and Islamic Authority: A Case Study of the European Council for Fatwa and Research' in Martin van Bruinessen and Stefano Allievi (eds), *Producing Islamic Knowledge: Transmission and Dissemination in Western Europe* (Routledge 2011) 122, 131.

30 Zaman, "Ulama" (n 19) 260.

> hitherto regulated by the foundational texts, the 20th century has seen increasing initiatives toward making this a collective venture.[31]

During the twentieth century, many Muslim countries formally launched their own religious establishments, with the consequence that the practice of *iftā'* (formulating an Islamic legal interpretation or opinion) became increasingly characterised by the emergence of *fatwā* committees, in which more than one *muftī*, or Muslim scholar, affirm the same *fatwā*. Skovgaard-Petersen has sought to discuss this process of institutionalisation with reference to modern states and their desire to monopolise the production of Islamic knowledge.[32] While the institutionalisation of the practice of *iftā'* has been generally undertaken by modern states, a number of other factors have an impact upon this process. Growing contemporary knowledge and the fact that Muslim scholars lack a general knowledge of the cultural, scientific and social contexts that relate to their fields have also contributed to the institutionalisation of producing Islamic knowledge and issuing *fatwās*.[33] These two factors are perhaps the clearer incentive to the desire to produce feasible, relevant and up-to-date *fatwās* in the modern world. Taking into account the fact that the practice of *iftā'* is a mechanism that applies Islamic law to existing realities, the institutionalisation of this practice may provide Muslim scholars with a scholarly forum in which they can practice collective *ijtihād*. These scholarly forums, which are brought into effect through the institutionalisation of the practice of *iftā'*, assist the issuance of applicable and viable *fatwās* that require the amalgamation of Islamic law and social realities, local customs and scientific/technological developments. It can accordingly be argued that modern Islamic institutions which issue *fatwās* embody the unification of Islamic legal theory and social practices in the modern world and therefore bring out continuity and change in clearer perspective.

The transition from imperialism to nation-states drastically changed the world. The new geopolitical, political, scientific and technological realities belonging to the changing world demand a fresh look at and a revaluation of the authentic texts, the Qur'an and Sunna, and some aspects of the Islamic legal tradition. Modern religious institutions were established in their regional environments in order to engage with these changes and produce applicable, appropriate and consistent *fatwās*. However, it is important to be aware that there are a number of contextual and environmental parameters and elements that implicitly shape the legal thought of Muslim scholars who function in these religious establishments. In his evaluation of the Islamic juristic tradition, Shah points out this when he writes:

31 ibid.

32 Skovgaard-Petersen (n 25) 22.

33 Zulfiqar Ali Shah, *Iftā and Fatwa in the Muslim World and the West* (The International Institute of Islamic Thought 2014) 1. For further insight into the factors that lead to the establishment of institutions that practice collective *iftā'*, see Imad-ad-Dean Ahmad, 'Shuratic *Iftā'*: The Challenge of Fatwa Collectivization' in Zulfiqar Ali Shah (ed), *Iftā and Fatwa in the Muslim World and the West* (The International Institute of Islamic Thought 2014) 33–34.

> But there were problems even with the original juristic tradition which was formulated and fixed during the first three Islamic centuries. There was so much political tumult and social turmoil going on during those years that the jurists' legal outlook and thinking process could not have escaped their surroundings.[34]

Even though Shah focuses upon the legal thought of early Muslim scholars, the particular context of each institution implicitly emerges as influential tacit elements that impact how the authentic texts are understood, interpreted and applied by these religious institutions. The implicit interactive relation between these contextual tacit elements and Islamic legal methodologies deployed by religious institutions is a key component of the book.

With the intention of demonstrating and justifying the connection between the methodologies of Islamic law and social surroundings, the book provides a methodological and contextual analysis of contemporary *fatwās* that have respectively been issued by the Dār al-Iftā' (the General Presidency of Scholarly Research and Iftā') in Saudi Arabia, the Diyanet (the Presidency of Religious Affairs) in Turkey and the FCNA (the Fiqh Council of North America) in America. These three institutions reflect a growing orientation to issue *fatwās* in a manner which enables them to function as a foundation for collective *fatwās* and collective *ijtihād*.

The "collective" character of *fatwās* fosters trusts in the authenticity and reliability of religious knowledge produced by these institutions. Zaman underscores the reliable dimension of collective *fatwās*, and he states:

> Collective *ijtihād* offers the possibility of pooling together the resources of scholars who would supposedly be inadequate on their own but are more credible as a collective.[35]

In common with Zaman, Qaraḍāwī prioritises collective *ijtihād* upon the grounds that it is more authentic and sounder than its individual counterpart. Earnestly, he proceeds to assert that addressing important legal problems, especially those pertaining to public affairs, and providing appropriate Islamic legal solutions for them require Muslim scholars' collective scholarly efforts.[36] In his view, the establishment of an international Islamic scientific council of *'ulamā'* (*majma' ilmī Islāmī*), an autonomous body that is independent of any governmental and political pressures, is an important precondition for the practice of collective *ijtihād*.[37] Those who advocate collective *ijtihād* as a means of determining new

34 Shah (n 33) 2.

35 Zaman, "Ulama" (n 19) 261.

36 Yusuf al-Qaraḍāwī, *Al-Ijtihād al-Mu'āṣir bayna al-Inḍibāṭ wal- Infirāṭ* (Al-Maktab al-Islāmī 1998) 103.

37 ibid 104.

Islamic legal opinions and interpretations in contemporary global societies frequently provide different supporting justifications. A number of scholars claim that this type of *ijtihād* is in harmony with the Qur'anic principle of consultation (*shūrā*)[38] and the practice of the Prophet's Companions. Qaraḍāwī, for instance, refers to specific traditions, such as the Prophet's response to 'Alī Ibn Abī Ṭālib, when he asked what should be done when the Qur'an and Sunna do not provide guidance upon a particular problem. The Prophet counselled 'Alī to consult scholars and other believers conversant with the problem and not to make any decision on his own.[39] Qaraḍāwī also points to several consultations conducted by Abū Bakr and 'Umar Ibn al-Khaṭṭāb, the first two caliphs.[40] As Qaraḍāwī and Zaman observe, the collective character of this type of *ijtihād* further reinforces its authenticity and credibility. Perhaps, the most incentive factor is conceivably based on the realisation that no single scholar is likely to be able to attain all knowledge that is required to resolve the contemporary challenges.[41]

The Dār al-Iftā', the Diyanet and the FCNA all embody the arena of collective *ijtihād* and function as institutionalised venues for the promulgation of *fatwās* in their regional contexts. However, it is first essential to acknowledge the differences within their cultural, legal, political and social environments. The Dār al-Iftā' is a state-dependent institution that has been selected with the intention of examining how the *fatwā* mechanism functions within the Saudi Islamic state and context. Its history can be traced back to the 1950s, when increasing oil revenues precipitated a series of administrative and bureaucratic reforms. The Dār al-Iftā' is the country's pre-eminent religious body that provides advice to the King and also issues official *fatwās* on behalf of the Saudi Government.[42] In 1971, it was restructured by a royal decree of King Fayṣal, and an unprecedented number of Saudi senior scholars were selected to serve in this religious body which operated within the scope of the Saudi state administration.

In Saudi Arabia, Islamic law has an essential and crucial place in state legislation, since the Saudi judicial and constitutional system depends on Islamic law. The Qur'an and Sunna constitute the foundational basis of its constitution. Article

38 This Qur'anic principle is based on the Q. 42: 38 which reads: "And those who have responded to the call of their Lord, and established regular prayer; And who (conduct) their affairs by mutual consultation; Who spend out of what We bestowed on them for living." This verse, motivating Muslims to conduct their affairs through consultation, is the main divine and legal ground for those who put forward the idea of collective *ijtihād*.

39 Al-Qaraḍāwī (n 36) 103.

40 ibid 103–104.

41 Taha Jabir al-Alwani, *Towards a Fiqh for Muslim Minorities: Some Basic Reflections* (Ashur A. Shamis (tr) The International Institute of Islamic Thought 2003) 34–35; Aznan Hasan, 'An Introduction to Collective Ijtihad (Ijtihad Jama'i): Concept and Applications' (2003) 20 (2) *The American Journal of Islamic Sciences* 34–38 <https://i-epistemology.net/v1/attachments/709_Ajiss20-2%20-%20Hasan%20-%20An%20Introduction%20to%20Collective%20Ijtihad.pdf> accessed 01 April 2018; Ahmad (n 33) 34; DeLorenzo (n 28) 68.

42 Al-Atawneh (n 24) 21.

7 of the Basic Regulations for Governance (*al-Niẓām al-Asāsī lil-Ḥukm*) clearly states:

> Government in the Kingdom of Saudi Arabia derives its authority from the Book of God and the Sunna of the Prophet (PBUH), which are the ultimate sources of reference for this Law and the other laws of the State.[43]

Taking into account Saudi Arabia's sharī'a-based legal system, it can be inferred that the Dār al-Iftā' and its *fatwās* play a crucial role within the country's legal and social system. Perhaps to a greater extent than any other country within the Muslim world, the Dār al-Iftā' is closely involved in the State's judicial, legal, political and social procedures – for this reason, its *fatwās* are pre-eminent in the formulation of Saudi Arabia's legal regulations and its cultural and social norms.

The Diyanet, in contrast, functions within an ultra-secular Muslim state. On March 3, 1924, the Caliphate, which had previously provided politico-religious leadership to the Muslim-Sunni community, was abolished, and then the Diyanet was established (on the same day) and tasked with conducting religious services in Turkey.[44] Even after Islam's constitutional status as the state religion was abolished (in 1928) and the principle of secularism was inserted into the Constitution (in 1937), the Diyanet continued, and still continues, to be directly engaged in religious affairs. Despite the incorporation of this religious institution into the State's administrative and institutional structure, secularism has remained a defining feature of the Turkish Republic. For example, Article 2 of the current Constitution (which was put in place in 1982, two years after an attempted military coup) clearly states:

> The Republic of Turkey is a democratic, secular and social state governed by rule of law, within the notion of public peace, national solidarity and justice, respecting human rights, loyal to the nationalism of Atatürk.[45]

The irrevocable status of secularism is very clearly established by Article 4 of the same Constitution ("the characteristics of the Republic in Article 2 … shall not be amended, nor shall their amendment be proposed").[46] However, even within

43 Basic Law of Governance (Article 1) (Royal Embassy of Saudi Arabia, 1 March 1992) <https://www.saudiembassy.net/basic-law-governance> accessed 08 October 2015.

44 Talip Küçükcan, 'Are Muslim Democrats a Threat to Secularism and Freedom of Religion? The Turkish Case' in Allen D. Hertzke (ed), *The Future of Religious Freedom: Global Challenges* (Oxford University Press 2013) 274; Gazi Erdem, 'Religious Services in Turkey: From the Office of Şeyhülislām to the Diyanet' (2008) 98 (2–3) *The Muslim World* 275 <http://onlinelibrary.wiley.com/doi/10.1111/j.1478-1913.2008.00216.x/full> accessed 01 February 2017.

45 The Constitution of Republic of Turkey, 1982 (Article 2) <https://global.tbmm.gov.tr/docs/constitution_en.pdf> accessed 16 September 2016.

46 The Constitution of Republic of Turkey, 1982 (Article 4) <https://global.tbmm.gov.tr/docs/constitution_en.pdf> accessed 16 September 2016.

a state that retains such a strong commitment to secularism, the practice of *iftā'* continues to directly apply to the Muslim segment of the society. The Diyanet's status as a state-dependent religious institution lends a quite different significance to Turkish secularism.

In Turkey, the Diyanet is the official voice of Islam, and it issues *fatwās* under the auspices of the democratic secular system. The transition from emperorship to republicanism changed the socio-cultural and socio-political realities of Turkey, and this system introduced new values that indelibly impacted the Diyanet's *fatwās*. A closer examination of the Diyanet, a state-funded institution of the Republic of Turkey, and its *fatwās* provides considerable insight into how Islamic law is adjusted to Turkish society in an attempt to bridge the gap between religious and secular values. The institution's official *fatwās* are in any case not formulated in a vacuum, as they are adjusted to Turkey's cultural, political and social realities. As a mechanism that conducts the issuance of *fatwās*, the Diyanet is a versatile institution that enables the Muslim community to retain an attachment to Islamic legal rulings and values within a democratic and secular system. A closer engagement with the Diyanet and its *fatwās* may provide considerable insight into how Islamic law retains its relevance for Muslims who live within a secular system.

As for the FCNA, it functions within the North American environment. The origin of this institution traces back to the Religious Affairs Committee that operated under the Muslim Students Association of America and Canada in the early 1960s. After the Muslim Students Association evolved into the Islamic Society of North America (ISNA) in 1980, the Religious Affairs Committee was reconfigured as the Fiqh Council of North America (FCNA) in 1986 and started to function as an Islamic jurisprudence department of the ISNA.[47] Since then, the main mission of the institution has been to provide Islamic legal guidance to the Muslim residents of North America through issuing *fatwās* and research papers and organising seminars and conferences regarding Islamic legal problems that American Muslims face in their daily lives.[48]

The FCNA is a religious institution that applies the concept of Islamic jurisprudence of Muslim minority (*fiqh al-aqalliyyāt*) within the scope of Islamic law, so the analysis of *fatwās* that are issued by this institution casts light upon how to put the concept of *fiqh al-aqalliyyāt* into practice. After the number of emigrant Muslims to non-Muslim countries increased and many of them became residents of non-Muslim countries, the concept of *fiqh al-aqalliyyāt* emerged as an important legal doctrine that was espoused by Muslim scholars to provide minority Muslims with *fatwās* that facilitate their engagement in their new environment,

47 Yvonne Y. Haddad and Jane I. Smith, *The Oxford Handbook of American Islam* (Oxford University Press 2014) 3; Mohamed Nimer, *The North American Muslim Resource Guide: Muslim Community Life in the United States and Canada* (Routledge 2002) 160.

48 Fiqh Council of North America, 'History of the Fiqh Council' <http://fiqhcouncil.org/wp-content/uploads/2018/09/FCNABrochure.pdf> accessed 21 August 2020.

without compromising their Islamic legal responsibilities and duties.[49] Examining the FCNA and its *fatwās* not only provides insight into the implementation of the concept of *fiqh al-aqalliyyāt* within real life but also sets a riveting precedent that demonstrates how a state-independent institution carries out the practice of *iftā'* in a non-Muslim democratic environment.

The Dār al-Iftā', the Diyanet and the FCNA, the main focus of the book, are particularly well-placed to provide institution-based models that demonstrate how the practice of *iftā'* is conducted in the modern world across different Muslim societies. More specifically, the three institutions address different audiences who live in socially, culturally, politically and legally divergent environments. As the sample of the state-dependent institutions, the Dār al-Iftā' and the Diyanet represent two extremes within the Muslim world – the Dār al-Iftā' vigorously functions under an explicitly theocratic monarchy, the Kingdom of Saudi Arabia, while the Diyanet influentially operates under an ultra-secular democratic system, the Republic of Turkey. Contrary to the Dār al-Iftā' and the Diyanet, the FCNA typifies a state-independent institution that voluntarily functions within a democratic non-Muslim environment. The three institutions and their associated *fatwās* help to bring out the interactions between the authoritative texts (Qur'an and Sunna), Islamic legal theories and methodologies that are used by the three institutions to derive *fatwās* from the authoritative sources and the respective social contexts in which the three operate. In simultaneously engaging with *fatwās* as legal discourses and social instruments, the book seeks to identify how Muslim scholars within these institutions tackle the exigencies and challenges of operating within these specific social environments.

The institutions that are examined in this work have received some scholarly engagement. This is especially the case with the Dār al-Iftā', where a substantial array of scholarly studies and literature about it already exists. However, the Diyanet's *fatwās* and the Islamic legal methodologies that it deploys in the process of issuing a *fatwā* have rarely been subject to close attention. As for the FCNA, its *fatwās* have been generally examined within the scope of the concept of *fiqh al-aqalliyyāt*, and there is almost no specific study that presents the institution's organisational structure and engagement with the practice of *iftā'*. In addition, to the best of the author's knowledge, the three institutions have never been directly compared to each other. In making this comparison, the book mainly adopts an analytical and illustrative, rather than exhaustively descriptive, approach. The three countries (Saudi Arabia, Turkey and America) provide important insight into the different functions, positions and status of *fatwās* issued by the three institutions within the national legal systems of the countries and their wider social context. In addition, the administrative, legal, political, social and cultural

49 Abdolmohammad Kazemipu, 'Reckoning with the Minority Status: On Fiqh al-aqalliyyat al-Muslema (Jurispurdence of Muslim Minorities)' in Mario Peucker and Rauf Ceylan (eds), *Muslim Community Organizations in the West: History, Developments and Future Perspectives* (Springer 2017) 13–14; Zaman, "Ulama" (n 19) 259.

attributes of the three countries potentially bring to light additional factors that influence the legal thought of Muslim scholars within the Dār al-Iftā', the Diyanet and the FCNA. Perhaps, the institutions brought together in this book epitomise a fairly broad picture of key trends, tensions and dynamics which surround the issuance of *fatwās* for various audiences living in distinct cultural, social, legal and political environments. This is the main reason why the three institutions have been selected – it is conceived that their *fatwās* and legal justifications align with the attributes of the respective environments and the precise exigencies that these communities encounter. This comparative examination of the *fatwās* provides new insight into the question of how Islamic legal methodologies are engaged to overcome legal problems that have been encountered by different audiences in divergent communities during the twenty-first century.

Researchers in Islamic studies have devoted a considerable amount of time to the understanding of Islamic legal sources, theories and methodologies (*uṣūl al-fiqh*) and analysis of judicial judgments – contemporary *fatwās* have also featured in these analyses, albeit to a lesser extent. Most of these studies tend to focus on written documents from pre-modern archives and some modern *fatwās*. However, these contributions are limited by the fact that they tend to focus upon the forms and procedures of *fatwās* rather than their contents and methodology. Of the studies that examine *fatwās*, few attempt to engage with the interaction between Islamic legal methodologies and social context. In engaging at this point, this book instead attempts to contribute to an improved understanding of the interpretative process and the possibility of legal change in the area of Islamic law.

Several recent works on *fatwās* have captured the attention of academics in both the Muslim world and the West. David S. Powers's ground-breaking study seeks to analyse a complex system of legal decision-making by drawing strongly upon *Kitāb al-Mi'yār*, a voluminous collection of *fatwās* that was compiled by al-Wansharīsī (d. 1508), a fifteenth-century Mālikī scholar.[50] His analysis of the *fatwās* highlights the complex and dynamic interplay between the legal and social values of society. Colin Imber examines the *fatwās* of Ebu's-su'ud (d. 1574), who is widely recognised as the jurist who successfully reconciled Ḥanafī law and Ottoman secular law. This evaluation of Ebu's-su'ud's *fatwās*, which were issued during the time of the Ottoman Empire, provide an overview both of the Ḥanafī legal doctrine and the interrelationship between sacred law (the Ḥanafī school) and secular law (derived from custom and developed through imperial decrees).[51] These two contributions demonstrate the importance of *fatwās* as a source for the study of Muslim legal and socio-cultural history. Brinkley Messick's *Calligraphic State: Textual Domination and History in a Muslim Society* (1993) approaches Yemenite *fatwās* from an anthropological perspective and focuses upon the close

50 David S. Powers, *Law, Society, and Culture in the Maghrib, 1300–1500* (Cambridge University Press 2002) 4.

51 Colin Imber, *Ebu's-su'ud: Islamic Legal Tradition* (Edinburgh University Press 1997) 24.

links between everyday workings of "sharīʿa society" and Yemenite Muslims' understandings of the written and spoken words. *Islamic Legal Interpretation: Muftis and Their Fatwas* (1996), which was compiled and edited by Masud, Messick and Powers, is perhaps the most important collection of *fatwā* studies which offers a comprehensive account of the political and social applications of *fatwās*.

It is something of a surprise to note that few scholars have engaged with the Dār al-Iftā' (literally "the house of *fatwās*"), *fatwās* and *muftīs*. Notable exceptions include Jakob Skovgaard-Petersen's history of the Dār al-Iftā' in Egypt and Muhammad al-Atawneh's engagement with the issuance of *fatwās* by the Dār al-Iftā' in Saudi Arabia, which were respectively published in 1997 and 2010.[52] Skovgaard-Petersen's *Defining Islam for the Egyptian State: Muftis and Fatwas of the Dār al-Iftā* established a valuable precedent for a more analytical approach to the contemporary Muslim legal systems; more specifically, to modern religious institutions in the Muslim world. The book introduces an elaborative analysis of the institution's relationship to Egypt's Islamic political discourse by examining representative samples of *fatwās* in their social and political context. Al-Atawneh's book examines the content and methodology of the *fatwās* of Saudi Arabia's Dār al-Iftā by evaluating the interaction between context and text with the intent of evidencing how the challenges faced by the Dār al-Iftā' are resolved by the *'ulamā'* while applying the Wahhābī interpretations of the sharīʿa to the new circumstance of the late twentieth century.[53] As for the Diyanet in Turkey, there is no detailed study of the Diyanet's *fatwās* or the process through which it issues *fatwās*. Mustafa Bülent Dadaş's recent article ("The Fatwā Policies of the High Board of Religious Affairs") is quite attention-grabbing due to its main subject. The article predominantly analyses *fatwās* issued by the Diyanet with the intention of identifying whether the High Board of Religious Affairs, the Diyanet's highest advisory and decision-making body, follows a specific and systematic procedure during the issuance of a *fatwā*.[54] When it comes to the FCNA, there are a few studies that examine *fatwās* issued by this institution, but these studies focus principally upon the concept of *fiqh al-aqalliyyāt* rather than the FCNA and its associated *fatwās*. However, Nadira Mustapha's thesis ("Islamic Legal Theory and Practice in the North American Context: An Epistemological and Methodological Analysis of the Fiqh Council of North America") deals specifically with the formation of the FCNA as the first Islamic jurisprudential body in North America and seeks to identify its Islamic legal methodology through analysing the *fatwās* issued by the FCNA.[55]

52 Skovgaard-Petersen (n 25); Al-Atawneh (n 24).

53 Al-Atawneh (n 24) XIII, XVII, 35–149.

54 Mustafa Bülent Dadaş, 'Kuruluşundan Günümüze Din İşleri Yüksek Kurulunun Fetva Siyaseti' (2015) 13 (25–26) *Türkiye Araştırmaları Literatür Dergisi* 37–68.

55 Nadira Mustapha, 'Islamic Legal Theory and Practice in the North American Context: An Epistemological and Methodological Analysis of the Fiqh Council of North America' (PhD thesis, McGill University 2013).

At the time of writing, there is no comprehensive comparative work of modern religious institutions and their *fatwās*. Within the literature, it is more usual for these institutions and their *fatwās* to be engaged with on an individual basis. A comparative framework that brings together different religious institutions operating within divergent contexts and that examines their *fatwās* helps in comprehending the interplay between Islamic legal methodologies and different contexts. Within the scope of the book, the Dār al-Iftā' in Saudi Arabia, the Diyanet in Turkey and the FCNA in America are selected to set a precedent for religious institutions that function in different contexts. In this regard, Saudi Arabia, Turkey and America are situated at three antipodal ends: Islamic theocratic monarchy, Muslim secular democracy and non-Muslim secular democracy, respectively. The three countries therefore exemplify the socially, politically, legally and culturally divergent societies. The influence of different contextual parameters and elements upon the practice of *iftā'* that is carried out by the Dār al-Iftā', the Diyanet and the FCNA is analytically examined in a comparative framework with the intent of bringing out the interaction between Islamic legal methodologies and environmental contexts.

Saudi Arabia is a country that uses Islamic law in its legal system, and Islamic legal issues therefore have a crucial bearing upon its governmental and legal system. In this system, the Dār al-Iftā' and its official *fatwās* represent the formal legal position of the state on issues relating to Islamic law. The official *fatwās*, in applying sharī'a in Saudi Arabia, normally assume a complementary role.[56] When the Dār al-Iftā' was established, the Saudi-Wahhābī *'ulamā'* were incorporated into Saudi Arabia's administrative and bureaucratic system. As al-Atawneh observes, this incorporation officially increased their authority and power within the state administrative machinery.[57] It is nonetheless clear that operating within the framework of an Islamic state provides the Dār al-Iftā' with a unique authority and power in several spheres, in particular those relating to legal, religious and social matters. *Fatwās* issued by the institution therefore have a crucial impact upon the Saudi judicial system and even political affairs.

Turkey represents a secular democratic country with its Muslim majority populace. The Turkish state, established upon the remnants of the Ottoman Sultanate, has espoused a secular democratic policy that aimed to cut off the political and legal influences of Islam.[58] In line with this policy, the Diyanet was founded to restrict Islam to only an institution under the auspices of the state within a Muslim majority society. Despite the fact that the influence of Islam upon the legal and political systems was incrementally deactivated, the secularisation of

56 Frank Vogel, 'The Complementarity of Ifta' and Qaḍā': Three Saudi Fatwas on Divorce' in Muhammad Khalid Masud, Brinkley Messick and David S. Powers (eds), *Islamic Legal Interpretation: Muftis and Their Fatwas* (Harvard University Press 1996) 262–269.

57 Al-Atawneh (n 24) 36–37.

58 Mustafa Koçak, 'Islam and National Law in Turkey' in Jan Michiel Otto (ed), *Sharia and National Law: Comparing the Legal Systems of Twelve Islamic Countries* (The American University in Cairo Press 2010) 233, 242.

social life could not be accomplished. The Diyanet has therefore been functioning within a politically secularised and socially Muslim environment. In this regard, the Diyanet, as a religious institution, does not have a clear counterpart in any other Muslim country. The presence of this official religious institution in a secularised country is unique to Turkey. In operating within a secularised environment, the Diyanet's engagement with Islamic legal issues conceivably takes into account a range of considerations which include Islamic legal methodologies and principles and also the political, social and legal structure and values of Turkish society.[59] The Diyanet emerges as an intellectual religious platform which seeks to bridge religious and secular values and which is underpinned by a holistic Islamic legal view that conjoins Islamic ethical values and legal principles.

America is a democratic secular country that has a wide range of diverse ethnicities and religions. The diversity in America forms a pluralistic social mosaic in which the Christian tradition has been predominant. Despite the dominance of the Christian tradition, freedom of religion and speech has been ensured by the US Constitution for every citizen.[60] This freedom of religion and speech attracted, and still attracts, many Muslims when they were choosing a country to which to emigrate.[61] Over time, the number of Muslims emigrating to this land increased and took the shape of a religious minority community that has become part of the pluralistic socio-religious American mosaic. Since the Muslim immigrants turned into a religious minority community, they have organised some institutional structures that enable them to participate in communal life in practicing their faith. The FCNA is one of these institutions that was established to provide Islamic legal information for American Muslims to overcome Islamic legal dilemmas that they encountered. The reality of Muslim existence in the American context has impelled the FCNA to develop a civilisational dialogue between the Islamic culture and American culture. The scholars functioning within this institution therefore espouse a positive integration methodology that helps them to provide *fatwās* in order to fulfil these American Muslims' roles both as good Muslims and as good citizens. *Fatwās* issued by the institution reflect the scholars' efforts that seek to establish an equation of identities (Muslim and American).

The society and state in which the Dār al-Iftā' operates diverge substantially from the framing context of the Diyanet and the FCNA. The Dār al-Iftā' works in a theocratic monarchical state and appeals to a society that affiliates

59 Emir Kaya, 'Balancing Interlegality Through Realist Altruism: Diyanet Mediation in Turkey' (PhD thesis, University of London 2011) 18.

60 The Religion Clauses of the First Amendment to the US Constitution states: "Congress shall make no Law respecting an establishment of religion, or prohibiting the free exercise thereof; or abridging the freedom of speech, or of the press; or the right of the people peaceably to assemble, and to petition the Government for a redress of grievances." See the Constitution of the United States, 'First Amendment' <https://constitution.congress.gov/constitution/amendment-1/> accessed 15 February 2021.

61 Khalid Duran, 'Demographic Characteristics of the American Muslim Community' (1997) 36 (1) *Islamic Studies* 57.

predominantly with the Ḥanbalī school while the Diyanet and the FCNA operate under the secular democratic state. Despite the fact that both the Diyanet and the FCNA have several similar characteristics in common in terms of functioning within secular democratic states, the Diyanet operates within a Muslim majority society that adheres principally to the Ḥanafī school while the FCNA functions within a non-Muslim society and appeals to Muslims that demonstrate diversity in their school affiliation. In terms of being a state-dependent institution, the Dār al-Iftā' and the Diyanet share similar aspects while the FCNA voluntarily functions as a state-independent institution. The aspect of being a state-dependent institution brings both the Dār al-Iftā' and the Diyanet close to their governments when they evaluate any issue related to politics. Conversely, the FCNA displays a more independent approach while issuing a *fatwā* regarding politics. All these contextual factors find their reflections in *fatwās* issued by the three institutions, so the practice of *iftā'* in all the three instances is accordingly defined by different aims, dynamics and impacts.

In comparing the three institutions, the book does not seek to determine the legal sustainability or validity of *fatwās*. Instead, it investigates the contextual and environmental factors that influence the Islamic legal methodologies adopted by the three institutions. In undertaking this investigation, the book examines *fatwās* issued by the institutions from a contextual and methodological perspective. The methodological evaluation reveals the juristic evidence and Islamic legal methodologies that establish the basis of argument in the examined *fatwās*; the contextual evaluation instead attempts to unravel the interpenetrating interplay between these Islamic legal methodologies that are applied in the *fatwās* and the contextual influences that shape the legal thinking of Muslim scholars in the three institutions.

The scope of the book (the Dār al-Iftā', the Diyanet and the FCNA, along with their legal products (mainly *fatwās*)) provides important insights into how the practice of *iftā'* has undergone important shifts in modern times. In the contemporary world, this practice started to become part of the state's political, legal or religious affairs in many Muslim countries, that is, it is no longer a matter for an individual *muftī* (Muslim scholar or jurisconsult), as it was before. It was previously the case that *muftīs* would pronounce *fatwās* in the absence of ties to the political authorities.[62] Independence from the state was therefore a defining attribute of previous *muftīs*. However, the individualised *iftā'* process began to be collectivised and institutionalised at the beginning of the twentieth century in many Muslim countries.[63] All three, the Dār al-Iftā', the Diyanet and the FCNA, are products of the twentieth century and are therefore linked to a wider context in which many Muslim and non-Muslim countries experienced bureaucratisation,

62 Masud, Messick and Powers (n 8) 3.

63 Skovgaard-Petersen (n 25) 21–22; Al-Atawneh (n 24) 6–7; Nico J.G. Kaptein, 'The Voice of the *'Ulamā'*: *Fatwas* and Religious Authority' (2004) 49 (125) *Archives de Sciences Sociales des Religions* 120 <http://www.jstor.org/stable/30119298> accessed 12 March 2018.

institutionalisation and modernisation in their economic, educational, legal and social fields. Since being established, the three institutions have actively issued *fatwās* with the intention of responding to religious questions directed by Muslims.

Methodology and structure

The study of modern Islamic religious institutions and the analysis of their *fatwās* require the application of varied methodologies at the same time. In the first instance, the historical descriptive methodology is largely used to describe and explain religious institutions along with their development within specific environments over time. In order to better address the development and functions of religious institutions in their regional settings, this method is employed in the book – it assumes a particularly prominent role in Chapter 1 (which traces the historical background of the Dār al-Iftā from the inception of the Saudi-Wahhābī alliance until 2015), Chapter 2 (which provides a detailed history of the Diyanet by mainly focusing upon the constitutional and legal regulations that establish the institution's administrative and organisational structure) and, additionally, Chapter 3 (which presents the historical development and organisational structure of the FCNA by referring to the concept of *fiqh al-aqalliyyāt*).

Fatwās are important religio-legal texts which provide a comprehensive understanding of the interrelationship between law and society. Scholars have recently become increasingly aware that the analysis of religious texts requires the application of multiple approaches in order to answer a particular question. Islamic legal texts, including *fatwās*, are multi-dimensional and multi-textured documents and should therefore be approached from multiple angles as this enables a fuller exploration of the interconnection of Islamic legal methodologies and social contexts. Contextual analysis and legal-hermeneutical analysis provide the second and third approaches that are largely applied in the analysis of *fatwās*. In acknowledging that the *fatwās* examined in the book are Islamic legal texts, both approaches are consciously applied in order to examine the interaction between legal methodologies and social contexts. The actual analysis of *fatwās* occurs across two levels. Firstly, analysis of the *fatwās* seeks to analyse their utilisation of Islamic legal sources, methodologies and theories (*uṣūl al-fiqh*) by undertaking a legal-hermeneutical evaluation of each *fatwā*. This legal-hermeneutical approach clarifies how *uṣūl al-fiqh* are used during the formulation of *fatwās*, and therefore implicitly seeks to answer the question of whether they are still applicable to the challenges which confront Muslims in the contemporary period. When evaluating the *fatwās* from a methodological perspective, Islamic legal theories and methodologies are systematically applied as a framework of reference. In the second instance, the social context is engaged in order to provide insight into the complex and dynamic interaction between *fatwās* and society. In each case, it is demonstrated how legal thought and society influence and shape each other. The analysis of social context helps to provide insight into a number of socio-cultural, socio-legal and socio-political factors which have influenced the *fatwās* issued by the three institutions – accordingly emphasis is mainly placed upon the textual interpretation of the examined *fatwās* and the contextual analysis of each *fatwā*.

In addition to historical descriptive, legal-hermeneutical and contextual analyses, a comparative methodology is used to make the influence of social context upon the practice of *iftā'* more explicit. In referring to the Dār al-Iftā', the Diyanet and the FCNA, this book is guided by the insight that the three institutions operate in fundamentally different societies (the Dār al-Iftā' operates under an extremely Islamic country, Saudi Arabia, while the Diyanet works in an ultra-secular Muslim country, Turkey, and the FCNA functions in a secular non-Muslim country, America). This allows for a comparison of how the practice of *iftā'* is implemented by the three institutions in these different societies; of what the role of *fatwās* is in these societies; and of to what extent the different social, cultural and legal environments affect the *fatwās* produced by the three institutions, along with the Islamic legal methodologies they follow.

As would be expected, it is necessary to set out specific criteria and points in order to compare the three institutions as the comparative possibilities are endless. In expanding from the aforementioned questions, four thematic areas have been identified in order to compare the three institutions. These are:

1. The interaction between the mainstream *madhhab* affiliation of society and Islamic legal methodologies, principles and theories adopted by the Dār al-Iftā', the Diyanet and the FCNA,
2. The influence of the cultural practices (or customary aspects) and social values of the three societies upon the issued *fatwās*,
3. The effect of the legal systems upon the function of *fatwā* in Saudi, Turkish and American societies,
4. The reflection of the political systems of the three countries within the issued *fatwās*.

The themes of this comparative analysis uncover the cultural, legal, political and social dynamics that underpin the relationship between the three institutions and their environments. In addition, they also provide insight into the contextual and textual components of the *fatwās* issued by the three institutions. A number of factors contribute to the formation of a *fatwā*, but the contextual and textual components are the main constitutive elements that combine Islamic legal methodologies and social realities in any given instance. In adopting an analytical and comparative method, the book demonstrates the interaction between the main constitutive elements of *fatwās* that have been produced by the three institutions within the respective societies. Textual legal analysis is also used as the main methodological tool which brings together relevant literatures with the intention of contextualising them. The advantage of the method is that it demonstrates the interactions and tensions between the authoritative texts and the intellectual, interpretative and legal communities in which these institutions function.

The book consists of five chapters. Chapter 1 examines Saudi Arabia's Dār al-Iftā', one of the most widely recognised institutions in the Islamic world. This chapter mainly focuses upon its history, and past and present products. It also mainly approaches the Dār al-Iftā' from two different angles: (1) its creation, environment (socio-legal and socio-political), functions and power structure; (2) its *fatwā* issuance procedure and *fatwās*. The practice of *iftā'* is discussed with reference to the pre-institutionalised period of the Saudi-Wahhābī *'ulamā'* (1744–1953), the institutionalisation of the Saudi-Wahhābī *'ulamā'* (1953–1971) and the reconfiguration of the Dār al-Iftā' (1971–1993) – each stage corresponds to the historical development of the practice of *iftā'* within Saudi Arabia. The socio-cultural, socio-legal and socio-political environment of the institution is emphasised to as great an extent as possible in order to demonstrate its influence upon the Dār al-Iftā' and its *fatwās*. The chapter places particular emphasis upon the authority and performance of the Dār al-Iftā', the institution's *fatwā* issuance procedure and the institution's symbiotic relationship with the Saudi Government.

Chapter 2 assesses Turkey's Diyanet from a historical perspective and outlines the purposes which have underpinned its creation, functions and power structure. Its historical development is divided into four periods. Each period reflects how political attitudes towards the institution changed – significant developments that influenced the institution's administrative and organisational structure during each period are highlighted and set out in more detail. In presenting the history of the Diyanet, the chapter sketches a general background by referencing political and socio-religious perspectives. The analysis of political background sets out the environment within which official legislation and regulations pertaining to the Diyanet have developed. The discussion of the Diyanet-related state laws and regulations both clarifies its administrative and organisational structure and also demonstrates how its activities have been impeded by the democratic secular state. The chapter then proceeds to delineate Turkey's religious and social structure, with the intention of demonstrating how the institution mediates between religion, society and state. In engaging at these points, the chapter sets out the wider context which the official *fatwās* were issued. The *fatwās* are then analysed in order to bring out the nebulous interaction between the Islamic legal methodologies applied in the examined *fatwās* and the secular democratic context of Turkish society. The procedure that this institution follows in issuing *fatwās* is then explained in order to demonstrate how it provides jurist-consultation to Muslims living in Turkey by technically formulating its *fatwās* in a collective manner within the scope of its own organisational structure.

Chapter 3 presents the historical developments and organisational structure of the FCNA with the intent of demonstrating the trajectory of Islamic law upon the institutional basis in America. Some analytical examinations of the *fatwās* are also incorporated into the chapter with the intent of ascertaining the Islamic legal methodology that is espoused by the FCNA during the process of issuing a *fatwā*. In this regard, the concept of *fiqh al-aqalliyyāt* is identified as an influential legal methodology when the institution engages with complex problems to issue a *fatwā*, so this concept is explained to clarify how it is put into practice by the FCNA. The chapter also places particular emphasis upon the American context with the intent of displaying the social, political, legal and cultural elements of this society upon the *fatwās* issued by the FCNA. While outlining the specific context of American Muslims, their dual identity (American and Muslim) emerges as one of the precise factors that the FCNA takes into consideration. The issues that confront American Muslims on account of their dual identity also reflect the pressure of contextual factors upon the lives of Muslims resident in America. This chapter sets out the analyses of *fatwās* regarding citizenship, integration and loyalty in order to display how the FCNA brings solutions to issues that trace back to the dual identity of American Muslims.

Chapters 4 and 5 compare the Dār al-Iftā', the Diyanet and the FCNA from different perspectives and elaborate each point with reference to the specific *fatwās* that the three institutions have issued on the same or similar issues. The examined *fatwās* provide insight into the contextual factors which influence the practice of *iftā'*, the manner in which the institutions interpret the authoritative texts and the functions of the *fatwā* within surrounding societies. A closer comparison is then made in parallel with the first three chapters, so direct references are made to the Islamic legal methodologies and procedures that are espoused by the three institutions, the contextual and cultural structures which frame the three institutions and the legal and political system that operates within the three countries. Chapter 4 specifically examines the influence of the predominant *madhhab* affiliation within the three societies upon the Islamic legal methodologies and theories adopted by the three institutions. It also evidences the reflection of cultural values and social perceptions upon the *fatwās* issued by the three institutions while most particularly engaging with the *fatwās* related to the relationship between Muslims and non-Muslims.

As for Chapter 5, it provides a comparative analysis that engages with the influence of the legal and political systems upon the practice of *iftā'* conducted by the Dār al-Iftā', the Diyanet and the FCNA. In the first instance, the influence of the legal systems of the three countries is thoroughly addressed to identify the role, authority and jurisdiction of the three institutions. Subsequently some *fatwās* issued by the Dār al-Iftā' are examined to allude to their transformation potentiality into royal decrees within the Islamic legal system of Saudi Arabia. Conversely, the secular legal system of Turkey and America induces the Diyanet and the FCNA to adopt a reconciliatory, or hybridising, approach. Some *fatwās* issued by the Diyanet and the FCNA are therefore also subjected to a variety of critical analyses in order to demonstrate their efforts that intend to reconcile Islamic legal norms and secular legal regulations. In the second instance, the political systems under which the three institutions operate are examined to demonstrate how the three institutions embark on different Islamic legal methodologies and principles with the intention of providing legal legitimisation to their countries' government systems. The separate political systems influence the manner in which the three institutions interpret the authoritative texts, so a legal-hermeneutical analysis is employed by focusing upon the Islamic legal methodological framework of the *fatwās* related to politics, government form and loyalty issued by the three institutions. The purpose of this analysis is to determine the extent to which differences in these *fatwās* can be linked to the interaction between the political contexts of the three institutions and the hermeneutical principles and Islamic legal methodologies applied by the three.

The study of the *fatwā* mechanism builds upon the scholarly works of the Dār al-Iftā', the Diyanet and the FCNA. It evaluates the *fatwās* issued by these institutions with reference to their formative legal methodology and the surrounding cultural, environmental, legal, political and social contexts. The former contributes to the understanding of *uṣūl al-fiqh* (Islamic legal theories and methodologies) and the latter to the comprehension of *fiqh* (Islamic jurisprudence). At a practical level, this analysis is focused upon the questions of how these modern religious institutions deal with the challenges of life and which contextual factors have influenced their *fatwās* during the modern period. The book engages with the Dār al-Iftā', the Diyanet and the FCNA from their establishment and extends up to 2015 – accordingly recent changes and developments within administrative arrangements, legal regulations and organisational structures remain beyond its scope. The *fatwās* that are engaged with in this book are generally selected from the Islamic legal decisions, resolutions, rulings and statements that were issued by the three institutions between 1970 and 2020. On rare occasions, reference is made to *fatwās* promulgated before 1970, but *fatwās* issued after 2020 fall beyond the scope of this study.

Disclaimer

The book is not normative. It does not seek to place a value judgement on the *fatwās* issued by the three religious institutions and nor does it seek to identify whether *fatwās* are "right" or "wrong." In evaluating the Islamic legal approaches, methodologies and theories applied by the three institutions, this book does not also seek to ascertain the authenticity, soundness or strength of these methods and theories; rather it is instead concerned with identifying how methods and theories applied by the three institutions are influenced by, and related to, their environments.

1 General Presidency of Scholarly Research and *Iftā'*

Islam is deeply embedded within Saudi Arabia's political settlement, and Islamic law (sharī'a) is the main foundation of its legal system.[1] Because power is rooted within an alliance between *'ulamā'* (religious scholars) and *'umarā'* (political leaders or the Saudi dynasty), the Saudi state combines religious and dynastic elements. Bureaucratisation, institutionalisation and modernisation, which were each sparked by the discovery of oil, have added a further layer of complexity to the relationship between the modern Saudi state and religion, and interactions between religion and society.[2] While the institutionalisation of the *'ulamā'* has undoubtedly heightened their dependency upon the Saudi Government, it is more likely that a symbiotic relationship conjoins the dynasty and *'ulamā'* in contemporary Saudi Arabia. The official religious institution puts in place the basis of this symbiotic relationship and bestows ideological and religious legitimacy upon the state.

The institutionalisation and modernisation process within Saudi Arabia has instituted an arrangement in which the official religious establishment has begun to be represented by the General Presidency of Scholarly Research and Iftā' (*al-Ri'āsa al-'Āmma lil-Buḥūth al-Ilmiyya wal-Iftā'*; henceforth: Dār al-Iftā'). This is an official entity whose *fatwās* and religious erudition have underpinned the Saudi legal system and social life since its establishment. The Dār al-Iftā' stands at the confluence point of the Saudi legal system, politics and society. The history of the Dār al-Iftā' is superimposed upon sustained interactions between the Dār al-Iftā' (the Saudi *'ulamā'*) and the Saudi dynasty. For this reason, the institutional history, religious predisposition and structure of the Dār al-Iftā' provide an insight into its socio-legal, socio-political and socio-religious positioning within the Saudi state.

1 Royal Decree A/90, 1 March 1992. See Basic Law of Governance (Article 1) (Royal Embassy of Saudi Arabia, 1 March 1992) <https://www.saudiembassy.net/basic-law-governance> accessed 08 October 2015.

2 Ayman al-Yassini, *Religion and State in the Kingdom of Saudi Arabia* (Westview Press 1985) 20, 32, 42–43, 59, 98–105, 109, 130.

DOI: 10.4324/9781003037637-1

This chapter addresses itself to the question of whether the Dār al-Iftā' implements a consistent, legitimate and coherent Islamic legal methodology within the Saudi state. It also asks a number of additional questions with the intention of bringing out the interaction between the Islamic legal methodologies adopted by the Dār al-Iftā' and the Saudi social context. These questions relate to the role of the Dār al-Iftā' and *fatwās* within the Saudi legal system, the independence of the Dār al-Iftā' from the Saudi dynasty during the issuance of a *fatwā* and the institution's engagement with Islamic legal challenges encountered by Muslims. A closer engagement with these questions provides insight into the interaction between the Dār al-Iftā' and the Saudi Government (or the King), along with the relationship between the Dār al-Iftā's Islamic legal methodologies and the social context.

This chapter is divided into three subsections. A brief history of the Dār al-Iftā' in Saudi Arabia brings out shifts within the relationship between Saudi *'ulamā'* and *'umarā'*. This demonstrates how the authority and power of the Dār al-Iftā' within the Saudi legal system, society and state have gradually reduced. Attention then turns to the institution's organisational structure. This is an essential contribution as it provides insight into the continued salience of *fatwās* within the law-making process. The discussion then engages with the process through which the institution issues a *fatwā*. In general terms, this chapter engages the Islamic legal understanding of the Dār al-Iftā. It also provides insight into the role of the institution and its *fatwās* in Saudi society, along with the jurisprudential system and social context of Saudi Arabia.

The formation of the General Presidency of Scholarly Research and *Iftā'* in Saudi Arabia

The historical alliance of 1744 between Shaykh Muḥammad ibn 'Abd al-Wahhāb, the founder of the Wahhābī movement, and Muḥammad ibn Sa'ūd, the predecessor of the Saudi dynasty, established the basis for the formation of the first Saudi state.[3] This alliance has since then remained intact. 'Abd al-Wahhāb's mission was sustained by his descendants, who are known as the Āl al-Shaykh family, and their authorisation as the Grand Muftī was handed down from father to son.[4] In furthering the Saudi dynasty, the Āl al-Shaykh family have actively participated in the practice of *iftā'* alongside other eminent *muftīs*, most of whom were

3 Al-Yassini (n 2) 25; Guido Steinberg, 'The Wahhabiya, Saudi Arabia and the Salafist Movement' in Frank Peter and Rafael Ortega (eds), *Islamic Movements of Europe: Public Religion and Islamophobia in the Modern World* (I.B. Tauris & Co. Ltd 2014) 38; John S. Habib, 'Wahhabi Origins of Contemporary Saudi State' in Mohammed Ayoop and Hasan Kosebalaban (eds) *Religion and Politics in Saudi Arabia: Wahhabism and the State* (Lynne Rienner Publishers 2009) 57–58.

4 Muhammad al-Atawneh, *Wahhābī Islam Facing the Challenges of Modernity: Dār al-Iftā in the Modern Saudi State* (Brill 2010) 42–47.

educated or trained by members of the Āl al-Shaykh family.[5] Although non-Āl al-Shaykh *'ulamā'* were included in the mutual interdependence between the Saudi dynasty and *'ulamā'*, the Āl al-Shaykh family maintained a historical monopoly over the highest religious posts within the state for a considerable period of time.[6] However, there has been a noticeable decline in the number of *'ulamā'* belonging to the family of Āl al-Shaykh since the 1940s.[7] Al-Yassini and al-Atawneh suggest that one possible reason for this decline is the desire of the Saud Government to weaken the monopoly and power of the Āl al-Shaykh family over religious discourses – this would be achieved by opening up the closed circle to less prominent families.[8] Shaykh 'Abd al-'Azīz ibn Bāz (d. 1999), for instance, was from outside this religious nobility, and yet ascended to the position of the highest religious authority (the Grand Muftī), a position he occupied until his death in Saudi Arabia. His ascent epitomises the opening up of this closed religious circle and the breakdown of the Āl al-Shaykh family's monopoly upon the religious establishment.

At the beginning of the establishment of the first Saudi state, the Āl al-Shaykh family were merely the class of the *'ulamā'* who had formed an alliance with Muḥammad ibn Sa'ūd and who espoused the Wahhābī religious ideology. The religious sphere was reserved for 'Abd al-Wahhāb and his descendants (the family of Āl al-Shaykh) – however, the Āl al-Shaykh family's privileged position was increasingly challenged once the official religious institution was established.[9] When Ibn Bāz was designated as the Grand Muftī, the position of privilege and its associated religious power most likely transferred to the official *'ulamā'*. Like the *'ulamā'* exclusively deriving from the Āl al-Shaykh family, the official *'ulamā'* would have been concerned with sustaining the mutual alliance and interdependence between *'ulamā'* and *'umarā'* within the wider context of the modern Saudi state. It is important to acknowledge this mutual dependence of *'ulamā'* and *'umarā'* because it continues to influence the interaction of religion and politics and provides considerable insight into the Saudi–Wahhābī interaction and their mutual co-existence as semi-autonomous bodies within contemporary Saudi Arabia. Al-Rasheed affirms this when she notes that: "in the twenty-first century, Wahhabiyya [official *'ulamā'*] continues to support the power it created and defended. In its official version, Wahhabiyya is the discourse of power legitimization."[10] The interdependency between the *'ulamā'* and Saudi ruling power, and the authority and legitimacy which derive from this interaction establish them as the principal agents charged with determining and controlling the

5 Al-Yassini (n 2) 44–48; Al-Atawneh, *Wahhābī Islam* (n 4) 5, 29; Madawi al-Rasheed, *Contesting the Saudi State: Islamic Voices from a New Generation* (Cambridge University Press 2007) 28–33.

6 Al-Atawneh, *Wahhābī Islam* (n 4) 11–12.

7 Al-Rasheed (n 5) 28–33; Al-Yassini (n 2) 71.

8 Al-Yassini (n 2) 71–72; Al-Atawneh, *Wahhābī Islam* (n 4) 29.

9 Al-Yassini (n 2) 42–43, 71–72.

10 Al-Rasheed (n 5) 4.

interpretation of Islamic legal sources and the content of legal regulations that govern the life of Saudi society. However, different circumstances and contexts have conceivably impacted upon their authority and legitimate scope of intervention.[11]

In Saudi Arabia, the established working relationship between *'ulamā'* and *'umarā'* at one point refers to the fundamental role of *fatwās*. This developed relationship fused politics and religion and instituted a comprehensive system of government that exerts control over Saudi political, public, religious and social life. The working agreement between *'ulamā'* and *'umarā'* established the practice of *iftā'* as a mechanism that formulises legal, moral and social codes. Because 'Abd al-Wahhāb's authority was as persuasive and dominant as that of the political leaders (Muḥammad ibn Sa'ūd and his son, 'Abd al-'Azīz Ibn Sa'ūd), his *fatwās* exerted an important influence over both socio-cultural norms and legal practice during the period 1745–1818.[12] These *fatwās* were usually implemented by the Committee for Commanding Right and Forbidding Wrong (*Hay'at al-Amr bil Ma'rūf wa al-Nahyī 'an al-Munkar*, whose members were selected by the Shaykh himself), and they functioned as an intermediary mechanism which consolidated the relationship between religion and politics.[13] During this period, the legitimacy of political power mainly derived from the *'ulamā'*, and the authority and prestige of the *'ulamā'* generally originated within the Saud dynasty's support. Al-Rasheed observes how religious indoctrination during this period provided a model of political subservience by producing "acquiescent" and "domesticated" subjects.[14] Following on from this observation, it may justifiably be asserted that these *fatwās* were consciously drawn upon in order to instil political compliance and loyalty to the Saudi state and political authority.

When King 'Abd al-'Azīz ibn Sa'ūd (r. 1932–1953) declared Saudi Arabia to be a unified Kingdom in 1932, there was not a noticeable impact upon the pre-existing traditional religious structure, which was grounded within the relationship between *'ulamā'* and *'umarā'*. It was actually the discovery of oil in 1937 that had a much more substantial impact upon the country's economic, religious, political and social development.[15] Economic prosperity necessitated the introduction of modern administrative systems. The institutional development of the state had a strong impact upon religious organisations and structures, and particularly upon the practice of *iftā'*. Mouline acknowledges this in noting that the religious space was, along with the petroleum industry, one of the first social sectors to adopt

11 Tobi Craig Jones, 'Religious Revivalism and Its Challenge to the Saudi Regime' in Mohammed Ayoop and Hasan Kosebalaban (eds), *Religion and Politics in Saudi Arabia: Wahhabism and the State* (Lynne Rienner Publishers 2009) 110–111.

12 Emine Enise Yakar and Sumeyra Yakar, 'The Symbolic Relationship between *'Ulamā'* and *'Umarā'* in Contemporary Saudi Arabia' (2021) 13 (1) *Ortadoğu Etütleri* 26; Al-Atawneh, *Wahhābī Islam* (n 4) 2; Al-Yassini (n 2) 31.

13 Al-Atawneh, *Wahhābī Islam* (n 4) 2.

14 Al-Rasheed (n 5) 29.

15 Afshin Shahi, *The Politics of Truth Management in Saudi Arabia* (Routledge 2013) 71–73; Yakar and Yakar (n 12) 32–33.

formal organisations.[16] The administration of oil revenues therefore produced a process of institutionalisation that in turn impacted the religious establishment.

During the 1950s, the country experienced a series of administrative and bureaucratic reforms. The institutionalisation of the practice of *iftā'* was part of this reform process which began when King 'Abd al-'Azīz designated Shaykh Muḥammad ibn Ibrāhīm Āl al-Shaykh as the State Grand Muftī on December 18, 1952. One year later, King Sa'ūd Ibn 'Abd al-'Azīz Āl Sa'ūd (r. 1953–1964), the King's successor, established the first official *iftā'* institution, which was entitled *Dār al-Iftā' wa al-Ishrāf 'alā al-Shu'ūn al-Dīniyya* (Institute for the Issuance of Religious Legal Opinions and the Supervision of Religious Affairs).[17] This was a significant development because, for the preceding centuries (1745–1953), following the well-known Saudi-Wahhābī pact of 1744, the practice of *iftā'* had been conducted informally.[18] The attempt to institutionalise the Kingdom's religious structure opened the way towards an official issuance of *fatwās* in Saudi Arabia. The Grand Muftī, Shaykh Muḥammad ibn Ibrāhīm,[19] was designated as the head of the newly established Dār al-Iftā', and the institution operated under his chairmanship until his death in 1969. Up until this point, the Dār al-Iftā' served an influential function in religious matters by issuing thousands of *fatwās* that played an important role in the formulation of the Saudi state's legal, social, cultural and moral norms.

The establishment of the Dār al-Iftā' was a significant moment in the relationship between the *'ulamā'* and the *'umarā'* because it marked the point at which the *'ulamā'* lost their independence and began to become a state-controlled institution that was subservient to the state, most notably in the field of politics.[20] With regard to political issues, it can be described as a manifestation of an official religious organisation that operates under the Saudi Government rather than as an autonomous association that is located within Saudi society. The Saudi Government reinforced its control over the political sphere by incorporating the *'ulamā'* into government institutions. However, the *'ulamā'* continued to exert political influence between the 1950s and the 1970s. The active participation of the *'ulamā'* in the struggle for power between King Sa'ūd and Crown Prince Fayṣal lends further credence to the proposition that the *'ulamā'* and their *fatwās* expedited to depose King Sa'ūd. On March 22, 1964, the senior *'ulamā'* issued a *fatwā* that provided an authoritative instruction that operated under the principle of *maṣlaḥa 'āmma*

16 Nabil Mouline, *The Clerics of Islam: Religious Authority and Political Power in Saudi Arabia* (Ethan S. Rundell (tr) Yale University Press 2014) 142.

17 'Abd al-Raḥmān al-Shalhūb, *Al-Niẓām al-Dustūrī fi al-Mamlaka al-'Arabiyya al-Sa'ūdiyya bayna al-Sharī'a al-Islāmiyya wal-Qānūn al-Muqāran* (Maktabat Fahd al-Waṭaniyya 1999) 218; Mouline, *The Clerics of Islam* (n 16) 138.

18 Al-Atawneh, *Wahhābī Islam* (n 4) 16.

19 Shahi (n 15) 73.

20 Al-Yassini (n 2) 78–79.

(general public interest) – this dethroned King Sa'ūd and legitimately enthroned Crown Prince Fayṣal.[21]

In the religious sphere, the bureaucratisation and modernisation could not be completed until 1971 for two reasons. Firstly, King Fayṣal (r. 1964–1975) required the support and endorsement of the *'ulamā'* in his struggle for power, and the Saudi Government seriously considered deploying the *'ulamā'*s religious authority in order to further its own goals. During the labour riots, which occurred between 1962 and 1966, the *fatwās* issued by the senior *'ulamā'* endorsed both the royal family and its continued authority.[22] King Fayṣal also drew upon the support of the *'ulamā'* to initiate a range of important innovations, which included the construction of Saudi Arabia's first television station in 1965.[23] Secondly, some reforms that were planned to modernise the *iftā'* council were also frustrated by Shaykh Muḥammad ibn Ibrāhīm, the Grand Muftī, and more specifically by his charismatic personality, broad institutional power and symbolic capital.[24] When Shaykh Muḥammad ibn Ibrāhīm ascended to become the head of the Dār al-Iftā', he also assumed the offices of Grand Muftī and Chief Qāḍī and was appointed as the supervisor of girls' education. Because Shaykh Muḥammad ibn Ibrāhīm struggled to prevent the government's intervention in the religious sphere, any action by the government would not only threaten its legitimacy but also its very existence.[25] Under his leadership, the Dār al-Iftā' became a highly personalised institution that was inseparable from his authoritative and strong leadership. At this point, King Fayṣal was probably reluctant to implement a reform of the *iftā'* council, for the reason that it would require directly intervening in the existing religious establishment.

On August 29, 1971, two years after the death of Shaykh Muḥammad ibn Ibrāhīm, King Fayṣal issued a Royal Decree that led to the formation of two new agencies: *Hay'at Kibār al-'Ulamā'* (Board of Senior *'Ulamā'*; henceforth: BSU) and *al-Lajna al-Dā'ima lil-Buḥūth al-'Ilmiyya wal-Iftā'* (Permanent Committee

21 Āmin Sa'id, *Fayṣal al-'Azim: Nashātuhu – Sīratuhu – Akhlāquhu – Bay'ahu – Iṣlaḥātuhu – Khaṭbuhu* (Maṭābi' Najd al-Tijārīyah 1970) 71–76; Simoon Henderson, *After King Abdullah Succession in Saudi Arabia* (The Washington Institute for Near East Policy 2009) 5.

22 Nabil Mouline, 'Enforcing and Reinforcing the State's Islam: The Functioning of the Committee of Senior Scholars' in Bernard Haykel, Thomas Hegghammer and Stéphane Lacroix (eds), *Saudi Arabia in Transition: Insights of Social, Political, Economic and Religious Change* (Cambridge University Press 2015) 54.

23 Mouline, 'Enforcing and Reinforcing' (n 22) 54; Emine Enise Yakar, 'The Influential Role of the Practice of Iftā' in Saudi Politico-Legal Arena' (2020) 16 (1) *Manchester Journal of Transnational Islamic Law & Practice* 44–45.

24 Mouline, *The Clerics of Islam* (n 16) 148–149. Shaykh Muḥammad ibn Ibrāhīm was an influential figure in Saudi Arabia during his term of office. As the Grand Muftī of Saudi Arabia, he informally heard appeals. Vogel points to his strong power when he says: "it seems a single scholar—again Muḥammad ibn Ibrāhīm—had all the powers of the supreme judicial authority." See Frank Vogel, *Islamic Law and Legal System: Studies of Saudi Arabia* (Brill 2000) 91.

25 Mouline, *The Clerics of Islam* (n 16) 149.

for Scientific Research and Legal Opinion; henceforth: CRLO).[26] King Fayṣal's reform policy, which was set out in his widely acknowledged "Ten Point Program,"[27] sought to restructure the Dār al-Iftā' by incorporating these two new agencies into its structure.[28] The proliferation of government agents and ministries made it possible to reallocate some functions of the *'ulamā'* among the newly established institutions and ministries; however, this did not make it possible to diminish or even eliminate the influence of the Dār al-Iftā' or the *'ulamā'* within Saudi public and legal life. Because the Saudi constitutional system and judiciary are grounded within the Qur'an and Sunna, Islamic law establishes the backbone of state legislation. This is unequivocally specified in Articles 1, 7 and 23 of the Basic Regulations of Governance (*al-Niẓām al-Asāsī lil-Ḥukm*), which were put into place in 1992. Article 1 states:

> The Kingdom of Saudi Arabia is a sovereign Arabic Islamic State. Its religion is Islam. Its constitution is Almighty God's Book, the Holy Qur'an, and the Sunna (Traditions of the Prophet (PBUH).[29]

Meanwhile, Article 7 clarifies:

> Government in the Kingdom of Saudi Arabia derives its authority from the Book of God and the Sunna of the Prophet (PBUH), which are the ultimate sources of reference for this Law and the other laws of the State.[30]

Finally, Article 23 states:

> The State shall protect the Islamic creed, apply the Sharia, encourage good and discourage evil, and undertake its duty regarding the Propagation of Islam (Da'wa).[31]

These Articles establish that the Dār al-Iftā' can be accepted as the main interpretative mechanism of Islamic legal sources – this applies because the institution is the highest official religious authority which is responsible for issuing *fatwās* based on Islamic law. The practice of *iftā* and the function of

26 Royal Decree A/137, 29 August 1971, See *Umm al-Qurā* (Mecca 4 April 1971) 2387; Anẓimat 'āmmat, 'Niẓām hay'at kibār al-'ulamā' wa lā'iḥat sayr al-a'amāl fī al-hay'at al-lajnat al-dāimat al-murtef'at 'anhā' <http://www.cojss.com/article.php?a=301> accessed 25 June 2016; Al-Shalhūb (n 17) 218–219.

27 Al-Atawneh, *Wahhābī Islam* (n 4) 9–10; Al-Yassini (n 2) 110. For an English translation of the programme, see 'Ministerial Statement of 06 November 1962 by Prime Minister Amir Faysal of Saudi Arabia' (1963) 17 (1/2) *Middle East Journal* 161–162 <http://0-www.jstor.org.lib.exeter.ac.uk/stable/pdf/4323561.pdf?_=1468274273021> accessed 03 June 2016.

28 Shahi (n 15) 75; Al-Atawneh, *Wahhābī Islam* (n 4) 9–10.

29 Royal Decree A/90, 1 March 1992.

30 ibid.

31 ibid.

adjudication (*qaḍā'*) implicitly complement each other.[32] This feature is further reiterated by Vogel's observation that the *qāḍīs* evidence, to at least some extent, a clear respect for the *fatwās* issued by the Dār al-Iftā' (in particular the BSU) and therefore seek to incorporate them into the Saudi judicial procedure.[33]

In addition, the Dār al-Iftā' maintains its connection with, and influence over, the judiciary system, and these two features take various forms. The fact that many members of the BSU have simultaneously served in high-ranking judicial positions could conceivably be interpreted as confirmation of the Dār al-Iftā's impact upon the judicial and legal system. For instance, Shaykh Ṣāliḥ b. Laḥaydān, one of the prominent members of the BSU, assumed the presidency of the Permanent Board of Supreme Judicial Council (*Majlis al-Qaḍā al-A'lā*) during the period 1992–2009.[34] Shaykh Bakr b. 'Abd Allāh Abū Zayd, one of the previous members of the BSU, served as a general deputy for the Ministry of Justice until the end of 1991, and was also appointed as a representative of the Kingdom at the International Islamic Fiqh Assembly.[35] Shaykh 'Abd Allāh b. Muḥammad b. Ibrāhīm Āl al-Shaykh, the current member of the BSU, was assigned to the Ministry of Justice by Royal Decree 2/125 in 1992;[36] in addition, Shaykh 'Abd Allāh b. Sulaymān al-Manī', one of the BSU's most prominent current members, has also served as a judge of the Western region of Mecca.[37] Al-Atawneh further reiterates the authority and power of the *'ulamā'* and, by extension, the Dār al-Iftā'. He observes:

> In any event, the 'ulamā' ... continue to exercise influence in several areas, including nearly all legal and religious affairs. They have even managed to gradually increase their power by expanding their control over other State ministries and various religious agencies, national and international, such as: the Ministry of Justice; the Ministry of Islamic Affairs and Endowments, Call and Guidance; the Ministry of Pilgrimage; the *Muṭawwi'a* ... and, finally, the World Muslim League and the World Assembly of Muslim Youth.[38]

32 Vogel, *Islamic Law and Legal System* (n 24) 115–116.

33 Vogel, *Islamic Law and Legal System* (n 24) 7–8, 115–117; Frank Vogel, 'The Complementarity of Ifta' and Qaḍā': Three Saudi Fatwas on Divorce' in Muhammad K. Masud, Brinkley Messick and David S. Powers (eds), *Islamic Legal Interpretation: Muftis and Their Fatwas* (Harvard University Press 1996) 262–263, 268–269.

34 Vogel, *Islamic Law and Legal System* (n 24) 83; Al-Atawneh, *Wahhābī Islam* (n 4) 23.

35 The General Presidency of Scholarly Research and Ifta' of Kingdom of Saudi Arabia, *English Translations of Permanent Committee for Scholarly Research and Ifta' of K.S.A: Second Collection*, vol 1 (CRLO 2012) 6.

36 Shaykh 'Abd Allāh b. Muḥammad b. Ibrāhīm Āl al-Shaykh, 'The Shūra Council' <https://www.shura.gov.sa/wps/wcm/connect/ShuraEn/internet/CV/Abdullah+Bin+Mohammed+Bin+Ibrahim+Al-Sheikh/> accessed 01 November 2017.

37 Member Scholars of the Permanent Committee for Ifta', 'His Eminence Shayhkh 'Abdullah ibn Mani'' <http://www.alifta.com/Fatawa/MoftyDetails.aspx?languagename=en&Type=Mofty&section=tafseer&ID=6> accessed 05 November 2016.

38 Al-Atawneh, *Wahhābī Islam* (n 4) 37.

Because the highest judicial and religious positions continue to be held by the BSU members, it is possible to assert that the Dār al-Iftā' still continues to maintain its influence and authority, at least over the Saudi judiciary and the religious and social spheres. In particular, it should be noted that the official *fatwās* of the institution, which are legally complementary, play a central role in shaping legal regulations and orienting internal policies.

The institutionalisation of the Dār al-Iftā' was largely completed by the 1993 recentralisation, in which King Fahd's royal decree reintroduced the office of Grand Muftī (*al-Muftī al-'Āmm*),[39] which had been suspended for roughly two decades after the death of Shaykh Muḥammad ibn Ibrāhīm in 1969. Shaykh Ibn Bāz was assigned to this position and served as the permanent chairman of both the BSU and the CRLO, representing the highest *iftā'* authority until his death. The reestablishment of this office resulted in the recentralisation of the contemporary practice of *iftā'*, and all *iftā'* institutions being placed under the office's control. When Ibn Bāz died in May 1999, Shaykh 'Abd al-'Azīz b. 'Abd Allāh Āl al-Shaykh was appointed as the State Grand Muftī and the chairman of both the BSU and the CRLO. These two public agencies are currently led by Shaykh 'Abd Allāh.

In the Saudi legal system, the *fatwās* issued by the Dār al-Iftā', in particular the BSU, perform a complementary role in the application process of Islamic law. Upon this basis, it may be asserted that there is established institutional cooperation between the Saudi courts (as the judicial authority) and the Dār al-Iftā' (as an interpretative authority of Islamic legal sources).[40] Al-Shalhūb explains two aspects of these *fatwās* and their operation within Saudi society. He states:

> when the issue is not related to an individual, the *fatwā* [on that issue] becomes general. In both individual and general *fatwās*, we ought to take two factors into account. Firstly, the religious aspect – this arises from the fact that the *fatwā* might not be legally binding, but it is religiously binding for the *mustaftī*. Secondly, the question is whether the issued *fatwā* is legally binding or not. For all individuals, the obligation to obey the issued *fatwā* becomes legally binding either through the verdict of the *qāḍī* or the approval of the King.[41, 42]

This statement establishes that the *fatwās* issued by the Dār al-Iftā' do not only guard public morality but also operate as the legal complementary within the Saudi legal system. For instance, the death penalty for drug traffickers and smugglers became the state law when King Fahd gave his assent. The legal code governing

39 ibid.

40 Al-Atawneh, *Wahhābī Islam* (n 4) 30–31; Vogel, *Islamic Law and Legal System* (n 24) 115–117; Vogel, 'The Complementarity of Ifta'' (n 33) 262–263, 267–269.

41 Al-Shalhūb (n 17) 221–222.

42 Author's translation.

this matter originates within the *fatwā* (the BSU's legal decision), which was discussed on February 2, 1987, at King Fahd's request.[43] In establishing execution as the last deterrent penalty for recidivist drug traffickers, smugglers and substance abusers, the BSU referred to the negative consequences of their actions on public health and the entire community. In setting out the legal rationale for this ruling, the BSU applies to the principle of the public interest (*maṣlaḥa*). The *fatwā* which sets out legal penalties for such crimes specifies:

> He who promotes drugs, whether by manufacturing, imports, sales or procurement, must be punished by imprisonment, whipping, financial penalty, or all the aforementioned, as per judicial discretion. However, repeat offenders must be punished most harshly, even by execution, in order to protect society from them.[44]

This suggests that the BSU evaluates the aforementioned crimes under the penal category of *ta'zīr* (in which punishments are left to the discretion of judges or rulers). The death penalty as the last option of penalisation has now been confirmed and put in place as a means to punish criminals who perpetrate drug abuse, smuggling and trafficking.[45] In quoting Ibn Taymiyya's approval for the execution of an individual who refused to give up the consumption of alcohol, BSU members sought to justify the inclusion of recidivist offenders within the *ta'zīr* penalty category.[46] This example reiterates that the Dār al-Iftā' actively influences Saudi society's laws, norms and regulations. In operating within a functioning Islamic legal system, the Dār al-Iftā' clearly exerts an intellectual effort to derive an Islamic legal opinion from the textual sources, and this sustains a smooth interaction between the religious scholars and rulers.

The symbiotic relationship between the *'ulamā'* and the *'umarā'*

Scholars who study Saudi Arabia tend to adopt two different approaches to the actions of the Saudi rulers regarding to the Dār al-Iftā's incorporation into the state administration. Firstly, some of them argue that the state sought to weaken

43 The BSU decision No. 138 of 02 February 1987 <http://ar.islamway.net/article/17711/%D8%AD%D9%83%D9%85-%D9%85%D9%87%D8%B1%D8%A8-%D9%88%D9%85%D8%B1%D9%88%D8%AC-%D8%A7%D9%84%D9%85%D8%AE%D8%AF%D8%B1%D8%A7%D8%AA> accessed 30 June 2016. See Al-Shalhūb (n 17) 223–224; Vogel, *Islamic Law and Legal System* (n 24) 266–267. For the translation of legal decision of the BSU, see also Al-Atawneh, *Wahhābī Islam* (n 4) 159.

44 Cited from Al-Atawneh, *Wahhābī Islam* (n 4) 160. See the BSU decision No. 138 of 02 February 1987 for the original Arabic text.

45 Vogel, *Islamic Law and Legal System* (n 24) 266–268.

46 In the *fatwā* probably to suppress and remove an excuse of doubt on the part of offenders of these crimes, it is stated: "It is essential that the aforementioned penalties be promulgated prior to their implementation, as educational and preventative measures." See the BSU decision No. 138 of 02 February 1987.

the *'ulamā'*s monopoly on politics by establishing the Dār al-Iftā'. In the second instance, others maintain that the state's termination of the *'ulamā'*s autonomy and its replacement by an official institution actually enabled the *'ulamā'* to increase officially their influence over social, political and legal spheres. Al-Yassini, in describing Saudi Arabia as one among a few extreme examples in which a given political authority uses religion to control and reshape society, leans towards the first perspective. He clarifies:

> The ulama became incorporated in state administration, and state laws regulate ulama activities. The state ... does not tolerate an autonomous religious domain that may compete with it for the loyalty of citizens. Thus, the state extended its jurisdiction to the religious domain and utilized religious leaders to legitimate its policies.[47]

Al-Yassini clearly takes the view that the state only left devotional matters and the social sphere in the hands of the Dār al-Iftā' through the initiated bureaucratisation and institutionalisation process across Saudi Arabia.[48] Al-Rasheed stingingly adds:

> The official *'ulama* failed to reflect on their own role in the modern Saudi state. They refrained from critically examining this role and tracing its evolving nature. Simply content with being guardian of the moral order while leaving political power in the hands of the ruling family and expanding class of bureaucrats and technocrats, they lacked self-consciousness and awareness. The Saudi *'ulama* accepted the *de facto* separation between religion and politics, while adopting a narrow definition of religion as all matters relating to personal conduct and *'ibadat* (worship).[49]

This suggests that the ruling family put into effect a *de facto* separation between politics and religion while establishing a politically secular state but socially an Islamic society. Steinberg similarly insists that the government's bureaucratisation and modernisation policies functioned to undermine the position and overall impact of the *'ulamā'* in both the political and religious spheres.[50] Over time, the institution and its scholars (*'ulamā'*) have come to focus upon issues which include the jurisprudence of the permissible and the forbidden (*fiqh al-halāl wa al-ḥarām*), the jurisprudence of worship (*fiqh al-'ibādāt*) and public morality, in the process becoming more removed from Saudi politics. The political isolation of the *'ulamā'* corresponds to a clear understanding between the *'ulamā'* and the government which envisions the separation of religion and politics. Consequently,

47 Al-Yassini (n 2) XI.
48 ibid 59–60, 75, 78–79.
49 Al-Rasheed (n 5) 57.
50 Steinberg, 'The Wahhabiya, Saudi Arabia' (n 3) 38.

what emerges from the first argument concerning the restructuring of the Saudi *iftā'* institution is that the *'ulamā'* have lost their power in the political sphere.

To a certain extent, the argument that the state restricted the political power of *'ulamā'* by subordinating them to an official institution appears to correspond closely to the range of bureaucratisation and modernisation activities. However, it is important to note that the official *'ulamā'*, conceived as guardians of religious legal interpretation, were never marginalised in the manner of their counterparts in the Arab-Muslim world. Although the incorporation of the *'ulamā'* into the state administration undermined part of their prerogatives during the twentieth century, the *'ulamā'* increased its authoritative position by occupying official posts and positions.

The second argument, which relates to the incorporation of the *'ulamā'* into the state administration, has been engaged by Mouline and al-Atawneh, who offer an influential account that correlates the issue with the basic Wahhābī doctrines of governance and politics, which designate both the *'ulamā'* and the *'umarā'* as authority-holders (*wulāt al-'amr*). Mouline reiterates that the incorporation of *'ulamā'* into the state administration increased their influence in official and social spaces. He observes:

> The ulama, as collective actors, did all they could to thwart Faysal's effort at fragmentation by individually overseeing the newly created institutions on behalf of the corporation. Starting in the late 1970s, they recuperated all of their prerogatives in the juridico-religious domain, strengthening their presence in the social space…
>
> In other words, the clerical corps very rapidly adapted to the new situation. More particularly, it once again adopted a strategy that would allow it, not only to preserve its interests by significantly reinforcing its social base and organizational frameworks, but also to impose itself as a reliable, long-term partner of the political power.[51]

Al-Atawneh lends further support to this argument by noting that the transformation of the religious establishment from informal to formal provides the *'ulamā'* an opportunity in maintaining their cooperation with the Saudi Government while enabling them, as an officially recognised religious actor, to continue to participate in the power structure.[52] However, al-Rasheed and al-Yassini, in their consideration of the political implications arising from the institutionalisation of the religious establishment, do not acknowledge the symbiotic relationship between the *'ulamā'* and the Saudi Government or its embodiment within the Wahhābī political doctrine. This is perhaps because the institutionalisation and

51 Mouline, *The Clerics of Islam* (n 16) 150.
52 Al-Atawneh, *Wahhābī Islam* (n 4) 36–37.

optimisation of the *'ulamā'* may be viewed as a reaction to ongoing socio-political changes which impacted Saudi Arabia and the wider world.

At this stage, it is important to focus upon how Saudi Arabia's official Wahhābī *'ulamā'* articulate the doctrine of *siyasa shar'iyya* (a fundamental legal doctrine that establishes the relationship between the ruler and its subjects in an Islamic state) over the twentieth century. It strongly stresses the importance of obedience and acquiescence to rulers and is therefore consistent with the traditional approach advocated by their predecessors.[53] This is also a feature of contemporary official *fatwās* and writings. During a symposium that was held in Riyadh's Fayṣal ibn Turkī Mosque, Ibn Bāz offered a legal explanation in response to a question which asked how the 'authority-holders' in the Q. 4:59[54] should be understood, along with the question of whether this term relates to the *'ulamā'* or the *'umarā'*, and even applies if they are unjust. In this symposium, Ibn Bāz states:

53 The Wahhābī doctrine has a political theory grounded upon Ibn Taymiyya's view, which upholds that Muslims must obey the ruler even if he is a sinner. This means that the Saudi Government is free to arrange governmental and political issues in a way that it sees fit, as long as it does not violate the sharī'a. In Ibn Taymiyya's view, the only ground for disobedience to a ruler emerges when he orders believers to violate the sharī'a – examples could include committing adultery (*zinā*), consuming alcohol or perpetrating theft (*sariqa*). Ibn Taymiyya's *al-Siyāsa al-Shar'iyya*, a famous treatise, provided the conceptual framework for contemporary Wahhābīs. He also defined the form of legitimate advice and exhortation by recognising the right and duty of qualified individuals to offer exhortation to a ruler. Ibn Aqil, Ibn Farḥūn and Ibn Qayyim al-Jawziyya all express similar views when addressing the *siyāsa shar'iyya* doctrine – this is shown by the fact that they all recognise and support the broad discretionary authority of the ruler while citing the principle of *maṣlaḥa* as a legal basis. In early Wahhābī political theory, the *'umarā'* and the *'ullamā'* emerge as the two foci of power. Shaykh Muḥammad Ibn 'Abd al-Wahhāb revivified the foundation of the bilateral relation between the *'ulamā'* and *'umarā'*; he did envisage the core feature of the Saudi-Wahhābī state. In line with his Wahhābī political theory, a temporal ruler becomes necessary to maintain and enforce the sharī'a and its dictates, and obedience to him emerges as a religious obligation. This suggests that the ruler must consult the *'ulamā* who are in charge of interpreting God's will and determining the sharī'a's dictates. Since then, this political theory has developed and maintained as the main legal doctrine regarding the politics and government by the contemporary official Wahhābī scholars. See Al-Atawneh, *Wahhābī Islam* (n 4) 37–42; Al-Yassini (n 2) 30; M.J. Crawford, 'Civil War Foreign Intervention, and the Question of Political Legitimacy: A Nineteenth-Century Sa'ūd ī Qāḍī's Dilemma' (1982) 14 (3) *International Journal of Middle East Studies* 227–248 <http://www.jstor.org/stable/pdf/163672.pdf> accessed 06 September 2016. For further insight into the similarity between the traditional Ḥanbalī *siyāsa shar'iyya* doctrine and the contemporary Wahhābī *siyāsa shar'iyya* doctrine, refer to Vogel, *Islamic Law and Legal System* (n 24) 204–205, 207–212; the sixteenth footnote of Al-Atawneh, *Wahhābī Islam* (n 4) 40. For an account of the progressive development of the doctrine of *siyāsa shar'iyya* from the time of the rightly guided four Caliphs to the twentieth century, refer to Vogel, *Islamic Law and Legal System* (n 24) 173–177, 185–221; Ann K.S. Lambton, *State and Government in Medieval Islam: An Introduction to the Study of Islamic Political Theory: The Jurists* (Oxford University Press 1981) 1–201, 242–264, 307–316.

54 The Q. 4:59 reads: "O who you believe! Obey Allah, and obey the Messenger (Muhammad), and those who charged with authority among you. If you differ about anything within yourselves, refer it to Allah and His Prophet (Muhammed) if you believe in Allah and the Last Day: That is the best and suitable final determination."

> Those in authority refer to Muslim scholars and rulers. Their orders should be followed if they agree with Shari'ah and should be disregarded if they disagree with Shari'ah. Thus, scholars and rulers should be obeyed in Ma'ruf because this serves to set things rights, spread security, help in carrying out the orders, give the oppressed their due rights, and deter the oppressors. On the other hand, disobeying rulers brings about corruption and injustice. Hence, those in authority – whether they are rulers or scholars – should be obeyed in Ma'ruf. The matter should go as follows: scholars shall explain the rulings of Allah, rulers shall enforce these rulings, and the people shall listen their scholars and follow the orders of their rulers. If orders involving disobedience to Allah are given, whether from rulers or scholars, these orders shall not be followed. For example, if a ruler orders you to drink Khamr (intoxicant) or consume Riba (usury), do not obey him. Likewise, if a scholar orders you to disobey Allah, do not obey that order. Pious scholars do not give such orders. In short, obedience is obligatory in Ma'ruf.[55]

In any event that relates to politico-religious issues, the doctrine of *siyāsa shar'iyya* is used both to buttress the Saudi Government's policy and also to ensure total obedience to the Saudi ruler and, by extension, the official *'ulamā'*.[56] This doctrine therefore establishes the relationship between the Saudi Government and its subjects by recognising the broad authority of the King and occasionally takes the form of a political weapon that seeks to consolidate the ascendency and authority of both the Saudi Government and the *'ulamā'*.[57]

The contemporary official Wahhābī scholars have sought to delineate an intricate model of cooperation that conjoins the Dār al-Iftā and the Saudi Government while constructing the structure of the Saudi-Wahhābī state and raising it over the alliance that combines these authority-holders.[58] This intricate cooperation

55 Obeying rulers and scholars in Ma'rūf to set things right, in *Fatwas of Ibn Baz*, 7:115–119 <http://www.alifta.net/Fatawa/FatawaChapters.aspx?languagename=en&View=Page&PageID=871&PageNo=1&BookID=14> accessed 21 August 2016. In the *fatwā*, the word *ma'rūf* is defined as "that which is judged as good, beneficial, or fitting by Islamic law and Muslims of sound intellect."

56 Fatwā No. 15631 in *Fatwas of the Permanent Committee*, 23: 401 <http://www.alifta.net/Search/ResultDetails.aspx?languagename=en&lang=en&view=result&fatwaNum=&FatwaNumID=&ID=3&searchScope=15&SearchScopeLevels1=&SearchScopeLevels2=&highLight=1&SearchType=exact&SearchMoesar=false&bookID=&LeftVal=0&RightVal=0&simple=&SearchCriteria=allwords&PagePath=&siteSection=1&searchkeyword=111098101100105101110099101032116111032114117108101114#firstKeyWordFound> accessed 06 September 2016.

57 Vogel, *Islamic Law and Legal System* (n 24) 173–175, 179.

58 The concept of cooperation between *'ulamā'* and *'umarā'* was originally outlined by Ibn Taymiyya in the Ḥanbalī school. He proposes a combination of power by construing the Q. 4:59 as entailing obedience to those in authority – this is achieved by interpreting the term *'ulī al-'amr* as covering both *'umarā'* and *'ulamā'*. He therefore supports a reunification of *fiqh* (Islamic legal understanding) and *siyāsa* (Islamic politics). See Vogel, *Islamic Law and Legal System* (n 24) 203–205.

establishes obedience to these authority-holders as binding, obligatory and akin to obeying God and his Prophet.[59] In this respect, it is possible to see that Ibn Bāz envisions obligatory obedience to royal decrees and rules not mentioned by the sharī'a – these could include regulations that govern employer–employee relations, traffic laws and other laws that have an individual or social benefit.[60] The only exception concerning the obligatory obedience is when the authority-holders issue a decree in violation of the sharī'a. However, Ibn Bāz persistently reiterates that a Muslim does not rebel against a ruler who does not comply with Islamic law. In his view, the only exception is when Muslims have sufficient power to overthrow the negligent government or authority: this establishes that the permissibility of rebellion is linked to the ability of Muslims to topple a regime. If success can be guaranteed in advance, then revolt is permissible. Ibn Bāz clarifies:

> If a ruler commits acts of clear disbelief, proven as such by evidence, and the people have the ability to topple him, to replace him with a pious ruler who enforces the Commands of Allah and supports the truth, they are permitted to do so.[61]

If this is not the case, a Muslim does not possess the right to actively oppose a ruler who violates the sharī'a; rather he should instead advise the ruler without violating the principle of Islamic law that relates to positive and negative commandments (*al-'amr wa al-nahy*).[62] Shaykh Ṣāliḥ b. Laḥaydān, an eminent member of the BSU and the head of the Supreme Judicial Council, further reiterates the confidential dimension of advice:

> *Nasiha* [advice, admonition] has certain conditions, principles, and rules of its own. One who wants to say everything that comes to mind without acting according to the rules of Islamic shari'a concerning *al-amr al-nahy* [positive and negative commandments] is one or the other: either a *jahil* [ignoramus], who must be taught; or an *'alim* [man of knowledge], who has gone too far and therefore must be debated until he understands; if he remains obstinate, he must be restrained.[63]

The prerequisite for advising a ruler by gentle means obfuscates the controversies, disagreements and strains between the Dār al-Iftā' and the Saudi Government. The cooperation between the Dār al-Iftā' and the Saudi Government upon the foundation of the doctrine of *siyāsa shar'iyya* has resulted in strong criticism being

59 Obeying (n 55).
60 ibid.
61 ibid.
62 Obeying (n 55); Al-Atawneh, *Wahhābī Islam* (n 4) 38–39; Joshua Teitelbaum, *Holier Than Thou: Saudi Arabia's Islamic Opposition* (The Washington Institute for Near East Policy 2000) 104–108.
63 Cited from Teitelbaum (n 62) 104.

directed towards the Dār al-Iftā' for issuing *fatwās* which support government policies during times of crisis. The prerequisite (any advice to a ruler should be given respectfully and in private) usually obscures the strained relations between these two authority-holders.[64] It is therefore not entirely accurate to assert that the relationship between the Dār al-Iftā' and the Saudi Government is coherent.

The doctrine of *siyāsa shar'iyya* sets out an ongoing reciprocal relationship between the official *'ulamā'* and *'umarā'* in the area of legislation and politics. The Dār al-Iftā', as the location of the official *'ulamā'*, performs an essential role in legitimising the Saudi Government's policies, particularly during times of crisis. However, the Saudi Government is also compelled to consult the *'ulamā'*, who are authorised to clarify the tenets of the sharī'a by interpreting God's will, and to oversee the implementation of these interpretations. Al-Atawneh further reiterates this reciprocal relationship between the Dār al-Iftā' and the Saudi Government. He writes:

> without the coercive power (*shawka*) of the state, religion is in danger; without Sharī'a, the state becomes a tyrannical organization. Thus, in an ideal state, the 'ulamā' and the 'umarā' cooperate: the former interprets God's will through the analysis and exegesis of His words, while the latter implements these interpretations. Consequently, authority is divided between the 'ulamā' and the 'umarā', both represented as authority-holders in Wahhabi doctrine.[65]

The harmonious relationship between the two emerges as a crucial factor that ensures the stability of the Saudi-Wahhābī state. The political integration of the Dār al-Iftā' is accordingly not conceived as a separate institutional entity that only provides religious legitimacy to government policies. To put it differently, the doctrine of *siyāsa shar'iyya* is conceivably the most important mechanism that helps to explain the reciprocal agreements and complementary cooperation between the Dār al-Iftā' and the Saudi Government. While it provides unlimited power to the ruler, this doctrine also establishes the basis for the independence of the *'ulamā'* on matters that fall within their jurisdiction.

The official *fatwās* issued by the Dār al-Iftā' provide a flexible legal mechanism that promotes the relationship between politics, religion and society; this institutes one of the most important legal sources of the Saudi state whose scope extends across a range of political, religious and social issues. The BSU and the CRLO currently operate under the leadership of the State Grand Muftī. They both constitute the Dār al-Iftā' and serve as the official representative of the religious establishment and the supreme authority for promulgating religious legal rulings or *fatwās*. Article 45 of the 1992 Basic Regulations explicitly confirms that this institution is dependent upon the state and also elevates the Qur'an and Sunna as the main textual sources that are consulted during the issuing of a *fatwā*. It states:

64 Al-Atawneh, *Wahhābī Islam* (n 4) 53.

65 ibid.

> The Holy Qur'an and the Sunna (Traditions) of God's Messenger shall be the source for fatwas (religious advisory rulings). The Law shall specify hierarchical organization for the composition of the Council of Senior Ulema, the Research Administration, and the Office of the Mufti, together with their functions.[66]

It is therefore apparent that in any event that requires a religious legal verdict and opinion, the Dār al-Iftā' continues to play an important role in structuring the modern Saudi legal, social and cultural spheres, and in turn impacting the Saudi Government's political policies. As stated in Article 45, this institution has a hierarchical structure and pursues a specific mode of operation.

Hay'at Kibār al-'Ulamā' (Board of Senior 'Ulamā' or BSU)

The BSU consists of 21 *'ulamā'* (including the chairman), and it is the highest religious authority that delivers ultimate legal decisions relating to the sharī'a in Saudi Arabia.[67] Royal Decree A/137 establishes the functions of the BSU. It states:

> [This institution] express[es] legal opinions based on the sharī'a regarding matters submitted to it by the King (*walī al-'amr*) and recommend[s] legal advice on religious matters [in order] to facilitate the King's decisions.[68]

Royal Decree A/137 also delineates that the BSU acts as an advisory body which provides assistance to the King's decisions on common law issues. It also decides whether any issue raised by the King and government fully complies with the sharī'a. Royal Decree A/137 specifies the issuance of legal opinions (on matters submitted by the King) and consultation as the BSU's foremost duties. In addition to these, it, in alliance with the Council of Ministers, functions as the country's pre-legislative mechanism and provides an ideological shield to the Saudi dynasty.[69]

As an established pre-legislative mechanism in Saudi Arabia, the BSU's *fatwās* perform a crucial role in legal, social and political areas. In a number of cases pertaining to social themes, the BSU's *fatwās*, which enjoy the approval of the King, underpin State laws. The BSU therefore actively participates in the legislation of the Saudi state when there are not any authoritative legal rulings or sources that relate to the subjects in question.[70] It has already noted that the death

66 Royal Decree A/90, 1 March 1992.

67 Seventeen *'ulamā'* were appointed to the first BSU, but this figure later increased to twenty-one. The other Royal Degree A/88 (of May 29, 2001) established a condition that the numbers of BSU members could not be lower than twelve or exceed twenty-two. See Royal Degree A/88, 29 May 2001 <http://www.cojss.com/article.php?a=301> accessed 25 June 2016.

68 Royal Decree A/137, 29 August 1971, 1.

69 Mouline, *The Clerics of Islam* (n 16) 150.

70 Al-Shalhūb (n 17) 222–224.

penalty for drug traffickers derives from the BSU's *fatwā* which was issued on February 2, 1987.[71] In addition, the BSU determined that anybody who was found to have committed sabotage would be executed, and this legal decision was later used to resolve two cases that came before a Saudi Arabian court.[72] The *fatwā* was issued by the BSU's own initiative rather than at any request of either the King or the government agencies, so it has a peculiar and specific character.[73] "Sabotage" is defined as actions which undermine the security of the state or property (private or public) and extended to activities such as the destruction of bridges, factories, hospitals, houses and mosques along with hijacking.[74] Emphatically referring to the much more harmful, severe and destructive character of sabotage activities than that of brigandage crimes and to the necessity of declaring a deterrent penalty for sabotage crimes, the BSU states that the saboteur "must be executed."[75] Defining the phenomenon of terrorism as a greater kind of "corruption on the earth than that of highway robbery," the BSU places any types of sabotage and terrorist activities under the category of crimes that shall be punishable with the death penalty. Even though there was no royal decree or circular letter that requested the implementation of this *fatwā*, the 1988 and 1989 cases ultimately referred back to it.[76] Closer inspection suggests that the BSU's *fatwās* perform a complementary role in the areas of adjudication and legislation although the approval of the King is usually a necessary precondition.

Although it is led by the State Grand Muftī, the Board is administratively directed by a Secretary-General (*'Amīn 'Āmm*), who is responsible for managing the BSU and establishing a connection between the BSU and the CRLO. The relevant Royal Decree states:

> A secretary-general of the Broad is to be appointed by the Council of Ministers … to be responsible for the Board's administrative system as well as for the coordination between the Board and the Presidency of CRLO.[77]

It was normally the case that members of the BSU would be appointed from amongst the Saudi senior *'ulamā'*. However, non-Saudi *'ulamā'* also have the

71 The BSU decision No. 138 of 02 February 1987.

72 Al-Shalhūb (n 17) 224–225.

73 The BSU decision No. 148 of 25 August 1988, <http://www.alifta.net/Search/ResultDetails.aspx?languagename=ar&lang=ar&view=result&fatwaNum=&FatwaNumID=&ID=3505&searchScope=2&SearchScopeLevels1=&SearchScopeLevels2=&highLight=1&SearchType=exact&SearchMoesar=false&bookID=&LeftVal=0&RightVal=0&simple=&SearchCriteria=allwords&PagePath=&siteSection=1&searchkeyword=217130216177216167216177032217135217138216166216169032217131216168216167216177032216167217132216185217132217133216167216161032216177217130217133#firstKeyWordFound> accessed 31 December 2017.

74 Vogel, *Islamic Law and Legal System* (n 24) 271–272.

75 The BSU decision No. 148 of 25 August 1988.

76 Vogel, *Islamic Law and Legal System* (n 24) 271–272.

77 Royal Decree A/137, 29 August 1971, 5–6.

right to become a member of the BSU with some certain conditions and the King's approval.[78] Being Wahhābī is one of the important conditions to be appointed as a member of the BSU.[79] Since 1971, membership of the BSU has been open to *'ulama'* from the four Sunnī schools; despite this, the Ḥanbalī-Wahhābī *'ulamā'* – upon account of historical, political and social factors – constitute the majority of members. The Royal Decree A/137 establishes that the members of the BSU should be appointed by the King with the option for an extension. The length of office term was determined to be four years, but the tenure of any member can be extended by a royal decree an extra four years.[80] The Royal Decree A/137 shifted the balance of power between the *'ulamā'* and Saudi Government. This instituted a new working arrangement in which many of the BSU's activities, most notably the appointment of its members, became directly subordinate to the King.[81]

The Board's *'ulamā'* meet twice a year to discuss topics submitted by the King and the CRLO, and to promulgate *fatwās* on an eclectic range of issues (which include the arts, politics, ritual practices, science, social life and technology).[82] The biannual meetings are generally held in the Dār al-Iftā' headquarters in Riyadh. Since the Dār al-Iftā' was reconfigured in 1971, the BSU has held more than 100 meetings. Proceedings and final decisions are recorded in a seven-volume edition ("*Abḥath Hay'at Kibār al-'Ulamā'* (*Research by the Board of Senior 'Ulamā'*)") which currently features on the organisation's website.[83] Some featured issues include:

- Ruling on banknotes,
- Conditions of penalties associated with contracts,
- Ruling on the utterance of three simultaneous divorces in one breath,
- Ruling on *nushūz* (disobedience, disloyalty and ill conduct to husband or vice versa) and *khul'* (right of a woman to seek divorce),
- Ruling on the dissecting of a dead body of a Muslim,
- Birth control,
- Codification of the most predominant statements of jurists (*fuqahā'*) concerning social transactions in order to oblige the judges to issue their verdicts accordingly,
- Insurance,
- Research on the ruling of relocating a part of a cemetery's location to implement public interest, such as a road extension or alike,
- Mortgage (*rahn*),
- Collection of alms-taxes (*zakāt*),

78 ibid 2.

79 ibid.

80 Royal Degree A/88, 29 May 2001, 1–3.

81 Shahi (n 15) 76.

82 Royal Decree A/137, 29 August 1971, 1–3; Al-Shalhūb (n 17) 220.

83 For these proceedings, see website at: http://www.alifta.net/Fatawa/FatawaChapters.aspx?languagename=ar&View=tree&NodeID=1&PageNo=1&BookID=1.

- Cornea transplantation,
- Writing the Qur'an in Latin script.

In addition to organising ordinary meetings, the BSU also has, subject to the coordinated contribution of the CRLO, the ability to arrange special meetings in exceptional cases. During the period 1971–1995, the BSU arranged nine such meetings in response to issues which encompassed domestic affairs, international relations and legal matters.[84] At the conclusion of one extraordinary meeting, a *fatwā* was promulgated to condemn a militant group's (Ikhwān) attack on Ka'ba, Mecca's Grand Mosque in 1979.[85] Prior to the Fourth International Conference of Women on September 15, 1995, another special meeting was arranged. At its conclusion, the BSU scholars harshly rejected the Conference's agenda upon the grounds that it contradicted Islamic legal principles and warned Muslims against attending this conference.[86]

The organisation's operating procedures clearly establish that at least two-thirds of the BSU membership must be present in a meeting that normally continues for a week or longer.[87] In instances where specialist input is required, external experts (in fields as diverse as commerce, economics, medical treatment, science and technology) have participated in BSU meetings; however, in these circumstances, they are not permitted to vote, and their recommendations are excluded from the BSU's promulgated *fatwās* and decisions. The Royal Decree A/137 observes:

> In examining issues related to economic and social affairs, and public systems including bank, commerce and labor, members of the BSU should consult one or more specialists in the required areas under the condition that they do not have the right to vote. Both the BSU's Secretary-General and the CRLO's chairman might select and summon these experts.[88]

Experts therefore contribute to the understanding of BSU members when the discussion extends to unfamiliar subject matter. Once decisions and *fatwās* are

84 Al-Atawneh, *Wahhābī Islam* (n 4) 23.

85 For an English translation of the *fatwā*, see Joseph A. Kechichian, 'The Role of Ulama in the Politics of an Islamic State: The Case of Saudi Arabia' (1996) 18 (1) *International Journal of Middle East Studies* 66–68 <http://0-www.jstor.org.lib.exeter.ac.uk/stable/pdf/162860.pdf> accessed 17 July 2016. For further explanation of the seizure of the sacred mosque, its organisers and militants, and their objectives and ideology, see Al-Yassini (n 2) 125–129; Yakar (n 23) 52–53; Pascal Ménoret, 'Fighting for the Holy Mosque: The Mecca Insurgency' in C. Christine Fair and Sumit Ganguly (eds), *Treading on Hallowed Ground: Counterinsurgency in Sacred Spaces* (Oxford University Press 2008) 118–135.

86 Declaration and warning against world conference on women, Beijing, in *Fatwas of Ibn Baz*, 9:203–204 <http://www.alifta.net/Fatawa/FatawaDetails.aspx?languagename=en&lang=en&IndexItemID=42704&SecItemHitID=46014&ind=20&Type=Index&View=Page&PageID=1209&PageNo=1&BookID=14&Title=DisplayIndexAlpha.aspx> accessed 01 November 2017. See also Al-Atawneh, *Wahhābī Islam* (n 4) 23.

87 Royal Decree A/137, 29 August 1971, 3.

88 Royal Decree A/137, 29 August 1971, 10.

confirmed by the absolute majority of BSU members, the BSU's Secretary-General and the CRLO initiate the publishing process. During the time when the office of the Grand Muftī was suspended, the biannual convention and its sessions were conducted and chaired by the five most senior members, with the first session of the meeting being presided over by the oldest BSU members.[89] After the Grand Muftī's office was re-established, the conventions have been overseen by the Grand Muftī.

A recent change in the BSU's membership occurred on December 3, 2016, when a royal decree was issued by King Salmān (r. 2015–), which appointed new members and extended the tenure of other members.[90] The current members (including the chairman) of the board are:

1. Shaykh 'Abd al-'Azīz ibn 'Abd Allāh Āl al-Shaykh (chairman)
2. Shaykh Ṣāliḥ ibn Laḥaydān
3. Shaykh Ṣāliḥ ibn Fawzān al-Fawzān
4. Shaykh 'Abd Allāh ibn Muḥammad ibn Ibrāhīm Āl al-Shaykh
5. Shaykh 'Abd Allāh ibn 'Abd al-Muḥsin al-Turkī
6. Shaykh 'Abd Allāh ibn Sulaymān al-Manī'
7. Shaykh Ṣāliḥ ibn Abd Allāh b. Ḥamīd
8. Shaykh 'Abd Allāh ibn Muḥammad al-Muṭlaq
9. Shaykh Aḥmad Sayr Mubārakī
10. Shaykh Sa'ad ibn Nāṣir Shathrī
11. Shaykh Muḥammad ibn 'Abd al-Karīm al-'Isā
12. Shaykh 'Abd al-Wahhāb ibn Ibrāhīm Abū Sulaymān
13. Shaykh 'Abd Allāh Muḥammad ibn Sa'ad Khanīn
14. Shaykh Ya'qūb ibn 'Abd al-Wahhāb b. Yusūf al-Bāhussayn
15. Shaykh 'Abd al-Raḥmān ibn 'Abd al-'Azīz Kulliyya
16. Shaykh Muḥammad ibn Ḥasan ibn 'Abd al-Raḥmān ibn 'Abd al-Laṭīf Āl al-Shaykh
17. Shaykh 'Abd al-Karīm ibn 'Abd Allāh ibn 'Abd al-Raḥmān al-Khuḍayr
18. Shaykh Muḥammad ibn Muḥammad al-Mukhtār Muḥammad
19. Shaykh Sulaymān ibn 'Abd Allāh Abā al-Khayl
20. Shaykh Jibrīl ibn Muḥammad ibn Ḥasan al-Baṣīlī
21. Shaykh Ṣāliḥ ibn 'Abd Allāh b. Ḥamid ibn al-'Aṣīmī.[91]

Most of the BSU's members have benefitted from a traditional education. Subsequent to being educated by an acknowledged Wahhābī scholar, the individual is established as an authoritative scholar to be regarded as a BSU

89 Al-Atawneh, *Wahhābī Islam* (n 4) 21.

90 Royal Decree A/48, 15 January 2013. See also 'Al-Tamdīd li-Arba'a A'ḍāi' fil-Lajna al-Ḍā'ima lil-Fatwā wa Amrun Malikiyyun: I'āda Takwīn Hay'at Kibār al-'Ulamā' bi-Ri'āsa Āl al-Shaykh wa 20 'Uḍwan' *Al-Jazīra* (Riyadh, 03 December 2016) <http://www.al-jazirah.com/2016/20161203/ln39.htm> accessed 24 October 2017.

91 Royal Decree A/48, 15 January 2013.

member.[92] They benefit from an informal network of scholarly lectures (which are known as *ḥalaqāt*) that provide education in diverse subjects which include *ḥadīth* (the report of a saying, action or acquiescence of the Prophet), *balāghat* (Arabic literature and rhetoric), *tafsīr* (Qur'anic commentary) and *usūl al-fiqh* (Islamic jurisprudence). A number of these scholars have proceeded to pursue higher degrees in Saudi universities or other academic institutions. Shaykh Ṣāliḥ ibn Fawzān al-Fawzān received instruction from Shaykh Hamūd ibn Sulaymān al-Ṭalāl before then attending and graduating from the Educational Institute of Buraydah and the Faculty of Sharī'a in Riyadh (from which he received an MA and PhD).[93] Shaykh 'Abd Allāh b. Muḥammad ibn Ibrāhīm Āl al-Shaykh initially received religious education from his father (Shaykh Muḥammad ibn Ibrāhīm Āl al-Shaykh, the State Grand Muftī) before then studying the interpretation of the Qur'an and Islamic jurisprudential principles under the guidance of Shaykh 'Abd al-Razzāq Afīfī.[94] He subsequently graduated from Sharī'a College in Riyadh (which later became the University of Imām Muḥammad Ibn Sa'ūd). He later studied at al-Azhar's University's Sharī'a and Law College, from which he received an MA and PhD.[95] Shaykh 'Abd Allāh ibn Sulamān al-Manī' is another scholar who received two degrees (undergraduate and MA) from Riyadh's University of Imām Muḥammad ibn Sa'ūd.[96] During the early 1950s, Islamic academic institutions and Saudi universities which provided sharī'a education began to be installed as part of the bureaucratisation and institutionalisation process,[97] and by the late 1990s the number of BSU members with MA and PhD degrees in religious studies had substantially increased.[98]

There are currently three sharī'a colleges that are located in three universities, specifically the Islamic University and Umm al-Qura University, both of which are based in Mecca, and the Riyad-based University of Imām Muḥammad ibn Sa'ūd.[99] The sharī'a education in these universities seeks to train scholars who are capable of exercising various degrees of *ijtihād*.[100] The appointment of graduates from these universities to the Dār al-Iftā' is one clear indication of how the

92 Al-Atawneh, *Wahhābī Islam* (n 4) 20.

93 Member Scholars of the Permanent Committee for Ifta', 'His Eminence Shaykh Salih ibn Fawzan Al-Fawzan' <http://www.alifta.net/Fatawa/MoftyDetails.aspx?languagename=en&ID=7> accessed 03 June 2016.

94 The Shura Council, 'Shaykh 'Abd Allāh b. Muḥammad b. Ibrāhīm Āl al-Shaykh' <https://www.shura.gov.sa/wps/wcm/connect/ShuraEn/internet/CV/Abdullah+Bin+Mohammed+Bin+Ibrahim+Al-Sheikh/> accessed 01 November 2017.

95 ibid.

96 The General Presidency of Scholarly Research and Ifta' of Kingdom of Saudi Arabia (n 35) 13.

97 Al-Yassini (n 2) 111–112.

98 Al-Atawneh, *Wahhābī Islam* (n 4) 20.

99 Mike Farquhar, 'The Islamic University of Medina since 1961: The Politics of Religious Mission and the Making of a Modern Salafi Pedagogy' in Masooda Bano and Keiko Sakurai (eds), *Shaping Global Islamic Discourses: The Role of al-Azhar, al-Medina and al-Mustafa* (Edinburgh University Press 2015) 27.

100 Vogel, *Islamic Law and Legal System* (n 24) 79–82.

'ulamā' have been institutionalised. The monopoly of the Āl al-Shaykh family, through the policy upheld by the Saud Government in an attempt to prevent any group accumulating more power than itself, has been substantially weakened by the institutionalisation process.

Al-Lajna al-Dā'ima lil-Buḥūth al-'Ilmiyya wal-Iftā' (Permanent Committee for Scientific Research and Legal Opinion)

The CRLO, the influential actor focused upon scholarly research and the practice of *iftā'*, is the second branch of the Dār al-Iftā'.[101] Its functions, as stated by the Royal Decree A/137, are to provide debates and discussions within the BSU with appropriate research materials and to conduct the practice of *iftā'* in matters of faith (*'aqā'id*), social transactions (*mu'āmalāt*) and worship (*'ibādāt*).[102] This clearly establishes that the CRLO's activities are confined to the micro-level social issues (e.g., everyday socio-religious questions). If the issue addressed to the CRLO falls outside of the micro-social domain and is beyond the CRLO's field of competence, a research report must be prepared and submitted to the BSU by the CRLO's members.[103]

Almost all the decisions taken by the BSU can be traced back to research prepared by the CRLO. Since being created in 1971, the CRLO has conducted extensive research that has fed into the BSU's discussions. The research frequently begins with a statement that explains the reason why the research has been prepared and then proceeds to set out its content. Then, the definition of specific words and terms associated with the research subjects is given generally from both lexical and legal points of view. For example, the research prepared for the BSU's discussion of banknotes begins with the lexical definition of banknotes, or money, and then proceeds to present Ibn Taymiyya's opinion that connects monetary unit and model with the customary practices of people and the public interest. Finally, the reader's attention is then drawn to a consideration of the origin and evaluation of the currency unit.[104]

Similarly, the research relating to issues of cornea transplantation, insurance, *khul'*, mortgage, *nushūz* and penal conditions of contracts begins with an introduction of both legal and literal definitions of relevant words and terms. After defining key terms and words, the prepared research proceeds to present relevant Qur'anic verses, *ḥadīths* and thoughts of earlier Muslim scholars from the four Sunni schools (*madhhabs*), with these contributions providing considerable

101 Al-Atawneh, *Wahhābī Islam* (n 4) 25.

102 Royal Decree A/137, 29 August 1971, 4–5. See also Al-Atawneh, *Wahhābī Islam* (n 4) 25; Mouline, *The Clerics of Islam* (n 16) 153–154.

103 Royal Decree A/137, 29 August 1971. See also Mouline, *The Clerics of Islam* (n 16) 154.

104 Hukm al-Awrāq al-Naqdiyya, in *Majallat al-Buḥūth al-Islāmiyya*, 1: 51–54 <http://www.alifta.net/Fatawa/FatawaChapters.aspx?languagename=ar&View=Page&PageID=18&PageNo=1&BookID=1> accessed 02 November 2017.

insight into the subject of discussion. These research contributions differ widely in terms of their depth and length and vary in accordance with the complexity of the research subject. The frequent allusions to the opinions and views of the other schools can be interpreted as a confirmation of the fact that the *'ulamā'* employ the practice of *tarjīḥ* (determining the preponderant opinion). To put it more concisely, the CRLO's research presents various and different opinions of other *madhhabs* to the BSU members before the preponderant opinion is determined by the *ijtihad* of the high-ranking official *'ulamā'*.

The practice of determining the preponderant opinion (*tarjīḥ*)[105] is not limited to a specific *madhhab*, as would be expected to be the Ḥanbalī *madhhab*. The material under the title "*Organizing Fatwas*" clearly establishes that the Dār al-Iftā' upholds inter-*madhhabs* interpretation and rejects the proposition of a commitment to a specific *madhhab* ("[t]he method of the Committee ... is to choose the opinion which is supported by the proof without being restricted to a specific Madhhab (School of Jurisprudence) or a certain scholar").[106] The CRLO therefore establishes that adherence to a single *madhhab*, which presupposed the disregarding of a correct, sound and valid opinion in another *madhhab*, is not an acceptable practice.[107] With regard to a particular legal issue, it is not appropriate to prefer an individual *madhhab* over another if the validity of opinion found in another *madhhab* is affirmed or discovered to be more just and accurate.[108] For example, during its biannual session of April 1976, the BSU authorised the CRLO to conduct detailed and comprehensive research on the issue of the dissection (or autopsy, for medical and forensic purposes) of the dead body of a Muslim – this research would be undertaken with the intention of providing a basis for the Ninth Biannual Session that would be held in August 1976.[109] The research paper breaks down into four main parts: (1) the dignity (*ḥurma*) and inviolability (*'iṣma*) of the

105 *Tarjīḥ* is defined as "the determining and ascertaining of the most preponderant and valid opinion" from amongst the Sunni Islamic legal schools (*madhhabs*), that is, the identification of the most valid opinion by evaluating evidence (*dalīl*) by means of the Islamic legal principles and methodologies. Fatwā No. 4172, Fatwā No. 11296, Fatwā No. 2815, Fatwā No. 9783, Fatwā No. 2573, Fatwā No. 5166, Fatwā No. 3323, Fatwā No. 2961, Fatwā No. 4522 and Fatwā No. 2872, in *Fatwas of the Permanent Committee*, 5: 28–46 <http://www.alifta.net/Fatawa/FatawaChapters.aspx?languagename=en&View=Page&PageID=1368&PageNo=1&BookID=7> accessed 27 November 2017.

106 Organizing Fatwas, in *Fatwas of the Permanent Committee*, 5: 1 <http://www.alifta.net/Fatawa/FatawaSubjects.aspx?languagename=en&View=Page&HajjEntryID=0&HajjEntryName=&RamadanEntryID=0&RamadanEntryName=&NodeID=4106&PageID=1345&SectionID=7&SubjectPageTitlesID=1364&MarkIndex=0&0#OrganizingFatwas> accessed 26 November 2017.

107 Fatwā No. 4172 (n 105).

108 Fatwā No. 3323 (n 105); Fatwā No. 2061 in *Fatwas of the Permanent Committee*, 5: 42–43 <http://www.alifta.net/Fatawa/FatawaChapters.aspx?languagename=en&View=Page&PageID=1377&PageNo=1&BookID=7> accessed 27 November 2017. See also Vogel, *Islamic Law and Legal System* (n 24) 78–79.

109 Hukm al-Tashrīḥ Jathat al-Muslim, in *Majallat al-Buḥūth al-Islāmiyya*, 2: 8–10 <http://www.alifta.net/Fatawa/FatawaChapters.aspx?languagename=ar&View=Page&PageID=126&PageNo=1&BookID=1> accessed 02 November 2017.

Muslim individual, whether alive or dead; (2) the different types of autopsy; (3) the legal views of earlier Muslim scholars in exceptional cases where an autopsy resulted in an organ being removed from a dead body; (4) the benefits of forensic autopsy for human beings in the modern world.[110] The inviolability of the Muslim body is underlined with reference to a number of Qur'anic verses, such as the Q. 4: 92 ("a believer should never kill a believer") and prophetic traditions that support the sanctity and inviolability of a human body ("[b]reaking the bone of a dead body is like breaking the bone of a live body").[111]

The CRLO clearly establishes that the mutilation and dissection of a body, whether a Muslim or a non-Muslim, is prohibited in Islamic law – the only exceptions are the three categories of punishments (*ḥudūd*, *qiṣāṣ* and *ta'zīr*) that are applied to adulterers, apostates, bandits, murderers, robbers and thieves.[112] The CRLO states that any failure to acknowledge the inviolability of the human body is, from the perspective of Islamic law, illicit. Despite this, the research seeks to identify the circumstances in which the dissection of a dead body or autopsy may be permissible. At the first instance, the CRLO distinguishes three kinds of autopsy: (1) forensic autopsy (*al-ṭib al-shar'ī*); (2) pathological autopsy (*al-tashrīḥ al-maraḍī*) that seeks to obtain medical knowledge about the cause of death, such as epidemic diseases; and (3) autopsies undertaken with the intention of obtaining medical and scientific knowledge (*al-baḥth al-'ilmī*).[113] After distinguishing these three separate examples, the CRLO attempts to identify which one is permissible by presenting five legal precedents that had been previously engaged by Muslim jurists and scholars from the four Sunni schools. The five legal precedents include: (1) opening fire on enemies hidden amongst Muslim prisoners of war; (2) cutting the womb of a dead pregnant woman to save her baby; (3) eating the flesh of a dead human in instances of starvation; (4) throwing a passenger (chosen by drawing lots) into the sea in order to save a sinking ship; and (5) firing missiles at enemies, even when women and children are amongst them.[114]

In referring to cutting the wombs of dead women in order to save the lives of their foetus, the CRLO evaluates the different approaches to this problem that have been taken by classical Muslim jurists and scholars, who include Ḥanafīs (such as Abū Ḥanīfa (d. 767)), Ḥanbalīs (such as Ibn Qudāma (d. 1283) and Ibn Ḥamdān (d. 1295)), Mālikīs (such as Mālik b. Anas (d. 795), Ibn al-Muwāq (d.1491) and al-Dardīr (d. 1768)) and Shāfi'īs (such as al-Māwardī (d. 1058), al-Nawawī (d. 1278) and al-Zarkashī (d. 1392)). These scholars adopted two different approaches.[115] The first stance, which was advocated by Ḥanafīs, Mālikīs and the majority of Shāfi'īs, permits the womb of a dead woman to be cut in

110 ibid.
111 ibid 11–14.
112 ibid 8–10.
113 ibid 15–17.
114 ibid 18–59.
115 ibid 33–41.

order to save the life of the baby – this is however dependent on the legal principles of necessity (*ḍarūra*) and public interest (*maṣlaḥa*). The second approach, which is instead advocated by the majority of Ḥanbalī and some Shāfi'ī scholars, emphasises the inviolability of the deceased and the uncertainty of the life of the foetus, whether alive or dead, and therefore prohibits the cutting of the womb in such instances.[116] It is noticeable that the CRLO appears to lean towards the first legal position by applying the legal maxims of "choosing the lesser of two evils" (*irtikāb adnā al-mafsadatayn*) and "necessities overrule prohibition" (*al-ḍarūrat tubīḥ maḥẓūrāt*).

In addition to the opinions of classical Muslim jurists, a number of contemporary *fatwās* issued by modern Muslim scholars, who include Rashīd Riḍā (d. 1935), Yūsuf al-Dajawī (d. 1948) and Ḥasanayn Muḥammad Makhlūf (d. 1990)), are introduced in order to provide a comprehensive overview of the issue. After acknowledging the long-term implications of the research, the BSU permits the first two types of autopsy (forensic autopsy and pathological autopsy) and cites their beneficial impacts upon justice, preventive medicine, public health and security.[117] In instances where it is a matter of choosing between life and death, the BSU argues that the protection and rescue of a life must prevail over the dignity of the deceased (*ḥurmat al-mayyit*). In addressing itself to autopsies for scientific research, the BSU maintains a cautious stance by setting out a number of conditions. It accepts the permissibility of conducting autopsies on human bodies for medical reasons as this could conceivably contribute to educational knowledge and therefore assist important scientific developments in the field of medical studies. This benefit notwithstanding, Islamic law is attentive to the dignity of human beings, and this type of autopsy could conceivably interfere with this imperative. It is also important to recognise that the *ḥadīth* in which the Prophet suggests an equivalence between breaking the bones of a dead and living person suggests that the third type of autopsy may not be allowed, lest it interfere with the dignity of the human body. While it is acceptable to use the cadavers of those who relinquish their faith and who become warriors against Islam (*ghayr ma'ṣūm*), it is not acceptable to use the cadavers of others (*ma'ṣūm*) in instances where there is no clear necessity.[118] In addressing itself to the dissecting of a dead Muslim's body, the BSU has leaned towards the legal position of the Ḥanafī, Mālikī, Shāfi'ī *madhhabs*, as opposed to the countervailing legal position of the Ḥanbalī *madhhab*.[119]

Even though the recognition of the three Sunni *madhhabs* (Ḥanafī, Mālikī and Shāfi'ī) may appear to hint at the liberation of the Dār al-Iftā' from the shackles

116 ibid.

117 ibid 59–65.

118 ibid 83–85.

119 For a more detailed CRLO analysis of the dissection (or autopsy for medical purposes) of a Muslim's dead body, refer to Al-Atawneh, *Wahhābī Islam* (n 4) 137–143; Muhammad al-Atawneh, 'Wahhābī Legal Theory as Reflected in Modern Official Saudi *Fatwās*: *Ijtihād*, *Taqlid*, Sources, and Methodology' (2011) 18 (3/4) *Islamic Law and Society* 349–352.

of the Ḥanbalī *madhhab*, it is important to acknowledge that there is a clear tendency towards the Ḥanbalī *madhhab*, which is attributable to its methodology (the direct use of original sources, such as the Qur'an, the Sunna and the traditions agreed upon by the Companions of the Prophet).[120] This preference for the sources of the Ḥanbalī *madhhab* and its methodology is clearly indicated in the Dār al-Iftā's *fatwās*, as al-Atawneh recognises ("the Ḥanbalī *madhhab*, as interpreted by Ibn Taymiyya and his disciples, is still preferred by the Dār al-Iftā' when strong evidence is lacking elsewhere").[121] The Dār al-Iftā's members continue to be faithful to the Ḥanbalī *madhhab* and its associated legal methodologies and principles – this is reflected in a continued adherence to the literal meaning of the sacred text (the Qur'an) and the transmitted tradition (*naql*), as opposed to the reason (*'aql*). The direct and frequent references to the Qur'an and Sunna in many *fatwās* on various subjects are indicative of placing the primary importance on the two main authoritative sources, before any other source. This continued commitment to the Ḥanbalī *madhhab* notwithstanding, it is possible to recognise a number of emerging tendencies in which the legal methodologies, principles and theories of the other three *madhhabs*, including *qiyās*, *maṣlaḥa* and *ḍarūra*, have been gradually drawn into mechanisms that the Dār al-Iftā' employs when it issues a *fatwā*.

The practice of *tarjīḥ* is particularly significant because it demonstrates that the Dār al-Iftā' does not limit itself to a certain *madhhab* (e.g., the Ḥanbalī school) and also illustrates that the institution addresses the challenges of modern life through a broad-ranging application of methodologies within the Islamic legal tradition.[122] The Dār al-Iftā's moderate approach towards the three *madhhabs* and their methodologies is easily observable when the BSU handles the controversial and intricate issues directed by the King or the government agencies. However, the CRLO generally follows the Ḥanbalī school's legal theories and methodologies when issuing *fatwās* for simple questions directed by individual questioners. This attests tenuously to the Dār al-Iftā's reluctance in adopting an inter-*madhhab* trend in the process of *fatwā*-making.

In addition to preparing research that establishes the basis for the BSU's discussions, the CRLO is also tasked with issuing *fatwās* (relating to faith, ritual practices and social transactions).[123] These questions are forwarded, whether through the internet, via post or through the telephone, by both members of the Saudi public and Muslims resident in other countries.[124] Specific questions tend to be answered on an individual basis, whereas those that occur with a greater frequency tend to be engaged during weekly sessions, which are generally held

120 Al-Atawneh, *Wahhābī Islam* (n 4) 75–76.

121 ibid 75.

122 ibid 81.

123 Royal Decree A/137, 29 August 1971, 5; Sherifa Zuhur, *Middle East in Focus: Saudi Arabia* (ABC-CLIO 2011) 96.

124 Al-Atawneh, *Wahhābī Islam* (n 4) 25.

on Sundays and Tuesdays.[125] On other weekdays, at least two *'ulamā'* should be available to either answer phone calls or receive visitors.[126] Royal Decree A/137 establishes the presence of at least three CRLO members and the passage of a majority vote as preconditions for the issuance of *a fatwā*. It states:

> Any *fatwā* must not be issued by the Permanent Committee unless the great majority of its members avow it. [In any event,] the number of *muftīs* must not be less than three. Under the condition of a tie on any issue discussed by *muftīs*, the vote of the chairman determines the outcome.[127]

The CRLO normally requires a single meeting in order to issue a *fatwā*; however, it is sometimes necessary to convene up to four further meetings if the key issue has not been resolved.[128] It is also possible to issue several *fatwās* during a single meeting.[129] Each *fatwā* has a serial number; however, the date of issuance and the name of the questioner are not generally included.

The four to seven members who work in the CRLO are selected from amongst the BSU's *'ulamā'*.[130] In addition to these prominent members, a number of research assistants are assigned to serve in the CRLO.[131] CRLO members meet twice a week. Recurrent *fatwās* are generated in a compendium before being published at the end of the year. At present, twenty volumes are dispersed through Islamic websites.[132] CRLO *fatwās* have also been compiled into periodic editions (entitled "*Fatawā al-Lajna al-Dā'ima lil-Buḥuth al-'Ilmiyya wal-Iftā'*") and published.[133] Since the CRLO's establishment, the issuance of *fatwās* has emerged as its main function although it has also undertaken numerous research projects.[134] While research project topics are generally determined by the BSU, CRLO and King, the King's priorities enjoy a clear pre-eminence.[135]

125 Mouline, *The Clerics of Islam* (n 16) 53.
126 Mouline, 'Enforcing and Reinforcing' (n 22) 60; Mouline, *The Clerics of Islam* (n 16)153.
127 Royal Decree A/137, 29 August 1971, 8.
128 Al-Atawneh, *Wahhābī Islam* (n 4) 26.
129 ibid 26.
130 Mouline, 'Enforcing and Reinforcing' (n 22) 59.
131 Al-Atawneh, *Wahhābī Islam* (n 4) 27.
132 Mouline, 'Enforcing and Reinforcing' (n 22) 59; al-Atawneh, *Wahhābī Islam* (n 4) 25. See http://www.alifta.net/default.aspx?languagename=ar and http://islamopediaonline.org/. See also private websites of prominent Wahhābī *muftīs*: Shaykh Ibn Bāz <http://www.binbaz.org.sa/> accessed 19 June 2016; Shaykh Ibn 'Uthaymīn <http://binothaimeen.net/index.php> accessed 19 June 2016; and others.
133 See online version <http://www.alifta.net/Fatawa/FatawaChapters.aspx?languagename=ar&MenuID=0&View=tree&NodeID=1&PageNo=1&BookID=3&Rokn=false> accessed 19 June 2016.
134 Al-Atawneh, *Wahhābī Islam* (n 4) 25.
135 Royal Decree A/137, 29 August 1971, 7.

Grand Muftī Office

In 1952, King 'Abd al-'Azīz established the Grand Muftī Office (*al-Muftī al-'Āmm*) and designated Shaykh Muḥammad ibn Ibrāhīm as the Grand Muftī. This provided the office with an official status within the Saudi administrative system. When Shaykh Muḥammad ibn Ibrāhīm died in 1969, his office was suspended for over two decades (1969–1993).[136] During this period, a new Dār al-Iftā', which was largely composed of the BSU and the CRLO, was established, and its structure was reordered in order to enable it to exert more complete control over the socio-religious domain. Mouline situates this reform within the wider context of institutionalisation.[137] It is likely that the Saudi Government did not wish to re-establish the Grand Muftī's office until the Dār al-Iftā' assumed its final form and attained public and religious recognition. Since Shaykh Muḥammad ibn Ibrāhīm held the juridical-religious offices and broad institutional powers, King Fayṣal's efforts to fragment and institutionalise the monopolistic religious establishment were complicated.[138] Shaykh Muḥammad ibn Ibrāhīm's dissenting statements and legal explanations, which confronted the positions of the courts and chambers of commerce, both of whom were responsible for addressing issues in the areas of positive law[139] and finance,[140] clarified the ongoing tension with the state policy. In his role as the Grand Muftī, Shaykh Muḥammad ibn Ibrāhīm presided over the *Dār al-Iftā' wal-Ishrāf 'alā al-Shu'ūn al-Dīniyya*,[141] a body with responsibility for issuing *fatwās* and managing religious affairs: he combined this role with various presidencies (of the al-Da'wa Foundation, the High Institute of the Magistracy, the Islamic University of Medina and the Religious Studies and Arabic Faculties).[142] These positions provided him with an opportunity to use state employment to dominate Saudi religious space. In addition to these religious positions, he was also responsible for the administration of girls' education and the leadership of the judicial system as a Chief *Qāḍī*.[143]

In suspending the Grand Muftī position for slightly more than two decades, the state brought the Grand Muftī's monopoly to an end and dissolved the vertical authority of this position, an action that was apparently undertaken in full awareness of the fact that any individual possessed of charisma and energy would have the ability to frustrate the reform and institutionalisation of the Saudi state. Even though the BSU, the CRLO, the newly created Ministry of Justice and the Supreme Judicial Council were essential components of the institutionalisation process, the suspension of the State Grand Muftī's office probably sought to

136 Al-Shalhūb (n 17) 218–219.
137 Mouline, *The Clerics of Islam* (n 16) 157.
138 Vogel, *Islamic Law and Legal System* (n 24) 92.
139 Mouline, *The Clerics of Islam* (n 16) 143.
140 ibid.
141 Al-Shalhūb (n 17) 218–219.
142 Mouline, *The Clerics of Islam* (n 16) 138.
143 ibid.

distribute the functions of the previous Dār al-Iftā' (which had operated under the leadership of Shaykh Muḥammad ibn Ibrāhīm) to these newly established (and state-dependent) agencies along with established ministries.

After limiting the office's authority and establishing a degree of collegiality within the religious establishments by fragmenting the juridical-religious structure, King Fahd issued a royal decree in July 1993 which declared the reestablishment of the Grand Muftī's office.[144] Shaykh 'Abd al-'Azīz ibn Bāz was then appointed to this position and also became the permanent chairman of both the BSU and the CRLO.[145] In Saudi Arabia, Ibn Bāz was widely respected among both Wahhābī scholars and the general public. Al-Atawneh affirms:

> Ibn Bāz's prodigious social activity and involvement caused him to be greatly esteemed in a wide range of Saudi circles, as can be clearly seen in the reactions following his death which proved a strong blow to Saudi society.[146]

In addition to his role as Grand Muftī, Ibn Bāz occupied a range of religious positions, at both the international and national levels. His religious career began when he worked as a *qādī* (judge) in the Al-Kharj area; he then became a lecturer in the College of Sharī'a (*Kulliyyat al-Sharī'a*) before becoming established as the president of the State Islamic University, the chairman of the World Muslim League (*Rābiṭat al-'Ālam al-Islāmī*) and the Chairman of the Islamic Jurisprudence Assembly in Mecca (*al-Majma' al-Fiqhī al-Islāmī fī Makka*).[147] These positions, in addition to his close relationship with the Āl-al-Shaykh family and the Saudi dynasty, enabled him to become an important religious and social figure within the society. His proximity to the Saudi throne also meant that he frequently acted as an intermediary between the Saudi Government and society.[148] Ibn Bāz retained the position of Grand Muftī until his death in 1999. Two days after his death, Shaykh 'Abd Allāh, the current Grand Muftī, was promoted to this position, along with the chairmanship of the BSU and the CRLO.

In contrast to his two predecessors, Shaykh 'Abd Allāh is not socially active or influential. He was born in Riyadh in 1941 with weak eyesight before, twenty years later, completely losing his sight.[149] In 1954, he attended the Imām al-Da'wa

144 Royal Decree, A/4, 9 July 1993.

145 Al-Shalhūb (n 17) 219.

146 Al-Atawneh, *Wahhābī Islam* (n 4) 33.

147 Member Scholars of the Permanent Committee for Ifta', 'Ibn Baz: Concise Biography' <http://www.alifta.net/Search/ResultDetails.aspx?languagename=en&lang=en&view=result&fatwaNum=&FatwaNumID=&ID=3&searchScope=14&SearchScopeLevels1=&SearchScopeLevels2=&highLight=1&SearchType=exact&SearchMoesar=false&bookID=&LeftVal=0&RightVal=0&simple=&SearchCriteria=allwords&PagePath=&siteSection=1&searchkeyword=105098110032098097122#firstKeyWordFound> accessed 11 November 2017.

148 Al-Atawneh, *Wahhābī Islam* (n 4) 32–33.

149 Member Scholars of the Permanent Committee for Ifta', 'His Eminence Shaykh 'Abdul-'Aziz ibn 'Abdullah ibn Muhammad Al Al-Shaykh' <http://www.alifta.com/Fatawa/MoftyDetails.aspx?languagename=en&Type=Mofty&section=tafseer&ID=8> accessed 11 November 2017.

Institute, before graduating from the Faculty of Sharī'a in 1962.[150] Subsequent to graduation, his vocational career in the area of religion began, and he worked as a teacher and lecturer at academic institutions in Riyadh, the Imām al-Da'wa Institute and the Faculty of Sharī'a, between 1971 and 1991.[151] In 1986, he was appointed as a member of the Dār al-Iftā' and became Ibn Bāz's deputy in 1995. In comparison to the previous two Grand Muftīs, whose exercise of religious authority derived from a variety of religious positions, Shaykh 'Abd Allāh holds few religious positions – he is therefore less active and less authoritative than his predecessors in the role. His membership of the Āl al-Shaykh family could be interpreted as the return of the Āl al-Shaykh to its historical religious post (the practice of *iftā'*) after it had been held for a substantial amount of time by a religious figure who was not linked to the family. Since being appointed to the role, Shaykh 'Abd Allāh has issued several controversial *fatwās* that have caused him to be labelled as conservative and xenophobic. (Brachman observes that Shaykh 'Abd Allāh "is known for his conservative positions on Islamic issues.")[152] His 2007 announcement upon the Green Dome on the top of the tombs of the Prophet and the first two Caliphs (Abū Bakr and 'Umar b. al-Khaṭṭāb) along with his 2012 declaration on the destruction of churches within the Arabian Peninsula attracted negative comments from both the Muslim and Western world.[153]

In conclusion, the reconstruction of the Grand Muftī's Office centralised the practice of *iftā'* after a substantial period of time by placing all *iftā'* institutions under its control and oversight.[154] As the permanent chairman of both the CRLO and the BSU, the Grand Muftī can open and manage sessions held within both institutions.[155] In addition, the Grand Muftī can also cast the decisive vote if the *'ulamā'* is unable to declare a clear majority when a *fatwā* is issued or legal advice is determined.[156] While the authority of the office is mainly restricted to the practice of *iftā'*, it has operated as the highest *iftā'* authority in the state since its establishment.

150 ibid.

151 ibid.

152 Jarret M. Brachman, *Global Jihadism: Theory and Practice* (Routledge 2009), under the title "Establishment Salafists."

153 Mark L. Samuel, *John's Assignment: A Satire on the Human Condition* (Author House 2013) 63–64. For the *fatwā* concerning the destruction of churches in the Arabian Peninsula, see Fatwā No. 21413 in *Fatwas of the Permanent Committee*, 1: 468–471 <http://www.alifta.net/Search/ResultDetails.aspx?languagename=en&lang=en&view=result&fatwaNum=&FatwaNumID=&ID=10807&searchScope=7&SearchScopeLevels1=&SearchScopeLevels2=&highLight=1&SearchType=exact&SearchMoesar=false&bookID=&LeftVal=0&RightVal=0&simple=&SearchCriteria=allwords&PagePath=&siteSection=1&searchkeyword=067104117114099104101115032105110032065114097098105097110032080101110105110115117108097#firstKeyWordFound> accessed 12 November 2017.

154 Al-Atawneh, *Wahhābī Islam* (n 4) 34.

155 Royal Decree A/137, 29 August 1971, 2.

156 ibid 3.

Table 1.1 The Dār al-Iftā's organisational structure and functions

The Grand Muftī of the Kingdom
(created in 1993)

The General Presidency of Scholarly Research and *Iftā'*
(Dār al-Iftā')
(active on a daily basis)

1. Defending, promoting and propagating the Wahhābism in Saudi Arabia and abroad,
2. Managing legal and theological scholars,
3. Providing administrative and logistic support to the BSU and the CRLO,
4. Supervising and inspecting the religious publications and translations (the printing and translation of the Qur'an, *fatwās* issued by the BSU and CRLO, its internet website, etc.)

***Hay'at Kibār al-'Ulamā'* (Board of Senior 'Ulamā)**
(meets biannually or more often in case of an urgent events)

1. Issuing public-type *fatwās,* particularly at macro-social and macro-political level,
2. Answering questions of legitimacy and public order,
3. Organising meetings and conferences on important religious, social and political issues,
4. Managing library

***Al-Lajna al-Dā'ima lil-Buḥūth al-'Ilmiyya wal-Iftā'* (Permanent Committee for Scientific Research and Legal Opinion)**
(meets twice a week and responses daily questions)

1. Issuing private-type *fatwās*, generally in the sphere of personal affairs (dogma, ritual, everyday life, etc.)
2. Preparing research reports for the BSU's discussions,

The process of issuing *fatwās*

In the contemporary period, the BSU and the CRLO, both of which operate under the leadership of the Grand Muftī, constitute the Dār al-Iftā', which is the highest official authority for Islamic legal interpretation and the issuance of *fatwās* in Saudi Arabia. Although possessing distinct roles and duties, these three agencies evidence complementary functions when deciding upon a *fatwā*. The process through which a *fatwā* is issued corresponds to a hierarchical system that conjoins the three agencies. The CRLO addresses a great number of questions which relate to all aspects of life, including, *inter alia*, economics, family planning, food, gender issues, marriage, medicine, Muslim minority groups, politics, technology and theology. Questions on these matters can be submitted by a legal professional or a lay Muslim. When a question relates to the administrative spheres, controversial and contradictive religious issues or macro-social and political realms, the question, along with a religious report prepared by the CRLO, is immediately transferred to the BSU.[157] The CRLO therefore sets the research agenda by selecting topics that derive from questions received on a daily basis. The research agenda is then submitted to the Royal Cabinet and is subject to the King's approval or veto.[158] Once this official process is complete, the research agenda is certified by the Royal Cabinet and subsequent to the King's approval, addressed to the BSU's members. The CRLO's functions can therefore be defined as the issuance of exhortations and *fatwās* that are addressed to personal religious inquiries that arrive at the CRLO on a daily basis. Furthermore, it also establishes the BSU's research agenda by preparing religious reports on a wide range of subjects. The BSU functions as a guardian against non-sharīʿa legislation. The Dār al-Iftā's hierarchical structure clearly establishes the BSU's status as the supreme religious *iftā'* authority in Saudi Arabia and also clarifies that the Dār al-Iftā' is subject to the authority of the political power when it comes to the determination of the research agenda that will be discussed by the BSU.

Correspondence and other communications between the BSU, the CRLO and the Royal Cabinet are the responsibility of the BSU's General Secretary, who is an official directly appointed by the Council of Ministers.[159] While the General Secretary is not a member of the BSU, he must have a diploma in religious studies. His function is to ensure that research reports, along with the CRLO's research agenda, are prepared and submitted to the BSU's members at least two weeks prior to the evaluative session.[160] He is also responsible for ensuring the effective coordination of the three state agencies and for processing the BSU's decisions and *fatwās*, with the cooperation of the CRLO's directorate.

In exceptional cases, the Royal Cabinet is entitled to ask the BSU to assemble special meetings and directly establish the research agenda.[161] These meetings are addressed to the condemnation of a dangerous event, the discrediting of an enemy of the Kingdom in the eyes of the public and/or the legitimisation of a decision generally regarding political matters.[162] Relevant examples include the 1979 seizure of Mecca, the 1990 deployment of American troops in Saudi Arabia and disconcerting "anti-government" tendencies.[163] The government petitioned the BSU on each of these issues with the intention of gaining support for its policies. However, because these *fatwās* possess a certain internal (legal and logical)

157 Mouline, *The Clerics of Islam* (n 16) 158.
158 ibid.
159 Royal Degree A/88, 29 May 2001, 4; al-Atawneh, *Wahhābī Islam* (n 4) 17.
160 Al-Atawneh, *Wahhābī Islam* (n 4) 21.
161 Mouline, *The Clerics of Islam* (n 16) 158.
162 ibid.
163 During the Ikhwān rebellion (1927–1930), the labour riots (1962–1966), the seizure of Mecca's Grand Mosque (1979) and the Arab-Israeli Peace Process (1991–1996), the official *'ulamā'* supported the Saudi Government by approving its political policies. See Teitelbaum (n 62) 17–66; Al-Atawneh, *Wahhābī Islam* (n 4) 45–54; Al-Rasheed (n 5) 80–133; F. Gregory Gause III, 'Official Wahhabism and the Sanctioning of the Saudi-US Relations' in Mohammed Ayoop and Hasan Kosebalaban (eds), *Religion and Politics in Saudi Arabia: Wahhabism and the State* (Lynne Rienner Publishers 2009) 135–144.

coherence, it would be inaccurate to criticise them for merely providing political support to the government; furthermore, the accusation that the BSU performs an essentially political function would also fall short of the objective requirements of Islamic legal analysis. Because cooperation (*ta'āwun*) and obedience (*ṭā'a*) are foundations of the Wahhābī doctrine of *siyāsa shar'iyya*, which reinforces the broad authority of the leader, the BSU presumably recognises the King's authority in identifying the state's interests.[164] In issuing a *fatwā* that relates to the political field, the Dār al-Iftā' acknowledges the existence of a separate field of authority and the need to offer allegiance (*bay'a*) to it. This politically autonomous field is however conceived in religious terms – this lends further strength to the proposition that the Wahhābī doctrine of *siyāsa shar'iyya* emerges through a traditional interpretation.

The coordinated effort of the Dār al-Iftā's three agencies produces *fatwās* that cover cultural, economic, legal, political, religious and social issues; however, they are only given legal effect by the King's endorsement. *Fatwās* lacking in legal effect touch upon subjects as diverse as celebrating the Prophet's Birthday (*al-Mawlid al-Nabawī*), gender confirmation surgery, female leadership, greeting Christians during their feast, marriage to obtain citizenship, listening to music, mobile ringtones, reading the Gospel and the Bible, shaking hands with women, treatment with blood and working in banks. Even though these *fatwās* are not legally binding, they make an important contribution to the country's religious and social life. It is normally the case that the BSU's decisions and *fatwās* are approved by the King. However, this approval is not forthcoming when the proposed measure runs counter to public welfare and/or state interests. Under some circumstances, state interests, as defined by the King, may take precedence over the BSU's decisions and *fatwās*.[165]

The BSU's *fatwā* upon the expansion of the circumambulation area around Ka'ba (*taw'siat al-maṭāf*) clearly demonstrates that the King or the government disregarded the BSU's decision due to the fact that it conflicted with public welfare.[166] In 2006, the King requested a *fatwā* from the BSU on the proposed enlargement of this area, with the intention of minimising any potential difficulties. The BSU members did not align their verdict with the Saudi Government's request and therefore highlighted the points at which the proposed measure conflicted with the authoritative texts. Particular controversy arose in relation to the expansion of the *mas'ā*, the circumambulation passage between the Hills Ṣafā and Marwa. In setting the BSU's *fatwā* aside, the King decided to seek the opinions of other Muslim scholars in the Muslim world. It was no surprise when other schol-

164 Vogel, *Islamic Law and Legal System* (n 24) 169–170.

165 ibid.

166 Jones (n 11) 112–119; Aḥmad Selāmat al-Gharyānī, 'Fatāwā al-'Ulamā' fī Ḥukm al-Tawsi'at al-Jadīda lil-Mas'ā wa 'Ademu Jawāzi al-Sa'ī fihā' <http://www.ahlalhdeeth.com/vb/showthread.php?t=199230> accessed 05 August 2016; Muṣṭafā Farḥāt, 'Akbar Tawsi'at lil-Ḥaramayn Tuthīru bayna al-'Ulamā' fī al-Sa'ūdiyya' <http://www.djazairess.com/echorouk/25380> accessed 06 August 2016.

ars within the Muslim world endorsed the King's proposal to enlarge Ka'ba's circumambulation capacity by appealing to the principle of *maṣlaḥa*.[167] Mouline suggests that the King's contra-decision was "an important economic and symbolic investment that would positively reflect on the kingdom and its rulers"[168] – however, this overlooks the fact that this cannot be solely considered from an economic perspective. By virtue of the fact that overcrowding and safety issues were also ongoing concerns for the Saudi state,[169] Mouline's assertion is quite narrow and restricted. The BSU's *fatwā* determines the areas which are encompassed by the *mas'ā* by referring to books produced by scholars of the *ḥadīth*, history and Islamic jurisprudence.[170] The scholars maintained that the area of the *mas'ā* can be ascertained through the measuring unit of arm's length (*dhirā'*), whose width was clearly documented in the books produced by the earlier scholars. Here it is established that the length of the *mas'ā* closely corresponds to the Hills of Ṣafā and Marwa and that its width is determined through the historical development and expansion of continuous generations that have passed since the Prophet Muhammad's time. After discussing this matter and deliberating upon it, the majority of scholars reached the following conclusion:

> Its current expansion exhausts in full the whole area of the *mas'ā*, and thus it is not permissible to extend its width any further. The problem can be solved by vertically adding building to over the *mas'ā* area under the condition of necessity (*ḍarūra*).[171]

In reaching their legal conclusion, the BSU's scholars therefore only emphasised religious considerations and the technical part of the question; in addition, reference was only made to the possibility of vertically constructing a building over the circumambulation passage which conjoins the Hills Ṣafā and Marwa. Although the BSU are generally supportive of the Saudi Government and its policies, this *fatwā* may potentially provide considerable insight into tensions between the official religious establishment and the Saudi Government in contemporary Saudi Arabia.

In addition, the *fatwā* addressed to the destruction of churches in the Arabian Peninsula was issued by the CRLO in 2012, when it operated under the chairmanship of Grand Muftī, Shaykh 'Abd Allāh. The question that is recorded asks whether it is acceptable for a company owner to establish a place of worship for his/her non-Muslim employees. The *'ulamā'* adopted a particularly interesting

167 Farḥāt (n 166).

168 Mouline, *The Clerics of Islam* (n 16) 161.

169 For other reasons of the expansion of circumambulation area around the Ka'ba, see Asghar Ali Imam Mahadi Salafi and Abul Hayat Ashraf, 'Expansion of the Mataaf," "Aiming High" and "Welcome Change,"' (2011) 5 (4) *The Simple Truth* 13–26 <http://www.ahlehadees.org/phocadownloadpap/april-11.pdf> accessed 04 August 2016.

170 Farḥāt (n 166).

171 Al-Gharyānī (n 166).

approach when authoring this *fatwā*, which is based on three central arguments, each of which is supported by the textual sources:

1. Building places of worship for non-Muslims in the Arabian Peninsula, such as churches and synagogues, is held to be almost equivalent to deviation from the right path or apostasy. This position is supported by a long list of Qur'anic verses that clearly establish that Islam is the last religion and the Prophet Muhammad is the last Prophet.[172] In referring to these verses, the *'ulamā'* establish their analogy (*qiyās*) by arguing that the acceptance of Christianity and Judaism as true religions will cause abjuration of one's own religion – this constitutes an effective cause (*'illa*). The *'ulamā'* therefore establish a clear analogy between the construction of houses of worship for non-Muslims and the endorsement of their faith. However, the *'ulamā'* signally fail to acknowledge that there is actually a significant difference between these two things (the endorsement of other religions as true and the construction of places of worship for non-Muslims). The profession of other religions as true is certainly related to faith or creed (*'aqīda*); however, the construction or maintenance of houses of worship belonging to non-Muslims is an issue that pertains to the Islamic legal rights of non-Muslims (*ḥuqūq ahl al-dhimma*).[173] Accordingly, from an Islamic legal perspective, the two cannot actually be held to be identical in order to draw an analogy,
2. The sacrosanct position of the Arabian Peninsula is held as the main ground to render the construction and maintenance of such temples as sinful. The *'ulamā'* attempt to support this position by citing a transmitted *ḥadīth*, in which the Prophet states that two religions should not co-exist in the Arabian Peninsula.[174] Although the *fatwā* cites this *ḥadīth* as a basis for refusing to allow non-Muslims to establish a foothold in the Arabian Peninsula, it overlooks the fact that it contradicts some Qur'anic verses,[175] which include the Q. 2:256 ("Let there be no force (or compulsion) in religion: Surely -Truth

172 The cited verses are the Q. 34:28, 7:158, 3:19, 3:85 and 98:6, respectively.

173 The term "*al-ahl al-dhimma*" literally means "the community of the covenant" – this is a term used to denote members of officially tolerated and protected religions under Muslim states in compliance with the agreements and contracts that are signed between Muslim states and non-Muslims.

174 Fatwā No. 21413 (n 153).

175 The Q. 10:99 reads: "If it had been your Lord's will all of them would have believed- All you are on earth! (But) will you then compel mankind, against their will, to believe?" According to this verse, mankind has been endowed with various faculties and capacities, and limited free will has been given to them, so they have the power and capacity to differentiate good from wrong. In the same vein with this verse, the *Sūra al-Kāfirūn* (the Disbelievers) refers to the very existence of freedom of religion in Islam. For further insight into a separate explanation that relates to the relationship between Muslims and non-Muslims, refer also to Said Hassan, 'Law-Abiding Citizen: Recent Fatwas on Muslim Minorities' Loyalty to Western Nations' (2015) 105 (4) *The Muslim World* 528–536 <http://onlinelibrary.wiley.com/doi/10.1111/muwo.12109/full> accessed 18 November 2017.

stands out clear from error"). This verse quite clearly recognises a right of freedom of religion, and it is therefore clear that not permitting the construction of places of worship can be said to represent a kind of compulsion. The contradiction between the textual sources can most likely be traced back to the fact that the *'ulamā'* adopt a literal interpretation. Rather than indicating the prohibition of the coexistence of one true (Islam) and one untrue religion, the *ḥadīth* clearly adopts an Islamic perspective to envisage the prospective impossibility of the simultaneous coexistence of two true religions in the Arabian Peninsula. Prior to the emergence of Islam, the Prophet Ibrāhīm and the Prophet Lūt simultaneously coexisted in the Arabian Peninsula.[176] In addition, this literal interpretation of the *ḥadīth* runs counter to other *ḥadīths* that explain the interaction of the Prophet with the People of Book and the political and religious policies that he applied to them.[177] The extant presence of the Christian and Jewish populations and their temples in the region may also lend further support to the proposition that the literal interpretation of the *ḥadīth* is questionable when perceived through the lens of Islamic legal history. In indicating the existence of *ijmā'* amongst Muslim scholars upon the need to destroy temples belonging to other religions, the *fatwā* states: "[s]cholars unanimously agreed on the obligation of destroying churches and other places of worship if they were built recently in the Muslim lands."[178] However, the claim that there is *ijmā'* on the destruction of temples of other religions suggests that the *'ulamā'* are blind to historical realities. For instance, 'Umar b. al-Khaṭṭāb, the second Caliph, granted freedom of religion to the Christian and Jewish population of Palestine and Syria and did not damage their temples when he conquered this land.[179] Upon this basis alone, it can be asserted that the claim of *ijmā'* is defective,

3. The last argument advanced by the *'ulamā'* is that allowing the construction of temples for other religions or allocating places for worship in any Muslim

176 In the Qur'an, the *Sūra al-Dhāriyāt* (the Scattering Winds) mentions that the prophecy was simultaneously given to both the Prophet Ibrāhīm and the Prophet Lūt. See the Q. 51: 24–37.

177 For the contradiction between the literal interpretation of the *ḥadīth* stated by the *'ullamā'* and other *ḥadīths* and the Covenants of the Prophet with the Christians of his time, see Abdur Rahman I. Doi, *Non-Muslims under Shari'ah (Islamic Law)* (Kazi Publications 1981) 62–84; Craig Considine, 'Religious Pluralism and Civic Rights in a "Muslim Nation": An Analysis of Prophet Muhammad's Covenants with Christians' (2016) 7 (15) *Religions* 6–13 <file:///C:/Users/emine%20enise%20yakar/Downloads/religions-07-00015.pdf> accessed 15 November 2017.

178 Fatwā No. 21413 (n 153).

179 Al-Ṭabarī, 'The Battle of al-Qādisiyyah and the Conquest of Syria and Palestine' in Ehsan Yar-Shater (ed), *The History of al- Ṭabarī*, vol XII (Yohanan Friedmann (tr) State University of New York Press 1997) 191–193. In referring to the existence of freedom of religion in Islamic law, Doi states: "It is interesting to note that all the old and famous Churches of Cairo were, according to al-Maqrizi, built during the Islamic period. For example, the famous church 'Mar Marcus' in Alexandria was built between 39–56 A.H. Similarly, the first church in Fusta, old Cairo, was built between 48–69 A.H. The Muslim rulers did not stop non-Muslims building the places of worship of their respective religions. Muslim rulers even provided them with facilities in building and preserving churches and synagogues." See Doi (n 177) 80–81.

country is tantamount to affirming disbelief, as these actions essentially confirm the truthfulness and authenticity of their religions.[180] The *'ulamā'* evaluated these claims under the concept of loyalty and disavowal (*al-walā' wal-barā'*).[181] In attempting to sustain their interpretations, they quote the Q. 5:2 out of context and with insufficient regard for its integrity. The cited part of the verse reads: "Help you one another in Al-Birr and At-Taqwâ (virtue, righteousness and piety); but do not help another in sin and transgression. And Fear Allâh. Verily, Allâh is Severe in punishment." However, the whole verse is concerned with the pilgrim (*ḥajj*) and the sacred symbols of God – the same Qur'anic verse also states: "And let not the hate of some people who earlier shut you out of the Sacred Mosque (in Makkah) lead you to overstepping your own limits (and bitterness on your part)." This is a clear warning that Muslims should bear in mind in their dealings with non-Muslims. Even if Muslims have previously encountered animosity and enmity in their relations with non-Muslims, they should endeavour to be fair, kind, modest and well-advised in their relations with their fellow non-Muslim citizens. It appears that the *'ulamā'* mainly rely on the specific Qur'anic verses and do not make reference to either their context or to other authoritative texts. The use of the stated part of the Qur'anic verse, which is clearly referenced out of context, may refer to the selectivity of the *'ulamā'* in adducing the textual legal evidence. Taking into account the selectivity and the rigid Wahhābī literal interpretation of the authoritative legal texts concerning the relationship between Muslims and non-Muslims, there are clear grounds for believing that the members of the Dār al-Iftā' or the official *'ulamā'* do not accept *ḥuqūq ahl al-dhimma* to be part of Islamic law. Although there are some defective points, the *fatwā* concludes with the statement that it is not permissible because the construction of temples for non-Muslims may result in accepting their faith, assisting their belief and strengthening their community.

The historical Wahhābī hostility towards other religious faiths therefore continues unabated, and this is clearly indicated in the fact that the official Wahhābī clerics call for discrimination and pressure to be exerted upon non-Muslims and restrictions to be placed upon their rights of religious freedom.[182] It also appears that this *fatwā* contradicts the interfaith respect and dialogue that King 'Abd Allāh

180 Fatwā No. 21413 (n 153).

181 Religious institutions have advanced different arguments and views on the concept of *al-walā' wal-barā'* (loyalty and disavowal). For example, the concept of *al-walā' wal-barā'* (loyalty and disavowal) is generally defined by the Saudi Arabia's Dār al-Iftā' in a way that suggests a Muslim should consider non-Muslims as enemies – accordingly, a Muslim should disassociate himself from them and their religions by submitting himself completely to God and being loyal only to Him. Hassan (n 175) 521–522, 527–528, 533–536; Sümeyra Yakar, 'The Consideration of *Bid'a* Concept according to Saudi and Iranian Scholars' (2020) 19 (2) *Mazahib Jurnal Pemikiran Hukum Islam* 237.

182 Quintan Wiktorowicz, 'Anatomy of the Salafi Movement' (2006) 29 *Studies in Conflict & Terrorism* 218.

(r. 2005–2015) sought to initiate. Since ascending to the Saudi throne in 2005, King 'Abd Allāh has prompted the modernisation of Saudi Arabia and its state apparatus (specifically a reform project focused mainly on freedom of expression, judicial fairness, religious tolerance and women's rights).[183]

In the area of religious tolerance, the Saudi state has initiated a number of significant projects. For example, in 2008, the Muslim World League, with the active encouragement of the King, began an interfaith dialogue discussion in Mecca.[184] The 2011 inauguration of the King Abdullah Bin Abdulaziz International Center for Interreligious and Intercultural Dialogue most likely derives from King 'Abd Allāh's reform policies which sought to promote inter-religious dialogue at the international level.[185] These initiatives, which were launched by the Saudi state, sought to bring together representatives of world faiths in order to increase mutual tolerance and respect both inside and outside Saudi Arabia.[186] It might therefore be argued that there is an ostensible clash between the King's reform policy and the position adopted by the high-ranking official *'ulamā'* or the Dār al-Iftā'. Many scholars, in contending that the *fatwā* contradicts the government policy, have precisely criticised it – those aligned with the dialogist and moderate government policy of King 'Abd Allāh have been particularly prominent in advancing this argument. Al-Alawi observes:

> The Saudi chief cleric then proceeded to conflict with repeated promises of the Saudi King, Abdullah, to foster interfaith respect and dialogue, by calling, in mid-March, for the destruction of all Christian churches in the Arabian Peninsula.[187]

Beside this, Esposito describes the *fatwā* as both a deviation from King 'Abd Allāh's reform policy and also a mirror that reflects the active and operative

183 Christoph Wilcke, *Looser Rein, Uncertain Gain: A Human Rights Assessment of Five Years of King Abdullah's Reforms in Saudi Arabia* (Human Rights Watch 2010) 1, 13, 16, 18–19, 20, 24, 33–34, 38–41, 48–49.

184 Wilcke, (n 183) 38; United States Commission on International Religious Freedom (USCRIF), *United States Commission on International Religious Freedom: Annual Report 2010* (U.S. Commission on International Religious Freedom 2010) 131; Yigal Carmon and Y. Admon, 'Reforms in Saudi Arabia under King 'Abdallah' (*The Middle East Research Institute (MEMRI)*, 04 June 2009) <https://www.memri.org/reports/reforms-saudi-arabia-under-king-abdallah> accessed 22 November 2017.

185 Abdullah al-Turki, 'Interfaith Dialogue: From Makkah to New York' in Muhammed al-Bishr (ed), *Interfaith Dialogue: Cross-Cultural Views* (1st edn, Ghainaa Publications 2010) 16–17; USCRIF (n 184) 131–133; Wilcke (n 183) 38–39.

186 Al-Turki (n 185) 15–18; Wilcke (n 183) 38–49; Carmon and Admon (n 184).

187 Irfan al-Alawi, 'Top Saudi Cleric: Ban Christian Churches in Arabia: Let Girls Marry at 10' (*Gatestone Institute International Policy Council*, 23 May 2012) <https://www.gatestoneinstitute.org/3073/saudi-fatwa-ban-christian-churches> accessed 20 November 2017.

role of the religious establishment in contemporary Saudi Arabia.[188] However, it should be noted that there is a statement in the *fatwā* ("[i]t is not permissible to oppose the Muslim ruler in destroying [churches], but you must obey him")[189] which clearly establishes the religious establishment's support for the policy pursued by King 'Abd Allāh's government and its unwillingness to become cast in an opposing role.[190] Although it has received little attention from scholars, this statement provides considerable insight into how the official *'ulamā'* function within the borders of the Wahhābī doctrine of *siyāsa shar'iyya* – in acting thus, the official *'ulamā'* helps to offset the threat of social unrest by preventing any clash between the Saudi Government, official religious establishment and wider society. This subtle undertone of support for the Saudi ruler notwithstanding, the *fatwā* clearly depicts the ongoing clash between the official *'ulamā'*s religious ideology and the Saudi Government policy. As Esposito emphasises, the fact that the government has proven to be reluctant to adopt legal measures that further entrench King 'Abd Allāh's reform policy can be interpreted as confirmation of the authority and power of the official *'ulamā'*, along with the continued salience of their religious discourses on the rights of non-Muslims. The fact that the limited reforms have not translated into state law further reiterates and underlines the King's reluctance to confront Saudi Arabia's religious establishment.

In addition to creating tension between the Saudi Government and the religious establishment, the *fatwā* also resulted in harsh criticism being directed at the Saudi state by Muslim scholars, other religious institutions and practicing Muslims across the world. Al-Azhar University, Jamal al-Shahab (Kuwait's Minister of Religious Endowments) and Mehmet Görmez (the president of Turkey's Presidency of Religious Affairs) all condemned the Saudi Grand Muftī and claimed that the *fatwā* clearly conflicted with Islam's peaceful teachings.[191] In undermining King 'Abd Allāh's commitment to promoting inter-religious dialogue and changing international perceptions of Saudi Arabia, the *fatwā* resulted in sustained criticism being directed towards the Saudi *'ulamā'*. In confirming that religious freedom continued to be suppressed in Saudi Arabia, the *fatwā* negatively impacted the religious foreign policy and religious reform that King 'Abd Allāh planned.

The relationship between the Dār al-Iftā' and the Saudi Government is not completely coherent and harmonious. However, it is difficult, if not impossible, to ascertain the precise status of the relationship between the two authority-holders (*wulāt al-'amr*), as the official *'ulamā'* have made it clear that they prefer to voice their criticism of the ruler in private.[192] Al-Yassini links the denoted

188 John L. Esposito, 'Exclusivist Muslims and the Threat to the Religious Reform' (*Religion and Ethics*, 15 May 2012) <http://www.abc.net.au/religion/articles/2012/05/15/3503503.htm> accessed 20 November 2017.

189 Fatwā No. 21413 (n 153).

190 ibid.

191 Samuel (n 153) 64; Al-Alawi (n 187); Esposito (n 188).

192 Al-Atawneh, *Wahhābī Islam* (n 4) 34; Chritopher Boucek, 'Saudi Fatwa Restrictions and the State-Clerical Relationship' (*Carnegie Endowment for International Peace*, 27 October 2010)

non-harmonic relationship (between the Dār al-Iftā' and the Saudi Government) to the King's actions towards the incorporation of the *'ulamā'* into the state administration.[193] Even though al-Yassini attributes these tensions and the Saudi Government's non-fulfilment of the Dār al-Iftā's decisions to the bureaucratisation and institutionalisation of the *'ulamā'*, it appears that this is not the case. The alleged argument that the institutionalisation of the *'ulamā'*, which occurred subsequent to the discovery of petroleum resources, rendered them ineffective and inoperative in Saudi Arabia is questionable precisely because the covert tensions between the *'ulamā'* and the *'umarā'* (in modern terms, the Dār al-Iftā' and the Saudi Government) have existed since the early period of the Saudi state. In 1927, for example, the Riyadh *'ulamā'*, who were predominantly drawn from the Āl al-Shaykh family, issued a *fatwā* that related to Saudi Arabia's Shī'i community.[194] The *fatwā* called for the Shī'is of Hasa to be prevented from worshipping publicly and from invoking the saintly members of the House of the Prophet (*Ahl al-Bayt*). It also called for this group to be prevented from visiting Karbala and Najaf, for them to be compelled to perform the five daily prayers in mosques and for their regional places of worship to be destroyed.[195] In setting aside the strong cooperation between the Saudi dynasty and the Āl al-Shaykh *'ulamā'* during this period, King 'Abd al-'Azīz refused to obey and enforce this *fatwā*. Instead of enforcing this oppressive *fatwā*, he chose to tax the protection that he provided to the Shī'is in the region.[196]

In addition, King 'Abd al-'Azīz's education policies and reforms that sought to include foreign language, geography and painting classes in public school curriculums created further tensions between the *'ulamā'* and him in 1930.[197] The *'ulamā'* issued a *fatwā* that protested against the King's education policies and in particular the inclusion of the aforementioned three subjects in the curriculum. The *fatwā*, which was probably grounded in the notion of *bid'a* (innovation) and the legal maxim of *sadd al-dharā'i'* (blocking means), objected to the study of foreign languages because it would enable Muslims to learn the religion of unbelievers; the painting classes because drawing and painting would also reproduce one of God's creatures; and geography because at that time, the *'ulamā'*'s interpretation of one of the Qur'anic verses regarding the earth indicated that it is flat.[198] King 'Abd al-'Azīz rejected this *fatwā* and decided to include the three sub-

<http://carnegieendowment.org/2010/10/27/saudi-fatwa-restrictions-and-state-clerical-relationship/6b81> accessed 23 September 2017.

193 Al-Yassini (n 2) 67.

194 Guido Steinberg, 'The Wahhabiyya and Shi'ism, from 1744/45 to 2008' in Ofra Bengio and Meir Litvak (eds), *The Sunna and Shi'a in History: Division in the Muslim Middle East* (Palgrave Macmillan 2011) 172.

195 Steinberg, 'The Wahhabiyya and Shi'ism' (n 194) 172–173; Raihan Ismail, *Saudi Clerics and Shī'a Islam* (Oxford University Press 2016) 108–109.

196 Steinberg, 'The Wahhabiyya and Shi'ism' (n 194) 170, 173–174; Mehmet Ali Büyükkara, *İhvan'dan Cüheyman'a Suudi Arabistan ve Vehhabilik* (Rağbet Yayınları 2016) 237–239.

197 Büyükkara (n 196) 154; Al-Yassini (n 2) 50.

198 Büyükkara (n 196) 154.

jects in the curriculum – in doing so, he argued that the *fatwā* failed to recognise the principle of Islam which encourages believers to obtain knowledge.[199] These examples provide grounds for the argument that the relationship between the *'ulamā'* and *'umarā'* (or the Dār al-Iftā' and the Saudi Government) has been demonstrating unbalanced fluctuations and abrupt tensions since the establishment of the Saudi state. This may be interpreted as implying that the role and activities of the *'ulamā'* in the present Saudi legal system and society have not been substantially diminished by the incorporation of the *'ulamā'* into the state administration.

In the absence of a constitutionally binding source of legislation, consensus is frequently achieved through the BSU, and the government may consult the BSU to issue a *fatwā* with the intention of standardising a legal ruling in the Saudi legal system. As Vogel notes, it appears that the BSU is one of the mechanisms of the Saudi legal system that provides uniformity and stability of rulings and judgments adjudicated by Saudi judges (*qāḍī*s).[200] For instance, the government requested a *fatwā* from the BSU that would ascertain delay penalties for construction contractors who fail to complete work on time when desiring *qāḍī*s to follow a single legal procedure on such matters.[201] Even though the ordinary *qāḍīs* are not officially liable for following *fatwās* issued by the BSU, they are reluctant to diverge from the senior *'ulamā'* when deriving a legal rule from the authoritative sources through their *ijtihād* efforts.[202] It is therefore possible to state that *fatwās*, in particular those issued by the BSU, have had an authoritative legal influence upon the *qāḍīs*' decisions. These types of *fatwās* are usually introduced and backed by the government, generally after the *'ulamā'* have first been consulted; in turn, the *qāḍīs* have begun to regard them as a single legal procedure that can be applied to the issue at hand.[203]

A further good example of these types of *fatwā*s is the BSU's *fatwā* that relates to two types of crimes (abduction/usurpation and drug/alcohol) and that was issued upon the request of King Khālid (d. 1982) in 1981.[204] When the incidence of these types of crimes noticeably increased, the King consulted the Dār al-Iftā' with the intention of bringing a deterrent legal regulation into effect and prevent-

199 ibid.

200 Vogel, *Islamic Law and Legal System* (n 24) 115–117.

201 ibid 124.

202 For further example on that issues, see Sümeyra Yakar, 'The Usage of Custom in the Contemporary Legal System of Saudi Arabia: Divorce on Trial' (2009) 6 (11) *Kilis 7 Aralık Üniversitesi* 386–387.

203 Vogel, *Islamic Law and Legal System* (n 24) 124.

204 The BSU decision No. 85 of 10 September 1981 <http://www.alifta.net/Search/ResultDetails.aspx?languagename=ar&lang=ar&view=result&fatwaNum=&FatwaNumID=&ID=1676&searchScope=2&SearchScopeLevels1=&SearchScopeLevels2=&highLight=1&SearchType=exact&SearchMoesar=false&bookID=&LeftVal=0&RightVal=0&simple=&SearchCriteria=allwords&PagePath=&siteSection=1&searchkeyword=217130216177216167216177032217135217138216166216169032217131216168216167216177032216167217132216185217132217133216167216161#firstKeyWordFound> accessed 10 December 2017.

Table 1.2 The process of *fatwā*-issuing by the Dār al-Iftā'

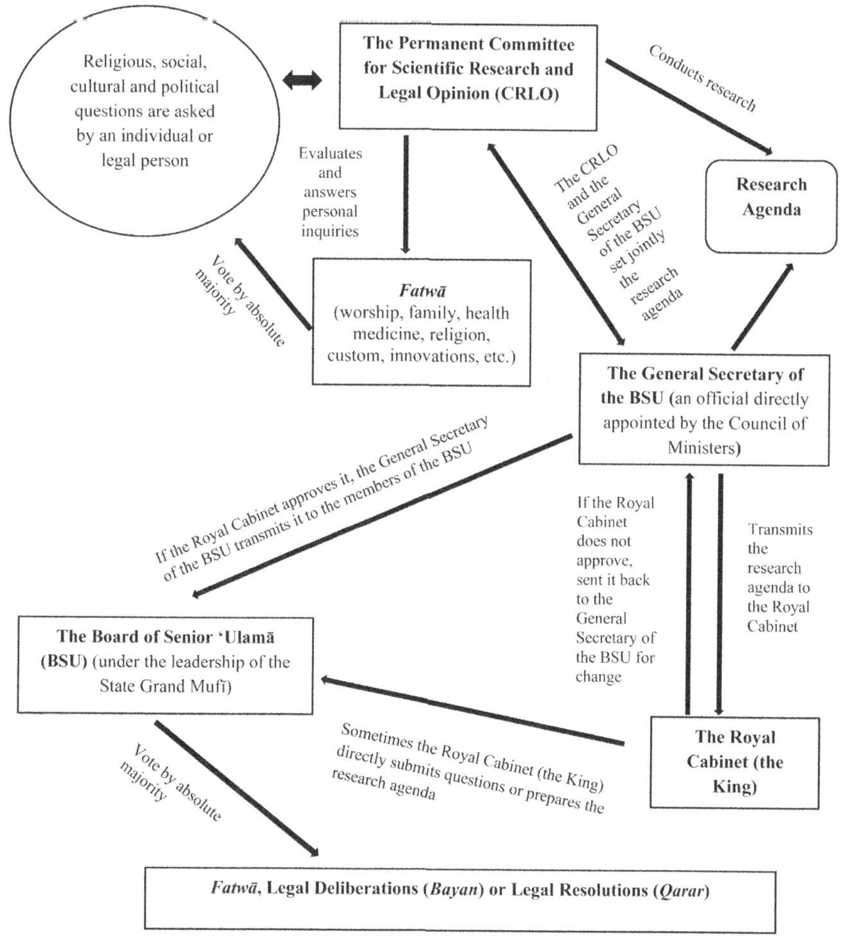

ing penalisations of these crimes from being delayed.[205] The *fatwā* that derives from the CRLO's preparatory study evaluates these crimes in two different sections: the first section addresses the issue of abduction and usurpation, and the second discusses the *apropos* penalty for crimes relating to alcohol and drugs. In putting in place the penalties for these crimes, the BSU's *fatwā* addresses itself to three points – firstly, the seriousness of the crimes; secondly, social welfare; and

205 The BSU decision No. 85 of 10 September 1981; Vogel, *Islamic Law and Legal System* (n 24) 252–253.

finally, the need for deterrent penalties for the offence. In referring to the first section, the BSU bases its argument upon the Q. 5:33 which reads:

> The punishment for those who wage a war against Allah and His messenger (Muhammad), and work hard with strength and taste for mischief through the land, is: Execution, or crucifixion, or the cutting off of hands and feet from opposite sides, or exile from the land. That is their disgrace in this word, and their punishment is heavy in the Hereafter.

This verse is the main authoritative text on which the *ḥadd* crimes and penalties of brigandage (*ḥirāba* or *muḥāraba*) are based. In the verse, the statement "work hard with strength and taste for mischief through the land" is interpreted as permitting the deputies of the ruler (judges) to extend the *ḥadd* penalties to people who cause harm to the Muslim community, create corruption on earth and fight against Islam. After citing this verse, BSU members further strengthen their argument by referring to the *ḥadīth* narrated by Anas and to Mālikī Ibn 'Arabī's legal ruling (*ḥukm*) that concerns defamatory and humiliating offences and abduction.[206] The *fatwā* then concludes the first section by accentuating three points. Firstly, it establishes that the person who commits an act of aggression, abduction and usurpation, whether in a city, desert, isolated place or village, should be convicted in accordance with the *ḥirāba* penalties. Secondly, the crimes committed against dignity have been understood to be equivalent to the offences that encroach upon other's lives and properties, or more heinous crimes than them. Thirdly, the judges have been bestowed the right to choose among the prescribed *ḥirāba* punishments when penalising the offenders of abduction and usurpation – however, the judge overseeing such a case must demonstrate that the offender wages a war against God and His Messenger and causes corruption on earth.[207] As the first and second

206 Abū 'Abdullāh Muḥammad ibn Ismā'īl al-Buhārī, *Ṣaḥīḥ al-Bukharī*, vol VIII (Muhammad Muhsin Khan (tr) Darussalam 1997) 416. Aforesaid Ibn 'Arabī' in the *fatwā* is Mālikī Ibn 'Arabī' (d.1148). In referring to the legal judgment of Ibn 'Arabī', BSU members conceivably intend to enrich their argument that puts the abduction offences under the category of *ḥirāba* crimes. The *fatwā* states: "Ibn 'Arabī' during his time of being a judge narrates one of his Islamic legal judgements as follows: "The case of a group of combatants were raised to me. One of the warriors forcefully abducted a woman regardless of her husband's attempts of rescuing her, along with some other people who were abducted as well. They brought the woman with them and they were taken to the court and I asked how the *muftīs* resolved the issue. They said: "the *muftīs* stated that those warriors who took the woman were not gangsters or brigands (*muḥārabūn*) because the *ḥirāba* crimes are concerned with looting properties, not transgressing against one's dignity." I replied in sadness, "we came from God and we only return to Him. Did not you know that violating one's dignity and honour is more horrendous than usurping one's money and that people are readier to let their money be looted and their properties be usurped rather than seeing their wives or daughters abducted and kidnapped? If there was any graver punishment prescribed by God, it would have been for those who transgress against dignity and honour."""" See the BSU decision No. 85 of 10 September 1981.

207 The BSU decision No. 85 of 10 September 1981. For further analysis of the *fatwā*, see Vogel, *Islamic Law and Legal System* (n 24) 254–276.

points clarify, the BSU places the crimes of assaulting, kidnapping and sexual harassment under the category of *ḥirāba* – this in turn paves the way for loosening the strict Islamic legal rules and conditions that relate to the application of the prescribed four *ḥadd* penalties that are specifically applied to the *ḥirāba* crimes set out in the cited verse. In the *fatwā*, the ambiguous and uncertain character of these crimes, as Vogel states, is obviated by designating and fixing them as the *ḥirāba* crimes.[208] With regard to the third point, the drawbacks which may conceivably derive from the *qāḍīs* applying the *ḥirāba* penalties for such offences are considerably mitigated by permitting them to sentence the offenders who commit the abhorrent and odious crimes with the *ḥirāba* penalties. The *fatwā* provides *qāḍīs* with a considerable facilitation and liberty in applying the *ḥirāba* penalties because Saudi *qāḍīs*, before the issuance of this *fatwā*, did not ordinarily impose death as a *ta'zīr* penalty by considering it an extraordinary and extreme penalty to be wielded only by the ruler.[209]

The *fatwā* does not only entrust the judges with full authority and discretion to choose among the four penalties in considering the character of the offender, the circumstance of the crime and its negative impacts on society; it also, in accordance with the King's desires, increases the deterrent effect of the punishments and expedites the legal process. In accordance with a later request by the King, the first part of this *fatwā* (which relates to abduction and usurpation) was implemented in Saudi Arabia's courts.[210] The transformation of *fatwās* into legal regulations provides considerable insight into not only the latent potentiality of a *fatwā* issued by the Dār al-Iftā' to become a legally effective regulation; to an equivalent extent, it also touches upon the complementary and cooperative partnership between the religious establishment and the Saudi Government in the field of legislation and adjudication. Vogel refers to this relationship when he observes:

> the king and the 'ulamā' cooperate in an effort to solve a complex contemporary problem, the rise of certain grievous crimes for which the classical fiqh has no ready, specific response.[211]

This suggests that some legal regulations are the products of reciprocal cooperation, efforts and interaction between the religious establishment and the State's administrative organisations. The effects of the dynamic cooperation between the Dār al-Iftā' and the Saudi Government are also clearly evidenced in social norms and regulations that control, regulate and shape many aspects of daily life in Saudi Arabia.

208 Vogel, *Islamic Law and Legal System* (n 24) 255.
209 ibid 254.
210 ibid 258.
211 ibid 222.

Many royal decrees that relate to social regulations and norms originate within the Dār al-Iftā's *fatwās*. This is particularly true of the regulations that govern the segregation of the sexes, a measure which has a direct daily impact upon the lives of Saudis. The religious establishment mainly draws upon the notions of *khalwa* (being alone in the company of an unrelated man) and *ikhtilāṭ* (intermingling of women with men) when evaluating issues that pertain to the education of women, the employment of women outside the home, interactions between men and women and the participation of women in social activities.[212] While the place of women is generally held to be the home, women are allowed to participate in social and working life, upon the condition that their occupations do not contradict the nature of woman; in addition, the permission of her husband should be obtained, and she should refrain from intermixing with unrelated men (non-*maḥram*).[213] It is possible to argue that the Dār al-Iftā' relies primarily on the legal principle of the blocking of illegitimate means (*sadd al-dharā'i'*) – this argument can be sustained by referring to the assumption that the intermingling of men and women may result in seduction and temptation (*fitna*) in any society. In referring to this argument, the Grand Muftī Ibn Bāz clearly states:

> It is better to block the means that lead to Fitnah than regretting it in the future ... Free intermixing of men and women in the workplace plays a major role in the deterioration and corruption of nations.[214]

This is the reason why the intermingling of men and women is restricted in many places, including hospitals, public libraries, public transportation, restaurants,

212 Danger of women joining men in their workplace, in *Fatwas of Ibn Baz*, 1:418–427 <http://www.alifta.net/Search/ResultDetails.aspx?languagename=en&lang=en&view=result&fatwaNum=&FatwaNumID=&ID=75&searchScope=14&SearchScopeLevels1=&SearchScopeLevels2=&highLight=1&SearchType=exact&SearchMoesar=false&bookID=&LeftVal=0&RightVal=0&simple=&SearchCriteria=allwords&PagePath=&siteSection=1&searchkeyword=119111091011100391150321191111114107#firstKeyWordFound> accessed 29 November 2017; Fatwā No. 7484 and Fatwā No. 2768 in *Fatwas of the Permanent Committee*, 17: 232–237 <http://www.alifta.net/Search/ResultDetails.aspx?languagename=en&lang=en&view=result&fatwaNum=&FatwaNumID=&ID=6509&searchScope=7&SearchScopeLevels1=&SearchScopeLevels2=&highLight=1&SearchType=exact&SearchMoesar=false&bookID=&LeftVal=0&RightVal=0&simple=&SearchCriteria=allwords&PagePath=&siteSection=1&searchkeyword=105110116101114109105110103108105110103032109101110032097110100032119111109101110#firstKeyWordFound> accessed 29 November 2017.

213 Fatwā No. 5082, Fatwā No. 4945, Fatwā No. 5512 and Fatwā No. 19359, in *Fatwas of the Permanent Committee*, 17: 54–55, 81–85 <http://www.alifta.net/Search/ResultDetails.aspx?languagename=en&lang=en&view=result&fatwaNum=&FatwaNumID=&ID=6509&searchScope=7&SearchScopeLevels1=&SearchScopeLevels2=&highLight=1&SearchType=exact&SearchMoesar=false&bookID=&LeftVal=0&RightVal=0&simple=&SearchCriteria=allwords&PagePath=&siteSection=1&searchkeyword=119111109101110039115032109105120105110103032119105116104032109101110#firstKeyWordFound> accessed 29 November 2017.

214 Danger of women (n 212) 424.

schools and universities.[215] The *fatwās* which restrict the mixing of men and women were transformed into a legal regulation by the Royal Decree 80/1631, which was issued in 1980.[216]

Similarly, the *fatwas* which refer to women's dress code in the country were transformed into legal regulations by two Royal Decrees (4/30820 and 8/1858).[217] *Fatwās* issued by the Dār al-Iftā' clearly state that Muslim women must present themselves in appropriate garments when in public and in the presence of non-*maḥram* men.[218] Women's attire is generally described in the following terms:

> The Islamic Hijab entails that a woman must cover all her body before a non-Mahram ... She should cover her head, face, bosom, feet, and hand, as all her body considered as 'Awrah (parts of the body that must be covered in public), which Ajanib (men other than a husband or permanently unmarriageable male relatives) should not see.[219]

215 Fatwā No. 4671 in *Fatwas of the Permanent Committee*, 17: 17 <http://www.alifta.net/Search/ResultDetails.aspx?languagename=en&lang=en&view=result&fatwaNum=&FatwaNumID=&ID=6301&searchScope=7&SearchScopeLevels1=&SearchScopeLevels2=&highLight=1&SearchType=exact&SearchMoesar=false&bookID=&LeftVal=0&RightVal=0&simple=&SearchCriteria=allwords&PagePath=&siteSection=1&searchkeyword=105110116101114109105110103108105110103032109101110032097110100032119111109101110#firstKeyWordFound> accessed 29 November 2017; Fatwā No. 20397 in *Fatwas of the Permanent Committee*, 24: 398–399 <http://www.alifta.net/Search/ResultDetails.aspx?languagename=en&lang=en&view=result&fatwaNum=&FatwaNumID=&ID=9660&searchScope=7&SearchScopeLevels1=&SearchScopeLevels2=&highLight=1&SearchType=exact&SearchMoesar=false&bookID=&LeftVal=0&RightVal=0&simple=&SearchCriteria=allwords&PagePath=&siteSection=1&searchkeyword=105110116101114109105110103108105110103032109101110032097110100032119111109101110#firstKeyWordFound> accessed 29 November 2017.

216 Al-Atawneh, *Wahhābī Islam* (n 4) 104.

217 ibid 107.

218 Fatwā No. 15885 in *Fatwas of the Permanent Committee*, 11: 317–319 <http://www.alifta.net/Fatawa/FatawaChapters.aspx?languagename=en&View=Page&PageID=14645&PageNo=1&BookID=7> accessed 02 December 2017; Fatwā No. 19478 in *Fatwas of the Permanent Committee*, 17: 207–208 <http://www.alifta.net/Search/ResultDetails.aspx?languagename=en&lang=en&view=result&fatwaNum=&FatwaNumID=&ID=6478&searchScope=7&SearchScopeLevels1=&SearchScopeLevels2=&highLight=1&SearchType=exact&SearchMoesar=false&bookID=&LeftVal=0&RightVal=0&simple=&SearchCriteria=allwords&PagePath=&siteSection=1&searchkeyword=087111109101110032099111118101114105110103#firstKeyWordFound> accessed 02 December 2017; Fatwā No. 2847 in *Fatwas of the Permanent Committee*, 17: 281–284 <http://www.alifta.net/Search/ResultDetails.aspx?languagename=en&lang=en&view=result&fatwaNum=&FatwaNumID=&ID=6540&searchScope=7&SearchScopeLevels1=&SearchScopeLevels2=&highLight=1&SearchType=exact&SearchMoesar=false&bookID=&LeftVal=0&RightVal=0&simple=&SearchCriteria=allwords&PagePath=&siteSection=1&searchkeyword=087111109101110032104105106097098#firstKeyWordFound> accessed 02 December 2017; Questions and Answers on 'Aqīdah, in *Fatwas of Ibn Baz*, 5: 298–299 <http://www.alifta.net/Fatawa/FatawaDetails.aspx?languagename=en&View=Page&PageID=531&PageNo=1&BookID=14#P298> accessed 02 December 2017.

219 Describing the proper Islamic Hijab, in *Fatwas of Ibn Baz*, 6: 19–20 <http://www.alifta.net/Fatawa/FatawaDetails.aspx?languagename=en&View=Page&PageID=624&PageNo=1&BookID=14> accessed 02 December 2017.

Generally speaking, the *fatwās* concerning the women's dress code are fundamentally based on three Qur'anic verses (the Q. 24:31, 33:53 and 33:59) and the Prophetic traditions. The instruction in the Q. 33:59 ("Tell your wives and daughters and the women of the believers to draw their cloak (veils) all over bodies") is interpreted by the Saudi official *'ulamā'* in a way that women should screen themselves and should only leave exposed the eyes or one eye in order to see the way.[220] The public attire of Muslim women should cover the whole body and should not be too tight or transparent; furthermore, it should not be too attractive and should not resemble men's dress in any respect. However, the *fatwās* do not explicitly indicate that the colour of this attire should be black. In fact, this is categorically denied ("It is not obligatory to dress in black; they can wear any other colour that is typical of women, provided that they do not attract attention or arouse Fitnah (temptation)").[221] Saudi women's common practice of wearing the black cloak (*'abāya*) therefore reflects personal preference rather than religious instructions or regulations issued by the Dār al-Iftā'. In complying with these decrees, even non-Muslim women who visit or reside in Saudi Arabia are required to present themselves in appropriate attire that will not conflict with Saudi custom and which will not violate legal regulations that pertain to the dress code of Muslim women.[222] The enactment of *fatwās* as legal regulations that relate to social issues (including appropriate attire for women outside the home, interaction between men and women and the right of women to work) may indicate that Saudi society's current legal and social structure may have been shaped by the Dār al-Iftā', as opposed to the state.

In addition, the Dār al-Iftā' sometimes introduces a bill to the Saudi Government. For example, in 1980, the Saudi state issued a royal decree, based on a relevant *fatwā* presented to the government as a legal recommendation, that would limit the number of students studying abroad.[223] The institution adopted a firm position upon a number of sensitive issues, and most notably, upon the imitation of the infidels. In order to prevent Saudi youth from being exposed to Western cultural and social norms, a *fatwā* was issued and submitted as a legal recommendation to the government.[224] This *fatwā* warned against travelling to infidel countries and opened the way for Royal Decree 19851, which limited foreign study to disciplines that could not be studied in Saudi Arabia. Several Qur'anic verses[225] were cited in

220 Questions and Answers (n 218) 298.

221 Fatwā No. 5363, in *Fatwas of the Permanent Committee*, 17: 109 <http://www.alifta.net/Fatawa/FatawaChapters.aspx?languagename=en&View=Page&PageID=6394&PageNo=1&BookID=7> accessed 02 December 2017. See also Fatwā No. 5089 and Fatwā No. 7523 in *Fatwas of the Permanent Committee*, 17: 108 and 109–110 <http://www.alifta.net/Fatawa/FatawaChapters.aspx?languagename=en&View=Page&PageID=6392&PageNo=1&BookID=7> accessed 02 December 2017.

222 Al-Atawneh, *Wahhābī Islam* (n 4) 107.

223 ibid 95.

224 ibid.

225 In the *fatwā*, the Q. 5:3, Q. 3:118, Q. 60:2, Q. 2:217 and Q. 2:120, respectively, are cited as the authoritative textual evidence.

order to lend further strength to the proposition that foreign study can result in the imitation of the infidels, with the consequence that the individual's Islamic ethics and creed are jeopardised.[226] The cited Qur'anic verses stress the excellence and perfection of Islam as a religion, while also alluding to the inappropriate attitudes, characters and conducts of infidels. The *fatwā* presents the prospect of imitation (cultural, religious or social) as the Dār al-Iftā's primary justification for limiting foreign study or travel.[227] Many *fatwās* that address similar issues explicitly clarify that Muslims ought to refrain from travelling to foreign countries in order to maintain their Islamic creeds and ethics.[228] In aligning itself with the Dār al-Iftā's religious recommendations, the government's legal regulation can be viewed as a legal precaution that seeks to prevent impressionable young people from being exposed to foreign cultures or deviating from the straight path (Islam).[229]

The aforementioned examples demonstrate that the BSU mainly functions as a pacifying mechanism that helps to overcome political obstacles that are in need of religious explanation and legitimacy, in addition to functioning as a pre-legislative mechanism. These examples also indicate that the BSU's *fatwās* and decisions, subsequent to the ratification of the King, are legally effective and authoritative. The Dār al-Iftā' therefore simultaneously functions as a watchdog agency that supervises the Islamic ethical dimensions of the state and society and as a pre-legislative mechanism in the Saudi legal system. The involvement of the *iftā'* institution in the legislative procedure can be theorised in two ways: either providing legal validity to an existing *fatwā* or issuing a new *fatwā* in the face of an unprecedented situation to fill a legal gap. For the most part, a royal decree functions as a mechanism that transforms a *fatwā* into a legally binding law. Official *fatwās*, in particular those issued by the BSU, have an important legal value in the judicial system because they essentially provide the legal foundation that underpins the legislative procedure in many cases.

226 Al-Taḥdhīru min al-Safar ilā Bilād al-Kafara wa Khaṭarahu 'alā al-'Aqīda wal-Akhlāq, in *Majallat al-Buḥūth al-Islāmiyya*, 16: 7–10 <http://www.alifta.net/Fatawa/FatawaChapters.aspx?languagename=ar&View=Page&PageID=2283&PageNo=1&BookID=2> accessed 18 November 2017.

227 Al-Taḥdhīru min al-Safar (n 226).

228 For other *fatwās* on the issue of travelling to and studying in infidel countries, see Fatwā No. 20968 in *Fatwas of the Permanent Committee*, 26: 93–96 <http://www.alifta.net/Search/ResultDetails.aspx?languagename=en&lang=en&view=result&fatwaNum=&FatwaNumID=&ID=10135&searchScope=7&SearchScopeLevels1=&SearchScopeLevels2=&highLight=1&SearchType=exact&SearchMoesar=false&bookID=&LeftVal=0&RightVal=0&simple=&SearchCriteria=allwords&PagePath=&siteSection=1&searchkeyword=115116117100121105110103032097098114111097100#firstKeyWordFound> accessed 29 November 2017; the interview of Okaz newspaper with His Eminence Shaykh 'Abdul- 'Aziz ibn Baz, in *Fatwas of Ibn Baz*, 5: 259–261 <http://www.alifta.net/Search/ResultDetails.aspx?languagename=en&lang=en&view=result&fatwaNum=&FatwaNumID=&ID=513&searchScope=14&SearchScopeLevels1=&Search-ScopeLevels2=&highLight=1&SearchType=exact&SearchMoesar=false&bookID=&LeftVal=0&RightVal=0&simple=&SearchCriteria=allwords&PagePath=&siteSection=1&searchkeyword=115116117100121105110103032097098114111097100#firstKeyWordFound> accessed 29 November 2017.

229 Al-Atawneh, *Wahhābī Islam* (n 4) 95.

Conclusion

Alongside the growth of the petroleum industry and its wealth, the structure of the religious establishment transformed from an informal to a formal organisation in order to meet the challenges of modernity and respond to the growing demands of Saudi society. In responding to modern exigencies, the *'ulamā'*, sometimes willingly and sometimes unwillingly, sought to accommodate this institutional and organisational development. This in turn enabled the institution to strengthen its authority and position in the socio-legal and socio-religious realms. The evolution of religious establishment from an ad hoc to a regular structure did affect the official *'ulamā'* by enabling their *fatwās* to penetrate further into Saudi society. The Dār al-Iftā', as the official Wahhābī religious establishment, certainly did not recede in the face of the tide of change advanced; on the contrary, it retained a strong and tenacious hold upon various dimensions of life (legal, normative and social) within the state. The socio-political context which has framed the developing relationship between religion and state has been mainly defined in relation to the contemporary Wahhābī doctrine of *siyāsa shar'iyya*, which institutes both the Dār al-Iftā' and the Saudi Government as authority-holders in Saudi Arabia. The former interprets textually authoritative Islamic legal sources by using legal methodologies, and the latter implements and enforces these interpretations as legal rulings.

The *'ulamā'*, or *muftīs*, recognise the broad authority of the King by applying the Wahhābī doctrine of *siyāsa shar'iyya*, which is derived from the classical Islamic model of the Caliphate in which the ruler represents the highest political and religious authority. In exercising the recognised power, the King governs the state in accordance with his own discretion while simultaneously resolving contradictions between governmental practices and Islamic legal principles by drawing upon the assistance of the Dār al-Iftā' and its *fatwās*. This affirms that the Dār al-Iftā' functions as an intermediary between Islamic law and Saudi politics, performing a conciliatory role on issues relating to the government and politics. Despite these benign interventions, the relationship between the government and the religious establishment has not been completely congruous and harmonious since the establishment of the Dār al-Iftā'. In their mutual interactions, there are veiled tensions which are not always straightforward to identify. This ongoing relationship further reiterates the indissoluble bonds which conjoin religious scholars and the Kingdom's rulers within the juridical, political, religious and social spheres.

In the contemporary period, the Dār al-Iftā' and its *fatwās* continue to perform a pivotal role in the formulation of cultural and social norms, along with legal regulations – this is clearly reiterated by the fact that the Saudi constitutional and judicial systems continue to be anchored in Islamic law and Islamic legal methodologies. The Dār al-Iftā's *fatwās* serve three main functions within the state. In the first instance, *fatwās*, in particular those issued by the BSU, help to legitimate the Saudi Government and provide political and social stability. In the second instance, transfers of political power within the Saudi dynasty have been generally subject to the *'ulamā's* anticipated consent; more recently, the *fatwā* has come to function as an official tool that indicates the *'ulamā's* unanimous approval. Lastly, the Dār al-Iftā's *fatwās* perform a complementary role in the judicial system. Clashes between the religious legal norms and the reality of an evolving society have been softened by the interventions of the official religious institution, which has repeatedly evidenced its ability to operate as a mediatory mechanism that establishes a robust connection between the society, state and religion. It is therefore likely that the Dār al-Iftā' will continue to perform an important role in the social-legal realm by issuing *fatwās* that have the potential to, subsequent to the King's approval, become religiously binding legal regulations.

Within Saudi Arabia's idiosyncratic Islamic legal system, the Dār al-Iftā's *fatwās* represent the initial stage of the law-making process. Once they are transformed into royal decrees, the Dār al-Iftā's *fatwās* have a considerable impact upon the different layers of the state. While the Dār al-Iftā' strives to preserve the religious character of the legal system, society and state, its *fatwās* are not always unquestioningly observed by the state. It is therefore possible to identify a number of contemporary cultural, legal and social practices within the country which incur the Dār al-Iftā's disapproval. The persistence of these practices could be interpreted as hinting at the institution's diminished significance, both within the Saudi legal system and in its relations with the Saudi Government.

With regard to Islamic legal methodology, the Dār al-Iftā' primarily follows in the footsteps of the jurists and scholars that belong to the Ḥanbalī *madhhab* – for this reason, it maintains a strict adherence to the two main authoritative textual sources (the Qur'an and Sunna), as opposed to other Islamic legal methodologies. In enacting the common methodological practice of the Ḥanbalī *madhhab*, the institution's members first refer to these two authoritative sources on various matters before then referring to other sources and reviewing the legal views of other *madhhabs*. Nonetheless, there are some very limited changes in the institution's affiliation to the *madhhab*. In some *fatwās*, the use of legal principles and legal maxims (such as *ḍarūra*, *maṣlaḥa*, *qiyās* and *tarjīḥ*) which are frequently applied by the other three *madhhabs* may justify this slight alteration in the affiliation to a specific *maddhab*, legal methodologies and theories. However, this more lenient and moderate attitude is generally espoused in order to accommodate Islamic legal rules to the modern world, and it has proven to be of particular utility when the institution engages with controversial or intricate questions that are generally asked by either the King or the Saudi Government.

2 Presidency of Religious Affairs

After the establishment of the Turkish Republic in 1923, the office of the Ottoman Sultanate's religious establishment (the office of the *Shaykh al-Islām*) was transformed into the Presidency of Religious Affairs (Diyanet İşleri Başkanlığı; henceforth: Diyanet). Since its establishment, the Diyanet has only been conducting religious affairs within the borders of secular Turkish state. The Diyanet, which is a state-dependent institution, consists of three main branches: the headquarters in Ankara, provincial branches across the country and overseas branches which generally provide religious services for Turks resident abroad. The structure of the headquarters in Ankara, which is the central body of the Diyanet, is the primary focus of this chapter. A closer engagement makes it possible to elucidate the Islamic legal positioning and mindset of the Diyanet because the High Board of Religious Affairs in the headquarters in Ankara is the official religious think-tank of the Turkish state. The most important responsibility of the High Board of Religious Affairs, which is the highest decision-making and advisory body within the Diyanet's administrative and organisational structure, is to provide decisions on religious matters, declare its opinion regarding religious issues and answer religious questions related to Islamic law by considering the current needs and circumstances of Muslims resident in Turkey. The chapter mainly examines Islamic legal decisions and *fatwās* issued by the High Board of Religious Affairs with the intent of determining the Islamic legal methodology implemented by that body, along with the social context in which *fatwās* were promulgated – this helps to identify the interaction between the Islamic legal methodologies and the social context in which the institution operates.

The institutional and intellectual history of Turkey's official legislative activities related to the Diyanet is explored with the intention of uncovering the institution's historical development. Although it developed within the specific context of Acts of the Parliament, by-laws, regulations and the boundaries of the Constitution, the Diyanet's particular Islamic legal mentality and methodology can only be fully comprehend with reference to the official *fatwās* issued by its highest decision-making body. The institution is engaged with from three separate angles. Attention initially focuses upon key historical events in the development of the Diyanet, with particular emphasis upon its intricate constitutional regulations. In the second instance, attention turns to its current organisational structure; this

DOI: 10.4324/9781003037637-2

is followed by a closer examination of the process by which a *fatwā* is issued. This contribution is of particular importance because, at the same time, some analyses related to *fatwās* are examined with the intention of evidencing the interaction between Islamic legal methodologies adopted by the Diyanet and its environmental context.

The historical evolution of the Presidency of Religious Affairs in Turkey

Modern Turkey was founded on the ruins of the Ottoman Sultanate, which had managed predominantly social structures which combined multiple cultures, languages and religions by deploying an assortment of agents and mechanisms.[1] In its aftermath, more than thirty states, which included the Republic of Turkey, were established in the Balkans, Middle East and North Africa.[2] These newly established nation-states, which gave birth to new political organisations and systems, sought to distance themselves from their immediate past by creating homogeneous political and social communities. Generally, these modern nation-states were established upon the basis of secularism rather than religion, and the key objective was to institute a political settlement in which loyalty was owed to secular states rather than religious establishments.[3] Over time, the Turkish model of the state-religion system has gradually transformed. Islam, which was established as a state religion in the first Turkish Constitution, therefore gave way to a secular state. This transformation resulted in a new relationship between the state, secular law and religion, along with the emergence of novel ideological, legal and religious trajectories, each of which anticipated a fundamentally altered future for the Republic of Turkey's predominantly Muslim population.

When a modern nation-state was established in Turkey, it was grounded within the radical secular ideology of the republican elite, along with the aspiration to reshape the state and its institutions and align them with Western modernism and secularism. This culminated in a range of radical secularisation reforms which were introduced during the first decade of the new Republic and which sought to curtail the role of religion in every single aspect of Turkish society. Küçükcan observes:

> Secularism was accepted as the state ideology above every other orientation at the expense of liberties as experienced especially during the single party rule in [Turkey] until 1950.[4]

1 Talip Küçükcan, 'Are Muslim Democrats a Threat to Secularism and Freedom of Religion? The Turkish Case' in Allen D. Hertzke (ed), *The Future of Religious Freedom: Global Challenges* (Oxford University Press 2013) 274; Gazi Erdem, 'Religious Services in Turkey: From the Office of *Şeyhulislām* to the *Diyanet*' (2008) 98 (2–3) *The Muslim World* 199–200 <http://onlinelibrary.wiley.com/doi/10.1111/j.1478-1913.2008.00216.x/full> accessed 01 February 2017.

2 Küçükcan (n 1) 274.

3 ibid.

4 ibid.

The social significance of religious influences, morals and values was diminished by removing cultural and political institutions that had been influenced by Islam from their official positions. The radical secularisation process sought to remove every symbol that had Ottoman-Islamic connotations.[5] Religious shrines (*türbeler*) and dervish lodges (*tekkeler*) were closed in 1925, a constitutional article that proclaimed Islam as the state religion was removed in 1928, the alphabet was overhauled (from Arabic to Latin) in 1928 and the call to prayer (*adhān*) was "Turkified" in 1932. Each intervention further reiterated how, during the first decades of the Republic, Tukey's political elites sought to systematically minimise the role of religion and sever Turkey's ties with the Ottoman-Islamic cultural and literary heritage.

The separation of religion from the body of Turkish politics was the first step in the process of radical secularisation. The Sharīʻa Courts were closed down, the Caliphate and the office of *Shaykh al-Islām* were abolished and the Unity of Education Law (*Tevhid-i tedrisat kanunu*)[6] was enacted on March 3, 1924, on the same day that the Presidency of Religious Affairs (henceforth: Diyanet) was established.[7] The management of religious affairs was placed under the control of a constitutional public body, as opposed to a ministry in the cabinet. The separation of religion from political authority was a core component of the project which sought to establish a secular state and transform Turkey into a modern society. However, this separation did not logically imply that religion would henceforth function as an autonomous sphere beyond the state's control. The Diyanet began to oversee religion in the name of the secular nation-state; over time, it became established as an effective institution that governed, promoted and managed religious affairs in the state.

In subsequent years, constitutional laws and regulations have established the Diyanet as a constitutional public institution that receives its entire budget from the state and which employs approximately 110,000[8] people from across the

5 Thijl Sunier and others, *Diyanet: The Turkish Directorate for Religious Affairs in a Changing Environment*, (VU University of Amsterdam and Utrecht University 2011) 10; Küçükcan (n 1) 275.

6 The Unity of Education Law (*Tevhid-i tedrisat kanunu*) was one of the main reforms of the Ataturk period which closed down all religious schools. This law, which sought to democratise and secularise the education system, established that all educational institutions, including medical and military schools, would henceforth be placed under the control of the Ministry of Education. See Act no. 430 dated 03 March 1924 <https://www.mevzuat.gov.tr/MevzuatMetin/1.3.430.pdf> accessed 30 September 2020.

7 Act no. 429 dated 03 March 1924. See Resmi Gazete (*Official Gazette*), 06. 03. 1924-63 <http://www.resmigazete.gov.tr/main.aspx?home=http://www.resmigazete.gov.tr/arsiv/63.pdf&main=http://www.resmigazete.gov.tr/arsiv/63.pdf> accessed 26 September 2016; Kuruluş ve Tarihi Gelişim, 'Türkiye Cumhuriyeti Başkanlık Diyanet İşleri Başkanlığı' <http://www.diyanet.gov.tr/tr/icerik/kurulus-ve-tarihce/8> accessed 26 September 2016; Emine Enise Yakar, 'A Critical Comparison between the Presidency of Religious Affairs (Diyanet İşleri Başkanlığı) and the Office of Shaykh al-Islâm' (2019) 6 (11) *Kilis 7 Aralık Üniversitesi İlahiyat Fakültesi Dergisi* 434.

8 İstatistikler, 'İstatiksel Tablolar (31.12.2015 tarihi itibariyle): Personel' <http://www.diyanet.gov.tr/tr/kategori/istatistikler/136> accessed 10 October 2016.

country. The eighty-two years of the Diyanet's existence can be divided into four periods. The first period begins with the formation of the Diyanet and concludes in the mid-1940s. During these years, the influence and importance of the Diyanet gradually declined in large part due to the radical secularisation reforms in many areas of public life. In 1924, the first article of Act 429 established the Diyanet but did not outlined its administrative and organisational structure.[9] It states:

> In the Republic of Turkey, the Grand National Assembly and the Cabinet, which is formed by the Grand National Assembly of Turkey, are responsible for the legislation and execution of provisions concerning the affairs of people, and an office (Diyanet İşleri Reisliği) has been formed to implement all provisions regarding the ritual practices (*'ibādāt*) of and faith (*i'tiqād*) of the religion of Islam and to administer religious organisations.[10]

This regulation established that religious affairs pertaining to faith (*i'tiqād*) and ritual practices (*'ibādāt*), along with the administration of all religious sites would henceforth be placed under the control of the Diyanet. Meanwhile, all other areas relating to the state and people were placed under the legislative power of the Grand National Assembly of Turkey.[11] Act 429 established the Diyanet as a religious administrative body by separating the politics of the new regime from religion and by undermining the influence of Muslim scholars (*'ulamā'*) within the state administration. This enactment also established that the head of the Diyanet would be, subsequent to a proposal by the Prime Minister, appointed by the President of the Republic of Turkey. The Diyanet, in operating as a constitutional body, was placed under the control of the Prime Minister's office.[12] This legislation demonstrates how the state deliberately sought to limit religion and the official institution responsible for its management. The 1927 Budget Act set out the administrative structure of the central and provincial branches of the Diyanet and declared its permanency for the first time.[13] However, the institution was not still an active or effective consideration in Turkey's public, religious and social life.

During the period 1924–1928, when the constitutional clause establishing Islam as the state religion remained in place, radical secularisation reforms continued

9 Act no. 429 dated 03 March 1924.

10 ibid.

11 Sönmez Kutlu, 'Diyanet İşleri Başkanlığı ve İslamiçi Dini Gruplarla (Mezhep ve Tatikatlar) İlişkileri' (2009) 12 (33) *Dini Araştırmalar* 108.

12 Act no. 429 dated 03 March 1924.

13 Act no. 1452 dated 30 June 1929. See Resmi Gazete, 30. 06. 1929-1229 <http://www.resmigazete.gov.tr/main.aspx?home=http://www.resmigazete.gov.tr/arsiv/1229.pdf&main=http://www.resmigazete.gov.tr/arsiv/1229.pdf> accessed 27 September 2016. Act no. 1452 elaborately sets out the organisational structure of the Diyanet and details the official positions which fall under it. The Permanent Table attached to Act 1429 sets out officialdom degrees, positions, salaries and the number of Diyanet's personnel in considerable detail.

apace. In 1928, the clause (which explicitly declared that "The religion of the Turkish Republic is Islam"[14]) was removed from the Constitution. Nine years later, the principle of secularism was established as a foundational constitutional principle.[15] This measure curtailed the authority and influence of the Diyanet to a greater extent. In its aftermath, the Turkish state has been frequently characterised as "secular." At the same time, the Diyanet's incorporation as a state religious institution into the state's bureaucracy furthered precisely the opposite impression (namely that, Islam was the country's de facto religion). After removing the Constitution's recognition of Islam as the state religion, the Turkish state sought to establish a more complex relationship with it by maintaining the Diyanet as a religious institution that would henceforth be responsible for Islamic religious affairs.[16] Since its establishment in 1924, the institution has therefore become established as a constitutional public body that possesses the authority to administer religious affairs for Turkish Muslims. In the immediate aftermath of its establishment, the Diyanet implemented a range of important multi-year research projects that enjoyed the financial support of the government. These projects included a translation of Muhammad Elmalı Hamdi Yazır's *tafsīr* (interpretation) of the Qur'an,[17] *Sahih-i Buhari Muhtasarı Tecrid-i Ṣarīh* (a revered collection of the Prophet Muhammad's Sunna)[18] and the publication of a number of religious education schoolbooks.

In this initial period, the most controversial Islamic legal explanation that was approved by Rıfat Börekçi (d. 1941), the Diyanet's first president, was a circular letter (*tamim*) possessing the status of *fatwā* that explored the possibility

14 The Constitution of Republic of Turkey, 1924 (Article 2) <http://www.anayasa.gen.tr/1924tek.htm> accessed 25 September 2016.

15 Act no. 1222 dated 10 April 1928. See Resmi Gazete, 14. 04. 1928-863, <http://www.resmigazete.gov.tr/main.aspx?home=http://www.resmigazete.gov.tr/arsiv/863.pdf&main=http://www.resmigazete.gov.tr/arsiv/863.pdf> accessed 26 September 2016; Act no. 3115 dated 05 February 1937. See Resmi Gazete, 13. 02. 1937-3533 <http://www.resmigazete.gov.tr/main.aspx?home=http://www.resmigazete.gov.tr/arsiv/3533.pdf&main=http://www.resmigazete.gov.tr/arsiv/3533.pdf> accessed 26 September 2016.

16 Ceren Kenar and Doğan Gürpınar, 'Cold War in the Pulpit: The Presidency of Religious Affairs and Sermons during the Time of Anarchy and Communist Threat' in Cangül Örnek and Çağdaş Üngör (eds), *Turkey in Cold War Ideology and Culture* (Palgrave Macmillan 2013) 26.

17 This *tafsīr*, which is entitled '*Hak Dini Kur'an Dili*' and which was published in 1936, was one of the most valuable works of the Diyanet that relates to the Qur'an. It was written by Muhammad Elmalı Hamdi Yazır (d. 1942). Yazır was a Turkish theologian and translator of the Qur'an, who was also, during the late Ottoman era and the early years of the Turkish Republic, renowned as one of the most prominent scholars interested in the Qur'anic exegesis, Islamic jurisprudence and theology.

18 *Sahīh-i Buhārī Muhtasarı Tecrīd-i Sarīh* by Zeynüddin Ahmed b. Ahmed Zebîdî (1488) was a twelve-volume *ḥadīth* work published by the Diyanet. Ahmed Naim (d. 1934) and Kâmil Miras (d. 1957) were commissioned by the Diyanet to translate this work into Turkish. This work presents *ḥadīths* with their commentary.

of performing the call to prayer (*adhān*) in Turkish.[19] This circular letter, which was issued in 1932, states:

> Some *muftīs* have hesitated on the issue of performing *adhān* and *qāmat* in Turkish on which there is no prohibition in terms of Islamic legal legitimacy (*şer'an*). Consequently, after the arrival of this circular to [the offices of *muftīs*], the general scientific officers (*umum ilmiyye memurları*) and *imāms* will be given a certain official notice [on that issue] and, thereon, ones who even slightly object to this [performing *adhān* in Turkish] will expose to the certain and severe penalties declared in the way of circular.[20]

It has already been noted that the historical connection between Turkey and Islam had proven to be a sensitive issue for the early republican elites who sought to create a homogeneous society that would only use Turkish as a common language. The desire to purify the Turkish language from the "taint of foreign languages (in particular Arabic and Persian)" culminated in some efforts to use the Turkish language during religious services.[21] However, calls to "Turkify" *adhān* did not initially command the support of the Diyanet. In 1926, for instance, Cemaleddin Efendi, the *imām* of Göztepe Mosque, was reported to the Diyanet for reciting *adhān* in the Turkish language, with the consequence that he was temporarily suspended from his office.[22]

During the 1930s, the pressure to use the Turkish language in religious services increased, largely as a result of direct pressure exerted by Mustafa Kemal Ataturk, the founder of the Turkish Republic.[23] In yielding to this pressure, the Diyanet ultimately provided legal approval in the form of a circular letter that conveyed its permission to perform *adhān* in Turkish. This letter raised contentious issues within Turkish society and its scholarly circles, such as the competence of the Diyanet's scholars, performing prayers in Turkish, the recitation of the Qur'an in Turkish and the reformation of Islamic practices (e.g., *adhān*). However, it is possible to argue that the rigid legal punishments that applied to those who

19 Bayram Koca, 'Diyanet İşleri Başkanlığı ve Aleviler Arasındaki Meseleye Liberal Bir Bakış' (2014) 19 (73–74) *Liberal Düşünce Yıl* 43; İsmail Kara, 'Din ile Devlet Arasına Sıkışmış Bir Kurum: Diyanet İşleri Başkanlığı' (2000) 18 *Marmara Üniversitesi İlahiyat Fakültesi Dergisi* 43–44.

20 Cited from Koca (n 19) 43; Kara (n 19) 43–44.

21 Hidayet Aydar, 'Türklerde Anadilde İbadet Meselesi -Cumhuriyet Dönemi-' (2007) 15 *İstanbul Üniversitesi İlahiyat Fakültesi Dergisi* 75.

22 ibid 78–79.

23 Subsequent to the establishment of the Turkish Republic, efforts to "Turkify" *adhān* attained renewed impetus, in particular amongst early republican elites. Mustafa Kemal Atatürk enthusiastically supported this reformation project, and this was reflected in one of his decrees which established a commission that brought together reformist religious figures of the time. It was tasked with translating *adhān* into Turkish. Henceforth, the Qur'an and *adhān* would be performed in Turkish. Prayers were also performed in Turkish for roughly the next twenty years. See Aydar 'Türklerde Anadilde İbadet' (n 21) 85–87.

failed to perform *adhān* in Turkish and Muslims who opposed the Turkification of *adhān* ultimately influenced the Diyanet's decision to allow *adhān* to be performed in Turkish.[24] A 1941 statement, which was added to Article 526 of the Turkish Criminal Code,[25] asserts that:

> Whoever performs *adhān* and *qāmat* in Arabic shall be punished either with imprisonment for a term which may extend to three months or with fine which may increase ten to two hundred Turkish currency.

In this regard, the legal restrictions encompassing the Diyanet and its personnel may be accepted as the key reason that impelled the Diyanet to issue the circular letter decreeing the *adhān* to be recited in Turkish.

The authority and jurisdiction of the Diyanet, in its initial phase, were curtailed to a great extent by the state's regulations. Okumuş further reiterates the limited authority of the Diyanet during the early Republican era. He observes:

> During the *single party period*, the state wanted to reform Turkey-religiosity in the mentality of reform in religion as it wished, and policies were followed in this direction. It was in this period that *Adhan* and daily prayers had to be performed in the Turkish language. It was a period of official restrictions, and things were difficult for the [Diyanet].[26]

The constitutional provisions relating to the Turkification of *adhān* could be interpreted as establishing that the early Republican government did not act in accordance with the law when engaged in the issue of *'ibādāt*. This impression persists despite the fact that the first article of Act 429 clearly states that all affairs regarding religion must be implemented and conducted by the Diyanet.[27] In reality, religious affairs were conducted by the early Republican government in accordance with its political and social policies, and the Diyanet just assumed the role of a confirmatory mechanism that provided religious legitimacy to regulations identified by the government.

On 8 June, 1931, another major change in the Diyanet's organisational structure was put into effect by the 1931 Fiscal Year Budget Law of the Directorate General of Foundations. This transferred the management of personnel and physical resources from the Diyanet to the Directorate General of Foundations,[28] with

24 Aydar 'Türklerde Anadilde İbadet' (n 21) 101–107.

25 Koca (n 19) 43. See also Hidayet Aydar, 'The Issue of Chanting the *Adhan* in Languages Other than Arabic and Related Social Reactions in Turkey' (2006) 13 *İstanbul Üniversitesi İlahiyat Fakültesi Dergisi* 60.

26 Ejder Okumuş, 'Turkey-Religiosity and the PRA' (2008) 98 (2–3) *The Muslim World* 354 <http://onlinelibrary.wiley.com/doi/10.1111/j.1478-1913.2008.00232.x/full> accessed 18 October 2016.

27 Act no. 429 dated 03 March 1924.

28 Act no. 1827 dated 8 June 1931. See Resmi Gazete, 13. 06. 1931-1821 <http://www.resmigazete.gov.tr/main.aspx?home=http://www.resmigazete.gov.tr/arsiv/1821.pdf&main=http://www.resmigazete.gov.tr/arsiv/1821.pdf> accessed 27 September 2016.

the consequence that its authority and functionality were considerably reduced. Act 2800 then proceeded to specify the organisational duties and structure of the Diyanet.[29] During this initial period, it would perhaps be inaccurate to describe the institution as being concerned with the religious affairs of Muslims; rather, it instead sought to inculcate the religious interpretations of the early Republican government within Turkish society; more episodically, the institution intervened, at the request of the state, in religious affairs.[30]

The second period extends from the late 1940s to the late 1970s, coinciding both with political liberalism and Islam's growing presence within the political arena. During this period, the Diyanet was accepted as a necessary institutional mechanism which would help to maintain public stability in the area of religious affairs while helping to meet public demand for organised and satisfactory religious services. During the 1940s, the Republic of Turkey's multi-party period began when the National Development Party (*Milli Kalkınma Partisi*) and the Democrat Party (*Demokrat Parti*) were established (in 1945 and 1946, respectively). In 1950, the Republican People's Party (*Cumhuriyet Halk Partisi*, or CHP), which had hitherto been the only governing party, lost the elections, and the Democrat Party assumed power.[31] Prime Minister Adnan Menderes relaxed the restrictions on Islam, with the consequence that the Diyanet's role and significance in Turkish state and society fundamentally altered. On 23 March, 1950, Act 5634, which reallocated the management of mosques and the conduct of *imāms* (prayer leaders) to the Diyanet, was passed.[32] This Act also changed the name of the Diyanet from Diyanet İşleri Reisliği to Diyanet İşleri Başkanlığı, and entrusted it with the organisation of a religious publication department that would examine, publish and translate religious articles, books, periodicals and sermons.[33]

Democrat Party policies facilitated the resurgence of Islam in political, public and social spheres, and this enabled the Diyanet to actively assist the promotion of Islam in Turkish public life. The removal of the legal penalty for *imāms* who perform *adhān* in Arabic,[34] the enforcement of compulsory religious education,

29 Act no. 2800 dated 14 June 1935. See Resmi Gazete, 22. 06. 1935-3035 <http://www.resmigazete.gov.tr/main.aspx?home=http://www.resmigazete.gov.tr/arsiv/3035.pdf&main=http://www.resmigazete.gov.tr/arsiv/3035.pdf> accessed 27 September 2016.

30 Kara (n 19) 43.

31 Sunier and others (n 5) 13.

32 Act no. 5634 dated 23 March 1950. See Resmi Gazete, 29. 03. 1950-7469 <http://www.resmigazete.gov.tr/main.aspx?home=http://www.resmigazete.gov.tr/arsiv/7469.pdf&main=http://www.resmigazete.gov.tr/arsiv/7469.pdf> accessed 27 September 2016.

33 Act no. 5634 dated 23 March 1950. See also Yüksel Salman, 'Diyanet İşleri Başkanlığının Kuruluşunun 81. Yıl Dönümü Üzerine' (2005) 171 *Diyanet Aylık Dergisi* 34 <http://www2.diyanet.gov.tr/DiniYay%C4%B1nlarGenelMudurlugu/DergiDokumanlar/Aylik/2005/mart_2005.pdf> accessed 19 February 2017.

34 Act no. 5665 was passed as an act of law on 16 June 1950. It amends Article 526 of the Turkish Criminal Code and implies the abolition of the ban on the Arabic *adhān*. Prior to this amendment, Article 526's legal penalty had applied to those who perform *adhān* in Arabic. See Resmi Gazete (Official Gazette), 17. 06. 1950-7535 <http://www.resmigazete.gov.tr/main.aspx?home=http://

the introduction of religious programmes to state radio and the initiation of an extensive programme of mosque-building were all significant developments that simultaneously attested to the re-emergence of both the Diyanet and Islam.[35] When a military coup removed the Democrat Party from power in 1960, the new military regime acknowledged the continued importance of religion by supporting the Diyanet and its existence in Turkey. The constitutional regulation relating to the Diyanet's organisational and personnel structure, which had been given legal effect by Act 5634 in 1950, remained in force until 1965.

The adoption of the 1961 Constitution gave rise to prolonged debates about the existence of the Diyanet and the representation of other religious communities and sects. In 1963, legislation was proposed to change the Diyanet to the Presidency of Religious Sects. This proposed legislation would move it away from the Ḥanafī-Sunni tradition and would establish it as an institution that would represent the other three Sunni schools, along with other religious denominations.[36] The proposal was rejected by the Constitutional Court on account of the fact that such a change could engender divisiveness, factionalism and discursion in the society.[37] As a consequence, this proposal did not impact on the Diyanet's regulations. In June 1965, a comprehensive law (Act no. 633) relating to the Diyanet was enacted by the coalition government made up of the Republican People's Party and the Justice Party (*Adalet Partisi*) (which was one of the offshoots which emerged after the Democrat Party was forced to close). This particular regulation tasked the Diyanet with "execut[ing] the works concerning the beliefs, worship, and ethical foundation of Islam, enlighten[ing] the public about religion and manag[ing] the places of worship."[38] This established the management of ethical principles and the education of the public on religious matters as two of the Diyanet's additional key functions.[39] This gave rise to the strenuous objection that the execution of the moral principles of Islam was not compatible with principles of democracy and secularism; this in turn extended to a more general objection that a secular state should not be concerned with the people's religious morals.[40] Despite these objections, "to manage what is related to the principles of ethics of Islam" was

www.resmigazete.gov.tr/arsiv/7535.pdf&main=http://www.resmigazete.gov.tr/arsiv/7535.pdf> accessed 01 October 2016.

35 Necati Aksanyar, 'Demokrat Partinin Din Politikalarının Türk Basınına Yansımaları (1950–1954)' (2007) 11 *Akademik Bakış* 12–15.

36 İştar Gözaydın, *Religion, Politics and the Politics of Religion in Turkey* (Friedrich-Naumann-Stiftung für die Freiheit 2013) 21–22; Kutlu, 'Diyanet İşleri' (n 11) 110–111.

37 Kara (n 9) 45; Kutlu, 'Diyanet İşleri' (n 11) 111.

38 Act no. 633 dated 22 July 1965. See Resmi Gazete, 02. 07. 1965-12038 <http://www.resmigazete.gov.tr/main.aspx?home=http://www.resmigazete.gov.tr/arsiv/12038.pdf&main=http://www.resmigazete.gov.tr/arsiv/12038.pdf> accessed 28 September 2016.

39 ibid.

40 Ahmet Hamdi Adanalı 'The Presidency of Religious Affairs and the Principle of Secularism in Turkey' (2008) 98 (2–3) *The Muslim World* 232 <http://onlinelibrary.wiley.com/doi/10.1111/j.1478-1913.2008.00221.x/full> accessed 17 October 2016.

added to the Diyanet's duties and responsibilities.[41] Act 633 admittedly tasked the Diyanet with educating the society on the subject of religion. In the aftermath of 1965, it was possible to observe an increase in religious conferences, publications and seminars across Turkey. This Act provided a concrete account of the institution and clearly sketched its legal parameters while setting out its personnel. It specifically tasked the institution with informing Turkish society about religion and consolidating the unity of the nation on matters of faith and moral principles; in addition, it was also tasked with purifying Islam of bigotry and superstition, both of which had no basis within the faith.[42]

In 1966, the constitutional basis of the Diyanet was interrogated by the Unity Party (*Birlik Partisi*), which was an Alevi-Turkish political party.[43] The Party filed a petition against the Diyanet in the Constitutional Court in which it argued that this form of religious institution was unconstitutional because Turkey was a secular state; upon this basis, it argued that the existence of such an institution simultaneously conflicted with the Constitution and the principle of secularism.[44] The Constitutional Court – which retained a strong commitment to secular principles – rejected the petition on the grounds that the institution was constitutionally necessary when the principle of secularism was understood with reference to the elevation of the Turkish nation and the accession of the status of modern civilisation, both of which were the overarching principles of the Turkish Republic.[45] The majority of the judges recognised that the Diyanet was a constitutional body and that its personnel were not a religious clergy; on the contrary, they were instead recognised as civil servants who worked on behalf of the state.[46]

Presidential and prime ministerial visits over the course of the 1960s and 1970s further reiterated the growing prestige of the Diyanet. Cevdet Sunay (Turkey's fifth president) and Fahri Korutürk (Turkey's sixth president) respectively visited

41 The decision to include the management of the moral dimension of Islam as one of the duties and responsibilities of the Diyanet continues to arouse strong criticism from some scholars. Savcı, for instance, argues that this is a deviation from Atatürk's principles, in particular from secularism. In his view, Atatürk had made it quite clear that religion should not be permitted to interfere in the domain of human relations. While Tarhanlı acknowledges that it is possible to – in both a legal and practical sense – incorporate an organisational religious institution into a secular system, he maintains that the situation is different in the case of the Diyanet. Tasking this institution with the management of ethical principles of Islam indicates that the state has come to espouse a particular religious ideology. In setting aside the ethical and moral values of religion, Gözaydin argues that the Diyanet should have been solely tasked with managing religious affairs. However, these assertions overlook the fact that the ethical and moral dimension is intrinsic to religion; it becomes clear that the task of separating ethics and religion may be impossible or discursive. İştar B. Tarhanlı, *Müslüman Toplum, "Laik" Devlet: Türkiye'de Diyanet İşleri Başkanlığı* (Afa Yayınları 1993) 71–150; Gözaydın, *Religion, Politics* (n 36) 14; Adanalı (n 40) 232–233.

42 Act no. 633 dated 22 July 1965.

43 Emir Kaya, 'Balancing Interlegality through Realist Altruism: Diyanet Mediation in Turkey' (PhD thesis, University of London 2011) 156–160; Adanalı (n 40) 234.

44 Adanalı (n 40) 234.

45 ibid.

46 ibid.

the Diyanet on 19 April, 1967, and 31 May, 1976.[47] Bülent Ecevit made the first prime ministerial visit to the institution on 01 April, 1978.[48] This genuflection to religion can be interpreted as part of a strategy in which the state, while seeking to maintain a secular image, sought to reach an accommodation with social and religious actors. The Diyanet can therefore be interpreted as a networked space in which a rapprochement between religion, society and state, along with a type of secularism exclusive to Turkey, was envisaged and enacted.

During the 1970s, when leftist-socialist activism was at its height, the sermons (*khuṭbas*), which Diyanet officials delivered in mosques across Turkey, warned the Muslim community to refrain from catastrophic or hazardous movements that could divide the society.[49] These sermons called upon people in attendance to obey the state. Gürpınar and Kenar refer to the language and textual references which the Diyanet used to promote the obedience of the community. They observe:

> Even here the selective … usage of hadith is noteworthy. For instance, the hadith "whoever separates the size of palm from the sultan then his death would be of Jahiliyya" was frequently quoted in sermons on "anarchy" to prove that obedience to state is an imperative in the Sunni tradition.[50]

During the second period, the Diyanet skilfully espoused Islamic teachings which related to the basis of legitimate authority in incorporating the Islamic legal doctrine upon obedience to authority into the social values of the society. Gürpınar and Kenar observe that the framing of a conciliatory Islamic legal view implies, in practical terms, the combination of Islamic and secular political cultures, which might otherwise be presumed to be irreconcilable or opposed.[51] It is therefore significant to note that *fatwās* issued by the Diyanet portray obedience as a moral religious responsibility towards the community/society, as opposed to the political authority. A recently published book by the Diyanet, for example, presents the fulfilment of civic duties (e.g., paying taxes and performing mandatory military duty) within a democratic secular state as part of a rightful due (*kul hakkı*) that is a moral and religious obligation for Muslim individuals.[52] Public peace, public order and social unity are the general foundations upon which the Diyanet constructs its Islamic legal perspective of obedience to the secular state.[53] At this point, it may be proposed that the Diyanet effectively assumes a placatory role

47 Ruşen Çakır and İrfan Bozan, *Sivil Şeffaf ve Demokratik Bir Diyanet İşleri Başkanlığı Mümkün mü?* (TESEV Yayinlari 2005) 65.

48 ibid.

49 For more detailed and further analysis of the sermons issued by the Diyanet, see Doğan Gürpınar and Ceren Kenar, 'The Nation and its Sermons: Islam, Kemalism and the Presidency of Religious Affairs in Turkey' (2016) 52 (1) *Middle Eastern Studies* 70–74; Kenar and Gürpınar (n 16) 27–35.

50 Gürpınar and Kenar (n 49) 70.

51 ibid 72.

52 M. Şevki Aydin and others, *Sorularla İslam* (Diyanet İşleri Başkanlığı Yayınları 2015) 172–178.

53 ibid 153–158, 172–178.

which becomes particularly pronounced during times of turbulence and crisis. This in turn motivates the community to demonstrate subservience to the state authority entrusted with the responsibility to govern society.

The third period of the Diyanet begins in the 1980s and concludes in the early 2000s. It can be argued that, during this period, the Diyanet helped to preserve state unity by promoting a variant of state nationalism that was heavily imbued with Islamic overtones. In the aftermath of the 1980 military coup, the Turkish elite increasingly gravitated towards an ideology known as Turkish-Islamic synthesis (*Türk-İslam sentezi*),[54] which sought to combine Islam, modernism and Turkishness through evidencing the connection between Islam and Turkish state nationalism.[55] This ideology enabled the elites (who were mostly secular) to use Islam to challenge communism and Kurdish nationalism, both of which jeopardised the Turkish state nationalism promoted by national and secular elites.[56] Islam was therefore drawn into the service of an ideology of Turkish state nationalism that sought to use it as a source of national solidarity and unity. The 1982 Constitution was the first instance in which this inclination towards the ideology of Turkish-Islamic synthesis became apparent.

In the aftermath of the 1980 military coup, a law was passed that forbade the verbalisation of any demand for a change in the Diyanet's status.[57] In addition to this, Article 136 of the current constitution, which came into force in 1982, was enacted, and it states:

> The Presidency of Religious Affairs, which is within the general administration, shall exercise its duties that prescribed in its particular law, in accordance with the principles of secularism, removed from all political views and ideas, and aiming at national solidarity and integrity.[58]

54 This is a theory or ideology that combines an Islamic element (with a thousand-year history), modernisation and a Turkish element (with a two thousand five hundred-year history). This ideology is predominantly concerned with the question of how Islam, modernity and Turkishness can be used to gather Turkish residents under a single rubric. The transformation from a multi-religious and multi-ethnic sultanate into a Turkish nation-state was achieved through the combination of Sunni Islam and Turkish nationalism. This application strengthened the formation of national identity and Turkey's territorial integrity. Emre Ünlücayaklı, 'The Official Discourse in Religion in post-1980 Turkey: The Official Boundaries of the Religious Field, National Belonging and Heritage' (PhD thesis, McGill University 2012) 99–108, 110; Sunier and others (n 5) 100.

55 Ünlücayaklı (n 54) 51; Sunier and others (n 5) 100.

56 Ünlücayaklı (n 54) 49, 51.

57 Act no. 2820 dated 22 April 1983. See Resmi Gazete, 24. 04. 1983-18027 <http://www.mevzuat.gov.tr/MevzuatMetin/1.5.2820.pdf> accessed 26 October 2016. In this Act, Article 89, which still is in use, aims to protect the legal status of the Diyanet and provides for the banning of political parties that call for the abolishment of the Diyanet. Gözaydın, *Religion, Politics* (n 36) 15; Ünlücayaklı (n 54) 65; Ufuk Ulutas, 'Religion and Secularism in Turkey: The Dilemma of the Directorate of Religious Affairs' (2010) 46 (3) *Middle Eastern Studies* 394 <http://www.tandfonline.com/doi/pdf/10.1080/00263200902899812?needAccess=true> accessed 12 October 2016.

58 The Constitution of Republic of Turkey, 1982 (Article 136) <https://global.tbmm.gov.tr/docs/constitution_en.pdf> accessed 16 September 2016.

This makes it clear that a theoretical wall of separation was implicitly established with a view to preventing religion from exerting influence upon the state. However, the converse does not apply – there is no restriction that limits the state interference in religious matters. This law establishes that the state viewed the Diyanet as an apolitical religious institution and clearly establishes the Diyanet as an institutional mechanism of national integrity and solidarity. This became apparent when the escalation of the internal Kurdish "problem" and the emergence of the Central Asian Turkic Republics during the 1990s resulted in the celebration of Nevruz being brought before the Diyanet. This was a particularly sensitive issue because the Nevruz was claimed as being of particular importance by both the Kurdish people of Turkey and the Turkish Republics, with which the country wished to establish special relations in the aftermath of the Soviet Union's collapse.

The Diyanet's official explanation claims that the Nevruz can be traced back to three separate epics (firstly, the Persian epic, which narrates the imaginary day on which the King of Küssi Empire entered into Babil; secondly, the Kurmanç and Zaza epic, which depicts the insurrection of a young blacksmith; and lastly the Ergenekon epic, which describes how Turks were released from the legendary Ergenekon valley where they had been stuck, in the aftermath of a military defeat).[59] The Diyanet establishes the Nevruz as an ancient Turkish and Kurdish festival which celebrated the seasonal change from winter to summer. The legal explanation also acknowledges the transformation of the Nevruz from the Zoroastrian religious festival, in which the coming of spring was celebrated and deceased ancestors were remembered. It is stated that it lost its ties with Zoroastrianism when it became adopted as an Iranian national holiday and became imbued with Islamic motifs and themes.[60] Despite acknowledging the importance of Nevruz in instilling national unity and solidarity, the Diyanet simultaneously recognises that it is not an Islamic festival.[61] The legal explanation states:

> In the time of the Ottoman, the Nevruz, the spring festival, was used as the beginning of the new year … it was also accepted as the official beginning of the financial year, and this has continued thusly until the 1980s.
>
> The custom of the Nevruz in Sunni communities has been seen as prevalently as in Shi'ī, Alevi, and Baktashi communities. As a matter of fact, it was used to be celebrated by Sunnis in the Ottoman Sultanate.[62]

The Nevruz emerges as a custom of both Kurdish and Turkish societies and also Shi'ī and Sunni Muslims; as such, it is interpreted as a common customary

59 Hayreddin Karaman, Ali Bardakoğlu and H. Yunus Apaydın, *İlmihal-II: İslam ve Toplum* (DİB 1998) 489–490.

60 ibid 490.

61 ibid 489–491.

62 ibid 491.

element that reunites divided groups within Turkish society with each other. Social harmony and unity emerge as key priorities of the Diyanet when it engages with issues that include social sensitivities and divisive provocations. After recognising this unifying dimension, the Diyanet emphasises the centrality of intent (*niyyat*) in relation to an Islamic ruling on whether it is permissible to participate in this kind of customary and traditional practice. It is emphasised that the content, purpose and reason of the Nevruz festival would have an important role in determining the legal ruling (*ḥukm*).[63] In stressing the principle of inner responsibility for every action, the Diyanet makes it clear that the individual is ultimately responsible for establishing the permissibility of participating in the Nevruz festivals and celebrations.

The Diyanet also sought to satisfy the religious needs of emigrant Muslim Turks who had relocated to Europe, other Muslim countries and the Turkic Republics during the 1950s and 1960s.[64] The temporary employment status of those Muslim Turks gradually transformed into permanent employment and permanent residence. Their religious needs encouraged the Diyanet to expand its role beyond Turkey. Fikret Karaman, one of the Diyanet's vice-presidents between 2003 and 2010, further reiterates the importance of this contribution:

> [the Diyanet] has increased its efforts to make religious services available to Turkish people living outside of the country. The Diyanet supports the integration of these people into societies in which they live, without losing their original identities, and religious and cultural values. The efforts of the Diyanet are especially important in introducing Turkish culture and Islam to new generations born abroad…
>
> Religious services are abroad also important in terms of world politics. Missionary activities are mostly located in regions where economic, social, health and education levels are low. The Diyanet maintains its services to protect and support the values of Islam both inside and outside the country.[65]

In order to further pursue these purposes, the General Directorate of Foreign Relations was established by a cabinet decree of May 25, 1971.[66] One key objective was to take necessary measures against destructive and divisive activities that

63 ibid.

64 In the late 1970s, the Diyanet began to extend its organisation and function abroad, most notably in Europe but also to other parts of the world. From the 1980s onwards, the Diyanet has sought to establish and develop connections with the Turkic Republics and Muslim countries. Kerem Öktem, 'Global Diyanet and Multiple Networks: Turkey's New Presence in the Balkans' (2012) 1 *Journal of Muslims in Europe* 42. See also Ünlücayaklı (n 54) 120; Fikret Karaman, 'The Status and Function of the PRA in the Turkish Republic' (2008) 98 (2–3) *The Muslim World* 286–287 < https://onlinelibrary.wiley.com/doi/10.1111/j.1478-1913.2008.00226.x> accessed 13 October 2016.

65 Karaman (n 64) 286–287.

66 Türkiye Cumhuriyeti Başkanlık Diyanet İşleri Başkanlığı, 'Tanıtım' <http://www2.diyanet.gov.tr/DisIliskilerGenelMudurlugu/Sayfalar/Tanitim.aspx> accessed 08 March 2017.

targeted Turkish citizens resident in foreign countries.[67] In further developing this dimension, the Diyanet opened the first consulate of religious affairs (which was also known as the Turkish-Islamic Union for Religious Affairs (*Diyanet İşleri Türk-İslam Birliği* or the DİTİB)) in Germany in 1984.[68] Subsequent to the collapse of the Soviet Union, the Diyanet also sought to fulfil the religious requirements of the six Turkic Republics which declared their independence.[69] By 2008, the Diyanet was expanded to thirty-four countries. The contemporary Diyanet has a separate Directorate-General which has five subordinate departments that conduct its affairs in the international arena. During this period, female preachers also began to be employed within the Diyanet, and they were tasked with giving religious sermons to women, leading women's pilgrimages and teaching in Qur'anic courses.[70] This represents a clear break with the androcentric stance upon the position and status of Muslim women. In most instances, traditional Islamic religious circles do not allow women to become religious leaders or preachers. This is despite an established history of learned Muslim women instructing men, which began with the wives of the Prophet Muhammad.

The last period corresponds to the growing power of the Justice and Development Party (*Adalet ve Kalkınma Partisi* or AKP) and stretches from 2002 to the current day. During this period, the Diyanet's influence, at both the national and international level, expanded. Until 2010, there were no constitutional regulations related to the institution. On 10 July, 2010, a new law (Act 6002) produced changes in its structure and status.[71] The first change resulted in it being raised to the undersecretary level, with the consequence that its bureaucratic status was significantly enhanced.[72] Although there have been changes within the institution's structure since it was first established, this Act makes a significant contribution by putting in place fourteen main departments in its structure. The second change expanded the institution's service area outside mosques and the Qur'anic courses – as a result it began to provide religious services to other state institutions, including hospitals, prisons, retirement homes and women's shelters.[73] In establishing the Bureau of Religious Guidance for Families (*Aile ve İrşat Rehberlik Bürosu*) in the *muftīs*' office in some cities and towns and the Religious

67 ibid.

68 Türkisch Islamische Union de Anstalt für Religion e.V./ Diyanet İşleri Türk-İslam Birliği, 'Kuruluş ve Teşkilat Yapısı' <http://www.ditib.de/default1.php?id=5&sid=8&lang=en> accessed 08 March 2017.

69 Salman (n 33) 35–36; Ünlücayaklı (n 54) 120.

70 Okumuş (n 26) 357.

71 Act no. 6002 dated 01 July 2010. See Resmi Gazete, 13. 07. 2010-27640 <http://www.resmigazete.gov.tr/main.aspx?home=http%3A%2F%2Fwww.resmigazete.gov.tr%2Feskiler%2F2010%2F07%2F20100713.htm&main=http%3A%2F%2Fwww.resmigazete.gov.tr%2Feskiler%2F2010%2F07%2F20100713.htm> accessed 10 October 2016.

72 Act no. 6002 dated 01 July 2010. Act 6002 clearly states that the existence of an intermediary state ministry is optional – this can be interpreted as establishing that the status of the Diyanet's President is comparable to that possessed by an undersecretary. See Kaya (n 43) 123.

73 Act no. 6002 dated 01 July 2010.

Services Development Project (*Din Hizmetleri Gelişim Projesi*),[74] the institution actively sought to engage with the community "to provide guidance under the light of the Qur'an and Sunna, based on morality-centred knowledge."[75] These activities sought to integrate people from every section of society into the religious services.

Table 2.1 The Diyanet's organisational structure

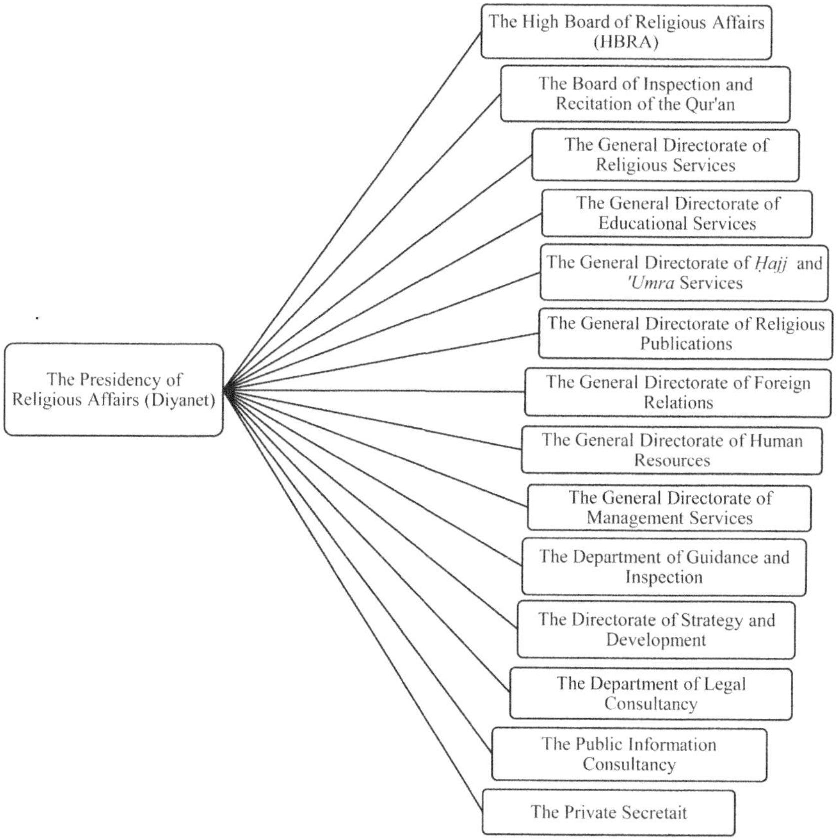

74 This is a project that sought to expand the area of religious services beyond the mosques by providing the people with necessary religious knowledge on various subjects, including the ecological environment, education and health. This project sought to counteract bad habits such as the consumption of alcohol, drug abuse, gambling and smoking and also possibly sought to spread a socio-religious morality that would be conducive to effective and efficient religious services. See Bryan S. Turner and Berna Zengin Arslan, 'State and Turkish Secularism: The Case of the Diyanet' in Bryan S. Turner (ed), *The Religious and the Political: A Comparative Sociology of Religion* (Cambridge University Press 2013) 220.

75 Turner and Arslan (n 74) 209.

In addition, this Act brings forth regulations that relate to the president of the Diyanet's appointment process (the same official can only be nominated twice) and term of office (five years).[76] The Religious Supreme Council (*Din Üst Kururlu*), which consists of one hundred and twenty individuals (including members of the High Board of Religious Affairs, regional *muftīs* and theologians) identifies three candidates for the Presidency before the Council of Ministers chooses one of the candidates and proposes his appointment to the President of the Republic of Turkey.[77] It is possible to argue that this new procedure represents an attempt to enhance the Diyanet's administrative autonomy.

During its last period, the Diyanet has experienced a transformation to a more autonomous institution that can produce and present religious information in isolation from government influence. Sunier et al. observe:

> Until recently, the Friday sermon (*hutbe*) was issued by the central Diyanet authorities on a weekly basis. This was one of the measures in which successive secularist governments tried to control local imams and religious practices. Decentralising the Friday sermons could thus also be interpreted as a move by the AKP to promote religious freedom: one of the political priorities of the AKP.[78]

Under the AKP government, the Diyanet began to become more autonomous, and the institution's president and scholars came to realise that they could declare opinions upon the truth of Islam without the threat of dismissal.[79] In 2002, the Turkification of *adhān* was revaluated during the Diyanet's "Consultation Meeting of Contemporary Religious Issues," in which a substantial number of Muslim scholars participated. The explanation relating to the Turkification of *adhān* focused upon the symbolic value and unifying influence of Arabic *adhān* for all Muslims around the world. It stated that *adhān* was an unchangeable symbol of Islam that refers to Muslim existence and identity, irrespective of where the individual is located in the world.[80] In the meeting, it was also underlined that both *sunna al-taqrīr* (a tradition of what the Prophet allowed to be said or done)[81] and consensus (*ijmā'*) related the performance of *adhān* in its original language, therefore reiterating Arabic language as an essential component of *adhān*. During

76 Act no. 6002 dated 01 July 2010.

77 Seda Dural, 'The Violence against Woman Policy of the AKP Government and the Diyanet' (MA thesis, Leiden University 2016) 18.

78 Sunier and others (n 5) 138.

79 Emine Enise Yakar and Sumeyra Yakar, *The Transformational Process of the Presidency of Religious Affairs in Turkey* (King Faisal Center for Research and Islamic Studies 2017) 23.

80 Türkiye Cumhuriyeti Başkanlık Diyanet İşleri Başkanlığı, *Güncel Dini Meseleler Istişare Toplantısı-I* (Diyanet İşleri Başkanlığı Yayınları 2004) 578–590.

81 Sunna simply means all the traditions of the Prophet Muhammad. It can be categorised into three parts: (1) all his deeds or what he did (*sunna al-fi'il*); (2) all his words or what he said/commanded (*sunna al-qawl*); and (3) everything that the Prophet allowed to be done in his presence – this is called *sunna al-taqrīr* or the confirmation (*takrīr*) or silence (*sukūt*) of the Prophet.

this consultation meeting, many Muslim scholars expressed the view that the legitimacy of *adhān* is established by three of the main sources of Islamic law, specifically, the sunna, *ijmā'* and the Q. 5:58 (which reads: "And when you recite your call to prayer they take it as a joke without (any) seriousness that is because they are a people without understanding"). After reference was made to these three sources, it was clearly and unequivocally stated that chanting *adhān* in languages other than Arabic is a negative innovation (*bid'a*) in religion and deviation from the Sunna – for this reason, it should not be performed by Muslims or permitted by Muslim scholars. In subsequent years, the same question arose in relation to the Kurdification of *adhān*. In a 2011 press release, Mehmet Görmez, the president of the Diyanet, states:

> *Adhān* is the mutual symbol and emblem of all Muslims. Every single word and sentence in *adhān* is "*shi'ar al-Islamiyya*". *Shi'ar* means a symbol that keeps alive our conscious of being and staying Muslim. Accordingly, translating *adhān* and performing it in any other language is not possible to amount to *adhān*, including the mutual belief and conscious of Muslims.[82]

Görmez's contribution clearly establishes that it is not permissible to recite *adhān* in a language other than Arabic because this will strip it of one of its distinguishing features that unifies and integrates Muslims.

In the years between 2000 and 2015, the Diyanet sought to engage different sections of society and enhance the efficiency of its domestic and international engagements. With this intention, the institution initiated the implementation of some innovations, projects and services. These innovations have included the establishment of a Diyanet TV channel that engages with a broad range of "consumer" groups including children, women and the elderly.[83] In addition to this, an internet website was organised to issue religious publications, receive questions and answer them, and a free call centre was also launched to facilitate the practice of *iftā'* and the mission of providing religious knowledge. Among some projects that extend the Diyanet's influence to the everyday lives of the citizens are the organisation of religious seminars and programmes for women and the direct encouragement of *imāms* (prayer leaders) to actively engage with their local congregation. The fourth period is therefore synonymous with the transformation of the Diyanet from a state-controlled institution to a more autonomous and active counterpart that possesses the ability to engage with large and diverse audiences.

82 Türkiye Cumhuriyeti Başkanlık Diyanet İşleri Başkanlığı, 'Başkan Görmez Kürtçe Ezan Konusunda TRT'ye Konuştu' <http://www.diyanet.gov.tr/tr/icerik/baskan-gormez-kurtce-ezan-konusunda-trt%E2%80%99ye-konustu-%E2%80%9Cezanin-herhangi-bir-dile-ve-lehceye-cevrilmesinin-ezan-olarak-kabul-edilmesi-asla-mumkun-degildir/6836> accessed 10 October 2016.

83 Turner and Arslan (n 74) 209.

Constitutional regulations and laws have entrusted the institution with administering all mosques, answering religious questions, organising educational religious facilities for youth and adults and training *vā'izs* (preachers) and *imāms* (prayer leaders). Nonetheless, it is particularly instructive to reflect upon the ruling parties' policies towards the Diyanet that have evidenced considerable variation over time, extending from strictly restrictive and nationalistic to somewhat autonomous. It is similarly possible to identify an equally wide variation in the constitutional regulations that pertain to the institution. Setting aside the different policies adopted by various administrations, the Diyanet, in complying with laws, regulations and standards, has strongly influenced the official discourse on the role of religion in public life, particularly in the period after the 1960s. The Diyanet's connections with the state confer considerable power and legitimacy upon the institution. Ünlücayaklı explicitly recognises this importance when he observes that the institution is "by far the most dominant agent in the bureaucratic-religious field and one of the most dominant ones in the vaster religious field."[84]

Amongst ordinary people of a religious persuasion, the Diyanet commands considerable stature and importance. Many Muslims refer to the Diyanet when performing their prayers (time of prayer), attending religious festivals (*'Īd al-Fitr* and *'Īd al-Adḥā*) or paying *zakāt* (religiously prescribed obligatory alms) and *fitr* (special form of Islamic alms-charity).[85] The institution also enjoys considerable renown in the production of *fatwās*. Taş, in highlighting his research group's recognition of the institution's production regarding Islamic law,[86] observes that 76 percent of participants follow the Diyanet's *fatwās*.[87] Despite the fact that the institution is a recognised authority within the field of religious scholarship, this status does not extend to the Turkish legal system. The Diyanet's *fatwās* just demonstrate an advisory, case-specific and optional character and do not have any sanctioning power.

Existence of a religious institution within the secular state

The existence of the Diyanet with its religious extensions and services within the secular state system raises questions about the precise relationship between the state and the Diyanet. There principally exist two arguments on that specific issue. The first contends that the state established the institution with the intention of promulgating its official religious ideology, a position which implies that the Diyanet cannot claim any religious authority to represent Islam. From this perspective, the Diyanet appears either as an administrative tool that is applied in order to inculcate the religious understanding of the state within Turkish society or as an organisational mechanism that assists in the arrangement of religious

84 Ünlücayaklı (n 54) 275.
85 Okumuş (n 26) 354.
86 Kemaleddin Taş, *Türk Halkının Gözüyle Diyanet* (İz Yayıncılık 2002) 161–162.
87 ibid 163.

services. Ismail Kara and İştar Gözaydın advance precisely this line of argument: the former contends that the Diyanet resembles other institutions of the Turkish state tasked with executing government policies. The institution lost its religious, sacred and prestigious status when the president of the Diyanet began to be appointed by the president of the secular Turkish Republic.[88] Gözaydın concurs:

> The state makes use of the Diyanet as an administrative tool to indoctrinate and propagate official ideology regarding Islam while fulfilling duties like "enlightening society about religion" and "religious education".[89]

Hence, in the view of Gözaydın, the Turkish state has had unrestricted authority over religious discourse and imposed the state's form of Islam by deploying the Diyanet as a religiously political apparatus. Turner and Arslan provide further clarification:

> To put it differently, we suggest the Turkish state's engagement with the field of religion has not been a case of flawed secularism, but on the contrary an example that fulfilled the basic practice of the secular nation-state – that is, to manage or govern religion in the name of national security and social unity. In this sense, the Diyanet is far from being an exception; it is an effective institution of the secular state.[90]

This reiterates that the Diyanet can be described as an ostensible representative of Islam and Muslims which is deeply bound up with the political authority. By logical extrapolation, the Diyanet enables the state to control the content of Friday sermons (*khuṭbas*), the curriculum of all Qur'anic courses and the institution's religious explanations and *fatwās*.

The second perspective maintains that the institution enables religion to emancipate itself from state control by promoting religious unity and solidarity amongst Turkey's Muslims. In the absence of a central and authoritative institution (e.g., the Diyanet), there would be innumerable religious controversies and discordances. The existence of a widely respected official religious authority would help to offset the danger that aims to fragment Muslims into assorted groups and sects. Ali Bardakoğlu (who served as the president of the Diyanet between 2003 and 2010), İrfan Bozan, Mehmet Ali Büyükkara, Ruşen Çakır and İzzet Er (a Diyanet vice-president between 2003 and 2010) directly challenge those who depict the Diyanet as a puppet of the secular state. These scholars observe that no politicians

88 Kara (n 19) 32, 38–39, 43, 45–50, 51–52.

89 İştar Gözaydın, 'Management of Religion in Turkey: The *Diyanet* and Beyond' in Özgür Heval Çınar and Mine Yıldırım (eds), *Freedom of Religion and Belief in Turkey* (Cambridge Scholars Publishing 2014) 17.

90 Turner and Arslan (n 74) 208.

have the right to force the Diyanet to issue a certain *fatwā* or religious decision aligned with the political authority's demands. Er further reiterates:

> [The Government] cannot tell Diyanet to give a certain fatwa. Even if they did, the Higher Council of Religious Affairs (the organ of Diyanet taking Decisions on Religious issues) would never accept it. They take their decisions according to the sources of Islam.[91]

Bardakoğlu also maintains that the institution evidences a liberal predisposition in producing and transforming religious knowledge. He observes:

> The second aspect of the Presidency of Religious Affairs is that it is free to choose scholarly and religious discourse it will use. Indeed, no matter how different things may appear … the Presidency of Religious Affairs has acted totally on its own initiative, its own scholarly competence and accumulation of knowledge and with Turkey's scholarly capacity while providing religious services, responding to religious questions that come from citizens or informing people of religious issues.[92]

In the same vein, Çakır and Bozan agree that the Diyanet has relative autonomy in the issuance of *fatwā* and public statements on religious matters. However, they contend that this "bounded" or relative autonomy should be transformed into "full" autonomy that is free from political influence and/or state interference.[93] Büyükkara, in the course of an interview that engaged with the interrelation of religion and the state, also highlights the importance of the Diyanet's unifying role when he demonstrates how it intercedes between the state and religious sects.[94]

The relative autonomy of the Diyanet in formulating and issuing its own decisions and *fatwās* on religious and religiously ethical issues engenders conflicts between the Diyanet and the government from time to time. It is quite clear that not all of the Diyanet's statements are in harmony with the state's secular regulations. Büyükkara observes:

> Each government desires to set its own seal on the Diyanet. We see these risks, but, in my view, the Diyanet makes the best of what it would do … for instance, even in the period in which there was rigid attacks [and a general ban] on wearing headscarf in public places on account of the influence of the

91 Cited from Sunier and others (n 5) 38.
92 Ali Bardakoğlu, *Religion and Society New Perspectives from Turkey* (Diyanet İşleri Başkanlığı 2009) 14.
93 Çakır and Bozan (n 47) 336–337.
94 Turgay Bakırtaş, 'Din ve Devlet Birlikteliği Bu Ülkenin Kaderidir' (*Gerçek Hayat*, 25 February 2016) <http://www.gercekhayat.com.tr/gundem/1050/> accessed 05 December 2016.

28th February, the Diyanet did not give any *fatwā* that would be used against wearing headscarf.[95]

While the Diyanet was often presented as the supreme religious authority, its *fatwās* on the headscarf were not acknowledged or engaged during this period. This official *fatwā* regarding the headscarf[96] would explicitly bring to light the contradictive relationship between the secular legal system and the Diyanet's *fatwās* within the Turkish Republic. Here it should be acknowledged that the political authority is not in a position to formulate religious opinions. The only way in which the government intervenes in the Diyanet's affairs is to appoint the president of the Diyanet and the members of the High Board of Religious Affairs. The Diyanet's expressed views on a wide range of subjects demonstrate its clear grasp of Islam and Islamic law and the relation of both to Turkish society. These contributions clearly demonstrate the institution's ability to surmount the limitations imposed by and the purposeful interventions of the administrative governments.[97]

The Diyanet's headquarters and the practice of *iftā'*

In the contemporary period, the Diyanet is still the main institution that is responsible for informing internal and external communities about Islam and Islamic legal issues, issuing Islamic legal decisions and *fatwās*, managing mosques and reviewing religious services, including the appointment of local religious representatives (*imāms* and *muftīs*).[98] Since being established, the Diyanet has issued thousands of Islamic decisions and *fatwās*, thus ensuring that the people of Turkey remain informed on Islam and issues pertaining to Islamic law. These contributions encompass a wide range of subjects, as diverse as the

95 ibid.

96 By the time that the Turkish Constitutional Court upheld the headscarf ban, it had already been in force for some time. At this juncture, the Diyanet acknowledged that the wearing of the headscarf is an Islamic legal ruling that is prescribed by the Qur'an and Sunna; this was however supplemented by the observation that there is no particular *naṣṣ* or *ḥadīth* that relates to the form of covering [*tesettür*]. The Diyanet's catechism establishes that each nation has its own particular characteristics, customs and traditions, each of which can be manifested in the wearing style of Muslims. However, the main norm to be taken into consideration by Muslim men and women is that covering or veiling oneself is a religious order and there is *ijmā'* (consensus) among Muslims on the issue. See Karaman, Bardakoğlu and Apaydın, *İlmihal-II* (n 59) 70–73; Hamdi Mert, 'Gündem: Alevilik ve Başörtüsü' (1992) 12 *Diyanet Aylık Dergisi* 6–30 <http://www2.diyanet.gov.tr/DiniYay%C4%B1nlarGenelMudurlugu/DergiDokumanlar/Aylik/1992/ocak_1992.pdf> accessed 19 February 2017; Çakır and Bozan (n 47) 331; Türkiye Cumhuriyeti Başkanlık Diyanet İşleri Başkanlığı, 'Basın Açıklaması' <http://www.diyanet.gov.tr/tr/icerik/basin-aciklamasi/6123> accessed 05 December 2016.

97 Sönmez Kutlu, 'The Presidency of Religious Affairs' Relationship with Religious Groups (Sects/Sufi Orders) in Turkey' (2008) 98 (2–3) *The Muslim World* 249 <http://onlinelibrary.wiley.com/doi/10.1111/j.1478-1913.2008.00223.x/full> accessed 23 October 2016.

98 Sunier and others (n 5) 108.

economy, sciences and social life. The Diyanet's official website features *fatwās* to individual religious questions, decisions of the Consultative Religious Council, online publications and reports on religious issues. Within the Diyanet, the High Board of Religious Affairs (*Din İşleri Yüksek Kurulu*) is the Presidency's most pre-eminent consultative and decision-making service which is tasked with conducting scholarship activities (answering religious questions, examining publications and undertaking research) and developing Presidency policies.[99]

The High Board of Religious Affairs

Since being established, the Diyanet has progressed and developed by enlarging and reorganising its institutional structure and religious services. Within the Diyanet, the High Board of Religious Affairs (*Din İşleri Yüksek Kurulu*) was, in 1965, instituted as the pre-eminent decision-making body whose scope extended to Islamic legal and social issues.[100] While it functions within the limits of official secularism, this Board promulgates the Diyanet's official opinions on religious issues. While performing its duties, the High Board of Religious Affairs (henceforth: HBRA) has undergone a name change. When the Diyanet was first established, it was known as the Board of Consultation (*Hey'et Müşavere*). It was responsible for answering religious questions, issuing Islamic legal explanations and managing personnel (including disciplinary duties).[101] The Board of Consultation was actively involved in all parts of the Diyanet's services until Act 633, which related to the institution's administrative and organisational structure, was accepted in 1965.[102] Even though the organisational structure of the HBRA was established in 1965, it was not fully active until the 1980s.[103] When the HBRA was established, the Diyanet assumed a clearer institutional role focused upon the production and transformation of religious knowledge. Act 633 was significant in this regard as it established the HBRA as the pre-eminent consultative and decision-making body tasked with producing Islamic knowledge that was directly addressed to the challenges that confronted Muslims within and outside Turkey.[104]

The constitutional laws and regulations establish the basis for the formation of the HBRA, the election and appointment of its members and the method through which the president of the HBRA and its members are elected. The duties and responsibilities of the HBRA, and the functions and tasks of the

99 Yaşar Yiğit, İbrahim Ural and Mehmet Bulut, *Diyanet İşleri Başkanlığı: Din İşleri Yüksek Kurulu* (Türkiye Diyanet Vakfı Yayınları 2009) 8.

100 Sunier and others (n 5) 40–41; 88–94; Yiğit, Ural and Bulut, *Diyanet İşleri* (n 99) 6–9; Adanalı (n 40) 230.

101 Mustafa Bülent Dadaş, 'Kuruluşundan Günümüze Din İşleri Yüksek Kurulunun Fetva Siyaseti' (2015) 13 (25–26) *Türkiye Araştırmaları Literatür Dergisi* 41.

102 Yiğit, Ural and Bulut, *Diyanet İşleri* (n 99) 8.

103 Kutlu, 'The Presidency' (n 97) 252; Yiğit, Ural and Bulut, *Diyanet İşleri* (n 99) 13.

104 Yaşar Yiğit, İbrahim Ural and Mehmet Bulut, *Religious Affairs Presidency: High Religious Affairs Committee* (Türkiye Diyanet Vakfı Yayınları 2010) 6.

commissions that operated under the HBRA are also set out in by-laws, constitutional laws and regulations. The Board consists of a president and fifteen members, four of whom are selected from a pool of university professors specialised in Islamic studies and whose Islamic works are widely recognised.[105] Twelve members of the HBRA are elected over the course of the election and appointment phases. The Candidate Designation Board, which was formed pursuant to the relevant regulation, selects twenty-four candidates through voting, a figure which is twice the actual number of HBRA members.[106] The president of the Diyanet submits twelve members from amongst these candidate members, along with four members who had to be elected amongst lecturers at faculties of theology, to the Council of Ministers because the appointment of all members is ultimately contingent upon the approval of the Council of Ministers.[107] It is normally the case that HBRA members would be well-educated scholars in Islamic sciences and Islamic law. Mehmet Görmez, who was the president of the Diyanet between 2010 and 2017, observes:

> The Religious Affairs High Council was responsible for defining, regulating, and improving religious affairs in Turkish society. Members of this council were to be elected from among people who had mastered both "*Akaid-i Islamiyye and Ulumu Şer'iyye*" (Islamic sciences and jurisprudence).[108]

This decision-making body is defined by the presence of competent individuals who possess the ability to provide religious knowledge and services. Act 633 restricts the number of HBRA members to sixteen (including the chairman) and limits their term to a five-year duration.[109] Members can only be appointed twice for the same position, although they are required to maintain office until a new member is assigned.[110] HBRA members select one president and one deputy chairman through a majority vote that is cast on a secret ballot.[111] If membership is terminated for whatever reason, a new member needs to be selected amongst either the candidate members who are identified by the Candidate Designation Board or lecturers at faculties of theology within thirty days.[112]

The 2015 HBRA committee took office with sixteen members on 28 August, 2015, and Dr Raşit Küçük, the vice-president of the president of the Diyanet, was

105 ibid 4–7.
106 Act no. 633 dated 22 July 1965.
107 ibid.
108 Mehmet Görmez, 'The Status of the Presidency of Religious Affairs in Turkish Constitution and Its Execution' (2008) 98 (2–3) *The Muslim World* 244 <http://onlinelibrary.wiley.com/doi/10.1111/j.1478-1913.2008.00222.x/full> accessed 20 October 2016.
109 Act no. 633 dated 22 July 1965.
110 ibid.
111 ibid.
112 ibid.

elected as the chairman of the HBRA on 05 September, 2015.[113] The other members of the HBRA are:

1. Zeki Sayar (the deputy chairman of the HBRA)
2. Mehmet Kapukaya (a HBRA expert)
3. Rifat Oral (a lecturer at the Directorate of Selçuk High Specialization Center)
4. Dr Muhlis Akar (a HBRA expert)
5. Dr Mehmet Canbulat (a HBRA expert)
6. Prof Dr Ahmet Yaman (a lecturer at the Faculty of Theology in Necmettin Erbakan University)
7. Doç Dr Cenksu Üçer (a lecturer at the Faculty of Islamic Sciences in Yıldırım Beyazıt University)
8. Prof Dr Zekeriya Güler (a lecturer at the Faculty of Theology in İstanbul University)
9. Prof Dr Ibrahim Hilmi Karslı (a lecturer at the Faculty of Theology in Recep Tayyip Erdoğan University)
10. Prof Dr Hüseyin Yılmaz (a lecturer at the Faculty of Theology in Yüzüncü Yıl University)
11. Prof Dr Mehmet Ünal (the dean of the Faculty of Islamic Sciences in Yıldırım Beyazıt University)
12. Prof Dr Mürteza Bedir (the dean of the Faculty of Theology in İstanbul University)
13. Prof Dr Kaşif Hamdi Okur (a lecturer at the Faculty of Theology in Hitit University)
14. Prof Dr Bünyamin Erul (a lecturer at the Faculty of Theology in Ankara University)
15. Prof Dr Cağfer Karadaş (a lecturer at the Faculty of Theology in Uludağ University)[114]

All of these scholars completed their studies at faculties of theology in Turkish universities, but some of them have combined their formal modern education with the traditional education (*medrese usulu eğitim*). In 1992, Zeki Sayar attended the eight-term specialisation course at Haseki Education Centre,[115] which primarily

113 Act no. 8044 dated 19 August 2015. See Resmi Gazete, 28. 08. 2015-29459 <http://www.resmigazete.gov.tr/main.aspx?home=http%3A%2F%2Fwww.resmigazete.gov.tr%2Feskiler%2F2015%2F08%2F20150828.htm&main=http%3A%2F%2Fwww.resmigazete.gov.tr%2Feskiler%2F2015%2F08%2F20150828.htm> accessed 07 November 2016.

114 ibid.

115 In 1976, Haseki Education Centre was established by the Diyanet to educate the Diyanet's personnel (particularly *muftīs* (specialists in Islamic law who issue *fatwās*) and *vā'izs* (preachers)). This centre makes an important contribution by offering the scientific substructure to *muftīs* and *vā'izs*, who both function as representatives of Islamic knowledge in Turkey. This substructure is probably programmed to provide traditional education (*medrese usulu egitim*), with a particular emphasis upon Arabic langue, Islamic jurisprudence, the Qur'anic commentaries (*tafsīr*) and *ḥadīth* traditions. See Haseki Dini Yüksek İhtisas Merkeziniin Tarihçesi, 'Merkezimiz' <http:

provides traditional education to the Diyanet's personnel. [116] Subsequent to completing his education in Selçuk University's Faculty of Theology, Rifat Oral also received instruction from well-known Turkish scholars who were considered to be authorities in Islamic studies. He took teaching permission (*ijāzat*) from them and also participated in an informal network of scholarly lecturers (*ḥalaqāt*) which included Fadl Abbas, Şuaybü'l Arnavud, Abdülaziz ad-Duri, Fethi Duveyni and Salah al-Halidi.[117] In common with Sayar, Muhlis Akar attended the sixth term specialisation course at Haseki Education Centre after earning his MA at the Faculty of Theology in Selçuk University in 1986; he later received his PhD degree from the Faculty of Economics in 2000.[118] During his early life, Zekeriya Güler received the classical traditional Islamic education (*klasik medrese egitimi*) and memorised the Qur'an by heart. He graduated from the Faculty of Theology in Selçuk University in 1986 and later received his PhD degree from the Faculty of Theology in İstanbul University before working as a lecturer at the Department of Ḥadīth in the same university.[119] The assignment of predominantly academic experts has increased global awareness of the Diyanet.

By virtue of the fact that the Diyanet is an administrative state institution, both its and the HBRA's organisational structures were regulated by constitutional laws and regulations. Act 633 depicts the duties of the HBRA in the following terms:

a) To make decisions on religious matters, express views concerning religious affairs, and answer questions relating to religion by taking into account current demand and requirements, historical experiences, the fundamental information sources and methodology of Islam,
b) To conduct, examine or translate research on religious matters. Benefit from competent people in the country, form research groups and purchase services when required and submit the results to the Directorate,
c) To examine and evaluate religious groups connected to Islam that produce different interpretations, religio-social associations and traditional religio-cultural formations inside and outside the country; also organize scientific and consultative meetings and conferences on these matters,

//www.hasekidiyanet.gov.tr/?pnum=122&pt=M%C3%BCd%C3%BCr%C3%BCm%C3%BCz%C3%BCn%20Kaleminden%20Merkezimizin%20Tarih%C3%A7esi> accessed 09 November 2016.

116 Din İşleri Yüksek Kurulu Başkanlığı, 'Kurul Üyeleri: Zeki Sayar' <http://www2.diyanet.gov.tr/dinisleriyuksekkurulu/Sayfalar/uyeler/ZekiSayar.aspx> accessed 14 November 2016.

117 Din İşleri Yüksek Kurulu Başkanlığı, 'Kurul Üyeleri: Rifat Oral' <http://www2.diyanet.gov.tr/dinisleriyuksekkurulu/Sayfalar/uyeler/RifatOral.aspx> accessed 14 November 2016.

118 Din İşleri Yüksek Kurulu Başkanlığı, 'Kurul Üyeleri: Muhlis Akar' <http://www2.diyanet.gov.tr/dinisleriyuksekkurulu/Sayfalar/uyeler/MuhlisAkar.aspx> accessed 14 November 2016.

119 Din İşleri Yüksek Kurulu Başkanlığı, 'Kurul Üyeleri: Zekeriya Güler' <http://www2.diyanet.gov.tr/dinisleriyuksekkurulu/Sayfalar/uyeler/ZekeriyaGuler.aspx> accessed 14 November 2016.

d) To follow developments associated with Islam (religious publications, religious and scientific activities and propagandas in the country), evaluate them and submit assessments to the Directorate,
e) To examine audio, printed and visual works sent by the Directorate and to decide, in the course of undertaking an analysis grounded within a religious perspective, whether or not they will be published,
f) To, subsequent to the payment of a fee, examine religious publications that individuals and particular institutions request to be examined,
g) To carry out works that relate to the Consultative Religious Councils,
h) To implement tasks and works assigned by the president of the Diyanet, and to express their views on these issues.[120]

At the level of both theory and practice, the HBRA functions as the highest religious authority whose decisions have crucial implications for public affairs that require religious explanation. In many cases, the Muslim society espouses and values Islamic legal decisions and *fatwās* issued by the HBRA – these extend to court divorce, inheritance, religious marriage (*nikāḥ*), ritual practices (*'ibādāt*) and superstitions.

HBRA members meet at least once a week to discuss and evaluate subjects on the agenda, and it is established that an absolute majority of the HBRA's members should attend these meetings. The president of the HBRA usually chairs meetings, but the president of the Diyanet presides when attending HBRA meetings. When the HBRA president is absent, the deputy chairman of the Board operates as the meeting chairman. The HBRA consists of five sub-commissions – these are set out in Table 2.2.[121] The subjects included in the meeting agenda are closely examined by the relevant commission/s before being evaluated within HBRA meetings. Discussions are usually based on the research and examination conducted by the commissions, which contain at least three members. Every commission selects a president, and HBRA members have the right to participate in more than one commission. During HBRA meetings, necessary decisions and *fatwās* are advanced by an absolute majority of members. The regulation establishes that HBRA members must sign the agreed decision subsequent to collective discussion and voting.

Table 2.2 The organisational structure of the HBRA

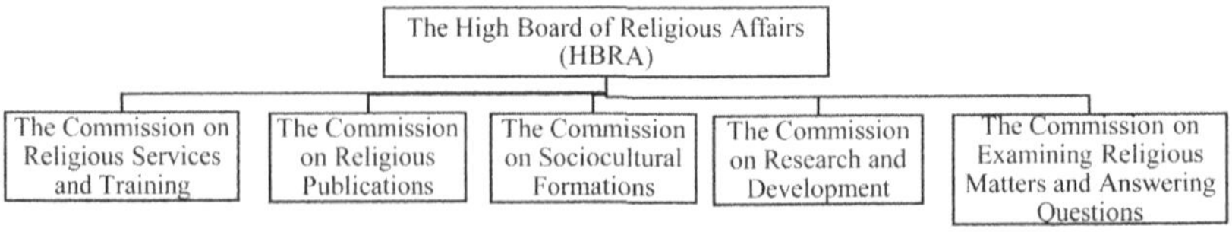

120 Act no. 633 dated 22 July 1965.
121 Republic of Turkey's Presidency of Religious Affairs (n 107).

At the beginning of the next HBRA meeting, a summary official report relating to the previous meeting's decision is read out. HBRA decisions and *fatwās* can therefore be interpreted as a collective *iftā* practice addressed to contemporary social, cultural, economic, technological and medical problems in need of more sustained scholarly engagement.

Every five years, the HBRA organises a Consultative Religious Council with the intention of improving the Diyanet's services.[122] Up to the contemporary period, the HBRA has organised five Consultative Religious Councils that address a wide range of subjects. Councils last normally for at least three days, although they can last sometimes for twice as long. The Council's members consist of the Diyanet president, along with current and former members of the HBRA. The attendees include a maximum of twenty religious and scientific scholars invited by the Diyanet, along with ten *muftīs* and five *vā'izs* selected by the HBRA. They extend to a member of each faculty of theology, a member of the Ministry of Education's Education and Training Board (*Milli Eğitim Bakanlığı Talim ve Terbiye Kurulu*), the director of the Religious Education General Directorate (*Din Öğretimi Genel Müdürü*) and one member of the Board of Trustees of Turkey's Diyanet Foundation (*Türkiye Diyanet Vakfı Mütevelli Heyeti*), who are required to attend as members of the HBRA's Consultative Religious Council.[123] In addition, one representative from the Directorate-General of Foundations, the General Secretariat of the National Security Council, the General Staff, the Ministry of Foreign Affairs, the Ministry of Interior, the Ministry of Tourism, the Radio and Television High Council and the State Planning Organisation, along with official guests invited by the president of the Diyanet are allowed to participate in and present a notification to the Consultative Religious Council. However, they are not entitled to vote.[124] The Council's agenda and the view of the Diyanet that would be presented in the Consultative Religious Council are prepared by the HBRA.[125] In every Consultative Religious Council, resolutions are, as determined by Act 93/4257, supported by the majority of members who attend the Consultative Religious Council ("In the Consultative Religious Council, decisions are taken by the great majority of joined members. Should the votes be tied, the President of the Diyanet determines the outcome").[126]

In 1993, the Council was, for the first time, organised under the name of "the First Consultative Religious Council" and tasked with examining "religious publications." In 1998, "the Second Consultative Religious Council" was convened

122 Act no. 93/4257 dated 19 February1993. See Resmi Gazete, 30. 04. 1993-21567 <http://www.resmigazete.gov.tr/main.aspx?home=http://www.resmigazete.gov.tr/arsiv/21567.pdf&main=http://www.resmigazete.gov.tr/arsiv/21567.pdf> accessed 18 November 2016.

123 Act no. 98/11479 dated 24 July 1998. See Resmi Gazete, 12. 08. 1998-23436 <http://www.resmigazete.gov.tr/main.aspx?home=http://www.resmigazete.gov.tr/arsiv/23436.pdf&main=http://www.resmigazete.gov.tr/arsiv/23436.pdf> accessed 19 November 2016.

124 ibid.

125 Act no. 93/4257 dated 19 February 1993.

126 ibid.

and its attention was directed towards the issue of "interreligious dialogue." In 2003, "the Third Consultative Religious Council" was established and asked to evaluate "the role of religion in Turkey's accession process to the EU." The HBRA also organised the fourth (addressed to "religion and society") and fifth (addressed to "contemporary religious education, knowledge, services and understanding") Consultative Religious Councils, which were respectively held in 2009 and 2014.[127] In addition to establishing ordinary Consultative Religious Councils, the HBRA is also entitled to, in urgent situations, call extraordinary meetings – these, however, require the coordinated effort of Board members, Diyanet personnel, the relevant ministries and representatives drawn from various institutions.[128] Up until the current date, the HBRA has held a single extraordinary Consultative Religious Council meeting, which was held on 04 August, 2016 in response to the bloody coup attempt of the preceding month.

The decisions of each Consultative Religious Council are recorded by the secretary-general (*Genel Sekreter*). Subsequent to the approval of the Diyanet's president, they are then published.[129] The secretary-general is also responsible for submitting the Council's agenda, date and place to the members of the Consultative Religious Council and to concerned institutions at least three months before any meeting.[130] In contrast to constitutional laws, judicial decisions and regulations, which are binding on all who are resident in Turkey, these Council resolutions, as Act 93/4257 establishes, instead possess an advisory, consultative and informative character ("The resolutions of the Consultative Religious Council have a consultative nature").[131] It is therefore important to note that the resolutions are not binding on members of the public, but are instead advisory and informative, with particular application to the ethical, religious and social realms.

The HBRA also organises Consultation Meetings of Contemporary Religious Issues which engage generally with contemporary problems related to Islamic law that currently confront Muslims at both the internal (within Turkey) and external levels. A list of subjects discussed and recorded in these consultation meetings follows:

- Correctly understand and interpret religious texts, women's problems and discussions on the pilgrimage (*ḥajj*) and prayer (*ṣalāt*),
- Medical developments, religious problems and social life originating within trade,
- Business life,
- Contemporary issues relating to *ḥalāl* food,
- Issues relating to family and prayers,

127 Din İşleri Yüksek Kurulu Başkanlığı, 'Din Şuraları' <http://www2.diyanet.gov.tr/dinisleriyuksekkurulu/Sayfalar/DinSuralarison.aspx> accessed 20 November 2016.

128 Act no. 93/4257 dated 19 February 1993.

129 ibid.

130 ibid.

131 ibid.

- Methods to understand and interpret the Qur'an and *ḥadīths*,
- Religious advisory services and the *fatwā* concept.[132]

In addition to these consultation meetings, the HBRA has organised various workshops that have engaged with astronomical observations, contemporary problems of belief, data bank projects, embryo research, esoteric comments in religion, *fatwā* projects, Islamic ethics, Islam and violence, the guided one (*Mahdī*) and Islam's outlook on different beliefs and races.[133] Last but not least, the examination of religious works remains the HBRA's core activity. Books and other written works that relate to religion are normally sent to the Commission on Religious Publications, which falls within the HBRA's structure. Commission experts are then responsible for examining the work and preparing a related report.[134] Commission experts then reconvene and re-engage the work, with a view to preparing a new report that will be presented to the HBRA.[135] After discussing the Commission report and analysing it from a religious perspective, the HBRA then makes a final decision on whether it will be published.[136] The works are therefore only published subsequent to an examination of whether they are consistent with an authentic and correct interpretation of Islam. In this manner, the HBRA operates as a board which is responsible for supervising religious publications within the Diyanet structure.

External experts have participated in certain HBRA meetings, projects and workshops, which have focused strongly upon contemporary problems and topics.[137] These experts have made an important contribution in areas where the scholars lack required knowledge, such as economics, medicine, technology and science. Between May 20 and 30, 2016, the Diyanet, working in cooperation with the Islamic Crescent Observation Project (ICOP), organised the International Lunar Calendar Unity Congress.[138] During the Congress, astronomical experts

132 Republic of Turkey's Presidency of Religious Affairs (n 107).

133 ibid.

134 Yiğit, Ural and Bulut, *Diyanet İşleri* (n 99) 19.

135 ibid.

136 ibid.

137 Act no. 633 dated 22 July 1965; Act no. 93/4257 dated 19 February 1993; Act no. 98/11479 dated 24 July 1998; Dadaş (n 101) 59.

138 The Congress, which was hosted by the Diyanet, was held in İstanbul between 28 and 30 May 2016. Scientific and religious scholars from roughly fifty countries, which included Egypt, Jordan, Malaysia, Saudi Arabia, Turkey, the United Arab Emirates (UAE) and the United States, participated in the Congress. The preparation of the Congress began three years in advance when a commission of scientists and scholars specialising in astronomy and Islamic jurisprudence (*fiqh*) began to explore views within the Muslim world at the international level. The Congress concluded with two main proposals: firstly, a dual calendar system that would entail a separate calendar for the Western Hemisphere, which would be of particular benefit to Muslims resident in North and South America; secondly, a single calendar system that Muslims in every part of the world would refer to when celebrating religious festivals (*'Īd al-Fitr* and *'Īd al-Adḥā*). These two proposals were put to the vote, and a clear majority of participants agreed to adopt a single Islamic lunar calendar system. See Din İşleri Yüksek Kurulu Başkanlığı, 'Uluslararası Hicri Takvim Birliği Kongresi Sonuç

made an important contribution by providing required knowledge to the participating scholars. The Congress decision derived from a Science Board that included scholars and scientists drawn from various countries.[139] In acknowledging that the issue of moonsighting has divided the Muslim community (*umma*), the Congress sought to develop a unified lunar calendar. It states:

> [I]t has been a real challenge for Muslims, particularly for the Muslim minority groups ... because, in one country, this results sometimes in celebrating the religious festivals (*'Īd al-Fitr* and *'Īd al-Adḥā*) in three different days amongst Muslims living in non-Muslim countries as well as Muslim countries ... This religion is the religion of oneness (*tawḥīd*) and has regarded unity and integrity as a legal obligation (*şer'i bir farz*) and a factual necessity.[140]

The Congress was justified by the fact that the celebration of religious festivals (*'Īd al-Fitr* and *'Īd al-Adḥā*) begins at different times in separate countries and sometimes even in the same cities. For this reason, it was imperative to work towards unifying the lunar Islamic calendar (*at-taqwīm al-hijrī*). The Congress noted that divisions amongst the Muslim community on the subject of local moonsighting (*ikhtilāf al-maṭāli'*) were contrary to the *tawḥīd* spirit of Islam; the need to achieve and uphold unity within the Muslim community came to provide the basis for the acceptance of a single lunar calendar system.[141]

In the Congress Resolution, the obligation regarding the viewing of the new moon (*hilāl*) was determined an obligatory and functional requirement for the verification of the birth of the new moon, so the witnessing of the crescent (*hilāl*) was established as a necessary precondition for the confirmation of the birth of the new moon.[142] If the crescent is viewed at any point of the world, whether through human sight or the use of modern astronomical instruments, it is conceivably sufficient for the discharge of religious obligations that the sighting of the crescent is considered the operative cause (*'illa*). Being grounded within the universal validity of sight (*ittihād al-maṭāli'*), the resolution does not appear to contradict the classical Islamic regulation which holds that the witnessing of the crescent is a form of worship and a prerequisite for devotional practices – this is the case because the visibility condition of the crescent is the resolution's main priority. The issue was resolved through an alignment with scientific opinion (astronomy) and Islamic jurisprudence (*fiqh*).

Bildirgesi' <http://www2.diyanet.gov.tr/dinisleriyuksekkurulu/Sayfalar/HaberDetay.aspx?rid=64&lst=HaberlerListesi&csn=/dinisleriyuksekkurulu> accessed 20 November 2016; Mehmet Çelik, 'Islamic Scholars Agree on a Shared Lunar Calendar for Muslim World' (*Daily Sabah Turkey*, 31 May 2016) <http://www.dailysabah.com/nation/2016/05/31/islamic-scholars-agree-on-a-shared-lunar-calendar-for-muslim-world> accessed 20 November 2016.

139 Din İşleri Yüksek Kurulu Başkanlığı, 'Uluslararası Hicri' (n 108)

140 ibid.

141 ibid.

142 ibid.

In the modern context, it can be asserted that economic, medical, sociological and technological sources grounded within empirical and scientific evidence emerge naturally and provide an essential data-base for the practice of *iftā'*. In common with other religious scholars, HBRA members cannot claim to possess a comprehensive knowledge of economic, medical, scientific or technological matters. The HBRA is, for this reason, frequently reliant upon external expertise. On medical questions, including the use of alcohol in medication, in vitro fertilisation, organ transplantation, plastic surgery and sterilisation, teams of doctors are, in advance of any Islamic legal explanation, asked to provide their specialised knowledge. On economic issues, including banking, commerce, interest/usury (*ribā*), life insurance and mortgages, economic experts substantially provide guidance to the HBRA. In addressing itself to the question of whether anaesthesia breaks the fast (*ṣawm*), for instance, the organisation refers to established medical and scientific truths.[143] After describing three types of anaesthesia (general, local and regional), the HBRA states:

> Anaesthesia is used to stop patients from feeling pain or other sensations during medical operations ... Anaesthesia is given as gas to breath in or injections into the human body. The anaesthesia through gas and injection does not carry a meaning of eating and drinking as it does not go down the stomach. However, regional and general anaesthesia sometimes necessitates to drip-feed the anesthetized person in order to establish vascular access in the case of emergency. Consequently, the fast breaks in the types of regional and general anaesthesia when the anesthetized patient drip-feeds, but the local anaesthesia does not cause to break the fast of the patient due to the fact that there is no mention of drip-feeding.[144]

Instead of referring directly to any textual evidence, HBRA members, in trying to identify which types of anaesthesia break an individual's fast, refer to medical knowledge on the subject. It can, upon this basis, be argued that medical knowledge is inserted into the *fatwā* to provide more detailed legal opinion. The knowledge of the external experts is generally cited and used as circumstantial and corroborative evidence in conjunction with the authoritative Islamic legal

143 Din İşleri Yüksek Kurulu, *Fetvalar* (Diyanet İşleri Başkanlığı Yayınları 2015) 286–287.

144 The *fatwā* sets out three types of anaesthesia. In the first instance, general anaesthesia is used for major operations, and an anesthetised (and entirely unconscious) patient does not feel pain and other signals passing along nerves to the brain. Local anaesthesia is the second type of anaesthesia which is used for minor medical procedures. While the person remains conscious (awake), he/she should not feel pain in the area being anesthetised. The third type (regional anaesthesia) is similar to local anaesthesia – however it anesthetises more broadly and in greater depth by injecting drugs into the specific nerves that are connected to the targeted part of the body. See Din İşleri Yüksek Kurulu (n 143) 286–287.

sources in many *fatwās* pertaining to issues as diverse as abortion, birth control, euthanasia and organ donation.[145]

Closer engagement suggests that the issuance of *fatwās* is among the HBRA's most important duties. It should be noted that these *fatwās* clearly address themselves to the task of constructing the religious consciousness and morality of the Muslims in the society. The following section sets out the HBRA's process of *iftā'* in greater detail.

The process of answering religious questions

The HBRA is the main component of the Diyanet, which functions as its executive agent in all matters pertaining to religious research, decisions and *fatwās* because Act 633 tasks the Diyanet with informing the society about religion.[146] Thousands of *fatwās* and decisions have been issued on various subjects which include culture, economics, food, gender issues, interfaith dialogue, marriage, medicine, Muslim minority sects, rituals, theology, the rights of non-Muslims, sophisticated technology and in vitro fertilisation.

It is generally the case that the questions directed by individuals and private/public organisations can be submitted through e-mail, fax, mail or telephone. However, some individuals do occasionally visit the Board to present their questions in person.[147] Answers to the questions asked by fax or mail are posted with a signed official letter by the HBRA's president or its deputy chairman. In the process of the practice of *iftā'*, questions are forwarded to the Commission on Examining Religious Matters and Answering Questions at the outset. The Commission then has the option of pursuing one of three courses of action. If the question is straightforward, it will receive a direct answer. If it is complicated, it will be sent to the commission's experts. While researchers initially conduct research independently, their final response to the question is issued on a collective basis. The prepared answer is submitted to the HBRA president who, in acting on behalf of the president of the Diyanet, then signs the document, which will later be forwarded to the initial applicant via fax or mail. The final course of action pertains to instances in which extra effort is required to deduce a *fatwā* or the issue has not arisen before. Here the Commission prepares research related to the question before this research is placed on the HBRA agenda, in the expectation that it will issue a *fatwā*.[148] After engaging with the issue on the basis of research prepared by the Commission, HBRA members then make a final decision, which is indicated by an absolute majority vote. HBRA members are therefore responsible for producing answers to religious questions in instances where the experts of

145 Din İşleri Yüksek Kurulu (n 143) 535, 538–540.
146 Yiğit, Ural and Bulut, *Religious Affairs Presidency* (n 104) 6.
147 Dadaş (n 101) 42–44.
148 ibid.

the Commission on Examining Religious Matters and Answering Questions are unable to respond.

In order to further engage (answer, publish and receive) questions and the practice of *iftā'*, the Diyanet also established a free call centre and launched an official website. In order to answer religious questions by phone, a private room (known as "the Room of Answering Religious Questions") was established within the HBRA.[149] It is estimated that the room answers a total number of between two hundred and two hundred and fifty questions per day.[150] During weekdays (from 09:00 a.m. to 17:00 p.m., with the exception of Ramadan, when it stays open until the later hours), two experts are deployed within the room.[151] Sometimes, if they require a clearer grasp of content or context, the experts will ask for questions to be put in writing.

E-mail enquiries submitted through the Diyanet's official website have recently increased in number.[152] The Commission on Research and Development (ARGED) is responsible for replying to these questions in addition to undertaking media outreach through consultative resolutions, journals, recommendations, reports and documentations of *fatwās*, television broadcasts and the Diyanet's official website. The ARGED transfers the questions to the relevant experts in the HBRA, before any answer is e-mailed to the petitioners.[153] After obtaining the experts' *fatwā* to the question, the ARGED e-mails the *fatwā* to the questioner. Frequently, those *fatwās* that have general contents and that are considered to be of importance not only to the individual questioner but also to the Muslims resident in Turkey are featured on the website (Table 2.3).

There are also questions that require a stronger grasp of the petitioners' situation or local cultural practices. In these instances, experts can adopt two approaches, which vary in accordance with the specific circumstance.[154] In the first instance, petitioners can sometimes be asked to present their question in person, a course of actions which could, under certain circumstances, help experts to provide a more authentic, reliable or specific religious answer.[155] In the second instance, the questions which include local or cultural correlations can be directed to the Office of Muftī in the petitioner's city.[156] In the process of answering a religious question, therefore, the investigation of the petitioners' conditions and of the local and cultural context emerges as a noteworthy criterion in order to ensure the religious answer's suitability to that specific case.

Within the structure of the HBRA, there is a systematic coordinative working relationship in the process of issuing *fatwā*. The Commission (on Examining

149 Yiğit, Ural and Bulut, *Religious Affairs Presidency* (n 104) 18.
150 Republic of Turkey's Presidency of Religious Affairs (n 107).
151 Yiğit, Ural and Bulut, *Diyanet İşleri* (n 99) 18–19.
152 ibid 18.
153 ibid 18.
154 ibid 18–19.
155 ibid.
156 ibid.

Table 2.3 The process of *fatwā*-issuing by the HBRA

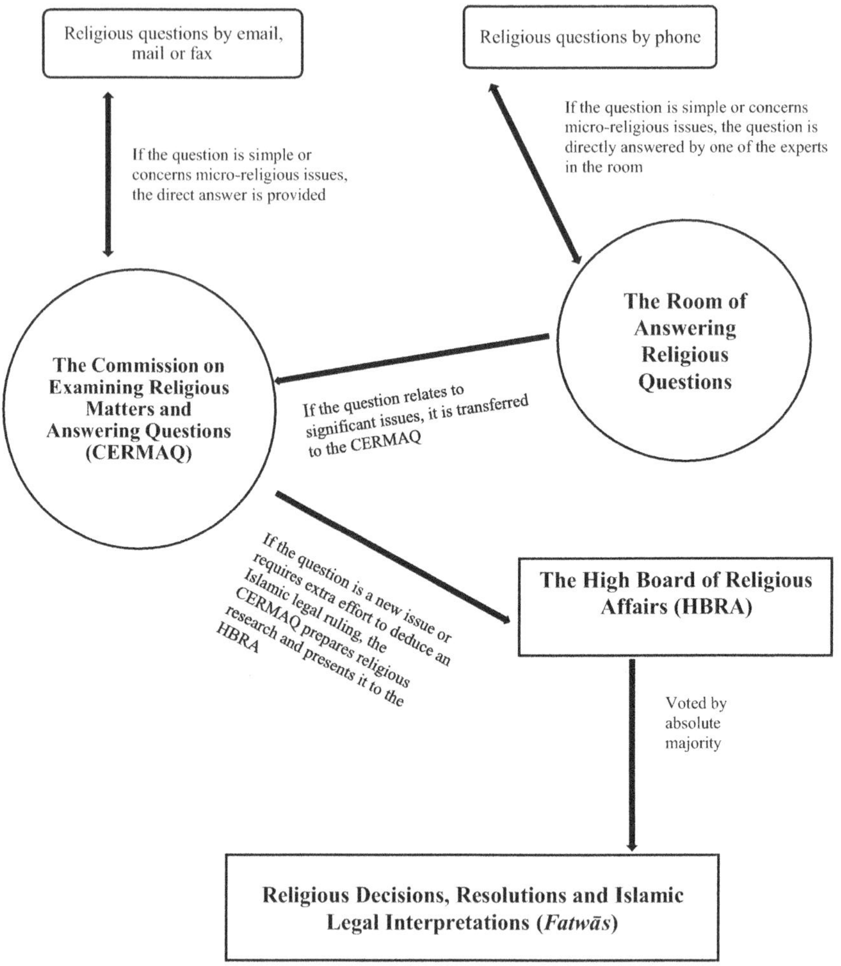

Religious Matters and Answering Questions) and the Room (of Answering Religious Questions) both seek to answer uncomplicated questions pertaining to Islamic legal and religious issues (e.g., ritual practices and their legal rulings) while HBRA members are primarily preoccupied with novel issues that have not been encountered before or complicated cases that require an intensification of existing scholarly efforts or a heightened level of collaboration in the practice of *iftā'*.[157] This clearly brings out the existence of a hierarchical administrative sys-

157 Dadaş (n 101) 43–44.

tem within the structure of the HBRA. In this system, the primary responsibility of the Board is to answer questions in a manner that closely corresponds to the essence of Islam and Islamic law.

In answering questions that have been presented to it, the HBRA has adopted two main strategies, which vary in accordance with question content. Firstly, if the content of the question is associated with ritual practices (*'ibādāt*) or classical Islamic legal issues discussed by earlier Muslim scholars, the HBRA normally refers to the views and methodologies of the Ḥanafī school (*madhhab*) – this entails a closer engagement with *fatwās* associated with *'ibādāt* and issues adjudicated by the earlier Muslim scholars.[158] It is occasionally the case that a *fatwā*, subsequent to introducing the Ḥanafī *madhhab*'s view, outlines the position of the three other Sunni *madhhabs* (with particular emphasis on the Shāfi'ī *madhhab*) without apportioning a clear preference.[159] This is especially true when: (1) the petitioner specifically requests the views of other Sunni *madhhabs*; (2) when the opinions of other Sunni *madhhabs* appear to be better suited to the immediate legal problem; (3) when the view of the Ḥanafī *madhhab* is not compatible with new circumstances; or (4) when a weakness is identified in the evidence (*dalīl*) of the Ḥanafī legal rule.

It is generally the case that the HBRA introduce the views of other legal *madhhabs* after mentioning the stance of the Ḥanafī *madhhab*, thus leaving the right of selectivity (*tarjīḥ*) to the discretion of the individual questioner.[160] The *fatwā* relating to the suckling number of babies that prohibits the marriage with milk siblings is one example of *fatwās* that encompass the views of other Sunni *madhhabs*.[161] As is usually the case, the *fatwā* presented the Ḥanafī *madhhab*'s legal ruling which holds that sucking is sufficient to establish milk kinship until the age of two. The *madhhab* maintains that the condition which institutes milk kinship is that the milk reaches the stomach of the baby this is the key consideration, as opposed to the consumed amount or the number of occasions on which the baby is breastfed by his/her milk mother.[162] After presenting the opinion of the Ḥanafī *madhhab*, the *fatwā* refers to the legal opinion of the Shāfi'ī and the Ḥanbalī *madhhabs* on the various conditions that establish milk kinship.[163] The two *madhhabs* agree that sucking less than five times does not institute milk kinship; suckling that takes place after two years of age does not result in marriage being forbidden.[164] To put it differently, the *fatwā* states that five times full breastfeeding before the age of two by the same wet nurse is certainly conditioned by the Shāfi'ī and the

158 Din İşleri Yüksek Kurulu (n 143) 46; Dadaş (n 101) 50.
159 Din İşleri Yüksek Kurulu (n 143) 46.
160 Dadaş (n 101) 50.
161 Din İşleri Yüksek Kurulu (n 143) 467.
162 ibid.
163 ibid.
164 ibid.

Ḥanbalī *madhhabs* to institute milk kinship that prohibits marriages among the milk siblings.[165]

Another *fatwā* relating to the legal ruling on the consumption of seafood, such as mussels, crab and lobster, also sets out a similar structure in which the legal views of the Ḥanafī and Shāfi'ī *madhhabs* are respectively presented.[166] These two *fatwās* and many others establish that the selection and implementation of the legal rulings, opinions and views of the four Sunni schools are generally contingent upon the discretion of the individual who asks the question. Mustafa Bülent Dadaş, one of the experts in the HBRA, explains why the institution offers different opinions of the four Sunni *madhhabs*. He states:

> The board conceivably aims to provide easiness and facility to the questioner (*mustaftī*) by mentioning the different views in a *fatwā*. Yet more, other *madhhabs*' legal views, along with the four Sunni law *madhhabs*, are introduced to the individual as practicable, valid and applicable Islamic legal options.[167]

However, several *fatwās* issued by the HBRA also make it clear that, after the relevant views of the *madhhabs* are conveyed, the Board assumes responsibility for determining the preponderant opinion. For example, the HBRA issued a *fatwā* relating to the issue of triple divorce (*ṭalāq*) by a single utterance.[168] The *fatwā* briefly sets out the legal view of the Ḥanafī and Shāfi'ī *madhhabs* at the beginning, before then engaging with two *ḥadīths* narrated by 'Abd Allāh b. 'Abbās, one of the Companions of the Prophet. These *ḥadīths* are referred to as the second Islamic legal opinion concerning triple divorce by a single utterance, a view which is, it should be noted, very much peculiar to the minority's stance within the Ḥanbalī *madhhab*.[169] The *fatwā* observes that the majority of scholars, including most Ḥanafīs and Shāfi'īs, maintain that this form of divorce has the same full effect as a triple divorce (the greater irrevocable divorce) – it does not matter whether the words of *ṭalāq* are pronounced three times in a single sitting or during the *'idda* period (the wife's waiting period after divorce).[170]

165 ibid.

166 ibid 531.

167 Dadaş (n 101) 53–54.

168 Generally speaking, there are two types of divorce (*ṭalāq*): revocable and irrevocable. In revocable divorce, the marriage does not terminate, and during the waiting period of the wife, the husband and the wife can reunite, without implementing a new marriage contract. Irrevocable divorce is classified into two types according to their degrees: the lesser, which permits the parties to remarry, and the greater, which prohibits remarriage of the parties until after the wife has married another man and that marriage is consummated and terminated.

169 Din İşleri Yüksek Kurulu (n 143) 444; Frank Vogel, 'The Complementarity of Ifta' and Qaḍā': Three Saudi Fatwas on Divorce' in Muhammad Khalid Masud, Brinkley Messick and David S. Powers (eds), *Islamic Legal Interpretation: Muftis and Their Fatwas* (Harvard University Press 1996) 265.

170 Din İşleri Yüksek Kurulu (n 143) 444.

The two *ḥadīths* narrated by 'Abd Allāh b. 'Abbās clearly state that the triple divorce in a single sitting previously only counted as a single divorce (revocable *ṭalāq*) during the time of the Prophet and Abū Bakr, the first Caliph. This was also true during the first two years of 'Umar b. al-Khaṭṭāb, the second Caliph.[171] In engaging with this issue, the HBRA evidenced a clear preference for the second view, namely that the multiple pronunciation of the *ṭalāq* formula in one sitting is considered to be the usage of only one divorce right, as opposed to the greater irrevocable divorce.[172] Even though this represents a minority view amongst Ḥanbalī scholars, the HBRA cites the two *ḥadīths* as the second view on triple divorce by a single utterance. It can therefore be argued that the HBRA applies the practice of determining preponderant opinion (*tarjīḥ*) as an Islamic legal methodology with the intention of broadening its spectrum. This establishes that the practice of *tarjīḥ* is not narrowly limited to the four Sunni *madhhabs*, but also extends to the opinions of the Companions, followers (*tābi'īn*) and even followers of followers (*tābi'ī al-tābi'īn*), along with the views of other Muslim scholars who are generally very interested in the area of Islamic law.[173]

By virtue of the fact that the HBRA expresses a clear preference for one of the legal opinions, the individual petitioner and other audiences are probably guided by the institution towards the second view, as opposed to its preceding (Islamic) counterpart. In this respect, the Diyanet can be interpreted as a religious institution that moderately follows a traditional Sunni interpretation of Islam.[174] Sunier et al. state:

> The picture that emerge[s] from our analysis of the religious information and guidance of Diyanet is one of institution[s] extensively engaged in the vocabulary, classical sources and methodologies available to Sunni religious authorities all over the world. Fatwas issued by Diyanet gain their legitimacy in the same way as other fatwa institutions, by interpreting the Quran, quoting authentic prophetic traditions and using analogous reasoning to address new

171 ibid.

172 ibid.

173 Dadaş (n 101) 48, 54. The *fatwā* relating to the legal ruling on inheritance between Muslims and non-Muslims can also be interpreted as an explicit confirmation that the decision was made with reference to the views of some of the Prophet's Companions (including Mu'āwiya b. Abī Sufyān and Mu'adh b. Jabal), as opposed to the general position of the four Sunni schools. In referring to the opinion of the two Companions, the HBRA assents to Muslims inheriting from their non-Muslim parents. In engaging with this specific issue, the majority of Muslim scholars from the four Sunni schools maintain that it is not permissible for a Muslim to inherit from a non-Muslim and vice-versa. Their argument is generally based on the two *ḥadīths* narrated from the Prophet: (1) "A Muslim does not inherit from an unbeliever and an unbeliever does not inherit from a Muslim" [narrated by Muḥammad b. Ismā'īl al-Buhārī]; (2) "People of different religions do not inherit from each other" [narrated by Ibn 'Īsā al-Tirmidhī and Aḥmad Ibn Ḥambal]. See Din İşleri Yüksek Kurulu (n 143) 487–488.

174 Turner and Arslan (n 74) 216.

> moral questions. In this sense, Diyanet works like an institution for Sunni orthodoxy.[175]

The Diyanet's decisions and *fatwās* are indebted to the Sunni tradition to a certain extent.[176] The classical Ḥanafī and Shāfiʿī traditions therefore provide an important basis for the legitimacy of the institution's official discourse and decisions, in particular *fatwās* relating to *ʿibādāt* and classical Islamic legal issues.

The second strategy adopted by the HBRA relates to novel and contemporary religious matters, along with issues pertaining to social transactions (*muʿāmalāt*). A question addressed to the institution may involve an issue that has not been extensively discussed by Muslim scholars or a subject that demands a review of an existing Islamic legal opinion.[177] In engaging with these two categories, the HBRA applies two different methods. In the first instance, it seeks to revise the issue by considering its extension and potential positive and negative effects. This is achieved by taking new circumstances into account with a view to reformulating existing rulings. In the second instance, it formulates new rules that relate to unprecedented cases, such as issues that are frequently encountered in the economic, medical and technological spheres.

To a substantial extent, the Diyanet deploys modern methods in order to adapt Islamic legal tradition to contemporary circumstances, an outcome which is predominantly achieved by prioritising the legal principle of public interest (*maṣlaḥa*), the highest objectives of Islamic law (*maqāṣid al-sharīʿa*) and the two main legal maxims (of necessity (*ḍarūra*) and customary practices (*ʿurf*)) over the specifics.[178] In describing the Diyanet's epistemological predisposition towards Islamic law, Kaya states:

> The Diyanet's Islamic legal approach is successful in reaching beyond formalistic tendencies and for seeking to materialise the spirit of religion rather than drawing judgements out of Muslim black boxes.[179]

Powel also accentuates the modern approach of the Diyanet, which places a particular emphasis upon the Ḥanafī *madhhab*, when he states:

> On many issues, [the Diyanet] relies on traditional *fiqh* rules; and it tends to refer to the *Hanafi* school for legitimacy. Even so, it is also modern in its attempts to harmonise the tradition with Turkish republicanism and secularism and to provide religious council to Turkish citizens.[180]

175 Sunier and others (n 5) 140–141.

176 Din İşleri Yüksek Kurulu Başkanlığı, 'İlkeler ve Hedefler' <http://www2.diyanet.gov.tr/dinisleriyuksekkurulu/Sayfalar/IlkelerVeHedefler.aspx> accessed 12 December 2016.

177 Din İşleri Yüksek Kurulu (n 143) 46.

178 ibid.

179 Kaya (n 43) 69.

180 Russel Powell, 'Evolving Views of Islamic Law in Turkey' (2013) 28 (2) *Journal of Law and Religion* 479.

The Diyanet's orientation towards Ḥanafī *madhhab*, which is clearly indicated in a number of its juristic publications and statements, is conceivably justified by the fact that many Muslim Turks follow the Ḥanafī school.[181] Even though there is not a specific official method or regulation identified by the Diyanet in the process of issuing *fatwā*, the institution's course does imply a particular approach to Islamic law which can be considered an alternative understanding that combines elements of the classical legal tradition (mainly Ḥanafī *madhhab*) with modernism.[182]

With regard to marriage, for instance, the transplantation of the Swiss Civil Code of 1926 made it a criminal offence to marry in a religious ceremony without executing civil marriage (Article 230/5 and Article 230/6) and to initiate multiple marriages (Article 230/12).[183] A civil marriage must first be confirmed by authorised marriage officers before a religious marriage (*nikāḥ*) is permitted. If this does not occur, the respective parties can be punished under Act no. 5237.[184] This is why a religious marriage without official registration was made optional and frequently operated in the absence of sanctioning power, generally in the Eastern part of Turkey. After the enactment of Act no. 5237, a religious marriage that has not registered by authorised marriage officers is not accepted as an official marriage in the law. Despite the fact this legal regulation renders a religious marriage into officially ineffective within the scope of state law, the religious marriage still remains a preferred form of marriage amongst many people in both rural and urban areas. A State Institute of Statistics publication observes:

> In 2011, the ratio of couple who employed both civil and religious marriage ceremonies is 93.7%, the figure for only civil marriages is 3.3%, and the ratio of only religious marriages is 3% in their first marriage.[185]

The data makes it clear that, for Turkish Muslims, the legitimacy of wedlock rests upon religious marriage. Yılmaz observes:

> "Many Turkish citizens still prefer the informal or consensual marriage, or *nikah*." Sometimes they marry with *nikah* only without registration, which is not recognised under the Civil Code. There are still some marriages performed by *imams* without the prior official celebration. In rural society,

181 It is important to note that a large majority of the Turkish population observes the Sunni tradition. A 2014 Diyanet survey found that almost 78 percent of Turkish citizens follow the Ḥanafī school while approximately 11 percent of the Muslim population adhere to the Shāfi'ī school. Din İşleri Yüksek Kurulu, *Türkiye'de Dini Hayat Araştırması* (Diyanet İşleri Başkanlığı Yayınları 2014) 8.

182 Türkiye Cumhuriyeti Başkanlık Diyanet İşleri Başkanlığı, 'Din, Yenileşme ve Modern Hayat' <http://www3.diyanet.gov.tr/tr/icerik/din-yenilesme-ve-modern-hayat-prof-dr-ali-bardakoglu-diyanet-isleri-baskani-istanbul/6217> accessed 25 February 2017.

183 Act no. 5237 dated 26 September 2004. See Resmi Gazete, 12. 10. 2004-25611 <http://www.mevzuat.gov.tr/MevzuatMetin/1.5.5237-20150327.pdf> accessed 03 November 2016.

184 ibid.

185 Türkiye İstatistik Kurumu, 'İstatistiklerle Aile, 2012' <http://www.tuik.gov.tr/PreHaberBultenleri.do?id=13662> accessed 03 November 2016.

the religious ceremony is still regarded as valid in itself, and a civil marriage alone is not regarded as valid by the Muslim community.[186]

However, religious marriages that are performed without prior official registration can conceivably give rise to familial, legal and societal complications: the custody, lineage and inheritance of children born into this marriage, the legitimacy of the marriage before the law, the maintenance of women in cases of divorce and the victimisation of women.[187]

In addressing itself to these social problems, the Diyanet has provided an Islamic legal decision (on the performance of marriage) which combines the requirements of Islamic and Turkish law. The Diyanet's Consultation Meeting addressed to familial problems states:

> On account of the [civil marriage] arrangements in our Civil Code, it can be easier to persuade our people for the necessity of the official marriage in today's Turkey than the past. It is possible to find negative examples that, in our society, have been faced by the families living only with the religious marriage. On this subject, it is primarily – in accordance with the principles adopted in Islamic legal methodology – necessary to generate the unity of the sensibility and understanding that all marriages must be officially registered in compliance with the principle of *maṣlaḥa mursala* (unrestricted public interest), and thence, no matter who implements such a regulation, it is necessary for the people to obey this … The official marriage in the Civil Code is the marriage of those who have no barriers to marriage; it means that the marriage is declared and freed from secrecy. This is in conformity with the Prophet's recommendation that the marriage must be public and be [publicly] announced.[188, 189]

This statement apparently refers to social problems that have the potential to manifest in instances in which religious marriage is performed without its civil accompaniment. In acknowledging associated familial, legal and social difficulties, the HBRA issued a *fatwā* that was addressed to the question of whether the person who performed the official marriage should perform the religious marriage (the *fatwā* states: "The civil marriage performed by fulfilling all the necessary conditions and requirements of *nikāḥ* (religious solemnisation) is a religiously valid marriage").[190] The *fatwā* strongly insists that the marriage

186 Ihsan Yılmaz, 'Secular Law and the Emergence of Unofficial Turkish Islamic Law' (2002) 56 (1) *Middle East Journal* 122.

187 İlker Çalışkan, Hasan Mollaoğllu and Muhammed Acar, *Aileye İlişkin Sorunlar: İstişare Toplantısı* (Diyanet İşleri Başkanlığı Yayınları 2009) 46; Sunier and others (n 5) 94.

188 Çalışkan, Mollaoğllu and Acar (n 187) 49.

189 Author's translation.

190 In the *fatwā*, religious marriage and its some conditions described as follows: "According to Islam, the religious solemnisation (*nikāḥ*) is a marriage of one woman and one man before wit-

should be publicly announced and officially registered, and should be undertaken with the full knowledge of parents and other relatives.[191] It is also implicitly asserted that a religious marriage ceremony should be conducted in the aftermath of its civil counterpart.[192] This suggests that the *fatwā* does not only address the religious needs of Muslims, but also offers a hybrid formulation that amalgamates Islamic law (informally practiced by the Muslims resident in Turkey) with the law of the secular state.[193]

The Diyanet's catechism observes that religious marriage is an individual responsibility that is enacted before God. However, it is occasionally misused by malevolent people – this results in familial problems and social disorders.[194] The civil marriage in which the rights of spouses are acknowledged by the state's legal system offsets the danger that these problems and misuses lead to.[195] The Diyanet's *fatwās* are instructive because they remind the reader of the possibilities of attempting to align Islamic legal rulings with contemporary trends and modern values. In developing a new technic which brings the secular Turkish legal system together with Islamic law, the Diyanet attempts to meet the demands of Muslims in a way that offsets the threat of legal and social conflict in Turkey. This reconciliatory approach is evidenced in the numerous *fatwās* that the institution provides in response to Muslims' problems. The Diyanet therefore seeks to overcome a range of contentious issues by amalgamating secular and Islamic law and arranging them around the principle of *maṣlaḥa*.

On rare occasions, the opinions of Ḥanafī, Ḥanbalī, Mālikī and Shāfi'ī scholars may be appealed in a discretionary manner. An opinion that had been previously acknowledged by Muslim scholars, irrespective of their affiliation to a particular school *madhhab*, can provide an initial point of engagement for the assessment and discussion of issues that have been addressed to the Diyanet. This may be interpreted as an indication that the Diyanet is following in the footsteps of the Ottoman Muslim scholars, their predecessors, in addressing themselves to some

nesses. In addition to this, both parties must have the capacity of marriage, must be free from any obstacles that might prevent the marriage from being valid, and must give their mutual consent in the form of a proposal (*ījāb*) and of an expression of acceptance (*qabūl*)." See Din İşleri Yüksek Kurulu (n 143) 439.

191 Din İşleri Yüksek Kurulu (n 143) 439.

192 ibid.

193 A similar approach is also adopted by the HBRA when answering a religious question concerning the court divorce. The question is of whether couples who are divorced by the court are religiously divorced or not. The *fatwā* regarding this question explicitly states that a court divorce is equivalent to the lesser irrevocable divorce within the scope of Islamic law. From the *fatwā*, it is possible to make an inference that a couple divorced three times by the court must follow the procedure of the greater irrevocable divorce according to Islamic law. That is to say, the couple must not remarry until after the wife has married another man and that marriage is consummated and terminated. See Din İşleri Yüksek Kurulu (n 143) 446.

194 Hayreddin Karaman, Ali Bardakoğlu and H. Yunus Apaydın, *İlmihal-I İman ve İbadetler* (DİB 1998) 220–223.

195 ibid.

specific questions. In discussing the traditional positions of Ottoman scholars on the legal maxims of "eclecticism" (*takhayyur*) and "combination of opinions" (*talfīq*), Ibrahim observes:

> Ottoman jurists from the provinces pushed these limits on the pragmatic selection of juristic views by expanding the permissibility of *tatabbu' al-rukhaṣ* and challenging the consensus over the prohibition of *talfīq*. This theoretical evolution also corresponded to the utilization of both legal techniques [*talfīq* and *takhayyur*], whereby legal subjects appealing to the courts were directed to the school that was more suitable for their legal transactions.[196]

The application of the Ottoman Muslim scholars to the legal maxims of *takhayyur* and *talfīq* can be taken as the justification of the Diyanet's use of the same legal maxims in some cases.

The presence of the ruler or his deputy, to take one example, is one of the necessary prerequisites for the establishment of the Friday prayer in the Ḥanafī *madhhab*.[197] The Diyanet's catechism makes it clear that many of earlier Ḥanafī scholars during the time of the 'Abbāsid made the permission and presence of the ruler a necessary condition for the performance of the Friday prayer. This established a link between the Friday prayer and the political authority, with the consequence that the Friday prayer, over time, came to attain a political meaning.[198] Earlier Ḥanafī scholars who were clearly influenced by this proposition later added a number of other conditions, which had no prior existence, as the necessary precursors to a valid Friday prayer. It is stated that the presence of the head of state or his deputy was one among a number of *post facto* conditions.[199] The Ḥanafī *madhhab* maintains that if none of these conditions are present, the Friday prayer is not obligatory (*wājib*/*farḍ*) for its adherents.[200] However, this prerequisite was softened by allusions to other *madhhabs* and later Hanafi scholars who did not impose the presence of the head of state or the permission of the government as preconditions for a valid Friday prayer. This suggests that the implicit permission is sufficient for the validity and establishment of the Friday prayer, as the catechism states:

196 Ahmed Fekry Ibrahim, 'Talfīq/Takhayyur', The Oxford Encyclopaedia of Islamic Law (2013) <http://www.oxfordislamicstudies.com/article/opr/t349/e0082> accessed 11 June 2017.

197 Karaman, Bardakoğlu and Apaydın, *İlmihal-I* (n 194) 289. Shams al-Dīn Sarakhsī (d. 1089), one of the most prominent Ḥanafī scholars, wrote *Kitāb al-Mabsūṭ*, in which he claimed that the presence of the *sulṭān* (the ruler of country) was one of the *wujūb* (conditions necessary for the establishment of the Friday prayer). See also Norman Calder, 'Friday Prayer and the Juristic Theory of Government: Sarakhsī, Shīraāzī, Māwardī' (1986) 49 (1) *Bulletin of the School of Oriental and African Studies* 35–36, 37 <http://www.jstor.org/stable/617667> accessed 27 March 2017.

198 Karaman, Bardakoğlu and Apaydın, *İlmihal-I* (n 194) 298.

199 ibid.

200 ibid.

> due to the fact that the prerequisite of the permission from the ruler for performing the Friday prayer lost its political connotations, there is no need to implement this condition in our day. On the other hand, if this prerequisite is still considered as a necessary condition for the establishment of the Friday prayer at the present time, the permission of building mosques, the salary payment to *imāms* by the state and the existence of the public institutions implementing such duties may be counted as a governmental permission, and hence it is possible to conjecture that the necessary condition has already fulfilled for the establishment of the Friday prayer.[201]

The first part of this statement can certainly be interpreted as delinking the Friday prayer from the government. This could conceivably be interpreted as a reflection of the Shāfi'ī *madhhab*'s condition for the establishment of Friday prayers. Calder makes this clear in his evaluation of Abū Isḥāq al-Shīrāzī (d. 1073), one of the pre-eminent Shāfi'ī scholars, when he addresses himself to conditions pertaining to the establishment of the Friday prayer ("The Shāfi'ī tradition looked much more to a sense of communal unity").[202] For this *madhhab*, it is therefore the existence of a settled community of Muslims, as opposed to a functioning authority or the permission of the government that was stipulated by the Ḥanafī *madhhab*, for the establishment of the valid Friday prayer. It can therefore be argued that the precondition of a functioning authority was adjusted according to prevailing conditions within contemporary Turkey when the Diyanet gravitated towards espousing the position of the Shāfi'ī *madhhab*.

Additionally, the traditional Ḥanafī legal position, which maintains that the Friday prayer can be held in more than one mosque in a city, is presumably upheld in recognition of its alignment with contemporary environmental, modern and social circumstances.[203] In this particular instance, the Diyanet combined Ḥanafī and Shāfi'ī legal views to argue that the Friday prayer can, particularly in megacities, be performed in more than one central mosque. Furthermore, the specific permission of the government is not a necessary condition because the existence of mosques, official religious institutions and state *imāms* can justifiably be regarded as the permission of the head of state or government.[204] At the level of Islamic legal methodology, these two legal maxims (*takhayyur* and *talfīq*) conceivably enable legal pragmatism up to a point; however, this feature becomes blurred due to the fact that the Diyanet does not develop a set of specific criteria that are addressed to the application of these two legal maxims.

The aforementioned cases presumably exemplify the approach that Diyanet officials adopt when providing religious counsel to Turkish citizens. A substantial number of questions presented to the HBRA involve issues previously addressed

201 ibid.
202 Calder (n 197) 41.
203 Karaman, Bardakoğlu and Apaydın, *İlmihal-I* (n 194) 298.
204 ibid.

by earlier Muslim scholars. When issuing *fatwās* on these issues, the Board usually presents Islamic legal rulings that have been adjudicated and decided by earlier scholars (in response to individual questions), instead of outlining a new legal ruling. The *fatwās* mostly convey Ḥanafī juristic views, which draw upon Ḥanafī scholars' *ijtihād* – this, however, is only the case when the views of the school are applicable to contemporary circumstances, conditions and realities.[205] Dadaş observes that there are several reasons why the Ḥanafī *madhhab* is privileged within the HBRA's Islamic legal methodology.[206] Firstly, a majority of Muslims resident in Turkey adhere to the Ḥanafī *madhhab*. Secondly, it was the official school of the Ottoman Sultanate, and courts of the time ruled in accordance with its *fatwās*, so the fact that the customs and traditions of those residents in the territory who identified themselves with the Ḥanafī *madhhab* are shaped in line with this *maddhab*. Thirdly, the scholars who work in the HBRA mostly trained in the Ḥanafī *madhhab*.[207] Finally, the HBRA presumably wishes to produce coherent and consistent Islamic legal knowledge and *fatwās*, and the Ḥanafī *madhhab* recommends itself on this basis.[208]

In some cases, the institution provides a religious consultation service in which it selects an alternative classical rule from among the four Sunni *madhhabs*. In other instances, it issues *fatwās* based on new interpretations of authoritative texts. Dadaş states that the HBRA in particular follows two types of *ijtihād* on contemporary religious issues that were not addressed by earlier Muslim scholars.[209] In the first instance, the HBRA adopts *ijtihād* through the *takhrīj* (extraction) method,[210] which is applied when evaluating contemporary religious issues that closely resemble the subjects that were previously adjudicated by Muslim scholars.[211] To take one example, the issue of organ donation was resolved by applying the *takhrīj* method in order to achieve *ijtihād*.[212] The HBRA's *fatwā* refers to a number of established legal rulings, which include the permission of earlier Muslim scholars for the wombs of dead women to be cut in order to save

205 Dadaş (n 101) 51.
206 ibid 50–51.
207 ibid 51.
208 ibid.
209 ibid 59–60.
210 Particular methods and technics are used to determine the effective cause (*'illa*). These methods are particularly important in the determination of *'illa* because the application of *qiyās* (legal analogy) requires the identification of the attributes of *'illa* and the ascertainment of the relationship which conjoins the original and new case. *Takhrīj*, which is generally known as *takhrīj al-manāt*, is one method that makes it possible to ascertain *'illa* through the identification of proper attributes and similarities. Dogan defines it in the following terms: "*Takhrīj al-manāt* is defined in *Uṣūl al-Fiqh* as identifying the proper attribute of the underlying cause for the ruling which is the mentioned in the text of the Qur'an, Sunna, and in *ijma*. In other words, *mujtahids* work to discover the *'illah* through examining the attributes of the ruling and find one of them to be a real reason for it." See Recep Doğan, *Usūl al-Fiqh: Methodology of Islamic Jurisprudence* (Tughra Books 2013) under the title "*Takhrīj al-Manāt*."
211 Dadaş (n 101) 59.
212 Din İşleri Yüksek Kurulu (n 143) 535–536.

the lives of their foetuses; for pathological autopsies to be performed in order to provide medical treatment for unknown diseases (on condition that permission was first forthcoming from the deceased's heirs); and for prohibited substances to be used for medication (upon the condition that no alternative medicines were available).[213] The HBRA adopts *qiyās* (legal analogy) as a legal methodology and this enables it to ascertain the similar effective causes between the cited cases and organ donation. The *fatwā* states that it is permissible to make organ donations, if certain Islamic legal conditions and criteria established in advance are met.[214]

Secondly, the HBRA also uses creative *ijtihād* (*ijtihād inshā'ī*) through applying certain legal principles and maxims which include the blocking of illegitimate means (*sadd al-dharā'i'*), necessity (*ḍarūra*) and public interest (*maṣlaḥa*), and this enables unprecedented and contemporary religious issues to be resolved.[215] This type of *ijtihād* requires the identification of legal opinions in response to new contemporary questions – it is not therefore sufficient to refer to the existing opinions of Muslim scholars with a view to establishing an analogy between earlier opinions and unprecedented cases (as was the case with the aforementioned issue of anaesthesia and the HBRA's decision on insurance, which was issued in 2005).[216] Dadaş, in engaging at a methodological level, observes that these are collective rather than individual *ijtihād*.[217] It is therefore possible to observe that the two types of *ijtihād* (*ijtihād* through *takhrīj* and *ijtihād inshā'ī*) are the main legal methods that the HBRA uses within the scope of collective *ijtihād* when engaging with novel or complicated issues.

In Turkey, the Diyanet is presumably acknowledged as a moral, legal and religious authority that educates and informs people about Islam and Islamic law. However, it should be recognised that Islamic legal decisions and *fatwās* provided by the institution are not imposed upon those who live under the state legal system. The level of popular acceptance of the institution probably determines its position and ability to engage with wider constituencies.[218] The legal function, status, structure and even name of the institution are grounded within by-laws, constitutional regulations and laws. At the administrative level, it is a state agency that does not exert any authority within the Turkish legal system. Its decisions and *fatwās* do not possess binding authority and can therefore be categorised as advisory and informative in character. Nonetheless, it could perhaps be argued

213 ibid.

214 The HBRA observes that organ donation is permissible under certain conditions. Firstly, it must be a matter of necessity (e.g., there must be no other treatment option available). Secondly, either the donor or his/her family must have consented to the removal and transfer of organs. Thirdly, organs can, under no circumstances, be exchanged for a financial reward. For further insight into additional conditions, refer to Din İşleri Yüksek Kurulu (n 143) 536.

215 Dadaş (n 101) 60.

216 For a more detailed analysis of the Islamic legal decision on the insurance question, refer to Dadaş (n 101) 62–63.

217 Dadaş (n 101) 59.

218 Din İşleri Yüksek Kurulu (n 143) 535–536.

that the institution has, through its involvement in the religious affairs of Muslims in Turkey, established a form of social legitimacy.[219] It is therefore instructive to note that the institution's detachment from state politics and its transformation into a more autonomous and competent religious institution has helped to sustain this legitimacy.[220] In remaining loyal to the scholarly heritage of Islamic law, it has also cautiously and gently advanced an Islamic legal reasoning that is simultaneously grounded within modern, religious and secular reference points. The Diyanet, as the main contributor to Islamic law and jurisprudence, can be said to represent a modern scholarly tradition that possesses three main trivets (Islamic legal tradition, modernism and secularism), each of which is exclusive to Turkey.

Conclusion

With the intention of establishing a modernised and secular state, the early Republican government implemented many reform projects, a number of which were explicitly modelled on Western counterparts. These included the abolition of the Caliphate, the abolition of sharīʿa courts, the extension of strict state control in the educational field, the nationalisation of the endowments (*awqāf*) that supported Muslim scholars and the replacement of the Islamic legal system with the secular legal system. The office of *Shaykh al-Islām* was not however abolished but was instead transformed into the Diyanet in 1924. In retaining the Ottoman Sultanate's religious establishment, the early Republican government subtly sought to appease the religious concerns and anxieties of its subjects. In the first instance, it applied restrictive policies to religion and religious structures. With its internal religious rivals silenced, the early Republican government clearly required a justification for the consolidation and maintenance of the implemented reforms. Nationalism and secularism asserted themselves at this point as a means through which ideological and political stability could be achieved within the newly established Republic. During the initial phases of the state-building process, the Diyanet was tasked with solidifying the state ideology and with standardising religious consciousness and aligning it with the secular narratives of the early Republican government. Although the Diyanet initially followed the request of the state by issuing and promulgating religious decisions and *fatwās*, it appears that, as time progressed, it became increasingly reluctant to pursue this course of action.

Over a roughly thirty-year period (1950s–1980s), the Diyanet began to be recognised as an institution of considerable significance by Turkish Muslims. It played an important role in producing religious knowledge and educating the public about Islam and Islamic legal rulings, at a time when the strict state policy towards religion that had been espoused by the early Republican government continually began to moderate. In recent years, the Diyanet has taken on the appearance of a more autonomous religious body that is primarily concerned

219 Dadaş (n 101) 64–65.
220 ibid.

with conveying religious knowledge and fulfilling popular religious needs, in comparison with its previous years. The transition away from a state-controlled institution founded by the early Republican elite has therefore been perhaps the most significant trend that has occurred during this period. This transformation can be traced back to political policies focused upon religion which have, both directly and indirectly, impacted the institution. Despite the ebbs and flows of changing political administrations, the Diyanet is now established as the only official institution that controls, manages and supervises religious affairs in Turkey. The Diyanet, and more specifically its decisions and *fatwās*, have made a vital contribution to the ethical, social and religious formulation of the Muslim component of Turkish society.

The Diyanet's *fatwās* are characterised by two main methodological approaches which the institution presumably adopts in accordance with the issue that is immediately in front of it. If the issue relates to classical Islamic legal rulings and *'ibādāt* established by classical normative Muslim scholarship, it will be engaged through the answering of questions. In the area of *'ibādāt*, the *fatwās* are generally framed against the backdrop of the Ḥanafī and Shāfi'ī *madhhabs*. A *fatwā* initially provides the Ḥanafī classical position and, presuming there is an observable difference between the two *madhhabs*, the divergent view of the Shāfi'ī *madhhab* is then presented to the questioner. Occasionally, the legal maxims of *takhayyur* and *talfīq* are applied by the institution to solve intricate issues and benefit the society (for instance, when the conditions that establish a valid Friday prayer are clearly re-determined within the context of contemporary Turkey through applying the principle of *talfīq*). These two legal maxims are however usually articulated against the backdrop of the legal principle of *maṣlaḥa*.

If the issue that is presented to the institution concerns contemporary religious issues and social transactions, the institution normally pursues a more moderate approach that combines democratic reference points, Islamic legal values and secularism. It may be presumed that the Diyanet has an important contribution to make to the balancing of these values and their adoption by the public. The institution also started to develop its own ideological, legal and theological approach to Islamic legal issues associated with social transactions. The Ḥanafī *madhhab*, by virtue of the fact that it commands the loyalty of a majority of Turkish Muslims, has been presumed to be the key reference point, with this *madhhab* providing the relevant legal methodology and jurisprudence. In addition to this Ḥanafī orientation, it should be recognised that the institution also seeks to develop a modern, overarching and progressive interpretative approach which takes into account Turkey's heterogenic and dispersed socio-religious structure. In this regard, it is important to note that the institution has, particularly when engaging with cultural and social themes, attempted to adopt a more conciliatory and moderate approach that is grounded within divergent cultural foundations, expectations, sensitivities and traditions. In articulating itself within a constructive and integrative language, the Diyanet invites Muslims to unite under the roof of Islam. In doing so, the institution extensively applies two main Islamic legal methodologies: firstly, the legal principle of *maṣlaḥa* and secondly *maqāṣid al-sharī'a*. One of the key concerns of the institution is therefore to promote and preserve social unity. At times when different religious groups and divergent interpretations of Islam threaten national unity or when political and social conflicts threaten solidarity and unity, the Diyanet brings the integrative, peaceful and unifying dimension of Islam to the forefront and cools the chaotic social mood through the direct application to the legal principles of *maṣlaḥa* and *maqāṣid al-sharī'a*.

The method of appointment of its highest administrators (including its president) and the constitutional regulations that relate to the institution's organisational structure may be understood to denote both its dependence upon the state and, by implication, the centrality of political influence. Notwithstanding all these ties, the institution has succeeded in gaining a high level of scholarly credibility and in acquiring freedom of speech; in addition, it has also attained a high level of public acceptance, particularly amongst the Muslim segment of society. In the aftermath of the 1970s, the Diyanet achieved considerable credibility by producing authentic, reliable and sound knowledge that related to Islam and Islamic legal issues. In normal circumstances, it acted, and still acts, as an independent public institution concerned with the production of religious knowledge and its dissemination to the society; clearly, any individual or state organisation is not able to compel this institution to issue a particular *fatwā*. Upon this basis, it is possible to conclude that the Diyanet enjoys, to a substantial extent, freedom in its scholarly and intellectual activities that pertain to Islam and Islamic legal and ethical issues.

3 The Fiqh Council of North America

The twentieth century witnessed the immigration of large numbers of Muslims to non-Muslim lands, particularly North America and Europe.[1] The notion of Muslims living in non-Muslim lands has increasingly come to be seen and examined as the Islamic jurisprudence of the Muslim minority (*fiqh al-aqalliyyāt*) within the scope of Islamic law. The exigencies and problems that confront Muslims resident in America and Europe have manifested as a challenge in formulating Islamic legal resolutions and *fatwās*. In America, Muslim scholars therefore established the Fiqh Council of North America (henceforth: FCNA) with the intention of providing appropriate *fatwās* to the problems that confront Muslims resident in America.

Like the previous two chapters, this chapter presents the FCNA with specific reference to its historical development, functional role amongst American Muslims and organisational structure, while mainly focusing upon the process through which the institution issues a *fatwā*. The analyses of *fatwās* also address the intention of evincing the Islamic legal understanding adopted by the FCNA. The institution represents a state-independent voluntary establishment that provides *fatwās* to religious questions related to Islamic law while considering the current needs and circumstances of Muslims resident in America. Its *fatwās* can therefore be perceived as main components within the developing process of the concept of *fiqh al-aqalliyyāt*.

This chapter is divided into three subsections. A general overview related to Muslims in America is presented with the intention of demonstrating the diversity amongst American Muslims in terms of their ethnicity, culture and Islamic school of law (*madhhab*) affiliation. This is followed by the objectives espoused by the FCNA to demonstrate the main concerns of the Council during the process of issuing *fatwās*. Attention then turns to the FCNA's history and organisational structure. This provides insight into the trajectory of Islamic law upon the institutional basis instead of individual grounds within the non-Muslim context. The discussion then engages with the process through which the institution issues a *fatwā* and the way

1 Amjad M. Mohammed, *Muslims in Non-Muslims Lands: A Legal Study with Applications* (The Islamic Text Society 2013) VII.

DOI: 10.4324/9781003037637-3

in which the institution transmits its outputs to the Muslims resident in America. Some deep analyses of *fatwās* are presented with the intention of identifying the Islamic legal methodology adopted by the FCNA, along with the social context in which *fatwās* were promulgated – this helps to identify the interaction between the Islamic legal methodologies and the social context in which the institution operates. These analyses also reveal the influence of the dual identity of American Muslims upon Islamic legal resolutions and *fatwās*. The objectives of Islamic law (*maqāṣid al-sharī'a*) and the legal principle of public interest (*maṣlaḥa*) emerge as main legal tools employed by the FCNA in the process of providing appropriate *fatwās*. In the last instance, attention therefore turns to these two legal principles with the intent of displaying the intertwining relationship between them and their substantial influences upon *fatwās* issued by the FCNA.

Muslims in America

Muslim immigration to America has a diachronic history that traces back to the first coerced West and North Africans who were brought to the continent through the transatlantic slave trade around the late eighteenth century.[2] Despite the fact that the presence of Muslims in America goes back to the late eighteenth century, the large-scale immigration of Muslims to America noticeably starts after the mid-twentieth century.[3] The presence of Muslims as a distinguishable community in the country began to become salient after this large-scale immigration. Muslims constitute a significant part of the socio-religious mosaic of America, but they are still a small minority living in a Christian majority country. Muslims as a religious minority have started to attain a place within American religious and social life through seeking to introduce themselves, along with their belief, to the diverse and comprehensive religious mosaic of the continent.[4]

Diversity is one of the characteristic features of the American Muslim populace. Muslims who chose to move to America for economic, political and religious reasons derive roughly from over thirty nations and represent various

2 Randa B. Serhan, 'Muslim Immigration to America' in Yvonne Y. Haddad and Jane I. Smith (eds), *The Oxford Handbook of American Islam* (Oxford University Press 2014) 30, 33–34; Slyviane A. Diouf, 'The First Stirrings of Islam in America' in Yvonne Y. Haddad and Jane I. Smith (eds), *The Oxford Handbook of American Islam* (Oxford University Press 2014) 16–17.

3 Yvonne Yazbeck Haddad, 'The Dynamics of Islamic Identity in North America' in Yvonne Yazbeck Haddad and John L. Esposito (eds), *Muslims on the Americanization Path?* (Oxford University Press 2000) 20–21; Khalid Duran, 'Demographic Characteristics of the American Muslim Community' (1997) 36 (1) *Islamic Studies* 57–59; Tauseef Ahmad Parray, 'The Legal Methodology of "Fiqh al-Aqalliyyat" and its Critics: An Analytical Study' (2012) 32 (1) *Journal of Muslim Minority Affairs* 89; Serhan (n 2) 31–33.

4 Mohamed Nimer, *The North American Muslim Resource Guide: Muslim Community Life in the United States and Canada* (Routledge 2002) XVII, 121–125, 171; Karen Leonard, 'American Muslims and Authority: Competing Discourses in a Non-Muslim State' (2005) 25 (1) *Journal of American Ethnic History* 5–6; Duran (n 3) 59–60.

ethnic, linguistic, national and cultural identities.[5] Afsaruddin simply depicts this characteristic aspect of the American Muslim community. She observes:

> The American Muslim community – estimated, according to various sources, to be between 3 to 8 million strong – is one of the most diverse communities in the United States. About half of American Muslims are immigrants from Asia and the Middle East, Africa, and Europe, while other half are indigenous African American and European Americans, Latinos, and Native Americans as well as second and third-generation children of immigrant parents.[6]

This diversity also includes immigrants and refugees who forced to move out of their homeland but still retain allegiance to it.[7] Muslims in this group have a strong inclination to return to their homeland with the intention of readjusting the order that they left behind. The African American and white converts who embraced Islam are another colour in this diversity.[8] Besides this, the second generation of Muslims whose forebears immigrated between the 1870s and 1950s can be mentioned as another layer of the multiplicity amongst Muslims resident in America.[9] A considerable national, cultural and ethnic diversity within the Muslim minority community in America is observable – this brings out the heterogenic, intricate composition of the American Muslims.

Like the American populace as a whole, American Muslims demonstrate differences in a variety of ways that include their ethnicity, language and country of origin. It is also possible to observe a variety in their school (*madhhab*) affiliation. Fallon states:

> Sixty-five percent of Muslims in the United States are affiliated with Sunni Islam, which follows the traditions and character of the Prophet Muhammad. Eleven percent are affiliated with Shia Islam (and are called Shiites), which mandates that the leader of the faith be chosen from among Muhammed's descendants.[10]

The schools of Ḥanafī, Mālikī, Shāfi'ī and Ḥanbalī constitute the Sunni block while the schools of Ja'farī, Ismā'ilī and Zaydī are the main schools within the

5 Bruce B. Lawrence, 'Islam in America' in Gary Laderman and Luis León (eds) *Religion and American Cultures: An Encyclopedia of Traditions, Diversity*, vol I (ABC-CLIO 2003) 123; Nimer (n 4) 21–27, 30; Duran (n 3) 59–63.

6 Asma Afsaruddin, 'Shari'a and Fiqh in the United States' in Yvonne Y. Haddad and Jane I. Smith (eds), *The Oxford Handbook of American Islam* (Oxford University Press 2014) 176.

7 Lawrence (n 5) 128.

8 Lawrence (n 5) 123–124; Duran (n 3) 63–64.

9 Haddad (n 3) 20; Serhan (n 2) 34–36.

10 Sarah M. Fallon, 'Justice for All: American Muslims, Sharia Law, and Maintaining Comity with American Jurisprudence' (2013) 36 (1) *Boston College International and Comparative Law Review* 156.

Shi'ī tradition. All schools, either Sunni or Shi'ī, have their adherents amongst American Muslims.[11] In addition to this Sunni-Shi'ī diversity, there are American Muslims who specifically identify themselves with Sufism. These followers of Sufism come from different backgrounds, but many of them are European and American converts.[12] There are also adherents of sects that include Ahmadiyya and Druze whose Islamic identity is controversial.[13] It is therefore possible to assert that American Muslims demonstrate a wide range of variety in terms of their *madhhab* affiliation. The multi-layered structure within the American Muslim community raises possible issues related to culture, law, politics and identity.

Questions of the integration and assimilation of Muslims into secular American society resulted in different tendencies being shaped by American Muslims. Haddad categorises these tendencies into three: the first category is called the "isolationist group" who desire to return to their homelands and make reforms regarding their countries' political, social and legal systems; the second is the "conciliatory or integrationist group" who resist assimilation but advocate the creation of a unified American Muslim community within the border of secular democratic society; and the third is the "apathetic group" that dissociates itself from any issue related to Islam while watching everything from the distance.[14] The integrationist group promotes the idea of engagement and peaceful coexistence while predominantly accentuating the universal Islamic values with the intention of providing a place for American Muslims within the multiple-religious, ethnic and cultural mosaic of America. This socially engaged group establishes institutions (e.g., mosques, schools, professional and social associations, charitable foundations and religious institutions).[15] Some Muslim scholars amongst the integrationist group have addressed themselves to issues regarding the meaning and nature of Islamic law, along with its place within the American legal and social system. Taking into consideration Haddad's classification of American Muslims, it is possible to assert that the FCNA, which is the immediate focus of this chapter, was presumably founded by the American Muslim scholars who adopted the reconciliatory views of the integrationist group.

Within the scope of Islamic law, the issue of Muslim residence in non-Muslim lands has led to ongoing discussions regarding the future of Muslim minorities in the West. The integrationist Muslim scholars have sought to provide appropriate responses to the questions of whether the residence of Muslims in non-Muslim countries is legitimate or illegitimate, whether Islamic law imposes an obligation upon all Muslims to migrate to the abode of Islam (*dār al-Islām*) and whether a Muslim subject can be loyal to a non-Muslim authority. The Islamic

11 Liyakatali Takim, 'Shi'ite Movements' in Gary Laderman and Luis León (eds), *Religion and American Cultures: An Encyclopedia of Traditions, Diversity*, vol I (ABC-CLIO 2003) 143; Leonard (n 4) 8–9.

12 Fallon (n 10) 156.

13 Leonard (n 4) 9; Duran (n 3) 66.

14 Haddad (n 3) 27–34. For further insight, refer to Nimer (n 4) 171–178.

15 Haddad (n 3) 33–35.

legal opinions provided for these questions have contributed to the formation and development of the concept of *fiqh al-aqalliyyāt* (Islamic jurisprudence of Muslim minorities).[16] The stance of these Muslim scholars probably challenges the classical Islamic legal views that perceive the world only through the lenses of the bi-prism of abodes (the abode of Islam (*dār al-Islām*) and the abode of war (*dār al-ḥarb*)) while adapting Islamic law to the realities of the modern nation-state.[17] Interestingly, the notion of the modern nation-state as a legal and social parameter begun to incrementally percolate into the Islamic legal discussions relevant to the issues of Muslim minorities. The integrationist American Muslim scholars meticulously make an effort to place the idea of "citizenship" and the sense of being "American" within the normative parameters of living Islamic law.

Within the American context, the field of Islamic jurisprudence (*fiqh*) was saliently activated by the integrationist American Muslim scholars' efforts and attempts, but the new questions regarding authority and consultation emerged to be addressed with the intention of providing Islamic legal solutions and responses to intricate problems that confront American Muslims. Satisfying answers should be provided to the questions of who should be authorised to develop Islamic jurisprudence in America and to whom American Muslims should consult and direct their problems associated with the understanding and practice of Islamic law. The FCNA was conceivably instituted to fill the authority gap within the area of Islamic jurisprudence in the continent. Despite the fact that the FCNA's authority over all American Muslims is questionable, the Council has obtained a substantial amount of authoritative prestige at least amongst integrationist and moderate American Muslims – this is because it publicly pronounced, and still pronounces, practicable and applicable *fatwās* that cover cultural, economic, technological, legal, political, religious, social and familial issues. The establishment of the FCNA as a representative council of Islamic law may therefore be accepted as the resulting output of the initiatives of the integrationist American Muslim scholars who intend to incorporate American Muslims into mainstream American life and who enhance social harmony and co-existence between Muslims and non-Muslims in the multi-cultural, multi-religious and multi-ethnic American society.

The Fiqh Council of North America

In America, the increase in the numbers of Muslims (through immigration, religious conversion and birth) formed a new identity that combines Muslimness and Americanness.[18] A representative of this identity may be denominated "American Muslim" or "Muslim American." The formation of this new identity

16 Uriya Shavit, 'The Wasaṭī and Salafī Approaches to the Religious Law of Muslim Minorities' (2012) 19 (4) *Islamic Law and Society* 417–420; Nimer (n 4) 129.

17 Leonard (n 4) 393.

18 John L. Esposito, 'Introduction: Muslims in America or American Muslims?' in Yvonne Yazbeck Haddad and John L. Esposito (eds), *Muslims on the Americanization Path?* (Oxford University Press 2000) 3.

gave rise to many questions for those who adopt it. These include: can a Muslim still be a Muslim in a non-Muslim state that is governed by secular law rather than Islamic law? How can they retain their Muslim identity without dissociating and injuring their American identity? Is it possible to produce applicable *fatwās* within the American context while, at the same time, considering specific settings, values and cultural aspects of that land? In developing an American Muslim community, these are the foremost crucial, central and critical issues that need realistic answers.

The dynamics of American Muslim identity are predominantly shaped by Islamic values, Christian-based American society and secular values.[19] It is obvious that the American Muslim identity encapsulates two types of sense of belonging: the sense of belonging to their homeland, America, and the sense of belonging to the global Muslim community (*umma*). American Muslims in a minority situation therefore have dual responsibilities and duties. In the first instance, they have certain legal, moral and social responsibilities towards their homeland.[20] In this regard, they are legally obliged to live according to the laws of the land. In the second instance, they should follow Islamic teachings and legal injunctions to fulfil their duties and responsibilities as part of their Muslim identity or as part of the global Muslim community.[21] The sense of belonging to America legally obliges them to abide by the laws and rules of that land, while the sense of being Muslim requires them to obey the teachings and legal prescriptions of Islam.

This dual identity sometimes generates intricate and complex dilemmas for Muslim minorities. The war on Afghanistan in 2001 may exemplify one of the paradoxical predicaments that confronted American Muslims. A Muslim religious functionary who serves in the US military sought a *fatwā* upon the legality of an American Muslim soldier's participation in the war against Afghanistan (a Muslim country).[22] The most sensitive point of the matter is what a Muslim's position, as a citizen of a particular non-Muslim country, should be when his/her country goes to war against a Muslim country. The dual identity of American Muslims drags them into a deadlock because their religious duty as a Muslim (that is to protect his/her fellow Muslims' lives, property and honour) and their legal liability to their country of residence (that is to defend it from its enemies) conflict with each other. To put it differently, issues of language, community, culture, politics, economics, legal regulations and secular values may be reckoned among other main factors that generate questions regarding the capacity of Islamic law in engaging with the life conditions and challenges of American Muslims. The presence of Muslims in America resulted in a new identity not only formulating

19 Esposito (n 18) 4.

20 Nimer (n 4) 14–15.

21 ibid 2.

22 Basheer M. Nafi, 'Fatwā and War: On the Allegiance of the American Muslim Soldiers in the Aftermath of September 11' (2004) 11 (1) *Islamic Law and Society* 78–79 <http://www.jstor.org/stable/3399381> accessed 10 July 2016.

but also bringing out the necessity of developing an Islamic jurisprudence that addresses the political, social, legal and cultural settings of the host country with the intention of issuing applicable *fatwās*.

Being a Muslim resident in a non-Muslim country is a more complicated and complex phenomenon than in the past. Social, cultural, religious and political problems that confront American Muslims are considerably different from the problems that Muslims resident in other Muslim countries face. They are also divergent from the challenges of the Muslim minorities who lived in non-Muslim lands in a time when the classical Islamic legal view of the world was formulated.[23] Being in a minority status, in addition to living in a non-Muslim country, has further complicated the lives of American Muslims and the solutions to their problems in terms of Islamic law.[24]

A group of prescient, integrationist American Muslim scholars realised that such difficulties and circumstances that confront American Muslims need and require up-to-date Islamic legal answers and opinions. With the diligent effort of these American Muslim scholars, the FCNA was established to provide practicable *fatwās* to intricate issues within the scope of Islamic law.[25] It is possible to state that the main inspiration behind the establishment of this Council is to provide indigenous *fatwās* to questions posed by American Muslims. These American Muslim scholars have two considerations. In the first instance, the traditional Islamic legal interpretations that divide the world into two (*dār al-Islām* and *dār al-ḥarb*) became disconnected from the reality of Muslim settlement in America, so the connection between the traditional Islamic legacy and the reality of the modern world should be reestablished by employing the traditional Islamic legal methodologies in providing practicable *fatwās* within the American context. In the second instance, the *fatwās* issued by Muslim scholars who live outside America are unsatisfactory in bringing appropriate practicable solutions to adversities that confront American Muslims on account of their inadequacies in comprehending the American context.[26] These two considerations induced the American Muslim scholars to establish the FCNA that intends to retain the link between Islamic law and American Muslims and that espouses the idea of reviving Islamic law and reactivating its legal methodologies within the American context. The incentive in organising an *iftā'* institution in America therefore recognises the fact that there is a need to fully serve the Muslim community in a minority situation and to consider the American context in the process of issuing a *fatwā*.

At this juncture, it may be beneficial to touch upon civil Muslim initiatives that reflect the institutionalisation of Islam in America because these institutionalising initiatives can be perceived as a "preparatory" stage in the establishment of the

23 Yusuf Talal DeLorenzo, 'Fiqh and the Fiqh Council of North America' (1998) 3 (2) *Journal of Islamic Law* 196.

24 Esposito (n 18) 6.

25 Yusuf Talal DeLorenzo, 'The Fiqh Councilor of North America' in Yvonne Y. Haddad and John L. Esposito (eds), *Muslims on the Americanization Path?* (Oxford University Press 2000) 68.

26 DeLorenzo, 'Fiqh and the Fiqh Council' (n 23) 193–194, 196.

Fiqh Council of North America. American Muslim students, scholars and leaders who often work on a volunteer basis have sought to open a place for Islam in the milieu of America. In the 1960s, there was an influx of Muslim students into America. These students' efforts to incorporate their Muslim identity in a Christian majority secular environment resulted in some Muslim organisations being established in America. The Muslim Student Association (henceforth: MSA) is an influential organisation that was established in 1963 on the initiative of these students.[27] The main objective of these students was to develop an Islamic understanding that is compatible with the democratic and secular values of American society.[28] Within the structure of the MSA, the Religious Affairs Committee was formed in the 1970s and entrusted primarily with the task of setting the dates of the lunar months.[29] At that time, determining the beginning and end of the religious festivals (*'Īd al-Fitr* and *'Īd al-Adḥā*) was the basic duty of the Religious Affairs Committee of the MSA. It is therefore possible to state that the scope of Islamic legal issues engaged by the Religious Affairs Committee of the MSA was very limited. The number of members was very few, possibly because it was an institution that was established upon the basis of voluntariness. Nonetheless, there were no clear criteria or qualifications that the members of the Religious Affairs Committee had to fulfil in implementing this function.[30]

In the late 1970s, the MSA laid the foundation of the Islamic Society of North America (henceforth: ISNA), which is now known as the "largest American Muslim organization."[31] When the ISNA was established in 1982, the Religious Affairs Committee evolved into the Fiqh Committee of the ISNA.[32] In 1986, the Fiqh Committee of the ISNA was reorganised and renamed the Fiqh Council of North America (FCNA) to better engage with the needs and problems of the growing American Muslim community.[33] The Council administratively constitutes a branch of the ISNA that provides non-binding Islamic legal resolutions and *fatwās* on issues raised by American Muslims. In a document in the files of the FCNA, the incentive behind this restructuring is stated as "to create a large and

27 R. Kevin Jaques, 'Islamic Organisations in America' in Gary Laderman and Luis León (eds), *Religion and American Cultures: An Encyclopaedia of Traditions, Diversity* Gary Laderman and Luis León, vol I (ABC-CLIO 2003) 140; Yvonne Y. Haddad and Jane I. Smith, *The Oxford Handbook of American Islam* (Oxford University Press 2014) 3; Jocelyne Cesari, *When Islam and Democracy Meet: Muslims in Europe and in the United States* (Palgrave Macmillan 2004) 81.

28 Haddad and Smith (n 27) 3.

29 DeLorenzo, 'The Fiqh Councilor' (n 25) 69; Nimer (n 4) 160; Karen Isaksen Leonard, *Muslims in the United States* (Russell Sage Foundation 2003) 90.

30 DeLorenzo, 'The Fiqh Councilor' (n 25) 68–69.

31 Haddad and Smith (n 27) 3; Cesari, *When Islam and Democracy* (n 27) 82; Jaques (n 27) 140.

32 Jocelyne Cesari, 'Islamic Organisations in the United States' in Yvonne Y. Haddad and Jane I. Smith (eds), *The Oxford Handbook of American Islam* (Oxford University Press 2014) 66; Afsaruddin (n 6) 179.

33 Nimer (n 4) 160; Afsaruddin (n 6) 178; Fiqh Council of North America, 'History of the Fiqh Council' <http://fiqhcouncil.org/wp-content/uploads/2018/09/FCNABrochure.pdf> accessed 21 February 2021.

Table 3.1 The development of the FCNA

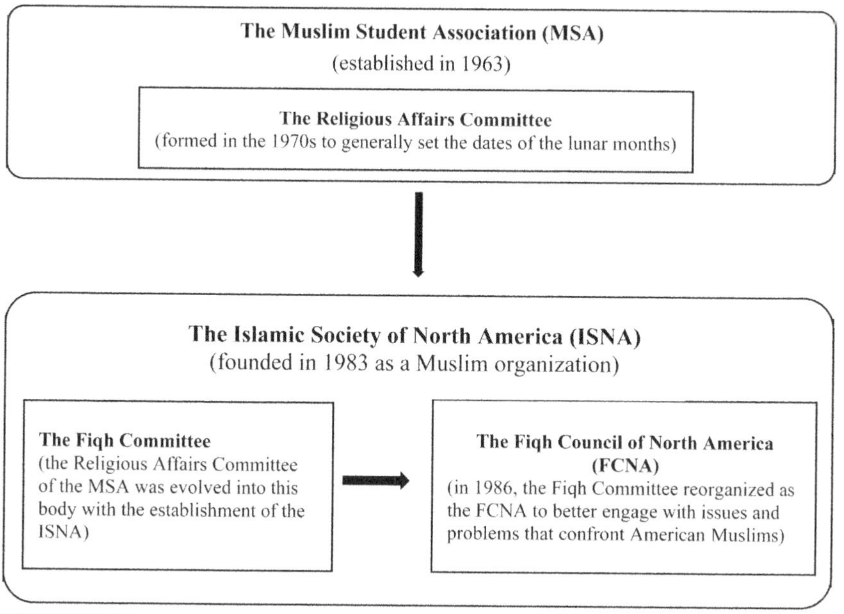

more authoritative body of Muslim scholars (ulama) to effectively confront the many legal issues facing Muslims in North America." [34] In considering the needs and exigencies of American Muslims, the FCNA assumes the mission of counselling these Muslims regarding how they should adhere to Islamic law. Over time, the Council obtained an influential authoritative position amongst American Muslims and began to counsel them upon the basis of Islamic law.

Since its reconfiguration, the FCNA has continued to be an affiliate of the ISNA. Within the structure of the ISNA, the main duty of the Council is to advise, counsel and educate American Muslims upon issues relevant to "the application of Islamic legal principles in their individual and collective lives within their respective North American societies."[35] After being reorganised as the FCNA, the membership of the Council has increased, and some certain conditions regarding qualifications of its members, meetings and the *fatwā* issuance process were duly identified.[36] Nonetheless, the scope of its activities and functions was certainly

34 This is cited from DeLorenzo, 'The Fiqh Councilor' (n 25) 69. According to footnote 14, this document is incomplete, and its authorship is unknown.
35 Fiqh Council of North America (n 33).
36 DeLorenzo, 'The Fiqh Councilor' (n 25) 69.

expanded as well. DeLorenzo, one of the former members of the FCNA,[37] accentuates the active and increasing role of the FCNA. He observes:

> Today, the council functioning extends to the needs of individuals and organisations within the community and to those with whom they interact, Muslim and non-Muslim alike. By way of example, over the past year the council has dealt with questions submitted by individual Muslims, by local and national Muslim organisations, by the Departments of Justice and Defense, by non-Muslim trial lawyers, by immigration lawyers, and journalists with interests as varied as biological engineering and third-world politics.[38]

Correspondingly, it is possible to state that the FCNA began to be acknowledged and recognised as an authority in reference to Islamic legal issues. With the progressive institutionalisation process, the FCNA presumably acquired one crucial form of religious and social authority amongst American Muslims, American individuals and American official bodies. In recent years, the FCNA has begun to be a point of contact for American courts on subjects that have Islamic legal implications.[39]

The FCNA is a state-independent institution that was established by American Muslims' voluntary efforts.[40] In the FCNA's brochure, it is explicitly stated: "FCNA is a fully independent 501(c)(3) non-profit organisation."[41] In this respect, the Council does not have any legal authority and does not exercise any coercive power over American Muslim individuals to enforce its legal resolutions and *fatwās*. The Council is therefore a voluntary state-independent organisation whose presence ordinarily depends upon "generous donations from the community and community-based organisations."[42]

Within the structure of ISNA, the FCNA was established to examine the possibilities of applying Islamic law as a legal framework that encapsulates the life of the Muslim community in America. The Council consists of twenty members who are generally selected from amongst prominent and erudite American Muslim scholars. However, non-American Muslim scholars can also become members

37 Yusuf Talal DeLorenzo is a financial consultant and an Islamic legal scholar. In the 1990s, he was one of the preeminent members of the FCNA. He resigned from his position in the FCNA due to his disenchantment regarding the FCNA and its role. See William Glaberson, 'Interpreting Islamic Law for American Muslims' (*The New York Times*, 21 October 2001) <http://www.nytimes.com/2001/10/21/us/interpreting-islamic-law-for-american-muslims.html> accessed 04 June 2017.

38 DeLorenzo, 'The Fiqh Councilor' (n 25) 69.

39 Afsaruddin (n 6) 179; Cesari, *When Islam and Democracy* (n 27) 60.

40 This online brochure is available in its official website. Fiqh Council of North America, 'FCNA Brochure' <http://www.fiqhcouncil.org/sites/default/files/FCNABrochure.pdf> accessed 23 April 2017.

41 ibid.

42 ibid.

of the Council with certain provisos and the approval of its members.[43] The FCNA's organisational structure consists of two bodies: the Council Executive Committee and the General Secretariat. The Council Executive Committee has eight members selected from amongst FCNA members. This Committee then selects one president, one vice-president and one secretary-general from amongst its members.[44] These eight executive members are:

1. Dr Muzammil Siddiqi (the president of the FCNA)
2. Dr Zainab Alwani (the vice-president of the FCNA)[45]
3. Dr Zulfiqar Ali Shah (the secretary-general/executive director of FCNA)[46]
4. Dr Mohamad A. El Sheikh[47]
5. Dr Jamal Badawi[48]
6. Shaikh Abdur Rahman Khan
7. Dr Muhammad Qatanani[49]
8. Dr Jaseer Auda[50]

43 The Statutes of the Fiqh Council of North America of 2014. The statutes were approved by the Council at the General Body Meeting held on February 28, 2014, and the author accessed these statutes via e-mail. Muzammil Siddiqi, Personal e-mail to the author, 10 May 2017.

44 The Statutes of the Fiqh Council of North America of 2014 (n 43).

45 Zainab Alwani is a figure worth mentioning on account of being the first female scholar amongst FCNA members. She received her PhD within the area of Islamic jurisprudence from the International Islamic University in Malaysia. Currently, she is the Assistant Professor of Islamic Studies at Howard University School of Divinity. Taking into consideration her membership in the Muslim Women Lawyers for Human Rights (KARAMAH) and the FCNA, it is quite possible to characterise her as a Muslim woman jurist and activist. See American Learning Institute for Muslims, 'Dr. Zainab Alwani' <https://www.alimprogram.org/scholars/dr-zainab/> accessed 01 July 2017.

46 Zulfiqar Ali Shah attended and graduated from the International Islamic University in Pakistan and earned his MA in the Fundamentals of the Islamic Religion (*uṣūl al-dīn*) at the same university. Later, he received his PhD in Theology and Religious Studies from University of Wales. For further insight, refer to Zulfiqar Ali Shah, *Iftā' and Fatwa in the Muslim World and the West* (International Institute of Islamic Thought 2014) IX.

47 Mohamad A. El Sheikh graduated from the faculty of Sharia and Law at Omdurman Islamic University in Sudan and was then appointed by the Sudanese Department of Justice to serve as a judge in the Sharia Court. In 1978, he received a scholarship to go to the United States in order to complete his further higher education. In 1980, he was awarded an MA by Howard University and later, in 1986, he received his PhD from Temple University. See al-Huda University, 'Dr. Mohamad Adam El-Sheikh' <http://alhudauniversity.org/dr-mohamad-adam-el-sheikh> accessed 01 July 2017.

48 Cesari, *When Islam and Democracy* (n 27) 150.

49 Muhammad Qatanani received three degrees (undergraduate, MA and PhD) from the Faculty of Islamic Legislation and Jurisprudence, the University of Jordan. He subsequently moved to the United States. Currently, he is working as a professor of Arabic and Islamic Studies at Montclair State University in New Jersey. See Graduate Theological Foundation, 'Mohammad Qatanani' <http://www.gtfeducation.org/faculty-staff/mohammad-qatanani.cfm> accessed 31 May 2017.

50 Fiqh Council of North America, 'Meet Our Council's Executive Members' <http://www.fiqhcouncil.org/node/13> accessed 13 September 2020.

These members have regular, close and frequent communications with each other. The selection of the president, vice-president and secretary-general depends upon the absolute majority of votes.[51] From the date of their election, the length of office term was determined to be three years, but members can also be appointed more than once to the same position. The president is the highest official of the FCNA and its spokesman, and s/he supervises all activities that are conducted by the Council. In addition to these, the president also calls for the regular and special meetings of the Council, and s/he conducts these meetings. Reviewing *fatwās* before their issuance and representing the Council among institutions and official bodies that have similar characteristics are also specified to be a part of his/her responsibilities.[52] In the event of the vacancy of the office of the presidency, the vice-president replaces his/her position until the Council's members elect a new president in the first forthcoming regular session. The president and the vice-president may be expelled from their positions by a reasonable decision that is issued by an absolute majority of the members if any of them (the president or the vice-president) acts in a way which requires them to take such action.

In addition to the Council Executive Members, the FCNA has twelve ordinary members. They are:

1. Shaikh Muhammad Nur Abdullah
2. Dr Yasir Qadhi
3. Dr Ossama Bahloul
4. Shaykh Mustafa Umar
5. Dr Deina Abdulkader
6. Dr Abdulbari Mashal
7. Imam Yahya Hendi
8. Imam Hassan Qazwini
9. Dr Ali Solaiman Ali
10. Dr Muddassir H. Siddiqui
11. Dr Ihsan Bagby
12. Sheikh Suhaib Webb[53]

An important characteristic aspect of these members is that they are well-known, influential and prestigious Muslim scholars and activists in their local environment in America. Many of these scholars received both traditional and modern education. Muzammil Siddiqi received his early traditional Islamic legal education in accredited religious institutions that include Aligarh Muslim University and Darul Uloom Nadwatul Ulama in India, before studying in the Islamic University of Medina in Saudi Arabia in 1965.[54] He subsequently received

51 The Statutes of the Fiqh Council of North America of 2014 (n 43).
52 ibid.
53 Fiqh Council of North America (n 50).
54 Islamic Society of Orange Country, 'Islamic Director's Biography Dr. Muzammil Siddiqi' <https

an MA in Theology from Birmingham University in England and earned a PhD in Comparative Religion from Harvard University in the United States.[55] Jamal Badawi graduated from Ain Shams University in Egypt. In the 1960s, he moved to the United States and received his MA and PhD from the Department of Business Administration, Indiana University.[56] Abdulbari Mashal received three degrees (undergraduate, MA and PhD) from Riyadh's University of Imām Muḥammad ibn Sa'ūd. His specialisation is in the area of Sharī'a audit and Islamic financial advisory. He has also many memberships in other institutions and organisations associated with Islamic banking and economics that include the Accounting and Auditing Organisation for Islamic Financial Institutions (AAOIFI), the International Islamic Fiqh Academy in Jeddah and the Center for International Private Enterprise (CIPE), US Chamber of Commerce.[57] Many FCNA members are resident in the United States and therefore immensely cognisant of American life, culture and environment. They are active and productive Muslim scholars who have been seeking to maintain an Islamic way of life in the non-Muslim American environment and promote it amongst American Muslims. In serving as members of the FCNA, they engage with their local Muslim and non-Muslim community and produce Islamic legal responses to the new challenges that confront American Muslims.

Considering the circumstances of American Muslims in a non-Muslim environment, the mission of "religious guidance" provides the FCNA and its members with a religiously authoritative status amongst Muslim residents in America. Although its members and leaders follow different *madhhabs*, the Council espouses a holistic approach towards them.[58] It is stated:

> The Fiqh Council of North America is a body of recognised and qualified Islamic scholars from the United States and Canada who accept the Qur'an and authentic Sunnah as the primary sources of Islam. Furthermore, FCNA is guided by the judicial heritage of the Prophet's companions and the legal rulings and methodology of established classical normative Muslim Scholarship.[59]

://web.archive.org/web/20070218010407/http://www.isocmasjid.com/Administration/dbio.htm> accessed 01 July 2017.

55 Islamic Society of Orange Country (n 54).

56 Dr Jamal Badawi, 'About Dr. Jamal Badawi' <http://jamalbadawi.org/index.php?option=com_content&view=category&layout=blog&id=2&Itemid=2> accessed 01 July 2017; Dr Jamal Badawi, 'A Guide to Political Left' <http://www.discoverthenetworks.org/individualProfile.asp?indid=1009> accessed 01 July 2017.

57 RAQABA: Shari'a Audit and Islamic Financial Advisory, 'Our Senior Professionals' <https://raqaba.co/en/> accessed 13 September 2020.

58 DeLorenzo, 'Fiqh and the Fiqh Council' (n 23) 196.

59 Fiqh Council of North America, 'About FCNA' <http://fiqhcouncil.org/about-fcna/> accessed 13 September 2020.

The holistic approach towards different *madhhabs* is also a result of the diversity of *madhhab* affiliation amongst American Muslims and increases the adoptability and admissibility of *fatwās* issued by the Council because if one *madhhab* was identified as the main epistemological approach, American Muslims adherent to other *madhhabs* can demonstrate a hesitative and reactive attitude in acknowledging the *fatwās*. In this regard, it is possible to state that the scholar's *madhhab* affiliation does not create an impeding factor in being appointed as a member of the Council. Diversity in their *madhhab* affiliation instead is acknowledged as an important factor in acquiring American Muslims' reliance and in increasing the acceptability of *fatwās*.

In the General Body Meeting held on February 28, 2014, the required qualifications that the FCNA's members must fulfil were specified. These are:

1. To be nominated by at least two permanent members of the Council or two of the knowledgeable scholars,
2. To have a university jurisprudential qualification or to be a disciple who should be a constant attendee of one prominent scholar's lectures and who should be graduated by his/her approval. He also has to have knowledge of the Arabic language and different Islamic sciences which indicate his capacity and ability within the area of Islamic law,
3. To be known for good conduct and character and to demonstrate commitment to the provisions of Islam and its ethics,
4. To be a resident in the American continent, but some non-resident scholars of the American continent who are interested in the jurisprudence of Muslim minorities in non-Muslim lands can be accepted as members of the Council,
5. To have a capacity that combines Islamic jurisprudence and knowledge of reality,
6. The membership of the candidate should be approved through the absolute majority of the Council's members.[60, 61]

Within the American context, some characteristics of a *muftī* in a traditional sense underwent, to a certain extent, an alteration.[62] It is explicit that in the second requirement, to have *ijāzas* (teaching licenses granted by a knowledgeable Muslim scholar) is equated with receiving formal and accredited training at university level in Islamic studies. In this sense, university degrees are replacing *ijāzas*, which are the certificates traditionally required to be a *muftī*. This change within the traditional accreditation notwithstanding, the phrase "to have knowledge of the Arabic language and different Islamic sciences" potentially necessitates that the qualified member should have knowledge of the classical Islamic disciplines which include Islamic jurisprudence (*usūl al-fiqh*), the Arabic language, the

60 The Statutes of the Fiqh Council of North America of 2014 (n 43).
61 Author's translation.
62 DeLorenzo, 'The Fiqh Councilor' (n 25) 67.

Qur'anic commentary (*tafsīr*), the reports of a saying, action or acquiescence of the Prophet (*ḥadīth*), Arabic literature and rhetoric (*balāghat*) and logic (*manṭiq*). This alludes unequivocally to the desire of the institution to identify an erudite member who has enough capacity in interpreting the authoritative texts and in accommodating Islamic law to the life of American Muslims. The designation of qualified scholars also promotes the credibility of *fatwās* issued by the FCNA.

The fourth and fifth qualifications can be perceived as a corollary of the fact that *fatwās* issued without taking into consideration the circumstances of America may lead to more problems than they solve. The emphasis upon the prospective members' familiarity with the local environment demonstrates a desire to produce *fatwās* that pay attention to the changing cultural, social and legal dynamics of the Muslim minority community because a growing number of American Muslims have been either born or raised in America and Canada. Despite the Council's desire to have members who actively engage in the lives of American Muslims, there exist some criticisms of the *post facto* acquired citizenship of some FCNA members. Leonard refers to the criticisms of African American Muslims, and she observes:

> ISNA's national Fiqh Council, however, has not been accepted as authoritative by all immigrant Muslim scholars, and it has been criticized by African American Muslims for being "overwhelmingly composed of naturalized Muslims," men who know little about U.S. family law and inheritance rights.[63]

These criticisms raise the question of whether the naturalised status of those members is an insurmountable hurdle to understanding the cultural, social and legal context of America. Nonetheless, the detailed analyses of *fatwās* issued by the FCNA from sociological, cultural and legal perspectives may diminish the negative influence of such criticisms because there are some specific references to the differentiating conditions and circumstances of American society in these *fatwās*. For instance, the *fatwā* regarding the permissibility of wearing dreadlocks when performing the prayer directly assesses contemporary American social life, and it states:

> Nowhere [is the wearing of dreadlocks stated] as being among the things that invalidate salah (prayer). So, in the modern North American context, where the fashion is so widespread, there is probably no reason to suppose it even makruh.[64]

This statement perceptibly indicates that FCNA members are conversant with American culture and recognise it as one determinative factor in the process of issuing *fatwā*. Dreadlocks are acknowledged to be a popular hairstyle amongst

63 Leonard (n 4) 10.
64 DeLorenzo, 'The Fiqh Councilor' (n 25) 77.

Americans that are worn especially by American Muslim youths, so it is stated that identifying this fashion as reprehensible (*makruh*) may discourage these youths from performing the prayer with congregation or engender a negative disposition amongst them towards performing the prayer.[65] This is the main consideration of FCNA members in issuing its *fatwā* related to wearing dreadlocks. It is also possible to identify the familiarity of FCNA members with American culture in some other *fatwās* issued as answers to the following questions: what are proper Islamic manners of dress and haircuts; how can Muslim marriages be terminated in the United States; is it permissible to accept Christmas gifts from Christian friends; and can a Muslim participate in work-related Christmas parties where alcohol is served?[66]

In considering the ethnic, social and regional diversity amongst American Muslims, the FCNA has sought to elect representative members from amongst different groups of Muslims living in the continent. In the Statutes of the FCNA of 2014, Article 15 states: "In electing its members, it is advisable to consider candidates who represent the different states of America in which Muslims have a visible presence."[67] Despite being resident in the United States and having American citizenship, many FCNA members come originally from a diverse background and represent different ethnic groups. This is acknowledged as an important advantage in considering the different needs of American Muslims who belong to diverse ethnic, cultural and social groups. Article 16 of the same statutes also specifies: "In electing its members, it is important to take into account that FCNA members should be representative of the various Islamic legal schools prevailing in the present world."[68] This article may imply that the FCNA equally recognises all schools of Islamic law, either Sunnī or Shi'ī *madhhabs*. It is therefore possible to state that the Council explicitly seeks to establish a bridge between American Muslims, at least on the denominational basis, through reinforcing unity and cooperation amongst the American Muslim scholars. Imam Hassan Qazwini,[69] for instance, is one attention-grabbing member of the FCNA because he is a distinguished active Muslim scholar, adherent to

65 ibid.

66 ibid 73–83.

67 The Statutes of the Fiqh Council of North America of 2014 (n 43).

68 ibid.

69 In 1980, Imam Hasan Qazwini joined the Islamic Seminary in Qum, Iran, and graduated from there in 1992, with a sound grasp of the fundamentals of Islamic jurisprudence and the Qur'anic commentary. After completing his education, Qazwini immigrated to America together with his family in late 1992. Soon after, not only did he become an effective figure amongst the American Muslims, adherent to Shi'ī tradition, but also drew the attention of some American political leaders. In particular, the youth community acknowledged him as their spiritual and religious guide. After noticing the energic, active and dynamic potential of the young generation, he, in 1998, established the Young Muslim Association (YMA) to create an environment in which the youth can be religiously educated and have their spiritual and religious needs catered to. See Imam al-Qazwini Sayid Hassan, 'Biography' <http://alqazwini.org/qazwini_org/biography.htm> accessed 01 July 2017.

Shi'ī tradition. The FCNA aims to engage and interact with American Muslims adherent to different *madhabs* through its members' capacity and fame. With this intention, the institution therefore specified that electing its members from different *madhhabs* so far as possible is a substantial criterion in the appointment of membership.

In addition to reaching out to the ethnically, culturally and socially diverse Muslim groups in America, the FCNA also concentrates on addressing the complex modern issues that trace back to living in non-Muslim contexts and the questions that were never engaged by earlier Muslim scholars. Cesari refers to this orientation of the FCNA, and she observes:

> [the FCNA] seeks to address novel conditions that emerge as a result of a unique North American-Islamic convergence in the light of historically accepted and honored legal methodology.[70]

Since its establishment, many questions ranging from economics to medicine, from ritual to social life, and from familial problems to political issues have been posed to the FCNA. Some of these questions have a complex and intricate nature that requires both reformatory skills and collective efforts of FCNA members in producing appropriate and practicable *fatwās*. In the FCNA's brochure, the necessity of "collective" effort in issuing a *fatwā* is precisely underscored. It states:

> FCNA attempts to harmonise varying jurisprudential views, scholarly opinions and exegetical interpretations in efforts to unify Muslim legal voices and issue mainstream collective decrees in matters of concern to Muslim life in North America.[71]

The Council is apparently aware of the fact that the complexities of modern life have required, to a substantial extent, interdisciplinary skills that are beyond the limit and competence of a single individual scholar.[72] Amongst Council members, this situation prospectively increases the demand for the production of "jointly considered legal advice and opinions that are based on the Qur'an and the Sunna."[73] In the Statutes of the FCNA of 2014, Article 4 specifies: "The Council shall collectively issue its *fatwās*, and it is not responsible for the opinions and *fatwās* of its members in their personal capacity."[74]

In the Council's efforts, a gradual tendency towards conducting more research, instead of practicing *iftā'* or producing *fatwās*, may be observable, but this does not mean that these research papers penned by the Council's individual members

70 Cesari, 'Islamic Organisations' (n 32) 68.
71 Fiqh Council of North America (n 40).
72 Esposito (n 18) 6.
73 DeLorenzo, 'The Fiqh Councilor' (n 25) 69.
74 The Statutes of the Fiqh Council of North America of 2014 (n 43).

are issued without the approval of its members. The consensus of FCNA members is one of the main *sine qua non* conditions before issuing any research paper and *fatwā*. Article 33 in the Statutes of the FCNA of 2014 precisely reiterates this prerequisite, and it states: "*Fatwās* issued on behalf of the Council shall be based on the unanimous vote of its members (or the consensus of its members), if possible, or by a two-thirds of quorum members in attendance."[75] However, the tendency towards conducting research has resulted in a partial decrease in the practice of *iftā'*. A quick glance at the FCNA's website may give a straightforward demonstration of the increasing tendency towards individual evaluations or research. This recent tendency towards individual research within the structure of the FCNA has very likely brought about different tones and literary styles in providing Islamic legal solutions and answers to questions posed by American Muslims.

Despite these different tones and literary styles, the FCNA usually seeks to retain legal principles and reasonings almost in the same manner, especially on gender issues. To set an example, Zainab al-Alwani, one of the members of the Council Executive Committee, refers to the concept of "complementary roles" when she writes on the issue of "the Quranic Concepts on Gender Relations."[76] Like al-Alwani, Jamal Badawi, another member of the Council Executive Committee, applies to the same concept – the concept of "complementary roles" – in his book, *Gender Equity in Islam: Basic Principles*, that was featured under the title "Gender Equity in Islam" as an answer to questions relevant to gender issues on the FCNA's website.[77] While restricting the Q. 4:34[78] to the particularity of family life, both of them interpret the word "*qawwāmūn*" in the verse as implying that it renders males financially responsible for the sustenance and maintenance of the family, alone. The very controversial term "*qawwāmūn*" is assertively re-defined by al-Alwani in the light of the objectives of Islamic law and some Qur'anic values that include God-consciousness (*taqwa*), doing good (*ihsān*), justice (*'adl*) and equality (*musāwa*). She observes:

> Qawwamun conveys the notion of providing for and that the term is used prescriptively to indicate that men ought to provide for women in the context of child-bearing and rearing … The term qawwamun is not an unconditional statement of male authority and superiority over all women for all time.

75 ibid.

76 Zainab Alwani, 'The Quranic Concepts on Gender Relations' <http://www.fiqhcouncil.org/node/12> accessed 13 May 2017.

77 Jamal Badawi, 'Gender Equity in Islam' <http://www.fiqhcouncil.org/node/26> accessed 20 September 2015; Jamal Badawi, *Gender Equity in Islam: Basic Principles* (American Trust Publications 1999) 13, 23–26, 38–41.

78 The Q. 3:34 reads: "Men are in charge of women because Allah has made the one of them to excel the other, and because they spend of their property for the support of women. So good women are the obedient, guarding in secret that which Allah has guarded. As for those from whom you fear rebellion, admonish them and banish them to beds apart, and chastise them. Then if they obey you, seek not a way against them. Allah is ever High Exalted, Great."

> This variance does not negate the principle of equality; rather it is a sign of social complement and solidarity between people.[79]

Similarly, Badawi readdresses the position and roles of women in society and their rights in Islamic law after accentuating the necessity of making a clear differentiation between the normative teachings of Islam and the various prevalent cultural practices amongst Muslim societies that are presumptively deemed as part of Islamic legal rulings and practices.[80] After underlying this crucial point, Baddawi principally defines the word "*qiwwāma*" as "responsibility for the family,"[81] and he then refers to the misinterpretation of scholars who construe the word "*qiwwāma*" as an unconditional statement of "male authority and superiority over all women." He puts emphasis upon the concept of "complementary roles between men and women," and he states:

> it is clear that in terms of spirituality and humanness, both genders stand on equal footing before Allah. It is clear also that nowhere in the primary sources of Islam (the Qur'an and Sunnah) do we find any basis for the superiority of one gender over the other. Human misinterpretations, culturally-bound opinions and manipulations are not congruent with what Islam teaches. The fully equality of all human beings before Allah is beyond doubt. This equality should not be confused, however, with role differentiation in the spirit of cooperation and complementary.[82]

The concept of "complementary roles" may be seen as a legal determinant that minimises the discrepancies between classical Islamic legal rulings and modern expectations – or American values – with regard to women's issues. Due to the fact that the status and rights of women are perhaps one of the politicised issues that confront American Muslims within the context of America, FCNA members predominantly apply this concept in formulating an Islamic legal resolution or *fatwā* regarding gender issues with the intention of satisfying American Muslim women's needs and forestalling potential negative criticism of Islamic law in reference to women's rights.

Despite the fact that the issuance of collective *fatwā* is determined to be the initial preference of the FCNA in the process of issuing *fatwās*, the Council's individual members have the right to present and prove their dissenting opinions on the matter of debate.[83] These individual opposing views, along with the

79 Alwani, "The Quranic Concepts."

80 Badawi (n 77) 1–2.

81 ibid 13.

82 ibid 13–14.

83 In the Statutes of the FCNA of 2014, Article 33 states: "An opposing member or a member abstaining from voting have the right to prove his position in the presence of the Council, and opposing views shall not be published. The Council may also adopt *fatwās* issued by qualified scholars and agencies after being presented to the Council and approved by it." The Statutes of

Council's collective *fatwās*, are also presented for the approval of the Council members before being posted to the questioner, but they are not published as they do not reflect the unanimous approval of Council members.[84] In doing so, the Council provides multiple-choice *fatwās* to the questioner who is the last resort in deciding which *fatwā* is more appropriate for his/her situation.[85] DeLorenzo notes one of reasons why the FCNA vests such a right to questioners, and he states:

> As a part of the process of *istifta'*, the *mustafti* (questioner) has the right to accept whichever opinion s/he feels the more valid. This is partly a function of the questioner's knowing better what his or her particular circumstances or *ahwal* might be.[86]

In situations in which the questioner is designated as the last resort in deciding whichever opinion is more applicable for his/her problem, the FCNA sets its sights on achieving two objectives: (1) the protection of the questioner's right to accept whichever opinion is more acceptable to him/her and (2) the removal of uncertainty regarding the questioner's particular circumstances that cannot be easily detected by FCNA members.

In some cases, one Islamic legal resolution or *fatwā* may present several alternative opinions to the questioner, and consequently, s/he decides which of them corresponds to his/her conditions and *madhhab* (if the issue is related to the ritual practices (*'ibādāt*)). The Islamic legal statement upon the question of how long a Muslim should fast in the summer of the northern regions of the world (above 48 degrees' latitude) is a perfect sample of multiple-choice *fatwās*. In leaving the right of selectivity to the discretion of Muslims resident in the northern regions, the *fatwā* outlines four alternative opinions regarding the issue without apportioning a clear preference, and states:

> To summarise, the alternative opinions that this article has presented to facilitate summer fasting for Muslims who live north of 48 degrees irrespective of the sunset are:
>
> (1) to fast according to the calendar of the Makkah and Medina;
> (2) to fast according to the calendar of the closest region with moderate timings;
> (3) to fast starting from Fajr for a maximum of sixteen hours based on 45 degrees of latitude;

the Fiqh Council of North America of 2014 (n 43). See also Afsaruddin (n 6) 179; Fiqh Council of North America (n 40).

84 The Statutes of the Fiqh Council of North America of 2014 (n 43); Fiqh Council of North America (n 40).

85 Afsaruddin (n 6) 180.

86 DeLorenzo, 'The Fiqh Councilor' (n 25) 71.

(4) to fast from Fajr to a maximum of eighteen hours based on 48 degrees of latitude.

... every Muslim must consider these opinions and follow that which will enable her or him to fulfil this fundamental pillar of our faith.[87]

This statement conflicts with *fatwās* issued by some other religious institutions that include the Dār al-Iftā' in Saudi Arabia, the European Council for Research and Fatwa (ECFR) in Dublin and the Islamic Fiqh Council in Mecca, all of which hold that Muslims should fast between the estimated dawn (*fajr*) and the actual sunset, even if this period is close to twenty-four hours every day.[88] These institutions, Auda states, suggest that Muslims should appeal to the concession (*rukhsat*) in cases of possible harm and hardship while implicitly grounding their arguments upon the assumption that Muslims in these regions are living there temporarily.[89]

To put it differently, Muslims should not fast if they find it too hard in the summer in the northern regions, but in another season and region, they must make up for the days that they could not fast.[90] This Islamic legal reasoning applied by the given institutions in employing the concession is precisely counteracted by the FCNA's statement upon the ground of the objectives of Islamic law (*maqāṣid al-sharī'a*) and the legal maxim of facilitation (*taysīr*). The FCNA states that the concession is by definition an exceptional and individual license in the case of necessity, so it is not appropriate to the general spirit of Islamic law to allow the overwhelming majority of Muslims permanently resident in these particular regions to use the concession.[91] Unlike the given institutions' stance, the FCNA intends to facilitate fasting during the holy month of Ramadan by encouraging not to avoid fasting or to postpone it for another time and place. Considering the permanent resident status of the Muslims in the northern regions, the FCNA presents the four options that allow Muslims to follow different calendars in performing the fast obligation in the month of Ramadan. The toleration of the active participation of the questioner in deciding which of the legal options presented to him/her is more valid may be an implicit indication that the FCNA tries to take into account even an individual Muslim's circumstances.

Within the American context, the FCNA plausibly developed, and still develops, its own methodology in answering questions, serving American Muslims and producing Islamic legal knowledge. The principal function of FCNA can be basically ascertained as to provide Islamic legal guidance to Muslims resident in America through answering their questions related to Islamic law, preparing

87 Jasser Auda, 'Should Muslim in the North Fast 23 Hours a Day?' <http://www.fiqhcouncil.org/node/82> accessed 22 August 2017.
88 ibid
89 ibid.
90 ibid.
91 ibid.

research papers and holding conferences and seminars regarding Islamic legal issues and subjects.[92]

The process of producing Islamic legal knowledge and fatwās

Since its establishment, the Council has answered questions from members of the community, issued important *fatwās* and conducted Islamic juristic research. It is generally the case that questions can be submitted through e-mail, fax, mail, website or telephone.[93] The Council intermittently disseminates academic articles, scholarly publications on various theological matters, Islamic juristic research and *fatwās*. Frequently, the *fatwās* and research that have general contents and that are considered to be of importance not only to the individual questioner but also to the Muslims resident in America are featured on its website. The FCNA has issued many *fatwās* related to both ritual practices (*'ibādāt*) and social transactions (*mu'āmalāt*) to provide the applicability and practicability of Islamic law within the context of a non-Muslim environment. The content of questions directed to the FCNA ordinarily includes the adaptations of classical Islamic legal rulings and norms to the American context. For instance, the questions of whether an American Muslim can join the American military to perform military service and whether it is permissible to utter the English translation or equivalent (I accept) instead of the exact words of the marriage contract (*'aqd al-nikāh*) in Arabic (*qābiltu*) are rooted in American Muslims' perplexity related to the clash between classical Islamic legal rulings and the American context.

Like many religious institutions, the FCNA received, and still receives, a considerable number of questions related to gender issues and familial problems that include marriage, alimony (*nafaqa*), dower (*mahr*), inheritance and bequest.[94] Especially, the questions pertained to women's issues perhaps form an area in which the divergences between classical Islamic rulings and modern expectations appear to widely increase. Questions related to economic issues, along with gender and familial issues, have constituted a considerable portion of questions asked by American Muslims. Economic problems are predominantly related to the questions of how to engage with the issue of interest/usury (*ribā*) in banking, mortgages, car loans, insurance and so on. Some questions also revolve around the relationship between Muslims and non-Muslims, especially Christians, and these questions have a special significance in the lives of Muslim minorities in a secular pluralistic society.

Once received by the FCNA, questions are primarily subjected to an analysis in accordance with three criteria. In the first instance, the Council examines the issue in terms of whether a satisfactory answer exists in the inherited Islamic legal rulings. The FCNA generally overviews the inherited rulings in this phase. If there

92 Fiqh Council of North America (n 40).
93 ibid.
94 Esposito (n 18) 6–7.

is a legally convincing and fulfilling legal ruling, the FCNA analyses whether that answer formulated by earlier Muslim scholars is practicable within the context of America. This is the second criterion that the FCNA takes into consideration in evaluating the questions that have been presented to it. In the last instance, the FCNA seeks to determine whether the issue is completely new within the area of Islamic jurisprudence. DeLorenzo outlines the preliminary examination of the questions that are forwarded to the FCNA. He observes:

> the council will only consider for which no satisfactory answers exist, either for the reason that it is a completely new one, or because the answer posed by the classical scholars seems clearly inapplicable, i.e., that their ijtihad become outdated.[95]

The Council does not apparently evaluate issues upon which clear Islamic legal rulings already exist and are applicable within the American context. Nonetheless, it very likely seeks to address novel issues that emerge as a result of the interaction or confrontation between Islamic legal values and American values.[96]

In order to further engage with the practice of *iftā'*, the FCNA reassesses and restructures the questions to provide appropriate answers – this enables an opportunity to people who have the same or similar problem as the questioner in benefiting from *fatwās* issued by the Council. Despite the fact that the reassessment of questions seems unremarkable, it is a significant procedure that potentially extends the jurisdiction of a *fatwā* beyond the circumstances of the single questioner to govern all equivalent cases. For Taha Jabir al-Alwani, the first president of the FCNA, redefining and reformulating the question are precisely crucial exercises in providing appropriate answers for specific circumstances that confront Muslim minorities. It is also considered an exercise which reflects the active dialogical network between questioner, Muslim scholar and social context.[97] In formulating realistic, authentic, constructive and practicable *fatwās*, Muslim scholars, al-Alwani states, should adopt a more logical and scientific approach that requires deep examination of the constituent elements of the question, the underlying social factors that cause the question to be raised and the questioner's intention.[98] After the preliminary examination, the questions that are selected to be answered are possibly rephrased and reconstructed by the Secretary-General in a way that prompts the response in a more constructive and positive direction within the American context.

The FCNA regularly receives questions from Muslims resident in America and Canada. Council members endeavour to answer these questions through

95 DeLorenzo, 'The Fiqh Councilor' (n 25) 70.

96 ibid.

97 Taha Jabir al-Alwani, *Towards a Fiqh for Muslim Minorities: Some Basic Reflections* (Ashur A. Shamis (tr) The International Institute of Islamic Thought 2003) 4–6.

98 ibid 5.

issuing Islamic legal resolutions, research and *fatwās* so far as possible. The Council's limited budget however restrains the FCNA's capacity to address all problems that American Muslims face.[99] DeLorenzo is critical of this point and claims that the Council frequently abstains from answering the difficult questions that confront American Muslims.[100] In this regard, DeLorenzo's criticism may be an acceptable reality that demonstrates the refrainment of FCNA members in responding to inherently controversial and intricate questions – these questions are not presumably answered on account of their political contents and implications. In consideration of the FCNA's limited budget as a voluntarily established religious institution, al-Alwani states that the FCNA has to select the questions in accordance with the capacity of its budget before answering them.[101] In this regard, it can be observed that some questions and issues, although they are relevant to the American Muslim community, can be left unanswered because of either the FCNA's limited budget or the reluctance of Council members in providing them with satisfying answers.

Council members regularly convene in general body meetings to discuss the topic on the agenda and to promulgate *fatwās* on an eclectic range of issues (which include arts, politics, ritual practices, science, social life and technology). Every year, the Council organises its general body meeting in the FCNA's headquarters in Virginia or in another place, and the president of the FCNA usually chairs these meetings.[102] The Secretary-General is responsible for submitting these general body meetings' agenda, date, duration and place to FCNA members and concerned attendees at least three months before any meeting.[103] In these meetings, discussions are usually based on research conducted and prepared by the Council's members and (if invited and attending) individual scholars, researchers and scientists.[104] In addition to organising ordinary meetings, the FCNA also has, at the request of the president or one-third of Council members, the ability to arrange special meetings in exceptional cases. The organisation's operating procedures clearly establish that at least more than half of the FCNA membership must be present at a meeting. In the Statutes of the FCNA of 2014, Article 37 specifies: "The general body meeting shall be considered legal if the percentage of attendant members of the Council exceeds the fifty percent of the total members of the Council."[105] It is obvious that the Council establishes the quorum as at least one more than half of its total members to discuss and evaluate any issue regarding

99 Glaberson (n 37).

100 The questions like whether suicide attacks are permissible with the intent of defending and protecting Muslims against their enemies are not generally engaged with by the FCNA. DeLorenzo links the reluctance of the Council in providing appropriate answers to these questions to their political implications and content. For further insight, refer to Glaberson (n 37).

101 Glaberson (n 37).

102 The Statutes of the Fiqh Council of North America of 2014 (n 43).

103 ibid.

104 ibid.

105 ibid.

Islamic law. The scholars are only allowed to consider, deliberate and discuss subjects included in the meeting's agenda, but some frequently asked questions relevant to the specified issue are occasionally sought to be answered.[106]

In many aspects, the general body meetings can be likened to a kind of academic conference format, but these general body meetings are very significant to the issuing of an Islamic legal resolution or a *fatwā* by the Council. In any case, *fatwās* are supported by the majority of members, as determined by Article 44 in the Statutes of the FCNA of 2014 ("The President of the Council and the *Fatwā* Committee are authorized to issue *fatwās* in the name of the Council if there exists the consensus of Council members").[107] It may be asserted that Islamic legal decisions and *fatwās* promulgated in the process of the practice of *iftā'* are explicitly the result of collective deliberations of FCNA members. The approval or consensus of the Council's members is therefore acknowledged as one of the determinative factors in the process of issuing a *fatwā*.

In instances where specialist input is required, external experts (in fields as diverse as commerce, economics, medical treatment, science and technology), as Article 13 establishes, have participated in FCNA meetings ("Advisors, experts, and translators who are considered to help in achieving the Council's objectives may be invited to participate in meetings and discussions, but they do not have the right to vote").[108] Although these experts are not permitted to vote, their recommendations, explanations and contributions are partly included as scientific evidence in the FCNA's promulgated research papers, Islamic legal resolutions and *fatwās*. It is therefore possible to state that these experts have made an important contribution in areas where the scholars lack the required knowledge and when the discussion extends to subjects with which they are unfamiliar. The Secretary-General in agreement with the president may invite experts, scientists and translators to the Council's regular and emergency meetings.[109] The participation of external experts, scientists and observers in FCNA meetings likely denotes that the Council intends to promote and improve the collective practice of *iftā'* in order to consider all aspects of the matter in question – this evidences that the Council adopts an approach that engages with the social, cultural, economic, scientific and legal dimensions and implications of the question as far as possible. The Council, for instance, has been working with a committee of Muslim astronomers (Moonsighting Committee Worldwide (MCW)) for many years to answer questions related to the lunar months and the sighting of the crescent.[110]

106 To take an example, the FCNA in its general body meeting in Virginia on June 10, 2006 approved the use of astronomical calculations in determining the beginning and end of the Islamic lunar months and also provided Islamic legal answers to some frequently asked questions regarding this issue. See the Islamic Center of Boston, 'Fiqh Council of North America: Regarding the Adoption of an Astronomically Calculated Islamic Calendar' <http://www.icbwayland.org/include/moonsightingdecisionweb.pdf> accessed 04 June 2017.

107 The Statutes of the Fiqh Council of North America of 2014 (n 43).

108 ibid.

109 ibid.

110 DeLorenzo, 'The Fiqh Councilor' (n 25) 70; Fiqh Council of North America, 'Moon Sighting

On September 11, 2006, the resolution issued by the FCNA exemplifies the way external experts have participated in the decision-making procedure of the Council upon the issue of "adoption of an astronomically calculated Islamic calendar."[111] The resolution seeks to respond to the question of whether the use of the astronomical calculation method in determining the beginning of lunar months is licit or illicit. Before issuing the resolution, the FCNA organised its general body meeting on June 10, 2006, in Virginia.[112] A number of Muslim scholars, *imāms*, astronomers and some other interested Muslims participated in this conference to present and discuss the Islamic legal dimension and astronomical aspect of the issue. When explaining the Islamic legal premises and astronomical considerations in the resolution, the FCNA states:

> 5. There are now many Muslim astronomers who have been working for many years to develop a global lunar Islamic calendar. Fiqh Council particularly appreciates the efforts of its consultants Dr. Imad ad-Dean Ahmad, Dr. Khalid Shaukat, Dr. Muib Durrani and Dr. Ahmed Salamah.
>
> 6. Dr. Salah Soltan and Dr. Zulfiqar Ali Shah also presented scholarly papers to give thorough evidence from fiqh perspective that the use of calculations is not against the Sunnah of the Prophet-peace be upon him.[113]

This is an explicit substantiation regarding the inclusion of external experts' knowledge in the FCNA's decisions upon issues with which its members are not familiar. After careful, elaborative and scientific discussions and deliberations in its general body meeting, the FCNA has revised its previous position that the conjunction (i.e., the new moon or the crescent) should take place before noon, Greenwich time. In the end, the Council adopted the *fatwā* issued by the European Council for Fatwa and Research (ECFR), and it states that the conjunction must occur before sunset in Mecca and that the moon must set after sunset in Mecca.[114] Providing greater harmony and unity amongst the Muslim communities in the West may be detected as part of the essential legal reasoning behind the adoption of the EFCR's stance by the FCNA.[115] Considering the recognition of the EFCR's

Calculations-1' <http://www.fiqhcouncil.org/node/31> accessed 01 May 2017; Fiqh Council of North America, 'Ramadan & Shawwal 1438 (2017)' <http://www.fiqhcouncil.org/node/83> accessed 01 May 2017.

111 Islam Online Archive, 'Fiqh Council of North America: Regarding the Adoption' <https://archive.islamonline.net/?p=15065> accessed 25 August 2017; Islam Online Archive, 'Astronomical Calculations for Islamic Dates Position of the Fiqh Council of North America' <https://archive.islamonline.net/?p=15065> accessed 25 August 2017.

112 Islam Online Archive, 'Fiqh Council' (n 111).

113 Islam Online Archive, 'Astronomical Calculations' (n 111).

114 Islam Online Archive, 'Fiqh Council' (n 111).

115 In this general body meeting, the adoption of an astronomically calculated Islamic calendar was discussed and a decision was made to adopt the position of the ECFR with the intention of bringing unity amongst Muslims resident in the West. After referencing how Muslims benefit from technological innovations (e.g., clock), the FCNA states: "the Prophet adopted [sighting the new

position on that issue by the FCNA, the resolution also refers implicitly to the Council's endeavour in developing interactive and collaborative relationships with other Islamic legal institutions.

The process through which an Islamic legal resolution or a *fatwā* is issued corresponds to a systematic cooperative working relationship amongst FCNA members.[116] The practice of *iftā'* starts with asking a question of the FCNA. It is the questioner's responsibility to depict his/her problem and circumstance. The concrete picture of the problem drew by him/her helps FCNA members to grasp better the presented problem and situation. After receiving questions, the Council seeks to categorise them in accordance with the three questions. These are: is the question related to *'ibādāt* or *mu'āmalāt*; is there any satisfying inherited legal ruling upon this specific issue; and if so, is the existing answer applicable within the American context? After being categorised, the questions that are simple and that have practicable inherited rulings within the American context probably receive direct answers from the Council. However, the questions that remain outside of this categorisation are accumulated in a pool because they are either novel issues that have not been encountered before or are subjects that require the reformulation of existing Islamic legal rulings. In accordance with the degree of urgency and the FCNA's financial budget, some of the new and controversial issues in the pool are selected, with the mutual agreement of the president and the Secretary-General, to issue a collective resolution or *fatwā* in the general body meetings organised by the FCNA. Nonetheless, some controversial and complicated questions in the pool are left unanswered on account of either the FCNA's shoe-string budget or its members' hesitation in answering them (e.g., the issue of suicide attacks).

The selected issues are generally evaluated and discussed in FCNA general body meetings upon the basis of research prepared by Council members and attendees. After careful scholarly deliberation and evaluation in the general body meetings, FCNA members make a final decision which is indicated by an absolute majority of votes of attendant members.[117] In the brochure of the FCNA, it is stated: "FCNA issues its legal opinions usually based upon the consensus of its distinguished members or a two-thirds super-majority of quorum members in attendance."[118] It is obvious that the approval of the absolute majority of FCNA

Moon with naked eyes] for the sake of making things easy for the Muslims … This method has been playing the havoc among the Muslims especially in the West for decades and is one of the sources of disunity and rift within the Muslim community." In considering the circumstances of the modern world, the fact that the use of technological tools and apparatus makes people's lives easy is implicitly underlined by the FCNA in the decision-making process upon the issue regarding the use of astronomical calculations in establishing the Islamic lunar calendar. See Islam Online Archive, 'Fiqh Council' (n 111).

116 The process of issuing a *fatwā* by the FCNA generally depends upon the author's critical and analytical thinking due to the lack of internal and even external sources on that issue.

117 Fiqh Council of North America (n 40).

118 ibid.

members in attendance is necessary to issue a *fatwā* or an Islamic legal resolution. While evaluating any issue in its general body meetings, the Council has pursued one of two courses of action in accordance with the questions' content. If the question is related to novel and contemporary issues, the Council formulates a new rule regarding this unprecedented issue – this requires an intensification of existing scholarly efforts and a heightened level of collaboration in the practice of *iftā'*. However, if the subject in the question demands a review of an existing Islamic legal ruling which is not applicable within the American context, the existing ruling is reformulated by taking the circumstances and conditions of American Muslims into account.

Once resolutions and *fatwās* are confirmed by the absolute majority of FCNA members, the Secretary-General records them and initiates the publishing process subsequent to the approval of the president. This was previously performed by one of its volunteer members who had more interest in and was specialised in the discussed subject. However, this duty was assigned to the Secretary-General at the general body meeting held on February 28, 2014, with the consequence that the Secretary-General began to record and edit the Islamic legal resolutions and *fatwās* issued by the FCNA. They are, subsequent to the president's approval, featured on the websites of the FCNA, the ISNA, Islamopedia Online[119] and other publications (e.g., *Islamic Horizons*). [120]

In America, the FCNA can be acknowledged as a religious authority that informs American Muslims about issues related to Islamic law. The acceptability of the Council as an authority depends upon its ability to provide *fatwās* that are applicable within the American context and in engaging with the wider people. Despite the fact that its legal resolutions and *fatwās* do not have any binding authority within the American legal system, they are advisory and informative for American Muslims who demand to arrange their lives in accordance with both Islamic law and American law.[121] The Council principally adopts an approach that

119 The FCNA is an affiliate of the ISNA, one of the largest Islamic organisations in North America. Its mission is specified as to contribute to the betterment of the Muslim society and foster the development of the Muslim community, interfaith relations, civic engagement and better understanding of Islam. Its website was launched to publish the activities and facilities of the ISNA; some of the FCNA's *fatwās* are issued on this website to reach more American Muslims. See Islamic Society of North America, 'Vision and Mission' <http://www.isna.net/mission-and-vision/> accessed 06 June 2017.

120 *Islamic Horizons Magazine* is the ISNA's renowned bi-monthly magazine. This magazine mainly gives information about the ISNA's activities, organisations and facilities. It also publishes some articles and papers related to political and social issues, Islamic legal subjects, international affairs, family life and culture. See Islamic Society of North America, 'Islamic Horizons Magazine' <http://www.isna.net/islamic-horizons-magazine/> accessed 06 June 2017. Islamopedia Online is a website that provides access to news and analysis regarding Muslim countries and Islamic subjects. It has a comprehensive database to which is contributed by many influential religious figures across Muslim countries. The website also provides access to some *fatwās* given by different Islamic institutions that include the FCNA. See Islamopedia Online, 'About Islamopedia Online' <http://www.islamopediaonline.org/about-us/about-islamopedia-online> accessed 06 June 2017.

121 Nimer (n 4) 160.

Table 3.2 The process of *fatwā*-issuing by the FCNA

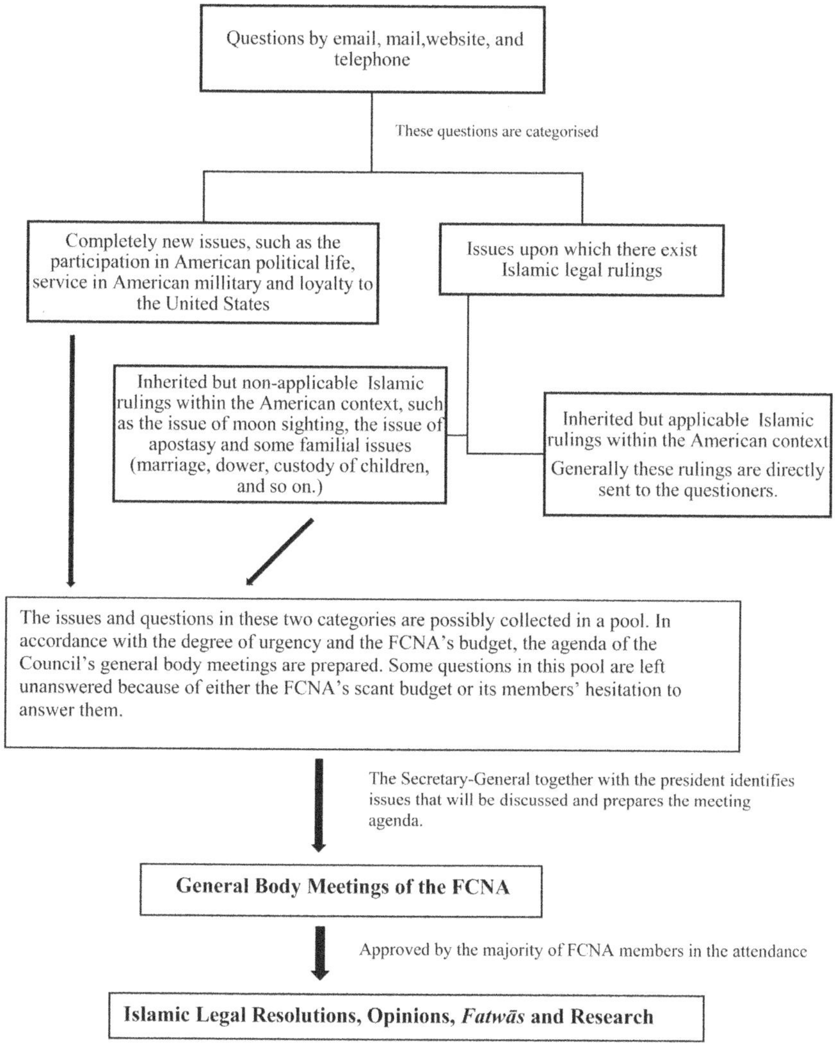

aims to advance an Islamic legal methodology that is simultaneously grounded within classical Islamic law, American values and the minority position of American Muslims.[122] This situation therefore evidences that the FCNA struggles to sustain the applicability of Islamic law amongst American Muslims.

122 ibid.

The influence of the concept of fiqh al-aqalliyyāt

After the presence of Muslim minorities became increasingly apparent in non-Muslim countries, the discussions and deliberations regarding the concept of *fiqh al-aqalliyyāt* within contemporary Islamic juridical and ethical thought have begun to increase. The incentive that ignites these discussions is to provide practicable *fatwās* for the myriad novel challenges that confront Muslims resident in non-Muslim countries. Over the last two decades, many Muslim scholars in both Muslim and non-Muslim countries have addressed the issue of the Muslim minority to devise an Islamic legal outline for them through delving into the Islamic legal, juridical and ethical tradition.[123] Here one can find a wide range of approaches that have been developed by Muslim scholars. The opinions of scholars can be classified into two categories in accordance with their stances related to the permanent residence status of Muslims in non-Muslim countries. The first group can be defined as "isolationist" scholars.[124] Scholars within this group generally counsel immigrant Muslims to return to Muslim countries as soon as they obtain an opportunity and to remain as segregated as possible from the wider aberrational non-Muslim society. These scholars advocate the applicability of the inherited Islamic legal rulings within non-Muslim contexts. Scholars in the second group can be qualified as "integrationist."[125] These scholars seek to facilitate the ethical, social, legal and political lives of Muslims instead of insisting upon applying the inherited rulings that lead to the isolation of Muslims from the wider society. In this regard, it may be stated that the minority and resident status of Muslims in non-Muslim countries has induced internal discussions amongst Muslim scholars – this also paved the way for formulating an "Islamic jurisprudence of Muslim minorities" (*fiqh al-aqalliyyat*).

In America, Taha Jabir al-Alwani (d. 2016) can be ranked amongst the prominent integrationist figures who led to the development of the concept of *fiqh al-aqalliyyat* and the establishment of the FCNA.[126] Hassan refers to al-Alwani's integrationist position. He observes:

> Al-ʻAlwani believes that Muslims in the United States need to establish themselves in the American public sphere. The channel for this integration is to create Muslim academic institutions that produce qualified graduates who understand the objective of their religion and appreciate the opportunity they have in the American land.[127]

123 Andrew F. March, 'Are Secularism and Neutrality Attractive to Religious Minorities? Islamic Discussions of Western Secularism in the "Jurisprudence of Muslim Minorities" (*Fiqh al-Aqalliyyat*) Discourse' (2009) 30 (16) *Cardozo Law Review* 2824–2825.

124 March identifies isolationist scholars as Salafī. See March (n 123) 2825.

125 March (n 123) 2825–2826.

126 Cesari, *When Islam and Democracy* (n 27) 146–147.

127 Salih Fares Hassan, *Fiqh al-Aqalliyāt: History, Development and Progress* (Palgrave Macmillan 2013) 90.

From Hassan's observation, it is quite possible to place al-Alwani amongst integrationist scholars. In addition to this, Fishman observes that the concept of *fiqh al-aqalliyyāt* envisaged by al-Alwani constitutes the ideological foundation of the FCNA ("Al-Alwani coined the term of *fiqh al-aqalliyyat* and used it for the first time in 1994 when the *Fiqh* Council of North America, under his presidency, issued a fatwa (legal opinion) allowing American Muslims to vote in American elections").[128]

Al-Alwani was born in Iraq in 1935, but his intellectual career as a Muslim jurist and scholar started to flourish in Egypt. He studied in al-Azhar University (from which he received his BA, MA and PhD in 1959, 1968 and 1973, respectively).[129] In 1975, he moved to Saudi Arabia, where he served as a lecturer in the Faculty of Sharī'a, Muhammad bin Saud University, and as a legal counsellor in the Saudi Ministry of Interior.[130] His stay in Saudi Arabia provided him with an opportunity to regularly attend international conferences, particularly those organised by Saudi-based institutions with the intention of developing an international invitation to Islam (*da'wa*). His participation in these conferences enabled him to engage with Muslims resident in non-Muslim countries. In 1977, he actively participated in the establishment of the International Institute of Islamic Thought (henceforth: IIIT), in Virginia, USA, and he then immigrated to the United States to assume the director position of the research unit in this institute in 1983.[131]

Al-Alwani's engagement with Muslims resident in America helped him to outline a model of Islamic jurisprudence that re-evaluates the inherited legal rulings and *fatwās* in the light of changing realities and that renews itself in order to adapt to the conditions of Muslim minorities. The "non-applicability" of the inherited rulings and *fatwās* within the context of America conceivably induced al-Alwani and scholars who had similar ideas to him to establish the FCNA, which aims to issue appropriate *fatwās* for American Muslims. The establishment of the FNCA in America sought to solve the predicaments that inherited and imported *fatwās* caused. In some sense, the formation of the FCNA may be seen as the actualisation of the concept of *fiqh al-aqalliyyāt* that was formulated by al-Alwani. He was elected as the FCNA's first president and stayed in this position during the years between 1986 and 2005.[132] The establishment of the FCNA has brought out an actual development that revives the interaction between the Islamic legal methodologies and the American contextual circumstances – this plausibly opens a space to re-evaluate the Islamic legal sources within their new context, America. In the resolutions and *fatwās* issued by the FCNA, there exist a number of signs which prove the methodological predisposition of the Council towards the concept of *fiqh*

128 Shammai Fishman, '*Fiqh al-Aqalliyyat*: A Legal Theory for Muslim Minorities' (2006) 1 (2) *Center on Islam, Democracy, and the Future of the Muslim World* 1.

129 Hassan (n 127) 88; Fishman (n 128) 2; Haida Mubarak, 'A Man of His Times: A Pioneer of Islamic Reform' (2016) 45 (3) *Islamic Horizons* 9–11.

130 Hassan (n 127) 88.

131 Mubarak (n 129) 10; Hassan (n 127) 88, 91.

132 Mubarak (n 129) 11.

al-aqalliyyāt. The FCNA can therefore be acknowledged as a religious institution which adopts the concept of *fiqh al-aqalliyyāt* in the process of issuing *fatwās*.

The concept of *fiqh al-aqalliyyāt* was used to prepare a substructure for the foundation of the FCNA. This concept conduces the FCNA to producing Islamic legal resolutions and *fatwās* that transform American Muslims from a silent, isolated and introverted minority position into an engaged community that has a sense of citizenship. The Council also contributes concurrently to the concept of *fiqh al-aqalliyyāt* in expanding it to a wider Muslim community, part of the American cultural and pluralistic milieu. Hassan observes:

> The study of the legal debate and the formation of Western-based fatwa institutions show little connection between local Islamic movements (e.g., African American groups) or individual native Westerners (e.g., converts) and the discourse of *fiqh al-aqalliyyāt*. It is difficult to locate an indigenous contribution to the discourse.[133]

Despite Hassan's argument, the Islamic legal resolutions and *fatwās* issued by the FCNA methodologically contribute to the development of *fiqh al-aqalliyyāt*. In the brochure of the FCNA, it is stated:

> FCNA gives great credence to the overall *maqasid* (objectives) of Islamic law; gives proper care and context to the soundness of textual evidences or contextual proofs, while also meticulously attributing the evidences to their original references. The fundamental governing principle of the Council is proper recognition of the new realities of Muslim life, a growing need for a newer and more enlightened jurisprudential outlook and facilitation of *yusr* (ease) within established boundaries and framework.[134]

The FCNA seeks to examine issues and problems that confront American Muslims and provides practicable *fatwās* upon the grounds of the concept of *fiqh al-aqalliyyāt* and the objectives of Islamic law (*maqāṣid al-sharī'a*).[135] In this regard, the legal maxim of facilitation (*taysīr*) and the "contextual examination" or "contextualisation" emerge as the main methodological tools which the FCNA applies in the process of issuing *fatwās*.

The Council employs certain standard sources of Islamic law to provide a practicable *fatwā* for any problem. Islamic legal methodology espoused by the FCNA is outlined in its brochure ("The Council depends upon authentic Islamic legal sources and sound and established legal evidences to derive its decrees").[136] When the Islamic legal resolutions and *fatwās* are elaborately analysed, it is

133 Hassan (n 127) 8.
134 Fiqh Council of North America (n 40).
135 DeLorenzo, 'The Fiqh Councilor' (n 25) 71.
136 ibid.

noticeable that the sources quoted by the FCNA predominantly are standard: the Qur'an, the Sunna, consensus of scholars (*ijmā*) and analogy (*qiyās*) – these are the main sources of classical Islamic law. Nonetheless, the Council applies the classical Islamic legal principles that include the public interest (*maṣlaḥa*), the presumption of continuity (*istishāb*), the blocking of illegitimate means (*sadd al-dharā'i*) and the customary practices (*'urf*).[137] This proves that all Islamic legal principles are used in accordance with the contextual circumstances that American Muslims face.[138] In applying all these legal principles, the Council espouses a liberal attitude that enables its members a wide scope of jurisprudence in practicing their duties. The liberality in using Islamic legal principles implicitly manifests the pragmatic orientations of scholars who advocate the concept of *fiqh al-aqalliyyāt* as the only mechanism in providing applicable *fatwās* to Muslims who permanently live in non-Muslim countries. March reiterates:

> *Fiqh al-aqalliyyat* tends to be a discourse where departures from traditional Islamic commitments are not seen as desirable, and certainly not goals in and of themselves, but where creative rethinking often occurs in subtle and pragmatic guises.[139]

Like March states, the main consideration of Council members generally emerges as the protection of the public interests of American Muslims. The FCNA seeks to activate the concept of *fiqh al-aqalliyyāt* through demonstrating its adherence to the classical Islamic legal methodologies and principles, but the liberality in applying them sometimes results in the Council issuing pragmatic *fatwās*.

Instead of theorising a new Islamic legal methodology (*uṣūl*), the FCNA applies the existing Islamic legal methodologies, but the inherited rulings are generally acknowledged as legal precedents that display how the legal methodologies are used in the process of deriving legal rulings from the authoritative sources. Al-Alwani observes:

> The aim should not be to apply the old fatwas literally, but to use them as a guide, learning how to obtain the original principles, the "roots" or *uṣūl*, from which earlier jurists derived and articulated them.[140]

The FCNA produced many *fatwās* that are different from the inherited legal rulings even though their contents are similar. To put it differently, the inherited rulings are drawn upon by the FCNA as legal precedents in relevant situations, but they are not acknowledged as fixed, unchangeable and perpetual.[141] For instance,

137 ibid.
138 The Statutes of the Fiqh Council of North America of 2014 (n 43).
139 March (n 123) 2826.
140 Al -Alwani *Towards a Fiqh* (n 97) 7.
141 Afsaruddin (n 6) 178.

the issue of alimony (*nafaqa*) after divorce was examined by the Council, and it issued the *fatwā* that concludes that a divorced woman has the right to receive alimony from the divorced husband. The amount of alimony should be adequate to maintain a decent living after the divorce.[142] It was stated that the Qur'an justifies offering such support to divorced women.[143] The Council identifies the higher principle of Islamic law regarding this issue as to financially support women in accordance with the Q. 4:34.[144] Divorced women can claim alimony after the annulment of marriage because, in the Q. 4:34, men are rendered as protectors and maintainers of women without there being any time and place restriction. However, earlier Muslim scholars who considered the dower (*mahr*) sufficient for the future living of divorced women inadvertently overlooked this legal principle. This is because protection and maintenance were offered to divorced women by their extended family in the time of those earlier scholars. In the *fatwā*, it is stated:

> The concern of Islamic law, before all else, is justice; and not the opinions of jurists who lived under circumstances very different from our own. Thus, if the dower was considered sufficient for the future of a divorced woman under social system in which the extended family provided for every manner of social service, including counselling, moral support, shelter, and so on it cannot be viewed as sufficient in twentieth century American society.[145]

In American society, it is all but impossible to find this kind of extended family structure. In general terms, the *fatwā* refers to the earlier Muslim scholars' opinions relevant to the issue and then implies the impracticability of these legal opinions in today's America while comparing the familial customary practices of those earlier Muslim scholars with the present-day common American family structure.[146] Despite the fact that the functionality and applicability of the classical Islamic legal methodologies are precisely accepted, it is underscored that the inherited legal rulings have lost to a substantial extent their practicability at the present time and the contexts in which they were formulated and regulated no longer exist. In the *fatwā*, it is explicitly reiterated that the inherited rulings, even though their methodologies were sound and functional, are too outdated to be applied within the present American context. Council members therefore acknowledge the inherited rulings as an intellectual source to demonstrate the divergences between the context of the American Muslims and that of the early Muslim scholars.

142 DeLorenzo, 'The Fiqh Councilor' (n 25) 74.
143 ibid.
144 The Q. 4: 34 reads: "Believing men are the protectors and maintainers of women, because Allah has blessed the one more than the other, because they support them from their means. Therefore, righteous women are devoutly obedient, and guard in their absence what Allah would have them guard."
145 DeLorenzo, 'The Fiqh Councilor' (n 25) 74.
146 ibid.

Despite the fact that the FCNA continuously accentuates the impracticability of the inherited rulings in the present context of America, this methodological approach is only adopted towards the inherited rulings regarding social transactions (*mu'amalat*). It can be observed that the FCNA unequivocally accepts the inherited rulings regarding ritual practices (*'ibādāt*) as fixed and immutable. The Council's methodological approach regarding the inherited rulings displays a variation in accordance with their content. DeLorenzo refers to this variation in the FCNA's methodology, and he reiterates:

> the issue of *madhhab* or affiliation to one legal school of thought or another is one which [the FCNA] considers valid only in regard to questions of worship or *'ibadat*. Yet, even within that restricted area, new developments have brought about questions that traditional imams never considered. For example, does possession of a credit card qualify one as having the means to undertake the hajj, even if one is not in possession of the requisite amount in cash?[147]

The detection of whether the problem pertains to the area of *'ibādāt* or *mu'āmalāt* emerges in the initial phase before issuing a *fatwā*. Even though the affiliation of a questioner to his/her respective *madhhab* plays a determinative role in the process of issuing a *fatwā* relevant to *'ibādāt*, new questions that were not addressed by earlier Muslim scholars may induce FCNA members to exert their mental energy (*ijtihād*) in issuing a *fatwā*, even sometimes within the restricted area of *'ibādāt*. If the issue is related to the area of *'ibādāt*, it is subject to the evaluation of whether the earlier Muslim scholars' opinions are available and applicable on that particular issue. If not, FCNA members engage with the issue to provide a practicable and legitimate answer in terms of Islamic law. It is therefore possible to state that it is highly likely that the Council leaves the door open to the application of *ijtihād* in the process of issuing *fatwā*s, even sometimes within the area of *'ibādāt*.

New determining factors, along with the classical legal methodologies, have been put into play in the process of practicing *iftā'* – these factors include common sense, presentation and representation of Islam in a good way, human rights, human equality, cooperation between individuals in a society for the general welfare, tolerance and civic duty. It is observable that these determining factors have been applied in the Islamic legal resolutions and *fatwās* issued by the FCNA. In the *fatwā* that was issued as an answer to the question regarding children's haircuts (point of dispute between their parents), the FCNA states:

> In forcing your will on your boys in the name of Islam they might very well (especially when we take their tender and impressionable ages into account) come to a number of faulty conclusions about Islam (conclusions which a secular and oftentimes hostile – toward Islam especially – society will

147 ibid 71.

> confirm them time after time, in school, on the street, on the playground, in the homes of friends and neighbours, and, most powerfully in the media):
>
> A. that Islam is cruel, unfeeling, and puritanical
> B. that Islam is authoritarian
> C. that Islam empowers men to ignore the wishes of their wives
> D. that Islam is somehow in conflict with the law of the land.[148]

Representing Islam in the best way as a legal consideration is systematically incorporated into the legal reasoning process of FCNA members. Some of these newly included legal considerations may be acknowledged as the social and contextual reflections of prevalent attitudes towards Islam, Muslims and Islamic law in America.

In unveiling the social and contextual influences upon the *fatwā*, it is essential to refer to the general impressions and attitudes of Americans regarding Islam and Muslims. Despite the fact that the number of American Muslims had increased enough to allow them to constitute a local presence in many major towns and cities of the continent, they were a relatively invisible community before September 11, 2001.[149] However, this invisible aspect of the Muslim minority community dramatically changed after the 9/11 terrorist attack in the United States.[150] This tragic event has therefore increased the visibility of American Muslims and their faith in the media and public sphere, but the representation of Islam and Muslims has generally included negative publicity mostly replete with either defamatory content regarding Islam or stereotypic images of Muslims.[151] Islamic law has also gotten its share of this detracting publicity. Afsaruddin alludes to how this negative publicity impinged adversely upon the representation of Islamic law, or sharī'a, within American society. She observes:

> post 9/11, in the media and the public sphere, the term shari'a has been much bandied about in connection with American Muslims, often with the intent of generating fear of a repressive Islamic theocracy that might be imposed on an unsuspecting American public. Highly charged rhetoric emanating from right-wing groups has referred to a "creeping shari'a," implying that it is a kind of contagion that will cripple American society.[152]

In incorporating the consideration of representing Islam well into its legal reasoning, the FCNA has sought to repulse the negative discourses that were launched as a result of the stigmatising representation of Islam and Muslims in America after 9/11.

148 Cited from DeLorenzo, 'The Fiqh Councilor' (n 25) 78–79.
149 Afsaruddin (n 6) 177; Fallon (n 10) 153–154, 161–163.
150 Cesari, *When Islam and Democracy* (n 27) 37–39; Cesari, 'Islamic Organisations' (n 32) 65; Afsaruddin (n 6) 177; Al-Alwani *Towards a Fiqh* (n 97) XX.
151 Nimer (n 4) 16–19, 77–78, 142, 149–152.
152 Afsaruddin (n 6) 177.

Furthermore, the citizenship status of Muslims raises questions regarding their liabilities and obligations towards America. In the context of a secular, liberal and democratic polity, the compact of citizenship is established through the legal and social contracts between Muslims and the American state.[153] The contract of citizenship means the recognition of the legal mechanisms and other institutions that are commanded by American law, so American Muslims must regard and obey the laws of this land as per the contract of citizenship. In this regard, the American laws, regulations and bylaws can be referred to as another consideration in the process of issuing *fatwās*. The *fatwā* related to marital status, alimony and custody of children, for example, states:

> Insofar as your marriage is considered, the Fiqh Council of North America has determined that no Muslim marriage may be terminated unless it is terminated through the court system of the state in which the Muslim is resident. This is an issue which has been discussed extensively by the Fiqh Council and, owing to the many ways in which the traditional Islamic formula for divorce has been abused by Muslims (and for many other reasons), the Council has given its opinion that divorce by Muslims living in the United States will not be recognised unless the divorce is recognised by the state. In this way the rights of all concerned, husbands, wives, children, and other relatives, may be protected; including religious rights, conjugal rights, property rights, custody rights, etc.[154]

The *fatwā* refers to the invalidity of marriages and divorces that are not recognised by the American Civil Code and that are not registered in accordance with the jurisdiction of state governments.[155] In America, marriage becomes legally valid when a marriage licence is obtained, and divorce receives state recognition when a judge or other authority dissolves the bonds of matrimony existing between two people.[156] American Muslims must therefore obtain a marriage licence and a divorce certificate in accordance with the jurisdiction of state governments in order for their marriage and divorce to be considered legitimate from the perspective of Islamic law.[157] This is probably because religious marriages and divorces that are performed in discordance with the jurisdiction of state governments give rise

153 Muzammil Siddiqi, 'Being Faithful Muslims and Loyal Americans' <http://fiqhcouncil.org/being-faithful-muslims-and-loyal-americans/> accessed 10 November 2020.

154 Cited from DeLorenzo, 'The Fiqh Councilor' (n 25) 73.

155 In response to the question of marriage, dower, a woman's right to seek compensation, the *fatwā* was issued by the FCNA. This *fatwā* was excerpted by DeLorenzo. See DeLorenzo, 'The Fiqh Councilor' (n 25) 73–74.

156 Public Health Service, Centers for Disease Control and National Center for Health Statistics, *Handbook on Marriage Registration* (U.S. Department of Health and Human Services 1988) 1; Public Health Service, Centers for Disease Control and National Center for Health Statistics, *Handbook on Divorce Registration* (U.S. Department of Health and Human Services 1988) 1–2.

157 DeLorenzo, 'The Fiqh Councilor' (n 25) 73–74.

to some insurmountable problems regarding the custody and inheritance rights of children born into these marriages, the legitimacy of marriage before the law, alimony and the victimisation of women. The *fatwā* apparently aims to surmount these familial, legal and social difficulties that confront American Muslims. It can be stated that the FCNA seeks strenuously to institute a congruence between Islamic and American legal regulations. DeLorenzo refers to American legal regulations as one of the criteria to which the FCNA should pay attention. He observes: "Suffice it to say by definition that Islamic law and American civil law represent the framework within which the American fiqh councillor operates."[158] The Council therefore continuously puts emphasis upon the fact that American laws, regulations and institutions are to be respected and obeyed with the intention of maintaining public interests and precluding chaos and disorder in society.[159]

American secular laws and regulations emerge as contextual elements that should be considered by FCNA members in the process of producing Islamic legal knowledge and *fatwās*. It is possible to state that the FCNA represents a religious institution that is overtly circumscribed by the American secular legal system. The necessity of obeying American laws is emphasised sometimes overtly, sometimes covertly in the *fatwās* issued by the Council. The legal reasoning is usually grounded upon the idea that the permanent residency of American Muslims denotes acknowledgement of a duty to obey American laws and regulations due to the process of the contract of citizenship.[160] The Council seeks to constitute a Muslim community that views itself as an integral part of American society and that has a sense of duty towards it. This is the result of the concept of *fiqh al-aqalliyyāt* that is adopted by the Council because this concept conduces Council members to engage with issues in a more flexible and pragmatic manner that focuses upon integrating Muslims into American society. It is therefore possible to state that the FCNA issued, and still issues, many *fatwās* that specifically provide solutions for American Muslims by developing a sense of belonging to America.

The concept of *fiqh al-aqalliyyāt* is grounded upon two premises: being a Muslim minority and having citizenship in a non-Muslim country. The simultaneous belonging of American Muslims to both Muslim and American identities incites the FCNA in espousing the concept of *fiqh al-aqalliyyāt* as its main methodological mechanism. While the FCNA contributes to the development of *fiqh al-aqalliyyāt* in the American context, the concept of *fiqh al-aqalliyyāt* enables the Council to provide *fatwās* that intend to integrate Muslims into American society as active citizens of the country. FCNA members therefore exert their efforts in providing *fatwās* that generally support the peaceful coexistence of American Muslims and non-Muslim Americans within the contemporary American context.

158 ibid 66
159 ibid 73.
160 Siddiqi (n 153).

The influence of the dual identity of American Muslims upon fatwās

The sense of simultaneous belonging to American and Muslim identities has raised some Islamic legal problems, including participating in the American political system, serving in the American military, being loyal Americans and contributing to American welfare. On these issues, the FCNA has moderately adopted a quite flexible, pragmatic and alternative approach that primarily evidences the possibilities of congruence between what the American democratic secular legal system guarantees for Muslims and what Islamic legal and ethical values desire for Muslims to live a sharī'a-oriented life. American Muslims reside in a society in which a secular legal system is applied by a non-Muslim authority and in which there is officially no room for the Islamic law. Within this society, the FCNA intends to provide applicable *fatwās* that take into account obligations and responsibilities rooted in the belongingness of American Muslims to both identities.

The fact of residing in a society where Islamic law is not applied has incited FCNA members to consider their citizenship rights and duties in terms of Islamic law. At the time, when the FCNA was under al-Alwani's presidency, the issue of the political participation of American Muslims in American politics was evaluated, and the Council issued a *fatwā* that allows American Muslims to vote in American political elections.[161] The *fatwā* upon this issue reflects the application of al-Alwani's concept of *fiqh al-aqalliyyāt*. It begins with a succinct statement regarding its topic and then refers to four premises upon which the *fatwā* is based. These are to protect and develop American Muslims rights as American citizens, to support Muslims around the world, to proselytise Islam's message and to demonstrate the universality of Islam.[162] The religious impartiality of the American secular system provides Muslims with opportunities of practicing their religion, conveying the message of Islam to non-Muslims and manifesting Islam's universal and humanitarian sides in this continent. All these possibly emerge as contextual factors that orient FCNA members to render the participation of American Muslims in American politics obligatory from the perspective of Islamic law. The *fatwā* states:

161 Taha Jabir al-Alwani, 'Muslims' Participation in the US Political Life' <https://archive.islamonline.net/?p=6367> accessed 13 September 2017; Ahmed Bedier, 'What Islamic Scholars Say about Voting' <http://unitedvoices.com/docs/Islamic-perspective-voting1.pdf> accessed 08 November 2020. Even though Hassan claims that this *fatwā* was issued by al-Alwani, Parray and Kutty propose that the FCNA issued the *fatwā* at the time when al-Alwani was the president of the Council. Therefore, the *fatwā* is evaluated as one of the FCNA's *fatwās* by the author. See Hassan (n 127) 114–117; Parray (n 3) 89; Faisal Kutty, '"Sharia" Courts in Canada: A Delayed Opportunity for the Indigenization of Islamic Legal Rulings' in Anna C. Korteweg and Jennifer A. Selby (eds), *Debating Sharia: Islam, Gender Politics, and Family Law Arbitration* (University Toronto Press 2012) 138.

162 Alwani, 'Muslims' Participation' (n 161).

> Our participation is an obligation in Islam, and not merely "a right" that we can choose to forfeit at will. It affords us the opportunity to protect our human rights, guarantee the fulfilment of our needs, and work for the improvement of living conditions for Muslims and non-Muslims in America and abroad.[163]

Political participation is described as an obligation (or a religious duty) that must be fulfilled by every American Muslim, so it is not a right that people can renounce. This makes political participation an individual obligation (*farḍ al-'ayn*) that enables American Muslims to protect their rights, disseminate the universal message of Islam and improve the interests of Muslims around the world.

The four premises in the *fatwā* are linked to the legal principle of *maṣlaḥa* and the legal maxim of opting for the lesser of two harms (*ikhtiyār akhaf al-ḍarārayn*). The legal principle of *maṣlaḥa* is applied with the intent of improving the welfare of not only American Muslims and other Muslims around the world but also non-Muslim Americans.[164] Political participation provides Muslims with many opportunities in maintaining their human rights, fulfilling their exigencies and improving their living conditions – this emerges as a main consideration in employing the legal principle of *maṣlaḥa*. The emphasis upon the betterment of the public interest of both Muslim and non-Muslim Americans can therefore be accepted as the influence of considerations regarding the belongingness of American Muslims to both American and Muslim identities. Additionally, the *fatwā* implies that the political participation of American Muslims provides more benefit to them than their non-participation.[165] In this regard, the legal maxim of *ikhtiyār akhaf al-ḍarārayn* is used as a legal methodology in identifying the choice less harmful to American Muslims. Al-Badawi, an executive member of the FCNA, observes:

> in terms of relative harm and benefit which is a rule of Shariah it may be collective wisdom, for example, of Muslim voters that one of them would do even greater harm to Muslim causes than the other … Well in that case, obviously, the lesser of two harms, i.e. electing or voting for someone who will do less harm to Muslims, obviously would be much better than sitting on the side-line and just criticizing both and doing nothing about it.[166]

American Muslims are counselled to participate in American politics with the intention of contributing to the wellbeing of this society as per their American identity. At the same time, they are also advised to fulfil their political participation right to promote the dissemination of Islam's universal values pursuant to their

163 Bedier (n 161).

164 ibid.

165 Uriya Shavit, '"The Lesser of Two Evils": Islamic Law and the Emergence of a Broad Agreement on Muslim Participation in Western Political Systems' (2020) 8 *Contemporary Islam* 245–246.

166 Bedier (n 161).

Muslim identity. Not only does such participation strengthen and enhance the welfare of Muslims and non-Muslims but it also helps to promote Islamic universal values in American society. The fact that actively engaging in the political process opens ways for Muslims to oppose religiously prohibited acts and wrongs (e.g., abortion and drug abuse) emerges as another legal reasoning for the obligation of American Muslims' political participation.[167] FCNA members therefore intend to integrate the American and Muslim identities of American Muslims instead of dichotomising them.

Another knotty issue that originates in the dual identity of American Muslims is the participation of Muslims in the American military. The Council received a question from Muhammad Abd al-Rasheed, a Muslim chaplain in the American military. The question is related to the permissibility of serving in the American military at the time when the United States waged war against the Taliban regime in Afghanistan.[168] After receiving the question, the FCNA did not immediately provide a direct answer to the question. Instead, the Council sought a *fatwā* from prominent Muslim scholars across the world, so the question was transmitted to some Muslim scholars from different Muslim and non-Muslim countries.[169] This may be the result of either the small size of the FCNA's budget or the difficult nature of the question and the Council's desire to obtain more credibility. A few weeks after the attacks of September 11, a group of prominent Muslim scholars across the world issued a *fatwā* that gives permission to American Muslim soldiers to participate in the efforts of the American military against the perpetrators of the attack, even if this involves a declaration of war against a Muslim country.[170] This *fatwā* was then sent by the FCNA to the questioner.[171]

167 Besides these Islamic legal principles and reasoning, the *fatwā* also refers to the first emigration of Muslims to Ethiopia as a legal precedent to justify its position, regardless of the categorical differences between the two experiences in terms of historical conditions. The objections of some Muslim scholars to the positive participation of Muslims in the politics of non-Muslim countries are evaluated in a critical way in the *fatwā*. This criticism may give a further insight into the importance of political participation and the convergence and divergence between the classical Islamic legal opinions and contemporary Islamic legal approaches. See Alwani, 'Muslims' Participation' (n 161). For a more detailed analysis of this *fatwā*, refer to Hassan (n 127) 114–117.

168 Nafi (n 22) 78–79; Nimer (n 4) 167–168; The Middle East Media Research Institute (MEMRI), 'Terror in America (23) Muslim Soldiers in the U.S. Armed Forces in Afghanistan: To Fight or Not to Fight?' <https://www.memri.org/reports/terror-america-23-muslim-soldiers-us-armed-forces-afghanistan-fight-or-not-fight> accessed 15 September 2017.

169 The Middle East Media Research Institute (MEMRI) (n 168).

170 It may be stated that the context and time in which the *fatwā* was issued have important influences and repercussions in shaping the mind of Muslims scholars who issued and approved this *fatwā*. Rather than focusing on this interplay between the context and *fatwā*, the author gives weight to how address the concept of citizenship in the *fatwā*. For more detailed contextual analysis, see Nafi (n 22) 78–116.

171 The *fatwā* was signed by five Muslim scholars, Yusuf al-Qaradawi, Tariq al-Bishri, Muhammad S. al-Awa, Haytam al-Khayyat and Fahmi Huwaidi. The approval of the five proficient Muslim scholars increases its credibility as a collective *fatwā*. However, some of the Muslim scholars who had signed the *fatwā* later changed their minds and issued a new *fatwā* that prohibits the participa-

The *fatwā* presents the legal effort of Muslim scholars who address some of the intricacies that ensue from the major changes in the world system (i.e., the concept of nation-state). It begins with condemning the September 11 attacks against America. This condemnation is grounded upon the Qur'anic principle related to the value and sanctity of human life. In accordance with the Q. 5:32, it is identified that killing one innocent human being constitutes an act of aggression against all humanity.[172] After being grounded upon the legal reasoning of the Q. 5:32, which prohibits the killing of innocents, the *fatwā* states that if this terrorist attack was evaluated from the perspective of Islamic law, the perpetrators and those who aided and abetted them through financing or other means would be punished in accordance with the rulings for the crime of waging war against society (*ḥirāba*).[173]

Instead of ascertaining the appropriate punishment for the perpetrators, the question is implicitly related to the loyalty of an American Muslim soldier as an American citizen: should his fidelity be to the Muslim *umma* as a whole or to his own country, America? In this regard, the *fatwā* implies that the loyalty of American Muslim soldiers in a time of war should be demonstrated to his own country. It is stated:

> The Muslim here is a part of a whole. If he resigns his position, his departure will result in a greater harm, not only for him but also for the Muslim community in his country – and here there are many millions of them. Moreover, even if fighting causes him spiritual or psychological discomfort, this personal hardship must be endured for sake of the greater public good, as the jurisprudential (*fiqhī*) rule states.
>
> Furthermore, the questioner inquiries about the possibility of the Muslim military personnel in the American armed forces serving in the back lines—such as in the relief services' sector and similar assignments. If such a request is granted by the authorities, without reservation or harm to the soldiers, or to other American Muslim citizens, then they should request that. Otherwise, if such a request raises doubt about their allegiance or loyalty, casts suspicions, presents them with false accusations, harms their future careers, raises misgivings about their patriotism, or similar sentiments, then it is not permissible to ask for that.[174]

---

tion of American Muslim soldiers in the war against Afghanistan and abrogated the previous one. See the Middle East Media Research Institute (MEMRI) (n 168).

172 The moral and legal foundation of this principle is the Q. 5:32. It reads: "On that basis, we ordained for the Children of Israel that if anyone killed a person – Unless it be for murder or for spreading mischief in the land – it would be as if he killed all mankind (the people): And if anyone saved a life, it would be as if he saved the life of all mankind (the people). Then although there came to them Our messengers with Clear Signs, yet even after that, many of them continued to commit excess (and do injustices) in the land."

173 Nafi (n 22) 80–81; the Middle East Media Research Institute (MEMRI) (n 168).

174 Cited from Nafi (n 22) 81–82.

The principle of *maṣlaḥa* and the two legal maxims (*ikhtiyār akhaf al-ḍararayn* and *ḍarūra*) are applied as methodological instruments in legitimating the participation of American Muslim military personnel in a war against other Muslim countries. In this case, the American Muslim community as a whole is acknowledged as a collective entity, so their collective interests are prioritised over the interests of other Muslim individuals. While the interests of the American Muslim community in their non-Muslim environment are at the centre of the *fatwā* upon the ground that the *maṣlaḥa* must secure benefit to the people as a whole,[175] the collective interests of the Muslim *umma* are inadvertently overlooked.

In the *fatwā*, some defects can be identified in the use of Islamic legal methodologies. In the first instance, the legal maxim of *ikhtiyār akhaf al-ḍararayn* is employed to ascertain the lesser harm, but the identification of the less detrimental one is partially obscured or mistakenly specified in some sense. If American Muslim soldiers feel conscientiously uneasy in fighting against other Muslims, they should prefer to choose one of the different taskings that include serving in non-combatant duties and using the right to conscientious objection. However, if such preference leads to a greater harm not only for him but also for the American Muslim community, it is not permissible to benefit from these different taskings.[176] It is tenuously determined that the harm that may be caused by the requests of American Muslim soldiers to serve in non-combatant positions may be greater than the harm that will ensue from the participation of American Muslim soldiers in a war against a Muslim majority country. The *fatwā* makes the defence of the home country morally and legally obligatory for American Muslim military personnel regardless of the religious composition of the country that commits aggression against the United States. The public interests of American Muslims are preferred instead of the common interests of the Muslim *umma*, so this infringes the generality condition of *maṣlaḥa*.[177]

In the second instance, despite the fact that the *fatwā* refers to the legal maxim of *ḍarūra* that necessity makes the forbidden permissible, this is a defective attribution. Bassam Jarar alludes to this obscure point in the *fatwā* and states: "it is known that the necessity does not permit murder."[178] Considering the restrictive conditions in applying the legal maxim of *ḍarūra*, it is paradoxical and defective to state that the participation of American Muslim soldiers in a war against another Muslim country is a necessity. This is because such fighting that causes the killing of innocent Muslims is clearly forbidden by Islamic law even under duress and necessity.[179] The *fatwā* therefore mistakenly overlooks that the involvement

175 Mohammad Hashim Kamali, *Principles of Islamic Jurisprudence* (St Edmundsbury Press 1991) 274.

176 Nafi (n 22) 81–83, 94–95, 113.

177 One of the conditions in applying the principle of *maṣlaḥa* is that "the *maṣlaḥa* must be general (*kulliyah*) in that it secures benefit, or prevents harm, to the people as a whole and not to a particular person or group of persons." Kamali (n 175) 241.

178 Cited from the Middle East Media Research Institute (MEMRI) (n 168).

179 Duress and necessity can be a justification for the suspension of the punishments related to the

of American Muslim soldiers would lead to the spilling of Muslim blood that includes innocent Muslims'. This raises a quandary regarding the use of the legal maxim of *ḍarūra*. Despite these methodological defects, the *fatwā* approved by the Council engages with the thorny issue regarding a clash between faith that originates in Muslim identity and patriotism that ensues from American identity. The *fatwā* is explicitly grounded upon the idea that citizenship in the nation-state system forms a covenant of rights and obligations between the individual and his country. It is therefore concluded that American Muslim military personnel should fulfil their duties with an unequivocal expression of loyalty to their home country.

The idea of being loyal to America that traces back to the concept of having citizenship therein brings out the difficulty in outlining a religious life that is formulated in accordance with the inherited Islamic legal rulings within the borders of this new environment. The secular legal system of America makes it necessary for American Muslims to pledge formal allegiance to the American state. The dual identity of American Muslims therefore engenders another collision between the allegiance to the non-Muslim state and the traditional Islamic allegiance to the Muslim *umma*.[180] On September 24–25, 2011, the FCNA's general body meeting was held in Virginia, and the resolution of the FCNA, titled "On Being Faithful Muslims and Loyal Americans," was issued at the end of the meeting. In the resolution, it is underscored that the consideration of being a resident in America explicitly entails an acceptance of obeying American legal regulations. It states:

> As a body of Islamic scholars, we the members of FCNA believe that it is false and misleading to suggest that there is a contradiction between being faithful Muslims committed to God (Allah) and being loyal American citizens.

ḥadd (fixed crimes) and *qiṣāṣ* (retaliation crimes). In accordance with the general rule, the person who unlawfully acts under duress is not punished with the penalties of *ḥadd* or *qiṣāṣ*, but the opinions of the earlier Muslim scholars differ upon the question of whether duress is also a justification (or one of the restrictive conditions) in homicide cases. Upon this issue, the majority of Muslim scholars state that "one may not sacrifice the life of another person in order to save one's own life, for it is generally accepted that during a famine it is not permitted to kill a person in order to survive by eating his flesh." Rudolph Peters, *Crime and Punishment in Islamic Law: Theory and Practice from the Sixteenth to the Twenty-First Century* (Cambridge University Press 2005) 23–24. See also Luqman Zakariyah, *Legal Maxims in Islamic Criminal Law: Theory and Applications* (Brill 2015) 139, 140–141, 150; Hayrettin Karaman, *İslam'in Işıginda Günün Meseleleri* (İz Yayınçılık 2012) 230–249; Emine Enise Yakar, 'The Concept of *Maṣlaḥa* in the Thought of Hayrettin Karaman' (MA thesis, University of Exeter 2014) 31–32; the Middle East Media Research Institute (MEMRI) (n 168).

180 Within the Islamic legal framework, one of the oft-cited traditional positions regarding loyalty and affiliation is to avoid establishing friendship with non-Muslims and obeying non-Islamic forms of legal and political authority. The traditional understanding is that *walā* (loyalty and affiliation) is exclusively between believers while the attitude towards unbelievers is *barā'* (disavowal and disassociation). See Nafi (n 22) 91; March (n 123) 2842–2843; Said Hassan, 'Law-Abiding Citizen: Recent *Fatwas* on Muslim Minorities' Loyalty to Western Nations' (2015) 105 (4) *The Muslim World* 516.

> Islamic teachings require respect of the laws of the land where Muslims live as minorities, including the Constitution and the Bill of Rights, so long as there is no conflict with Muslims' obligation for obedience to God.[181]

The consideration of being loyal to the United States by American Muslims is grounded upon a kind of contractual belonging. The fulfilment of obligations and duties which ensue from the compact of citizenship is acknowledged as a religious obligation that requires loyalty to contracts.[182] In the resolution, the permissibility of the permanent residency of Muslims in America is precisely attributed to the reality of their right to freely practice their religion therein. It is not permissible for Muslims to reside in non-Muslim countries in accordance with the inherited rulings if they are prevented from freely observing their religious duties. The operative legal reasoning of these inherited rulings loses its validity due to the fact that the American secular legal system provides Muslims and other religious communities an opportunity to freely practice their respective religions. The resolution reiterates that the modern understanding of loyalty (national loyalty) does not clash with religious loyalty insofar as the contract of citizenship does not constrain one from practicing religion or the freedom of a Muslim to live his or her faith. It can be stated that the religious neutrality of the American secular legal system allays FCNA members' apprehension in expressing that American Muslims should offer their loyalty to America.

The resolution explicitly incorporates "respect to human, civil and political rights," "imperative of just and peaceful coexistence" and "rights of legitimate self-defence against aggression and oppression" into the principle of *maqāṣid al-sharī'a* which is basically to protect religion, life, reason, lineage and property.[183] It is possible to assert that a systematic expansion can be observed within the scope of *maqāṣid al-sharī'a*. FCNA members continuously accentuate the confluence between the principle of *maqāṣid al-sharī'a* and the US Constitution by alluding to the universally accepted values of the two. American Muslims are induced to obey American legal regulations through the idea of confluence between democratic values and Islamic legal principles that is corroborated by the expanded principle of *maqāṣid al-sharī'a*. Nonetheless, American Muslims are also exhorted to maintain their distinctive Muslim identity. The resolution states:

> It is fully compatible with Islam for Muslims to integrate positively in the society of which they are equal citizens, without losing their identity as Muslims (just as Jews and Christians do not lose their religious identity doing the same).[184]

181 Siddiqi (n 153).

182 Even though the Qur'anic verse is not directly cited, the related verses on this issue are highly likely the Q. 2:177, 5:1 and 17:34.

183 Siddiqi (n 153).

184 ibid.

It is therefore plausible to assert that the main consideration of FCNA members can be identified as integrating Muslims into American society and developing a collaborative dialogue with other American citizens – this reflects the intention of the FCNA to form an identity that equally considers the responsibilities that ensue from both American and Muslim identities.

Generally, the Council states that the secure American environment that recognises the freedom of Muslims in practicing their religion obliges American Muslims to respect the legal regulations of this system and to fulfil their citizenship duties towards their home country. Meanwhile, American Muslims are also counselled to protect their Muslim identity by abstaining from those secular values and social practices that transgress and obliterate their Islamic legal and ethical values.[185] Even if the three *fatwās* appear to bring American identity into the forefront rather than the Muslim identity in many respects, the actual aim can be identified as to provide Islamic legal solutions for the complexities that are rooted in both the modern concept of citizenship and the dual identity of American Muslims. With regard to this point, El Fadl laments the partiality and sympathy of the Council to the American legal and political system ("[The FCNA] is known for analysing Islamic law for the American military and media and other non-Muslim organizations rather than responding to the needs of Muslims").[186] From some perspectives, El Fadl's criticism may echo the political motivations behind the *fatwās*, but he inadvertently overlooks the Council's effort in addressing the most controversial issues that confront American Muslims. He describes the FCNA as a religious institution that just produces Islamic legal justifications for obedience to the American political policies and legal regulations. Unlike El Fald, Afsaruddin alludes to the integrative and ethical orientation of the FCNA's *fatwās*. She observes:

> The fatwas [issued by the FCNA] stress the compatibility of basic Islamic juridical principles and practices and the objectives of Islamic law with those of secular American law, creating a legal and moral rationale for American Muslims to be loyal to their country and fostering an ethic of committed citizenship.[187]

In accordance with Afsaruddin's statement, it may be asserted that the Council displays a diligent and consistent predisposition to produce *fatwās* for the likely complexities that originate in the dual identity of American Muslims and their relationships with American political authority.

The examined *fatwās* evidence that the FCNA pursues a strategy that intends to gain American Muslims an identity that combines their American and Muslim belongingness. In this regard, American Muslims are counselled to adopt a

185 Al-Alwani, *Towards a Fiqh* (n 97) XVII, 33.
186 Cited from Glaberson (n 37).
187 Afsaruddin (n 6) 181.

positive, confident and integrationist approach regarding their place in society by forsaking the notion of minority status. The Council also provides more concrete and realistic *fatwās* related to the appropriate Islamic legal attitudes towards non-Muslim forms of rule. It is possible to infer that the role of the FCNA, when evaluating issues that ensue from the dual identity of American Muslims, is to determine which cultural and secular values and legal regulations of America to be adopted are obligatory, recommended, neutral, reprehensible and forbidden in accordance with the authoritative texts of Islamic law, the Qur'an and Sunna. The legal principles of *maqāṣid al-sharī'a* and *maṣlaḥa* are mainly employed when FCNA members engage with the problems of political participation in a non-Muslim polity, contribution and fidelity to a non-Muslim state, along with the issues regarding citizenship. These two emerge as the key Islamic legal principles in providing appropriate *fatwās* while the FCNA engages with questions that are directed by American Muslims.

Conclusion

The twentieth century witnessed the immigration of large numbers of Muslims to America. The increase in the number of Muslims generated an American Muslim identity that combines the belongingness of these immigrated Muslims to American and Muslim identities. Muslims who have this identity have begun to face new problems that need practicable *fatwās* to maintain their lives in accordance with both Islamic and American legal regulations. The Fiqh Committee of the ISNA was reorganised as the FCNA in 1986 with the intention of better evaluating these problems of American Muslims within the scope of Islamic law. Since its establishment, the FCNA has served as an Islamic legal establishment that exerts a substantial effort in producing sound and authentic Islamic legal knowledge and *fatwās* with regard to the social, cultural, moral and legal dilemmas and contemporary issues that American Muslims face.

The requirement of applicable *fatwās* induces the FCNA to evaluate issues by taking into consideration contextual factors of American Muslims. The Council members earnestly seek to provide Islamic legal solutions that reconcile Islamic legal principles with American legal regulations and democratic values. It can be precisely asserted that the FCNA develops a complex stance towards the role and function of Islamic law in American Muslims' lives through applying mainly the legal principles of *maqāṣid al-sharī'a* and *maṣlaḥa* in the process of issuing Islamic legal resolutions and *fatwās* in response to the questions directed by American Muslims. In accordance with the concept of *fiqh al-aqallliyāt* that was envisaged by al-Alwani, the FCNA focuses primarily upon two things: understanding the circumstances of American Muslims who desire to live a sharī'a-oriented life and providing practicable *fatwās* for American Muslims within American secular democratic society.

In the *fatwās*, the emphasis upon the dual identity of American Muslims may be detected as a reflection of the social, national, legal and political influences of American society. This reflection possibly implies a paradigm shift that evidences a predisposition towards the acceptance of America as a "homeland" instead of a "non-Muslim land." With the intention of instituting a balance between Muslim and American identities, the FCNA espouses the legal principle of *maqāṣid al-sharī'a* that is extended with the incorporation of other considerations (i.e., respect to human, civil and political rights, protection of Muslims' interests and good representation of Islam). The *fatwās* issued by the Council meet the exigencies and needs of American Muslims while providing insight into the scholarly efforts of FCNA members in dispelling the misperceptions related to Islamic law that qualify it as a hegemonic, anti-democratic, anti-liberal and patriarchal legal system.

Within the context of America, the FCNA espouses a methodology that accommodates Islamic law to the society in which American Muslims reside – this can be termed a practice of adaptation to and negotiation with the contextual realities. The Islamic legal resolutions and *fatwās* issued by the Council reaffirm the flexible character of Islamic law, so they are not a production of newly invented Islamic legal methodologies. Instead, the FCNA predominantly employs the legal principle of *maqāṣid al-sharī'a* that had already existed in the classical Islamic legal methodology. This principle is rejuvenated to issue applicable *fatwās* for American Muslims within the scope of *fiqh al-aqalliyyāt*. In this regard, the FCNA has espoused the concept of *fiqh al-aqalliyyāt* in the process of issuing *fatwās* and developed an intermeshing tripartite mechanism. In the first instance, the Council accentuates the necessity of contextualising the Islamic legal tradition and reiterates that the inherited Islamic legal rulings, especially those concerning *mu'āmalāt*, are the result of their own contexts. In the second instance, the permanent resident status of American Muslims is normalised through the acknowledgement that American secular, democratic and liberal values are in harmony with Islamic legal principles and ethical values. In the last instance, the Council adopts a form of legal thought that reconciles the American and Muslim identities of American Muslims and that accommodates Islamic legal principles to American secular democratic society while issuing its *fatwās*.

4 Influence of *madhhab* affiliation and social values

Saudi Arabia's Dār al-Iftā', Turkey's Diyanet and America's FCNA have been selected as case studies with the intention of bringing out interactions between Islamic legal methodologies and divergent cultural, legal, political and social contexts. As the first, second and third chapters have demonstrated in more detail, they provide very different styles of producing Islamic legal decisions, resolutions and opinions (*fatwās*) in the twenty-first century. There is a dynamic, fluid and organic connection between these institutions and the contexts in which they function – this highlights the importance of distinguishing one's *fatwā* from the context in which one operates and the influence of contextual elements upon the use of Islamic legal methodologies.

The three institutions hold different Islamic legal positions upon issues which include celebrating the Prophet's birthday and other religiously important days, performing religious marriage and divorce, establishing relationships with non-Muslims, participating in politics, donating and transplanting organs, accepting democracy and approving Muslim women's leadership. In evaluating these and other issues, the institutions sometimes formulate different and even diametrically opposed *fatwās*. This raises the question of whether they can even be considered to be part of the same religious tradition. Although all the three institutions refer to the foundational authoritative sources (Qur'an and Sunna) and put in place Islamic legal methodologies that enable the resolution of problems confronting Muslims, they diverge in their analysis of how the foundational texts should be applied and their assessment of contemporary Islamic legal issues.

Differences of opinion (*ikhtilāf*) between the three institutions essentially link to the four main thematic factors set out in the introduction of the book. This chapter and the next chapter compare the three institutions by referencing the four thematic perspectives and intend to bring out the interaction between Islamic legal methodologies and social context in clearer perspective. These four thematic factors are:

1. The interaction between the *madhhab* affiliation in Saudi Arabia, Turkey and the American Muslim community and the Islamic legal methodologies, theories and principles adopted by the Dār al-Iftā', the Diyanet and the FCNA,

DOI: 10.4324/9781003037637-4

2. The influence of cultural and social practices within the three societies upon the issued *fatwās*,
3. The impact of the legal systems upon the functioning of *fatwās* in Saudi and Turkish societies and the American Muslim community,
4. The influence of the political systems of the three countries upon the issued *fatwās*.

Through a more sustained engagement with these thematic elements, the interaction between the Islamic legal methodologies espoused by the three institutions and their different social contexts is analysed. With the intent of evincing this interaction, specific emphasis is placed on the issue of how the three institutions interpret the fundamental sources and which Islamic legal methodologies are applied in their respective environments.

Scholars working in these institutions seek to apply the immutable and fundamental principles of the authoritative sources to their respective environments – this requires a deep knowledge of Islamic law and also an understanding of a particular issue or problem in its specific context. When scholars evaluate context-specific problems in order to provide applicable *fatwās*, their juristic legal thinking and outlook are influenced – whether directly or indirectly – by the cultural, social, legal and political context of the institutions. To take one example, the Dār al-Iftā', the Diyanet and the FCNA adopt the jurisprudential view that Muslims should be fair, kind and righteous in their dealings with non-Muslims.[1] However, in applying this principle in Saudi Arabia, Turkey and America, they are most likely influenced by their respective environments which

1 In addressing the relationship with non-Muslims, the Dār al-Iftā' places a particularly strong emphasis upon just and fair dealings with non-Muslims. See Muslims Dealing with Non-Muslims, in *Fatwas of Ibn Baz*, 6: 283–285 <http://www.alifta.net/Search/ResultDetails.aspx?languagename=en&lang=en&view=result&fatwaNum=&FatwaNumID=&ID=735&searchScope=14&SearchScopeLevels1=&SearchScopeLevels2=&highLight=1&SearchType=exact&SearchMoesar=false&bookID=&LeftVal=0&RightVal=0&simple=&SearchCriteria=allwords&PagePath=&siteSection=1&searchkeyword=116104101032112101111112108101032111020321161041010320981111111107#firstKeyWordFound> accessed 03 April 2018. The Diyanet's position upon this issue was partially revealed when the decision "the Religious and Legal Position of Houses of Worship pertaining to Non-Muslims in Islamic Tradition" was published in 2012. Here the Diyanet commits to protecting the rights of non-Muslims resident in a Muslim country and counsels Muslims to demonstrate justice, morality and righteousness in their relationships with non-Muslims. See Din İşleri Yüsek Kurulu Kararları, 'İslam Geleneğinde Gayr-ı Müslim Mabetlerin Dini ve Hukuki Durumu' <https://kurul.diyanet.gov.tr/Karar-Mutalaa-Cevap/4373/islam-geleneginde-gayr-i-muslim-mabetlerinin-dini-ve-hukuki-durumu> accessed 03 April 2018. The FCNA issued an article ('Muslim/Mon-Muslim Relations') that outlines the general Islamic principles regarding the relationships with non-Muslims. At the outset, it puts an emphasis upon the importance of interfaith dialogue and then identifies a methodology to understand the Qur'anic principles regarding the relationships between Muslims and non-Muslims. It is stated that peace, coexistence, justice, respect and compassion should be the main principles related to the engagement with non-Muslims. See Jamal Badawi, 'Muslim/Non-Muslim Relations' <http://fiqhcouncil.org/muslim-non-muslim-relations/> accessed 23 November 2020.

function to both customarily and socially delineate the scope of possible relations with non-Muslims.

More specifically, the question of protecting non-Muslim sanctuaries (e.g., churches and synagogues) and of allocating places of worship to non-Muslim citizens was evaluated by the Dār al-Iftā' and the Diyanet, but they formulated antipodal juristic views upon this specific issue. The *fatwā* issued by the Dār al-Iftā' clearly states that it is forbidden to build houses of worship for religions other than Islam – this applies because such initiatives may be taken to indicate an acceptance of their faith, along with an associated commitment to their community.[2] The Diyanet's decision (upon "the Religious and Legal Position of Houses of Worship Pertaining to Non-Muslims in Islamic Tradition") can be directly contrasted with the Dār al-Iftā's *fatwā*. Here the Diyanet implicitly argues that it is obligatory for a Muslim state to protect sanctuaries belonging to non-Muslims and to allocate places of worship to non-Muslims resident in the state.[3] Despite the fact that the FCNA does not specifically address the issue related to sanctuaries belonging to non-Muslims, the issue of the relationship between Muslims and non-Muslims is evaluated by the Council. It refers indirectly to the necessity of recognising the freedom of religion of non-Muslims and respecting their belief upon the ground of the Qur'anic general principles (acceptance of plurality and diversity in human societies, prohibition of compulsion in faith, universal peaceful coexistence and peaceful dialogue).[4]

Even though the institutions referred to similar Islamic legal proofs (the Qur'an and Sunna) and concurred upon the basis that Muslims should engage justly, kindly and righteously with non-Muslims, the Dār al-Iftā' issued fundamentally opposed *fatwās*. Despite the fact that the Diyanet and the FCNA converged upon the same stance, their interpretations of the Qur'an and Sunna displayed some differences. The Diyanet adopts a more traditional understanding that holds the Muslim state responsible for protecting and providing places of worship belonging to non-Muslims while the FCNA engages with the issue within the scope of plurality and diversity in human societies. This divergence can be attributed to the interaction between Islamic legal methodologies and different cultural, legal, political and social contexts.

2 Fatwā No. 21413 in *Fatwas of the Permanent Committee*, 1: 468–471 <http://www.alifta.net/Search/ResultDetails.aspx?languagename=en&lang=en&view=result&fatwaNum=&FatwaNumID=&ID=10807&searchScope=7&SearchScopeLevels1=&SearchScopeLevels2=&highLight=1&SearchType=exact&SearchMoesar=false&bookID=&LeftVal=0&RightVal=0&simple=&SearchCriteria=allwords&PagePath=&siteSection=1&searchkeyword=067104117114099104101115032105110032065114097098105097110032080101110105110115117108097#firstKeyWordFound> accessed 12 November 2017. This *fatwā* was discussed in Chapter 1 when explaining the clashes between the Saudi Government's policies and the Dār al-Iftā's legal stances. For more detailed analysis of this *fatwā*, see Chapter 1.

3 Din İşleri Yüsek Kurulu Kararları (n 1).

4 Badawi, 'Muslim/Non-Muslim' (n 1).

The divergence of *fatwās* pertaining to similar and almost identical questions is particularly pronounced in relation to social transactions (*mu'āmalāt*). This can be understood as a further demonstration of how context impacts on *fatwās* issued by the three institutions. It seems plausible that the sources of divergence within *fatwās* do not originate within fundamental Islamic principles and sources but can instead be traced back to interpretative technics and legal methodologies which derive from wider contextual influences upon the three institutions. While the Dār al-Iftā', the Diyanet and the FCNA are evaluated in relation to each other with reference to the four thematic factors, the official Islamic legal decisions, resolutions and *fatwās* issued by the institutions are used to provide additional insight into each thematic comparative point. The chapter focuses specifically upon the influence of the *madhhab* affiliation within the societies and the effect of prevalent social and cultural practices within the three countries over the three institutions and their *fatwās*. In engaging with these points, the chapter seeks to identify differences within the *fatwās* issued by the Dār al-Iftā', the Diyanet and the FCNA and attempts to ascertain the extent to which these differences can be attributed to these two thematic contextual factors.

The influence of *madhhab* affiliation

The *madhhab* affiliation within the societies has served, to a greater or lesser extent, to shape the jurisprudential methodologies of Muslim scholars. Abdul Rahman et al. explicitly point to the possible effect of the *madhhab* affiliation in a society on the practice of *iftā'* by arguing:

> If the dominant legal mindset in a society is tied to the doctrine of a certain *mazhab*, then it will absorb into any activities related to law because fatwa is a reflection of the doctrine of the prevailing legal practice.[5]

With regard to jurisprudential methodologies that are espoused by the three institutions, it is possible to identify a number of differences which have been partially influenced by the *madhhab* affiliation of the Muslim population within the three countries. The Ḥanbalī *madhhab* is the legal school which is predominant within Saudi society.[6] In addition, Saudi Arabia's cultural, political and social environment has been influenced by the Wahhābī movement, which emerged from central Arabia in the mid-eighteenth century.[7] The Ḥanbalī *madhhab* and the Wahhābī religious movement have markedly shaped both the Dār al-Iftā's

5 Noor Naemah Abdul Rahman, Asmak Ab Rahman and Abdul Karim Ali, 'A Study on Students' Research Related to Fatwa Summited at Malaysian Public Universities' (2012) 2 (18) *International Journal of Humanities and Social Science* 129 <http://www.ijhssnet.com/journals/Vol_2_No_18_October_2012/15.pdf> accessed 02 March 2018.

6 Ahmed Akgunduz, *Islamic Law in Theory and Practice* (IUR Press 2010) 285; Frank Vogel, *Islamic Law and Legal System: Studies of Saudi Arabia* (Brill 2000) XV.

7 Vogel (n 6) XVI, 44.

religious understanding and interpretation technic of the authoritative texts. The Dār al-Iftā' has tended to emphasise the jurisprudential methodologies of the Ḥanbalī *madhhab*, in addition to creating an opening for three Sunni *madhhabs*' opinions and methodologies upon controversial issues. This has been done under the practice of determining the preponderant opinion (*tarjīḥ*) if the strongest proof (*dalīl*) is identified in another *madhhab*'s legal ruling or opinion.[8]

Conversely, Turkey's Diyanet chooses to silently pursue the jurisprudential methodologies and legal views of the Ḥanafī *madhhab* – the institution maintains that this is particularly necessary because the majority of the Turkish Muslim population adheres to the Ḥanafī *madhhab*, which has historically exerted a strong influence over mainstream custom, social practices and tradition.[9] Despite the fact that the Ḥanafī *madhhab*'s legal methodologies and opinions have been predominant within the practice of *iftā'*, the needs of followers of other *madhhabs*, other religious groups and sects are taken into account to as great an extent as possible. When the opinions and views of other Sunni *madhhabs* appear better suited to the immediate issue at hand, most notably in ritual practices (*'ibādāt*) or classical Islamic legal issues discussed by the earlier Muslim scholars, the Diyanet generally presents the views of these schools along with the position of the Ḥanafī *madhhab* by leaving the final decision to the individual.[10] When contemporary religious issues are instead the main preoccupation, the Diyanet mainly practices two variations of *ijtihād* (*ijtihād* through the *takhrīj* method and *ijtihād inshā'ī*) upon a collective basis.

In contrast to Saudi and Turkish societies, American Muslims demonstrate diversity in their *madhhab* affiliation, so it is quite difficult to identify the dominant *madhhab* affiliation within the American Muslim community.[11] This diversity implicitly induces the FCNA to espouse the concept of the Islamic jurisprudence of Muslim minority (*fiqh al-aqalliyyāt*) in the process of issuing *fatwās*.[12] The embrace of the concept of *fiqh al-aqalliyyāt* alleviates the possible complexities that will ensue from the *madhhab* affiliation of American Muslims. Within the scope of *fiqh al-aqalliyyāt*, the FCNA pursues a jurisprudential methodology that is underpinned by the two legal principles of *maqāṣid al-sharī'a* and *maṣlaḥa* while considering the realities and circumstances of American Muslims.[13] While the mainstream *madhhab* affiliations within Saudi and Turkish societies press

8 Muhammad al-Atawneh, *Wahhābī Islam Facing the Challenges of Modernity: Dār al-Iftā in the Modern Saudi State* (Brill 2010) 77–81.

9 Mustafa Bülent Dadaş, 'Kuruluşundan Günümüze Din İşleri Yüksek Kurulunun Fetva Siyaseti' (2015) 13 (25–26) *Türkiye Araştırmaları Literatür Dergisi* 50–51.

10 ibid 53–54.

11 Sarah M. Fallon, 'Justice for All: American Muslims, Sharia Law, and Maintaining Comity with American Jurisprudence' (2013) 36 (1) *Boston College International and Comparative Law Review* 156.

12 The chapter only refers to the concept of *fiqh al-aqalliyyāt* that was designed by al-Alwani because the FCNA was established under his presidency and adopted his concept of *fiqh al-aqalliyyāt*.

13 Fiqh Council of North America, 'FCNA Brochure' <http://fiqhcouncil.org/wp-content/uploads/2018/09/FCNABrochure.pdf> accessed 26 December 2020.

themselves with various degrees of intensity upon Islamic legal decisions and *fatwās* issued by the Dār al-Iftā' and the Diyanet, the two institutions' evaluations regarding contemporary issues demonstrate their clear awareness that Islamic law should adjust to changing circumstances. The two institutions therefore adopt a more inclusive approach towards Sunni *madhhabs* (Ḥanafīsm, Mālikīsm, Shāfi'īsm and Ḥanbalīsm) when evaluating new and complex issues. As for the FCNA, it evaluates any issue within the scope of the questioner's *madhhab* while only answering specific questions related to *'ibādāt*. Issues related to *mu'āmalāt* are however generally evaluated by the Council within the scope of *fiqh al-aqalliyyāt*.[14] The diversity in the *madhhab* affiliation of American Muslims emerges as one of the incentives that directs the FCNA to espouse a more tolerant approach towards the affiliated members to the Sunni and Shi'ī *madhhabs* compared to the Dār al-Iftā' and the Diyanet.

The influence of the predominant *madhhab* affiliation of Saudi and Turkish societies can be clearly identified within the *fatwās* issued by the Dār al-Iftā' and the Diyanet. It is possible to identify a number of references, both direct and indirect, to the Islamic legal views of the renowned Muslim jurists and scholars that respectively belong to the Ḥanbalī and Ḥanafī *madhhabs*. The Dār al-Iftā', for example, refers to Ibn Taymiyya's view that sanctioned the execution of a person who refused to give up drinking alcohol when issuing a *fatwā* upon the application of the death penalty to drug smugglers. In the *fatwā*, the Dār al-Iftā's main concern, in referencing Ibn Taymiyya's view, is whether execution is a penalty suited to the penal category of *ta'zīr* (punishments left to the discretion of the ruler or judge). Ibn Taymiyya permitted the ruler a wider scope in exercising his discretionary power to punish miscreants who disrupted law and order, with this even applying in instances where they had not committed murder. While scholars of Ibn Taymiyya's time allowed the death sentence to be applied in instances of spreading anarchy, chaos and sedition (*sā'un fī'l-arḍ fasād*) only if murder had been committed, Ibn Taymiyya allowed the ruler to prescribe death sentence to conspirators (*su'at*), supporters (*a'wina*) and transgressors (*ẓalama*) upon the basis that they were attempting to spread anarchy and terrorise society. With regard to offences where punishment was not fixed, Ibn Taymiyya therefore asserted that the ruler was permitted to punish a culprit through *ta'zīr*, including execution.[15]

In drawing upon Ibn Taymiyya's view, the Dār al-Iftā' places execution within the scope of *ta'zīr* punishments and establishes that relevant judicial agencies, such as the courts, jurisdictional bodies and the Supreme Judicial Council must, once proof of criminal offences was demonstrated, possess the right to sentence drug smugglers and traffickers to the death penalty.[16] To the

14 Yusuf Talal DeLorenzo, 'The Fiqh Councilor of North America' in Yvonne Y. Haddad and John L. Esposito (eds), *Muslims on the Americanization Path?* (Oxford University Press 2000) 71.

15 ibid 72.

16 The BSU decision No. 138 of 02 February 1987 <http://www.alifta.net/Search/ResultDetai

same extent, the *fatwā* calling for the demolition of all churches in the Arabian Peninsula is consolidated by Ibn Taymiyya's legal opinion. Ibn Taymiyya issued a number of rulings which extended to those who believe that churches are Allāh's houses and serve as places for His worship, or those who believe that the worships of the Christians and Jews are true and constitute obedience to His prophets, or those who actively enable places of worship to be opened for them to perform their religion, or those who think their religious practice to be closeness and obedience to Allāh. He qualified all of them as disbelievers.[17] Ibn Taymiyya's legal opinion is used as a supplementary indication in the *fatwā* that further consolidates the legal ruling calling for the removal of churches in the Arabian Peninsula. Islamic legal opinions of Muslim scholars who belong to the Ḥanbalī *madhhab* therefore occupy a privileged place in modern-day official *fatwās* issued by the Dār al-Iftā'.

Similarly, the influences and reflections of the Ḥanafī *madhhab*, which is adhered to by a large majority of the Turkish population, are discernible in the *fatwās* officially issued by the Diyanet. In both theory and practice, the Diyanet (modern neo-Ḥanafī scholars) remains faithful to the doctrines and tenets of Ḥanafīsm by primarily privileging this *madhhab*'s legal opinions – this, however, depends upon the prior condition that these classical views are applicable to contemporary problems confronting Turkish Muslims. To give an example, the Diyanet grounds its *fatwā* upon the Ḥanafī legal opinion when addressing the question of how religious marriage (*nikāḥ*) between a Muslim man and a non-Muslim woman from the People of the Book should be performed, along with the question of whether non-Muslims from the People of the Book can witness this marriage. The *fatwā* states:

> A religious marriage with a non-Muslim woman from the People of the Book is in almost all respects identical to the religious marriage contracted with a Muslim woman – this applies to its form, rulings and implementation. In direct opposition to a marriage in which both parties are Muslims, the Ḥanafī *madhhab* establishes that the witnesses in the marriage of a Muslim man and a non-Muslim woman can be from the People of the Book. Except this, there is no difference in terms of Islamic legal rulings and conditions of marriage while the religious marriage is conducted between the two parties [a Muslim man and a non-Muslim woman].[18]

---

ls.aspx?languagename=ar&lang=ar&view=result&fatwaNum=&FatwaNumID=&ID=3101&searchScope=2&SearchScopeLevels1=&SearchScopeLevels2=&highLight=1&SearchType=exact&SearchMoesar=false&bookID=&LeftVal=0&RightVal=0&simple=&SearchCriteria=allwords&PagePath=&siteSection=1&searchkeyword=217130216177216167216177032217135217138216166216169032217131216168216167216177032216167217132216185217132217133216167216161#firstKeyWordFound> accessed 30 June 2016.

17 Fatwā No. 21413 (n 2).

18 Din İşleri Yüksek Kurulu, *Fetvalar* (Diyanet İşleri Başkanlığı Yayınları 2015) 443.

Taking this *fatwā* and others into account, the Diyanet primarily refers to the position of the Ḥanafī *madhhab* rather than other *madhhabs* when answering questions directed to it. This feature apparently attests to the influence of the mainstream *madhhab* tendency of Turkish society. In a number of official *fatwās*, the Diyanet's approach to the Ḥanafī *madhhab* is generally presented as an act of "imitation (*taqlīd*)" rather than a method of argument (*ṭarīqat istidlāl*) that is applied with the intention of investigating the authoritative texts.[19]

A question pertaining to the neutering of animals is also answered by the Diyanet with direct reference to the traditional Ḥanafī legal opinion. In addressing this issue, it primarily focused on extracting the general principle of Islamic law related to animal rights. The fact that all animals, like humans, have reproductive rights is identified to be the main legal principle associated with the issue. After determining this general legal principle, the Diyanet categorically condemns the neutering of animals without any valid reason and asserts that such actions were legally prohibited by Islamic law ("If there is no valid and legitimate reason, it is illicit to neuter or sterilise animals").[20] However, while the neutering of animals is not encouraged in Islam, it is not completely forbidden. In referring to *al-Fatawā al-Hindiyya*,[21] the Diyanet clarifies that it is acceptable for pets to use contraceptives to prevent their pregnancy, and stray animals (abandoned and homeless animals) can be sterilised in order to control their reproduction upon the condition that this does not damage the ecological balance. The legal views of both Marghīnānī (d. 1197) and Ibn Māza (d. 1141) clearly establish that it is permissible for animals (e.g., calves and goats) to be neutered if it will produce some benefits which include improvement in the animal's health or the production of meat.[22] In referring directly to widely acknowledged *fiqh* works of the Ḥanafī *madhhab*, which include *al-Fatāwā al-Hindiyya*, Marghīnānī's *al-Hidāya*[23] and Ibn Māza's *al-Muḥīt*,[24] the Diyanet grounds its *fatwā* upon the traditional legal

19 Emir Kaya, 'Balancing Interlegality through Realist Altruism: Diyanet Mediation in Turkey' (PhD thesis, University of London 2011) 156–160; Ahmet Hamdi Adanalı 'The Presidency of Religious Affairs and the Principle of Secularism in Turkey' (2008) 98 (2–3) *The Muslim World* 204–205 <http://onlinelibrary.wiley.com/doi/10.1111/j.1478-1913.2008.00221.x/full> accessed 17 October 2016.

20 Din İşleri Yüksek Kurulu (n 18) 556.

21 *Al-Fatāwā al-Hindiyya*, which is also known as *al-Fatāwā al-'Ālamgiri*, is a collection of Islamic legal rulings that have been issued and compiled by many scholars, principally from Ḥanafī scholars in India. It was created at the request of the Mughal Emperor Aurangzeb (who was also known as Alamgiri) in the late seventeenth century.

22 Din İşleri Yüksek Kurulu (n 18) 556.

23 *Al-Hidāya fī Sharḥ Bidāyat al-Mubtadī'* is commonly referred to as *al-Hidāya*. It is a twelfth-century legal manual by Burhān al-Dīn Abu'l-Ḥasan 'Ali bin Abī Bakr bin 'Abd al-Jalīl al Farghānī al-Marghīnānī, and it is considered to be one of the most influential compendia of Ḥanafī jurisprudence.

24 *Al-Muḥīḍ al-Burhānī fī Fiqh al-Nu'mānī* was authored by Ibn Māza al-Bukhārī (d.1141), one of the prominent scholars of the Ḥanafī school. Ibn Māza is more frequently referred to as "al-Ṣadr al-Shahīd."

view of the Ḥanafī *madhhab*, which was constructed upon the Islamic legal principle of need (*ḥāja*), necessity (*ḍarūra*) and public interest (*maṣlaḥa*).

The same question was presented to the Dār al-Iftā', and the institution provided a clear answer that was grounded upon the jurisprudential methodology of the Ḥanbalī school.[25] It states:

> [The castration of animals] is permissible if there is public benefit, based upon the evidence reported by Imām Aḥmad and al-Ḥākim on the authority of Abū Rāfi' … who said {The Prophet … sacrificed two white, castrated rams with big horns.} He said (in *Majma' al-Zawāid*) the *isnād* (chain of narrators) of this *ḥadīth* is *ḥasan* (good).[26]

Although the two *fatwās* issued by the Dār al-Iftā' and the Diyanet appear very simple and straightforward, they perfectly exemplify the differences between the legal methodologies applied by the two institutions and the influence of the predominant *madhhab* tendency within both societies upon the Dār al-Iftā' and the Diyanet. It can be observed that the Dār al-Iftā' methodologically follows the jurisprudential methodology of the Ḥanbalī *madhhab* by prioritising the text and elevating tradition (*naql*) over reason (*'aql*). As the *fatwā* clearly reiterates, the Dār al-Iftā' bases its legal opinion upon the *ḥasan ḥadīth*, instead of aligning itself with the legal view of the Ḥanbalī *madhhab*. In the traditional Ḥanbalī *madhhab*, it is permissible to castrate animals, such as sheep and rams, upon the basis that this will improve the quality of the meat; this course of action is however held to be reprehensible (*makrūh*) when applied to horses and other animals.[27] This methodological approach of the Dār al-Iftā' most likely derives from the fact that Wahhābī-Ḥanbalī scholars (the majority of the scholars in the Dār al-Iftā') distinguish between "following (*ittibā'*)" and "imitation (*taqlīd*)" in accordance with the deeply embedded predisposition within the Ḥanbalī *madhhab* that rejects blind *taqlīd*.[28]

25 The question is: what is the Islamic legal ruling on the castration of animals? See Fatwā No. 6341 in *Fatwas of the Permanent Committee*, 26: 162–163 <http://www.alifta.net/Fatawa/FatawaChapters.aspx?languagename=en&View=Page&PageNo=1&FromMoeasrID=26068&PageID=10212&BookID=7> accessed 08 April 2018.

26 Fatwā No. 6341 (n 25).

27 'Abd al-Rahmān ibn 'Abd Allāh al-Ba'lī al-Ḥanbalī, *Kashf al-Mukhaddarāt wal-Riyāḍ al-Muzhirāt lil-Sharḥ Skhṣar al-Mukhtasarāt* vol II (Dār al-Bashaer al-Islāmiyya 2001) 695. For further insight into this issue, also refer to Abū Zakriyyā Yaḥyā ibn Sharaf al-Nawawī, *Al-Majmū' Sharḥ al-Madhhab (Irshād)* vol XI (Maktabat al-Irshād 2008) 154–155; 'Abd al-Raḥmān ibn Muḥammad ibn Sulaymān al-Mad'ū Bashī Zāda, *Majmū' al-Anhir fī Sharḥ Multaqā al-Abḥar* vol IV (Dār al-Kutub al-'Ilmiyya 1997) 224; Abū al-Walīd Muḥammad Ibn Aḥmad Ibn Rushd, *al-Bayān wa al-Taḥṣīl wa al-Sharḥ wa al-Tawjīh al-Ta'līl fī Masāil al-Mustakhraj* vol XVII (Dār al-Gharb al-Islāmī 1988) 436; Wazāra al-Awqāf wa al-Shu'ūn al-Islāmiyya-Kuwait, *al-Mawsū'a al-Fiqhiyya* vol XIX (Wazāra al-Awqāf wa al-Shuūn al-Islāmiyya 1983) 125–126.

28 Al-Atawneh (n 8) 71–74.

The Dār al-Iftā' draws certain lines between the two (*taqlīd* and *ittibā'*) upon the basis that a *muqallīd* (imitator) adheres strictly to an *imām* or a *madhhab*; in contrast, a *muttabī'* (follower) closely aligns him/herself with the Prophet, including his behaviours, moral advice, norms and statements. The *fatwā* that indirectly relates to *taqlīd* states:

> [A] person has not to imitate any scholar. Rather, opinions of scholars have only to be followed when there is evidence for them. All Muslims must follow the Messenger (peace be upon him) for he is the model to be emulated by all believers.[29]

A separate *fatwā* that directly addresses the issue of *taqlīd* divides it into four categories. The first category is the independent *taqlīd* of an individual qualified to employ his own *ijtihād* after deriving his own rules from the textual sources.[30] If a person is sure of the truth and evidence that derive from his own *ijtihād*, it is not appropriate for this person to follow an opinion that conflicts with his own ruling. This type of *taqlīd* is unequivocally forbidden because it contradicts the juristic consensus of scholars upheld by the Dār al-Iftā'.[31] The second category is the *taqlīd* of those who are capable of *ijtihād* but who imitate other *mujtahīds* without exercising their own *ijtihād* in order to derive a legal ruling from the legal sources. Shāfi'ī (d. 820) and Ibn Ḥanbal (d. 855) both maintain that this type of *taqlīd* is prohibited.[32] In addition, the Dār al-Iftā' argues that it is incumbent upon those skilled in *ijtihād* to derive legal rulings from the authoritative texts. The third category is *taqlīd* practiced by a lay Muslim who is not qualified to derive rules through his own efforts as he lacks the ability to examine legal evidence and then deduce rules. The Dār al-Iftā' only permits a type of *taqlīd* in which a lay person who does not know how to deduce rules is allowed to follow a skilled *mujtahīd*. The final category is the *taqlīd* of those who ignorantly follow their predecessors and leaders in matters which violate Islamic law – a consensus amongst Muslim scholars establishes that this type of *taqlīd* is unlawful.[33] While the Dār al-Iftā' does not forbid the practice of *taqlīd* in its entirety, it nonetheless restricts its application by only permitting the third. Depending upon the approach

29 Fatwā No. 17831 in *Fatwas of the Permanent Committee*, 2: 168–172 <http://www.alifta.net/Fatawa/FatawaSubjects.aspx?languagename=en&View=Page&HajjEntryID=0&HajjEntryName=&RamadanEntryID=0&RamadanEntryName=&NodeID=4100&PageID=10898&SectionID=7&SubjectPageTitlesID=11293&MarkIndex=8&0#ImitatingtheFourMadh-habs(Hanafi> accessed 20 April 2018.

30 Fatwā No. 11296 in *Fatwas of the Permanent Committee*, 5: 29–31 <http://www.alifta.net/Fatawa/FatawaSubjects.aspx?languagename=en&View=Page&HajjEntryID=0&HajjEntryName=&RamadanEntryID=0&RamadanEntryName=&NodeID=4098&PageID=1369&SectionID=7&SubjectPageTitlesID=1388&MarkIndex=0&0#Whatisthemeaningandformsof> accessed 20 April 2018.

31 ibid.

32 ibid.

33 ibid.

that the Dār al-Iftā' adopts towards *ittibā'* and *taqlīd*, it may be observed that the institution attempts to retain the jurisprudential methodology of the Ḥanbalī *madhhab* to as great an extent as possible.

Despite the fact that the mainstream *madhhab* affiliation in Saudi and Turkish societies influences the jurisprudential methodology of the Dār al-Iftā' and the Diyanet, the diversity in American Muslims' *madhhab* affiliation orients the FCNA to adopt the concept of *fiqh al-aqalliyyāt* as a jurisprudential methodology. The Council initially identifies the general principles of Islamic law regarding the issue and then usually evaluates the circumstances of American Muslims when answering any question. In 2019, the FCNA, for example, issued a resolution that calls for divestment from fossil fuels and investment in renewable energy sources.[34] At the outset, the Council refers to the existing threat of consuming fossil fuels to the health, wellbeing and continuity upon earth and then identifies the general principle of Islamic law upon the ground of the Qur'anic verses (the Q. 55:5–9, 30:41, 45:12–13, 6:141 and 7:31). It states that the maintenance of the delicate ecological balance, biodiversity and sustainability of all forms of life upon earth is the individual and collective responsibility of humanity because God designated human beings as His trustees (guardians and care-takers) of earth.[35] In referring to the detrimental impacts of consuming fossil fuels on the environment, the output of climate scientists has been incorporated into the Resolution. It is stated that the consumption of fossil fuels endangers all human civilisation and planetary life, so all humans should lean urgently towards investing in renewable and clean energy sources and solutions. Remissness in protecting the environment means the omission in the principle of *maqāṣid al-sharī'a*. In the Resolution, it is stated:

> From an Islamic perspective, the supreme objectives [Maqaasid] of Islamic Shari'ah are: to project faith; freedom of belief and worship for all; sanctity of human life, reason; progeny and private property. Failure to deal with the environmental dangers undermines those key objectives including life itself.[36]

In applying the principle of *maqāṣid al-sharī'a*, the Council induces the use of and investment in renewable and clean energy sources, but it is possible to observe an expansion in the volume of this principle. After putting emphasis upon the necessity of investing in the green economy, the availability of technology and devices to turn the entire energy systems in America into renewable energy systems is referred to.[37] Upon the ground of the existence of necessary potentiality in America to switch to renewable energy systems, the FCNA invites all American

34 Resolution, 'Statement of Fiqh Council of North America on Fossil Fuel Divestment' <http://www.crescentsofbrisbane.org/00%20Files%20&%20Images/CCN783/FIQH%20Climate%20Change.pdf> accessed 28 November 2020.

35 Resolution (n 34).

36 ibid.

37 ibid.

citizens, organisations and companies – both Muslim and non-Muslim – to contribute to the development, establishment and support of these systems.

The issue of the inclusion of women in mosques was also evaluated by the FCNA and the three questions associated with this issue were answered upon the ground of the same jurisprudential methodology. In the first instance, when answering the first associated question regarding the attendance of women at mosques, the Council refers to the time and practice of the Prophet. The active and free participation of women in mosques during the time of the Prophet is ascertained as the general principle.[38] Some *ḥadīths* related by Bukharī, Muslīm and Tirmidhī are referred to as the basis of this general principle. After determining the general principle, the FCNA states that the *ḥadīths* that allude to the exclusion of women from mosques were uttered because of the fear of seduction (*fitna*) in the society. The *fatwā* states:

> The hadith that "the best prayer of a woman is in her house," cannot be taken as a general guideline, because the great female companions, including the Prophet's wives, prayed in the Prophet's masjid. If the hadith was supposed to apply to all women, the wives of the Prophet (saaws) and the female companions would not have gone to the masjid.[39]

The *ḥadīth* that designates the best prayer place for women as their houses is interpreted as a restriction to women who have specific circumstances, so the FCNA restricts its meaning to specific circumstances. In the second instance, the American social context is evaluated and alluded to as the factor that diminishes American Muslims' connection to Islam. The FCNA concludes that the greater attendance of women at mosque will provide a continuous bond with Islam and strengthen the solidarity within the American Muslim community.[40]

Similar questions were answered by the Dār al-Iftā'. The question regarding the attendance of women at mosques to offer the Friday and funeral prayers was affirmatively answered. It is directly stated that there is not any restriction that prevents women from performing their prayers in mosques.[41] However, the Dār al-Iftā' demonstrates its tendency towards the *ḥadīth* that designates the best place for women to pray as their houses when answering the question of whether Muslim women can go to mosques without covering their faces. It is stated:

38 Fatwa, 'The Inclusion of Women in Masjid' <http://fiqhcouncil.org/the-inclusion-of-women-in-masjids/> accessed 26 November 2020.

39 ibid.

40 ibid.

41 Fatwā No. 20836 in *Fatwas of the Permanent Committee*, 17: 226–227 <https://www.alifta.gov.sa/En/IftaContents/PermanentCommitee/Pages/FatawaSubjects.aspx?cultStr=en&View=Page&HajjEntryID=0&HajjEntryName=&RamadanEntryID=0&RamadanEntryName=&NodeID=682&PageID=6492&SectionID=7&SubjectPageTitlesID=6544&MarkIndex=17&0#Isitpermissibleforwomento> accessed 27 November 2020.

> It is forbidden for them to go to Masjids without covering their faces. The Prophet (peace be upon him) prohibited that. As for women who cover their faces and do not cause temptation, there is no impediment that they go to the Masjid, but her home is better for her.[42]

Even though the Dār al-Iftā' does not refer to the legal ruling of the Ḥanbalī *madhhab* regarding the attendance of women at mosques, this is the accepted view within the *madhhab*.[43] Referring to Aḥmad Ibn Ḥanbal's opinion regarding the private parts of women, Ibn Taymiyya states that a woman does not have to cover her face when she prays at home, but when going out, she must wear loose garments and a special face veil (e.g., *niqāb*) because her entire body is considered her private parts.[44] From this statement, it can be inferred that women should wear a face veil when they pray outside their home. After adducing the *ḥadīth* that prescribes not to prevent women from going to mosques, both Ibn Taymiyya and Ibn Qudāma state that the attendance of women at mosques is licit.[45] In the *fatwā*, the Ḥanbalī legal rulings related to the private parts of women and their attendance at mosques are combined without referencing the accepted view of the *madhhab*. Despite the emphasis upon the permissibility for women to attend mosques, the Dār al-Iftā' implicitly encourages women to perform prayers in their home.

Like the Dār al-Iftā' and the FCNA, the Diyanet also engaged with the issue of women's attendance at the Friday, funeral and *'Īd* prayers, and then issued a decision upon this issue.[46] However, the issue is evaluated in terms of the acts of subjects (*af'āl al-mukallafīn*) and the place of women in the row (*ṣaf*). While referring to the categories of *af'āl al-mukallafīn*, the Diyanet specifically uses the categorisation of the Ḥanafī *madhhab*. It is stated that the attendance at funeral prayers is collective duty (*farḍ al-kifāya*) upon both women and men, so women can perform funeral prayers. The attendance at the Friday and *'Īd* prayers is neutral (*mubāḥ*) for women while being obligatory (*farḍ*) and necessary (*wājib*),

42 Fatwā No. [Absent] in *Fatwas of the Permanent Committee*, 17: 53–54 <https://www.alifta.gov.sa/En/IftaContents/PermanentCommitee/Pages/FatawaSubjects.aspx?cultStr=en&View=Page&HajjEntryID=0&HajjEntryName=&RamadanEntryID=0&RamadanEntryName=&NodeID=682&PageID=6330&SectionID=7&SubjectPageTitlesID=6382&MarkIndex=16&0#Isitpermissibleforwomento> accessed 27 November 2020.

43 Ahmad Ibn 'Abd al-Ḥalīm Ibn Taymiyya, *Majmū' al-Fatāwā* vol XII (Majmu' al-Malik Fahd 2004) 109–111, 146–147; Ahmad Ibn 'Abd al-Ḥalīm Ibn Taymiyya, *Majmū' al-Fatāwā* vol XIII (Majmu' al-Malik Fahd 2004) 245–246; 'Abdullah ibn Aḥmad ibn Muḥammad Ibn Qudāma, *al-Kāfī fī Fiqh Ahmad Ibn Ḥanbal* vol I (Dār al-Kutub al-'Ilmiyya 1994) 287–288.

44 Ahmad Ibn 'Abd al-Ḥalīm Ibn Taymiyya, *Fatwas of Muslim Women* (Sayed Gad (tr) Dar al-Manrah 2000) 37–41.

45 Ibn Taymiyya, *Fatwas* (n 44) 39; Ibn Qudāma (n 43) 287–288.

46 Din İşleri Yüsek Kurulu Kararları, 'Kadınların Cuma, Bayram ve Cenaze Namazı Kılıp Kılamayacağı ve Bunların Saflardaki Durumu' <https://kurul.diyanet.gov.tr/Cevap-Ara/2747/medyada-tartismasi-yapilan-bazi-konular?enc=QisAbR4bAkZg1HImMxXRn2t8ij%2beDtMkJdRGirgyeb8%3d> accessed 28 November 2020.

respectively, for men. In evaluating the place of women in the row, it is stated that in prayers that have bowing down (*ruku'*) and prostration (*sajda*), men's prayers become invalid (*fāṣid*) if women are adjacent to or amongst them in accordance with the Ḥanafī *madhhab*.[47] However, if this situation occurs in funeral prayers that do not have *ruku'* and *sajda*, men's prayers become reprehensible (*makruh*). After referencing the women's place in the row in accordance with the Ḥanafī *madhhab*, the Diyanet concludes that the attendance of women at mosques depends upon their preference, so there is no impediment for women to go to mosques in order to perform prayers as long as they comply with the moral instructions of attending mosques.[48] Although the three institutions concur upon the permissibility of women's attendance at mosques, they espouse the different jurisprudential methodologies that have been shaped in their respective environments.

While the dominant *mahdhab* affiliation within Saudi and Turkish societies implicitly orients the Dār al-Iftā' and the Diyanet towards adopting the jurisprudential methodologies of Ḥanbalī and Ḥanafī *madhhabs*, respectively, the diversity in American Muslims' *madhhab* affiliation induces the FCNA to espouse the concept of *fiqh al-aqalliyyāt*. The methodological influence of the Ḥanbalī *madhhab* most likely impels the Dār al-Iftā' to adopt a text-centric approach when issuing *fatwās*. This approach can be identified in many *fatwās* that have been officially issued by the institution. Rather than referring to the opinion of the Ḥanbalī *madhhab*, the Dār al-Iftā' provides direct references to the Qur'an and the *ḥadīth* literature – the neutering of animals is an instructive example in this regard. The Dār al-Iftā' does not therefore present its *fatwās* as legal opinions that derive from *taqlīd* but instead renders them as a search for textual evidence that is achieved through *ijtihād*. Taking into account the Dār al-Iftā's attempts to separate *ittibā'* and *taqlīd*, it is possible to observe that the Diyanet adopts *taqlīd* as a methodology when addressing itself to questions that concern *'ibādāt* and classical legal issues evaluated by the earlier Muslim scholars.[49] This feature of the Diyanet's approach is evidenced in its many *fatwās*. The Diyanet therefore presents its *fatwās* by directly referring to the commonly accepted legal opinion that is embodied within the Ḥanafī *madhhab*, and, to a lesser extent, the Shāfi'ī *madhhab*.[50] However, rather than extracting direct evidence from the Qur'an and the *ḥadīth* corpus in the same manner as the Dār al-Iftā' does, the Diyanet generally grounds its *fatwā* within a legal opinion provided by a prominent and recognised Muslim scholar in the Ḥanafī *madhhab* – this applied to the above-examined *fatwās*. When finding a classical legal ruling applicable to contemporary issues, the Diyanet does not refer to

47 ibid.
48 ibid.
49 For the Diyanet, the term "*taqlīd*" means presumably following or embarking on the best suited legal opinion among the views of the Ḥanafī school or the Sunni schools.
50 Kaya (n 19) 124.

the foundational sources in an effort to rederive a legal opinion from them. It is conceivable that the existence of applicable legal opinions removes the necessity for *ijtihād* – this applies because the legal opinion regarding the issue that has been directed to the institution was already decided by earlier Muslim scholars.

Compared to Saudi and Turkish societies, the American Muslim community contains adherents of different *madhhabs* within itself – this directs the Council to pursue a more holistic approach that addresses all American Muslims. The concept of *fiqh al-aqalliyyāt* emerges as the main jurisprudential methodology that is consolidated through the three legal principles (the contextualisation of circumstances (*siyāq al-ḍurūf*), the objectives of Islamic law (*maqāṣid al-sharī'a*) and the public interests (*maṣlaḥa*)). In the first instance, the Council seeks to identify the general principle of Islamic law in accordance with the foundational sources and then generally corroborates it with the principle of *maqāṣid al-sharī'a*. Rather than applying the fixed *maqāṣid al-sharī'a* in a classical sense, it can be observed that the Council explicitly extends the scope of *maqāṣid al-sharī'a*. The freedom of religion for all people and protection of the environment, for example, have been incorporated into the scope of *maqāṣid al-sharī'a* when the FCNA evaluates the issue of investing in green energy. Instead of pursuing a formalistic jurisprudential methodology, the FCNA demonstrates a predisposition towards espousing a more contextual approach when evaluating any issue related to Islamic law. In the second instance, the Council issues *fatwās* by taking into consideration the circumstances of American Muslims, so the contextualisation emerges as a significant legal tool in the process of issuing Islamic legal resolutions and *fatwās*. This jurisprudential methodology can be identified in many *fatwās* that have been issued by the Council.

A further notable difference between the *fatwās* issued by the three institutions perhaps arises out of their hermeneutical approaches towards the fundamental sources of Islamic law. This can be linked to the influence of the predominant *madhhab* adherence in the Saudi and Turkish societies upon the Dār al-Iftā' and the Diyanet, respectively, because their hermeneutical approaches have been substantially shaped by the two *madhhabs* (Ḥanbalīsm and Ḥanafīsm). While the Dār al-Iftā' literally interprets the authoritative sources, the Diyanet generally focuses upon the intent and purpose of these sources. As for the FCNA, the traditionally inherited jurisprudential methodologies are applied as main interpretative tools, but the FCNA espouses a holistic interpretative approach while interpreting the authoritative sources. Like the Diyanet, the FCNA also puts excessive emphasis upon the objectives of the authoritative sources. The different hermeneutical approaches espoused by the Dār al-Iftā', the Diyanet and the FCNA emerge as another reason why such a clear divergence can be observed between the three institutions' Islamic legal decisions, resolutions and *fatwās*. Due to the fact that the Ḥanbalī *madhhab* and the Wahhābī religious movement have markedly impinged upon the Dār al-Iftā', the wording of the Qur'an and the *ḥadīths* presents, without necessary resort to exegetic interference or rational interpretation, the absolute basis upon which the institution conducts the practice of *iftā'*. Wiktorowicz reflects upon the strong Wahhābī tendency towards a literal interpretation of the authoritative texts. He observes:

> [Wahhābī] publications eschew human systems of argumentations, preferring instead to make a point and follow it with series of direct quotes from the Qur'an and sound hadith collections ... But it reflects the [Wahhābīs'] rejection of human logic and their objective of undermining the rationalists.[51]

This feature is exhibited in a considerable number of *fatwās*, and it can be said to be a defining feature of Wahhābīsm. The Dār al-Iftā's rulings in many *fatwās* are stated in one or two sentences and are supported by a number of direct quotations from the Qur'an and *ḥadīth* literature. This can be attributed to the impact of the Ḥanbalī legal doctrine on the Wahhābī juristic and legal views. Al-Atawneh reflects upon the link between Ḥanbalīsm and Wahhābīsm when he writes:

> A quick glimpse at classical Wahhābī methodology and fatwā sources indicates that they follow Ḥanbalī legal doctrine, as elaborated by Ibn Ḥanbal's disciples, especially Ibn Taymiyya (d. 1328) and Ibn Qayyim al-Jawziyya (d.1350).[52]

Taking into account the earlier Wahhābī affiliation to the Ḥanbalī *madhhab*, it can be observed that the Ḥanbalī *madhhab* still continues to exert influence upon the contemporary Saudi-Wahhābī scholars that operate within the Dār al-Iftā'.[53] Ibn Qayyim al-Jawziyya lists Ibn Ḥanbal's legal sources (*uṣūl*) as the following: (1) the texts of the Qur'an and the Sunna; (2) the legal opinions of the Companions (*fatāwā al-ṣaḥāba*); (3) in instances where there is disagreement between the Companions, the legal view that most closely resembles the Qur'an and the Sunna; (4) certain weak (*ḍa'īf*) or weakly attested *ḥadīths* (*mursal aḥādīth*); and (5) sound analogy (*qiyās ṣaḥīḥ*) when no other source exists.[54] Taking Ibn Qayyim's account as a point of reference, it can be identified that the first four of Ibn Ḥanbal's *uṣūl* only rely on texts, whether these are provided by the Qur'an, the *ḥadīth* reports from the Prophet or the *fatwās* from his Companions. This list of Ibn Ḥanbal's *uṣūl* engenders a text-centric legal methodology that ascribes a broad authority to *naql* when deriving Islamic legal rulings. Vogel observes that the text-centric *uṣūl al-fiqh* approach of the Ḥanbalī *madhhab* is actually still

51 Quintan Wiktorowicz, 'Anatomy of the Salafi Movement' (2006) 29 *Studies in Conflict and Terrorism* 212.

52 Al-Atawneh (n 8) 14.

53 For the historical interaction and interconnection between Ḥanbalīsm and Wahhābīsm, see Vogel (n 6) 3–165.

54 Ibn Qayyim al-Jawziyya, *I'lām al-Muwaqqi'īn 'an Rabb al-'Ālamīn* vol I (Dār al-Jīl 1973) 29–33; Abdul Hakim I. al-Matroudi, *The Ḥanbalī School of Law and Ibn Taymiyya* (Routledge 2006) 34–35; Muhammad Abu Zahra, *The Four Imams: The Lives and Teachings of Their Founders* (Aisha Bewley (tr) Dar Al Taqwa 2001) 473–474.

practiced by the Wahhābī scholars and, by extension, the Dār al-Iftā's official *'ulamā'* – in both instances, the authoritative legal texts precede other sources.[55] Accordingly, the Dār al-Iftā' outlines the methodological rules and procedures in the practice of *fatwā* by generally acting in accordance with the Ḥanbalī *madhhab*. When discussing any question directed to the institution, the *'ulamā'*, in the form of the Dār al-Iftā', generally adduce proofs directly from the Qur'an and Sunna. If the first two sources do not provide legal evidence, the legal opinions reached by the consensus of the Prophet's Companions are applied upon the basis that they are the legally authoritative sources of Islamic law.

In common with many Ḥanbalī scholars, the *'ulamā'* that function in the Dār al-Iftā' generally insist upon the literal application of the injunctions of the Qur'an and *ḥadīths* – for this reason, any interpretative mechanism is held to be superfluous. In addition, whenever an issue is not addressed in the Qur'an and the authentic *ḥadīth* literature, they bring *āḥād ḥadīths* (solitary reports) as the legal evidence, with this being preferred over analogical legal reasoning and methodologies.[56] However, the text-centric approach adopted by the Dār al-Iftā' has gradually transformed into a Sunna-centric approach that privileges the *ḥadīth* over the Qur'an. To take one example, the Dār al-Iftā' bases its legal ruling referring to the construction of non-Muslim houses of worship in Muslim countries (particularly those being part of the Arabian Peninsula) on the *ḥadīth* which establishes that two religions cannot co-exist in the Arabian Peninsula.[57] The *ḥadīth* is understood in its literal meaning which states that only Islam can be practiced in the region, without being subject to a further assessment of its authenticity or further interpretation. The issue of female leadership is evaluated on a similar basis with reference to the *ḥadīth* narrated by Abū Bakra ("Never will succeed such a people who place a woman to be in charge of their affairs").[58] In taking this *āḥād ḥadīth* as its point of reference, the Dār al-Iftā' clearly and unequivocally states that it is not acceptable for women to assume a leadership role within their own communities.[59] The two *fatwās* clearly establish that the official *'ulamā'* directly refer to the Qur'anic verses and *ḥadīth* literature without interpreting them. It may therefore be conjectured that the *ḥadīth* literature, when being engaged in its literal meaning, assumes a critical role in issuing a *fatwā* that relates to contemporary questions directed to the Dār al-Iftā'.

55 Vogel (n 6) 73.

56 For further insight into the role of a *āḥād ḥadīth* in the Ḥanbalī *madhhab*, refer to Abu Zahra (n 54) 479–490.

57 Fatwā No. 21413 (n 2).

58 Fatwā No. 11780 in *Fatwas of the Permanent Committee*, 17: 13–16 <http://www.alifta.net/Fatawa/fatawacoeval.aspx?languagename=en&View=Page&HajjEntryID=0&HajjEntryName=&RamadanEntryID=0&RamadanEntryName=&NodeID=4660&PageID=6300&SectionID=7&SubjectPageTitlesID=6352&MarkIndex=19&0#Inwhichwomenareprohibitedto> accessed 25 August 2015.

59 ibid.

In contrast to the text-centric approach of the Dār al-Iftā', the Diyanet, when issuing a *fatwā*, normally attempts to identify the guiding principles and overarching legal objectives of the authoritative texts. If the Diyanet is regarded, to a certain extent, as maintaining the Ḥanafī *madhhab*, this provides *'aql* with an important role in helping to determine and understand the main aims and fundamentals of the authoritative texts. Upon this basis, it may be asserted that the Diyanet, in common with its predecessors, aspires to the active participation of *'aql* in the process of producing *fatwās* that relate especially to social transactions. In principle, the modern neo-Ḥanafī scholars in the Diyanet remain faithful to the tenets of Ḥanafīsm and the classical Ḥanafī legal epistemology – this is evidenced in the cautious application of a singular *ḥadīth* (*khabar al-wāḥid*) and the use of legal reasoning in the process of making *fatwās*, in particular those that relate to contemporary issues.

The Ḥanafī *madhhab* is adhered to by a large majority of the Turkish population. It was constructed upon the teachings of Abū Ḥanīfa (d. 767), affiliated to the group of scholars who were "less receptive to solitary *ḥadīths* and relied much more on the use of legal reasoning and sound judgement."[60] This group of scholars are commonly known as the People of Opinion (*ahl al-ra'y*). Vogel defines the People of Opinion and their legal approach in the process of law-making and observes:

> [The People of Opinion] understood the Islamic law as an all-embracing corpus unfolding first from the example of the Prophet and his Companions and then from the experience and wisdom of the pious lawyers of succeeding generations. They exhibited lawyerly concerns for stability, continuity, logical coherence, and practicability of their laws and for accommodating secular sources of law, such as custom, local consensus, and administration.[61]

As a member of the People of Opinion, Abū Ḥanīfa gave secondary importance to *'aql* and contrasted in this respect with his counterparts in the process of law-making. Vogel suggests that the Ḥanafī *madhhab* mostly reflects the characteristic aspects of the People of Opinion and can clearly conflict in this respect with the three other Sunni schools (Ḥanbalīsm, Mālikīsm and Shāfi'īsm).[62] Within the Ḥanafī *madhhab*, Qur'an, Sunna, *ijmā'* (consensus) and *qiyās* (analogy) are listed as the four fundamental sources of law, with two main secondary sources (*istiḥsān* (juristic preference) and *'urf* (custom)) being added to the Ḥanafī legal sources with the intention of supplementing those primary four sources. Abu Zahra's *The Four Imams: The Lives and Teaching of Their Founders* refers to seven fundamental sources of jurisprudence used by Abū Ḥanīfa. These are: (1) the Book, (2) the

60 Vogel (n 6) 40. See also Taha Jabir al-Alwani, *Source Methodology in Islamic Jurisprudence: Usul al-Fiqh al-Islami* (The International Institute of Islamic Thought 2003) 62.

61 Vogel (n 6) 40.

62 ibid 43.

Sunna, (3) *Fatwās* of the Companions, (4) *ijmā'*, (5) *qiyās*, (6) *istiḥsān* and (7) *'urf*.[63] The ordering of these Ḥanafī sources clearly demonstrates that while the scriptural sources remain essential for the Ḥanafī *madhhab*, the context and the use of legal reasoning also have an important influence upon the formulation of law. Nonetheless, the most distinctive character of the Ḥanafī *madhhab*'s legal methodology is its approach to a singular *ḥadīth* (*khabar al-wāḥid*).[64] Within the Sunni *madhhabs*, there was a long and contentious debate upon the probative value of *khabar al-wāḥid*.[65] While the Ḥanbalī *madhhab*, which was associated with the People of *Ḥadīth* (*ahl al-ḥadīth*) considered these reports to provide more reliable guidance than human reasoning, the Ḥanafī *madhhab*, which was connected to the People of Opinion, did not accept *khabar al-wāḥid* as a sound basis for extracting legal rules – for this reason, they set out a number of conditions which applied to its application.[66] Within *'Uṣūl al-Shāshī* (one of the well-known Ḥanafī *uṣūl* works attributed to Nidhām al-Dīn al-Shāshī (d. 955)), three conditions were stipulated in accepting the *khabar al-wāḥid* as a legal source within the Ḥanafī legal tradition. These are:

1) It does not contradict the Book of Allah,
2) It does not conflict with a *mashhūr ḥadīth*,
3) It does not conflict with the *dhāhir* (the known norms in society).[67]

Taking these three conditions into account, it may be asserted that the Ḥanafī *madhhab*, in applying rational criteria, ranks the probative value of *khabar al-wāḥids* below the verdicts of systematic legal reasoning. This should be considered alongside a relevant assertion ("When a *khabar wāḥid* goes against the status quo of a *dhāhir*, one cannot act upon it").[68] With regard to matters of public importance, a *khabar al-wāḥid* that contradicts a well-known practice in society cannot be accepted as a legally valid source. This applies because a *ḥadīth*, if valid, would have been widely circulated and acted upon.

In aligning itself with many Ḥanafī scholars, the Diyanet takes the view that applying *āḥād ḥadīths* to contemporary issues requires a critical assessment that is, by necessity, preceded by an examination of the legal validity or applicability of the *ḥadīth*.[69] This critical assessment process requires both having the knowledge of the *ḥadīth* and interpreting the context in which the Prophet uttered the *ḥadīth* and the contemporary context to which the *ḥadīth* will be applied. In addition, the

63 Abu Zahra (n 54) 244–245.

64 A *ḥadīth* only has a single transmitter in a particular generation.

65 Vogel (n 6) 44.

66 Abu Zahra (n 54) 244–245.

67 Nidhām al-Dīn al-Shāshī, *Introduction to Usul Ul-Fiqh: According to the Hanafi School* (Abdul Aleem (tr) Cordoba Academy 2015) 123.

68 ibid 124.

69 More detailed explanation of the position of the Ḥanafī *madhhab* regarding a singular *ḥadīth* (*khabar al-wāḥid*), see Abu Zahra (n 54) 251.

Diyanet evaluates *āḥād ḥadīths* by directly comparing them to the authoritative texts (the Qur'an and Sunna) with the intention of ensuring that they do not conflict with any authoritative text and the objectives of Islamic law.

To take one example, the Islamic legal decision that relates to the issue of "the religious and legal position of houses of worship belonging to non-Muslims" can provide further insight into the hermeneutical and methodical approach towards the *ḥadīth* literature adopted by the Diyanet. In evaluating the *ḥadīth* that the Dār al-Iftā' used to establish its *fatwā* forbidding the construction of non-Muslim houses of worship in Muslim countries, the Diyanet subjects the *ḥadīth* to a critical assessment that is consistent with the fundamental Qur'anic principles and the life of the Prophet.[70] After referring to a long list of Qur'anic verses that recognise the right to freedom of conscience, religion and thought, the Diyanet draws upon proofs from the life of the Prophet and his Companions to demonstrate that the Prophet desired a pluralistic society in which citizenship and equal rights were guaranteed to all people irrespective of their religious beliefs and practices.[71] The *ḥadīth* which establishes that no religion apart from Islam may reside in the Arabian Peninsula is also categorised as a strange or rare *ḥadīth* (*gharīb ḥadīth*) with regard to its location within the chain of transmitters (*isnād*).[72] In taking these reasons into account, the Diyanet unequivocally states that the *ḥadīth* cannot be appropriately used as legal evidence when it is compared with the general Qur'anic principles. To the same extent, when discussing the issue of female leadership, the Diyanet, in the same manner as the Dār al-Iftā' did, refers to the *ḥadīth* narrated by Abū Bakra. However, it restricts the application of the *ḥadīth* to the time of the Prophet. The *fatwā* clearly states that the Prophet remarked upon the apparently imminent collapse of the neighbouring Sassanid Empire, whose ruler was a woman.[73] In contrast to the Dār al-Iftā', which accepts the *āḥād ḥadīth* concerning the female leadership in its literal meaning as legal evidence, the Diyanet examines the same *āḥād ḥadīth* in the context of statement and restricts it to the time in which the Prophet uttered it. The *fatwā* clearly states that the fundamental rights and liberties that are provided to men are understood to extend to women – by implication, it is not appropriate to restrict judicial capacity and *jus capiendi* upon the basis that the object of reference is a woman. The Diyanet precisely states that no objection can be legitimately made to women who possess the required qualifications to undertake all kinds of administration and even assume the role of head of state.[74] After many *āḥād ḥadīths* are considered with reference to the Qur'anic principles and historical context, they are either

70 Din İşleri Yüsek Kurulu Kararları (n 1).

71 ibid.

72 ibid.

73 Din İşleri Yüsek Kurulu Kararları, 'Kadınların İş Hayatında ve Siyasette Yer Almaları' <https://fetva.diyanet.gov.tr/Karar-Mutalaa-Cevap/2913/kadinlarin-is-hayatinda-ve-yonetimde-yer-almalari> accessed 27 August 2015.

74 ibid.

accepted or rejected by the Diyanet as a legally valid source during the issuing process of *fatwās*.

Like the Diyanet, the FCNA generally establishes the general principles in accordance with the authoritative sources and then grounds its *fatwās* upon them. The permanent residence status of Muslims in non-Muslim countries has resulted in the concept of *fiqh al-aqalliyyāt* being introduced within the scope of Islamic law in the 1990s.[75] This concept has been grounded upon the idea that Muslims resident in non-Muslim countries, especially those in the West, require a new jurisprudence that specifically engages with their problems because the *fatwās* issued upon the ground of the inherited legal rulings do not correspond to the contemporary circumstances of Muslim minorities. However, it is not a completely new jurisprudence detached from the classical Islamic jurisprudence. Al-Alwani states: "The theory of fiqh for minorities does not ignore the reasoning of fiqh of science or the rules of extrapolation. It is exercised within the established rules of ijtihad, or those interpretative analysis."[76] The traditional legal principles and interpretative methodologies are used with the intention of revivifying the functionality of Islamic law and establishing a vital link between contextual circumstances and *fatwās*.[77] The principles of *maqāṣid al-sharī'a*, *maṣlaḥa* and *siyāq al-ḍurūf* emerge as the main pillars of *fiqh al-aqalliyyāt*. In applying these principles within the borders of *fiqh al-aqalliyyāt*, the FCNA espouses a holistic interpretative approach towards the authoritative sources in the process of the issuance of *fatwās*. The general principles are initially identified through a holistic reading of the authoritative texts, and then they are linked to the contemporary issues in accordance with the principle of the universality of Islam. The link between general principles and social realities is generally established through applying the principles of *maqāṣid al-sharī'a*, *maṣlaḥa* and *siyāq al-ḍurūf*.

In the process of formulating a *fatwā*, divine revelation and reason are put into play together because they are designated as the fundamental sources of law that complete each other.[78] Even though the origin of Islamic law is divine, its application to the real world and human actions is grounded upon the effort of the human mind. Al-Alwani stresses the correlative relationship between the two in the process of applying the Islamic legal principles and values to the current social realities, and he observes: "The purpose of reading revelation is to apply the general 'key principles' to specific situations and link the absolute to the relative, as far as our capabilities allow."[79] Reason therefore assumes a substantial role

75 Shammai Fishman, '*Fiqh al-Aqalliyyat*: A Legal Theory for Muslim Minorities' (2006) 1 (2) *Center on Islam, Democracy, and the Future of the Muslim World* 5.

76 Taha Jabir al-Alwani, *Towards a Fiqh for Muslim Minorities: Some Basic Reflections* (Ashur A. Shamis (tr) The International Institute of Islamic Thought 2003) 12.

77 Al-Alwani, *Towards a Fiqh* (n 76) 12; Dina Taha, 'Muslim Minorities in the West: Between Fiqh Minorities and Integration' (2013) 1 *Electronic Journal of Islamic and Middle Eastern Law* 2.

78 Al-Alwani, *Towards a Fiqh* (n 76) 13.

79 ibid 15.

in the process of identifying the general principles and applying them to human behaviours and contextual circumstances.

Within the scope of *fiqh al-aqalliyyāt*, the holistic interpretative approach is primarily espoused to derive the general principles from the authoritative sources. In the first instance, the Qur'an is read in its structural unity to identify the general principles, and the Sunna is evaluated in accordance with these general principles and aligned with them. This obviates misunderstandings that ensue from the tendency of equating the Qur'an and Sunna. Although the Qur'an and Sunna originate in the same source, there is a nuanced difference between them. Al-Alwani refers to this and states that the Qur'an is the source that establishes general principles, values and standards and the Sunna explains how to apply them to real-life circumstances.[80] The Sunna is therefore accepted as the practical interpretation of the Qur'an. In the second instance, the Sunna is closely examined with the intention of understanding the revealed context of the Qur'an and identifying the methodology of how the Prophet applied the general principles to the real situations.[81] The understanding of the Sunna facilitates the establishment of a two-dimensional link between the authoritative texts and the real-life circumstances.

To take one example, the issue of the relationship between Muslims and non-Muslims is examined by the FCNA. The answer to the question of how the verses (the Q. 9:5, 29 and 123) that order to fight against non-Muslims including Jews and Christians should be understood can provide further insight into the hermeneutical approach towards the authoritative sources espoused by the FCNA.[82] At the outset, the general principles are ascertained in regulating the relationships between Muslims and non-Muslims through the holistic interpretative approach that provides a reading to understand the Qur'an in its structural unity. They are specified as the dignity of human beings, sanctity of human life, justice, acceptance of plurality and diversity in human societies, prohibition of compulsion in faith, universal peaceful co-existence and peaceful dialogue. The dignity of human beings and the sanctity of human life are grounded upon the Q. 17:33, 5:32 and 17:70 while justice is derived from the Q. 4:134 and 5:8 as a universal principle.[83] It is stated that each human being must be dignified and respected on account of being human regardless of his/her religion. People are created as free agents who are individually responsible before God with regard to their beliefs and moral choices. The *fatwā* states that people can only be judged on account of their infringement of the rights of individuals and society, so no human can be discriminated against and punished because of their religious belief in this world.[84] Justice is described as a universal concept that should be observed without any

80 ibid 16–20.
81 Al-Alwani, *Towards a Fiqh* (n 76) 22; Badawi, 'Muslim/Non-Muslim' (n 1).
82 Badawi, 'Muslim/Non-Muslim' (n 1).
83 ibid.
84 ibid.

nepotism and enmity. Persecuting and penalising any person because of his/her religious conviction therefore conflict with the universal justice that is prescribed by the authoritative sources. These three general principles denote that the acceptance of diversity in human societies, prohibition of compulsion in faith, universal peaceful co-existence and peaceful dialogue are the principles that are prescribed in the Qur'an. The principles of acceptance of diversity in human societies and prohibition of compulsion in faith are identified in accordance with the Q. 49:13, 5:48, 11:118, 10:99 and the Q. 88:21–26, 10:99, 42:48, respectively. The plurality and diversity in human societies are interpreted as the reflection of God's will – this means that God recognises the free will of His believers. Coercing people to believe in God therefore explicitly contrasts with His decree of free will. It is stated that the ultimate reward and judgement regarding people's belief will be on the Day of Judgement and belongs to God, so acceptance of plurality means to coexist with people who hold different beliefs without being judgemental and biased against them.[85] The last two principles (universal peaceful coexistence and peaceful dialogue) refer to ethical values that Muslims should espouse in their engagement with non-Muslims. The principle of peaceful co-existence is grounded on the Q. 60:8–9 while the principle of peaceful dialogue is identified in accordance with the Q. 98:1, 3:64 and 29:46. Muslims in their relationships with non-Muslims must be kind, just and peaceful because this is a duty that is decreed by God.[86] In the *fatwā*, it is stated that all principles, except the last, apply to all non-Muslims, but the principle of peaceful dialogue is restricted merely to the People of Book (Jews and Christians). In the Qur'an, a special position is allocated to them that distinguishes them from the Arab idolaters – this is because their faiths, like Muslims', are based upon revealed books and scriptures and share similar moral teachings and values. Muslims are counselled to establish peaceful dialogue specifically with the People of Book.[87] All verses related to the relationships between Muslims and non-Muslims are therefore interrelatedly construed with the intention of forestalling selectivity from the authoritative sources which leads to manipulation and misinterpretation in the process of identifying the general principles.

In accordance with the general principles, the Q. 9:5 is interpreted with reference to its historical context, so the meaning of this verse is restricted to the specific circumstances in which people oppress and tyrannise Muslims. The permission to fight against non-Muslims in the Q. 9:5 is associated with the aggressive and oppressive behaviours of those people against the Muslims. The ruling of the verse therefore does not include Jews and Christians who do not fight against Muslims.[88] The FCNA considers the meaning of the verses in the structural unity of the Qur'an, that is, only a part of a verse or one verse in

85 ibid.
86 ibid.
87 ibid.
88 ibid.

an interrelated section cannot be considered without referring to the section in which a particular verse belongs. All the three verses (the Q. 9:5, 29 and 123) are evaluated with reference to their historical contexts, and it is stated that the generalisation of the meaning of these verses invalidates many other verses that decree the freedom of conscience, peaceful coexistence and universal justice to Muslims in their dealings with non-Muslims. In providing further insight into the historical contexts and circumstances related to the verses, the *ḥadith* literature is alluded to, and it is stated that in the time of the Prophet some antagonists who include idolater Arabs, some Jews and Christian oppressed, tortured and attacked Muslims because of their faith. The legal reasoning in permitting war against non-Muslims is linked to injustice, oppression and aggression that are committed against Muslims instead of their religious conviction.[89] The FCNA therefore applies to the *ḥadith* literature to explain the historical context in which the verses were revealed and to clarify the conditions in which Muslims are allowed to wage war against their antagonists.

The issue of female leadership is also evaluated by the FCNA upon a similar basis through the holistic interpretative approach. In the first instance, the general principle is identified as the mutual participation of men and women in social and political affairs in accordance with the Q. 9:71.[90] The historical realities in which women assumed different duties, including teaching, nursing, administering and law-making, are alluded to. In the second instance, the inherited legal rulings that inhibit women from designation as the head of state are critically examined. It is stated that there is not any authoritative text that precludes women from assuming leadership positions.[91] The rulings that categorically exclude women from leadership positions are generally grounded upon three assumptions. The first assumption is that the Q. 4:34 designates men as the protectors and maintainers of women – this excludes women from a leadership position in political life. However, this verse is related to the particularity of family and only arranges its associated issues which include the complementary role allocation between men and women. It is stated that the scope of the verse is restricted to family issues, so it cannot extend to the political participation of women. The second assumption is grounded upon the *ḥadīth* narrated by Abū Bakra ("Never will such a nation succeed as makes a woman their ruler").[92] Taking this *ḥadīth* as a reference point results in its wording generalising, but the *ḥadīth* cannot be generalised because the Prophet uttered it to allude to the imminent collapse of the Persian Empire which demonstrated an ingrained enmity towards him. The meaning of the *ḥadīth* is limited by the FCNA to the time of the Prophet, and the *ḥadīth* is accepted as inconclusive and insufficient evidence when evaluated and analysed in accordance

89 ibid.

90 Jamal Badawi, 'Gender Equity in Islam' <http://fiqhcouncil.org/gender-equity-in-islam/> accessed 05 December 2020.

91 ibid.

92 ibid.

with its historical context. The third assumption establishes an analogy between leading the prayer and presiding over the state. Since women are precluded from leading the prayer, they cannot assume the position of leadership in state affairs. This assumption is refuted upon the ground of disanalogy because leading the prayer is purely an act of *ibādāt* while leading the state is related to political affairs. The exclusion of women from leading the prayer does not refer to the proscription of their political rights. In the last instance, the role of 'Umm Salama, one of the Prophet's wives, during the negotiations of the Treaty of Hudaybiyya is referred to, and it is stated that she acted as a chief advisor of the Prophet.[93] The general principle is corroborated by referencing the role of 'Umm Salama with the intention of adducing the active participation of the women in political affairs during the time of the Prophet. The holistic interpretative approach espoused by the FCNA dissipates any conflict in the authoritative sources.

Taking into account the interpretative approach adopted by the three institutions towards the authoritative texts, it may be inferred that the Diyanet explicitly approves reason as one of the main instruments that can be used to produce Islamic legal knowledge and *fatwās* – this clearly contrasts with the preference of the Dār al-Iftā' that implicitly pushes it into the background. Like the Diyanet, the FCNA applies to both the authoritative sources and reason together in the process of formulating *fatwās* because both are identified as the sources that plausibly complete each other. Both the Diyanet and the FCNA issue their *fatwās* upon the basis of the fundamental principles reached through examining the circumstances in which the Qur'an was revealed and the *ḥadīths* were uttered by the Prophet, so their *fatwās* generally converge upon similar legal interpretations. In contrast, the Dār al-Iftā' answers the religious questions presented to it by relying largely on the literal meaning of the authoritative texts, so its *fatwās* diverge generally from the *fatwās* issued by the Diyanet and the FCNA.

Even though it is apparent that the dominant *madhhab* in Saudi and Turkish societies has substantially influenced the methodological procedure applied to the practice of *iftā'* by the Dār al-Iftā' and the Diyanet, there are certain indications that the two institutions extract considerable advantage not only from the predominant *madhhab* affiliation in their respective societies but also from other sources and methodologies that are endorsed and recognised by other *madhhabs* and prominent Muslim scholars. The tolerance that the two institutions exhibit towards the other Sunni *madhhabs* can be observed in the frequent references that they make to the other *madhhabs* in their Islamic legal decisions and *fatwās*. For example, the Islamic legal decision that the Dār al-Iftā' issued on autopsies derives, to a substantial extent, from the legal opinions accepted by predominantly Ḥanafī, Shāfi'ī and Mālikī *madhhabs*.[94] With regard to Islamic legal methodology,

93 ibid.

94 Hukm al-Tashrīḥ Jathat al-Muslim, in *Majallat al-Buḥūth al-Islāmiyya*, 2: 83–85 <http://www.alifta.net/Fatawa/FatawaChapters.aspx?languagename=ar&View=Page&PageID=126&PageNo=1&BookID=1> accessed 02 November 2017.

the Dār al-Iftā' mainly resorts to *qiyās*, *maṣlaḥa* and *tarjīh*. Subsequent to finding the legal views of earlier Muslim scholars that had similar effective *'illa* related to the issue, the *'ulamā'* within the Dār al-Iftā' review these views with the aim of determining the preponderant opinion amongst them. The Dār al-Iftā' then constructs its Islamic legal decision upon the mainstream view of the given three *madhhabs*, and this enables it to allow for violating the inviolability of a deceased Muslim body in order to uphold the public interest. Upon the grounds of *maṣlaḥa* and *ḍarūra*, the institution permits forensic and pathological autopsies, while autopsy for the purpose of research is allowed only if the cadaver is a non -Muslim.[95] Similarly, the Dār al-Iftā' approves the use of the Internet and applies the principle of *maṣlaḥa* while arguing that it can serve as an effective tool that helps to disseminate beneficial information for religious, social and educational purposes.[96] While warning against its immoral contents (including pornography) and negative influences, it encourages Muslims to use it for the benefit of Islam and Muslims.

In a similar manner, the Diyanet also draws upon the other three Sunni *madhhabs* and the legal views of the Companions and other independent scholars and applies the legal theories and principles that have been approved by the other three Sunni *madhhabs*. For example, the Diyanet answered the question of whether it is necessary to perform a funeral prayer for a deceased individual when part of their body has been found by drawing upon the Shāfi'ī *madhhab*. In accordance with the Shāfi'ī *madhhab*, it is necessary to perform a funeral prayer when even a small part of the body of the deceased has been found. This contrasts with the view of the Ḥanafī *madhhab* which establishes that when the head of the dead body is found, half of the dead body must also be found to perform the funeral prayer for the deceased; however, if the head of the dead body is absent, then more than half of the body has to be present for a funeral prayer to be offered. Subsequent to presenting the Ḥanafī *madhhab*'s position, the Diyanet suggests that it is preferable to adopt the legal position of the Shāfi'ī *madhhab* when taking into account the psychological well-being of the deceased's relatives.[97] Turkish Muslims are apparently directed to adopt the position of the Shāfi'ī *madhhab* on this specific issue. The issue of organ donation was also evaluated by the Diyanet. In drawing upon the principles of *ḍarūra* and *maṣlaḥa*, the Diyanet endorses organ donation and accentuates that saving the lives of living people is one of *maqāṣid al-sharī'a*.[98] These *fatwā* samples attest to the expedient use of Islamic legal legacy through eclecticism (*takhayyur*) or the legal maxim of combination of opinions (*talfīq*). The legal views of the four Sunni *madhhabs* and other prominent Muslim scholars therefore potentially assist the Diyanet in developing

95 ibid.
96 Al-Atawneh (n 8) 118–120.
97 Din İşleri Yüksek Kurulu, *Fetvalar* (Diyanet İşleri Başkanlığı Yayınları 2015) 549.
98 ibid 535–536.

a pragmatic legal method in the process of issuing *fatwās* in response to modern problems that confront Turkish Muslims.

The practice of choosing among the Islamic legal views of Muslim scholars in accordance with the strength of their proofs is often referred to as *tarjīḥ*. This is a kind of legal methodology that enables Muslim scholars to review the legal views expounded by earlier Muslim scholars in declaring the most preponderant among them. In the contemporary period, both the Dār al-Iftā' and the Diyanet appear to be pursuing a form of eclectic *ijtihād* when utilising *tarjīḥ*, which is one of the essential tools of *ijtihād*. It can be assumed that both institutions do not restrict themselves to any particular *madhhab*; rather, they instead decide with reference to the question of which *madhhab*'s opinion is better suited to their respective environments. In this point, the Diyanet demonstrates a greater degree of flexibility than the Dār al-Iftā'.

The legal reasoning upon which the institutions base their *fatwās* sometimes emerges as a methodological factor that engenders different *fatwās*. It is therefore crucial to ascertain the legal reasoning upon which the institutions ground their *fatwās* when employing a specific legal maxim or principle. For example, the Dār al-Iftā' and the Diyanet, when discussing the permissibility of using contraceptives, resort to the legal maxim of blocking of illegitimate means (*sadd al-dharā'i'*). However, different legal rationales asserted by the two institutions result in two fundamentally opposed *fatwās* being issued. The Dār al-Iftā' employs the legal reasoning that the use of contraceptives may inflict harm upon the cultural, ethical, familial and social spheres by promoting adultery and the spread of sexually transmitted diseases in society. This destroys the supreme value of the family unit, which is an integral underpinning of the Islamic social structure.[99] It is necessary to restrain whatever may be conducive to this prohibited action because adultery (*zinā*) is forbidden in Islam. In citing this legal rationale along with a range of others, the Dār al-Iftā' asserts that all birth control and contraception methods are totally forbidden, but they are permitted in exceptional cases.[100] It appears that the opinion of the Dār al-Iftā' that relates to the illicitness of birth control and contraception derives from a prior assumption that the use of contraceptives results in fornication increasing within society.

A similar issue was also evaluated by the Diyanet. The *fatwā* concludes that it is acceptable to use contraceptives (e.g., *coitus interruptus* (*al-'azl*), copper-T (contra-implantation) and condoms) that prevent pregnancy upon a temporary but

99 Taḥdīd al-Nasl, in *Majallat al-Buḥūth al-Islāmiyya*, 2: 525–527 <http://www.alifta.net/Fatawa/FatawaChapters.aspx?languagename=ar&View=Page&PageID=207&PageNo=1&BookID=1> accessed 02 November 2017.

100 The *fatwā* states that contraception methods are only permissible when there is a potential for harm to be inflicted upon the woman as a result of pregnancy. If the life of the mother is endangered because of the continuation of pregnancy or another pregnancy, the woman can have her baby aborted or use a permanent method of contraception in order to save her life. In the case of necessity, the woman's well-being is prioritised by the institution. See Taḥdīd al-Nasl (n 99) 529–531. For more detailed analysis of this *fatwā*, see Al-Atawneh (n 8) 134–137.

not permanent basis. The legal rationale that the Diyanet uses to construct its *fatwā* derives from a prior conjecture that the prohibition of using contraceptives may contribute to an increased rate of abortion, which is prohibited by Islamic law, in the society.[101] In accordance with this specific legal rationale, the Diyanet conceivably confirms the use of temporal contraception methods in order to prevent the occurrence of unlawful things (the killing of unwanted babies or embryos).[102] In common with the Dār al-Iftā', the Diyanet also applies the legal maxim of *sadd al-dharā'i'* – however, here it is essential to note that the main concern of the Diyanet differs from the Dār al-Iftā's. While the Dār al-Iftā' seeks to prevent the spread of fornication in society by employing the legal maxim of *sadd al-dharā'i'*, the prevention of killing innocent babies through abortion presents itself as the Diyanet's main preoccupation when it resorts to the same legal principle.

In both Saudi Arabia and Turkey, the challenges of the modern period probably motivate the two institutions to develop an inter-*madhhab* approach when issuing appropriate *fatwās* to the problems of their respective societies. Both the Dār al-Iftā' and the Diyanet display some tolerance towards the four Sunni *madhhabs*, and this moderate proclivity adopted by the two institutions is triggered by pragmatic considerations, which encompass a range of cultural, legal, political and social concerns. Despite the moderate tolerance towards the four Sunni *madhhabs*, the predominant *madhhabs* within both societies – Ḥanbalīsm in Saudi Arabia and Ḥanafīsm in Turkey – have, to a substantial extent, shaped the Islamic legal methodologies, principles and views espoused by the two institutions. Nonetheless, the diversity in American Muslims' *madhhab* affiliation incites the FCNA into designing and adopting the concept of *fiqh al-aqalliyyāt*. With the intention of addressing all American Muslims, the FCNA abstains generally from demonstrating a predisposition towards any particular *madhhab*.

The influence of social values and cultural practices

Fatwās do not exist in a vacuum. They are instead produced within particular social environments and cultures. The influence of cultural practices and social values upon *fatwās* can help to explain the issuance of diametrically opposed *fatwās* by the three institutions. Even though the Qur'an and Sunna, as the fundamental sources of Islamic law, are the fixed and immutable authoritative texts, their interpretation in different social contexts and application to different societies are not impervious to the influences of social values and cultural practices. An-Na'im explicitly stresses:

101 Din İşleri Yüksek Kurulu (n 97) 540. In a separate *fatwā*, the Diyanet states that permanent methods of birth control, such as tubectomy and vasectomy, are completely prohibited if there are no health grounds for their application. It can be deduced that in cases of absolute necessity, permanent methods of contraception can be practiced by Muslims. See Din İşleri Yüksek Kurulu (n 97) 539.

102 Din İşleri Yüksek Kurulu (n 97) 540.

> Although derived from the fundamental divine sources of Islam, the Qur'an and Sunna, Shari'a is not divine because it is the product of *human interpretation* of those sources. Moreover, this process of construction through human interpretations took place within a specific historical context which is drastically different from our own.[103]

In an extension of this view, it can be argued that the issuance of *fatwās* through human interpretation occurs within a specific social context which most likely shapes the legal understanding of Muslim scholars. This establishes the possibility that cultural assumptions and social perceptions can influence the interpretation of the authoritative texts and the application of Islamic legal principles and methodologies. The contents of *fatwās* and the applied legal concepts indicate that cultural values, customary practices and social perceptions are effective, albeit invisible, elements in the construction of *fatwās*. Upon this basis, it can be argued that *fatwās* issued by the three institutions potentially bear the imprint of their society's cultural practices and social perceptions.

The influence of cultural values and social perceptions can be most easily observed in the *fatwās* associated with the role, status and rights of women in religion and society, along with those that relate to remembrance celebrations and the relationships between Muslims and non-Muslims. In attempting to uncover the indirect influence of cultural practices and social presumptions upon *fatwās*, several *fatwās* regarding the relationships with non-Muslims are thoroughly examined and analysed in a comparative framework. A range of issues and questions that relate to the relationships between Muslims and non-Muslims were discussed and evaluated by the Dār al-Iftā', the Diyanet and the FCNA. These include the acceptance of the testimony of non-Muslims in marriages of non-Muslim women and Muslim men; attendance at a non-Muslim funeral; loyalty to a non-Muslim polity; residence within a non-Muslim country; the allocation of places of worship to non-Muslims and the establishment of friendship with non-Muslims upon the basis of intimacy, fidelity and affection. In each of these respects, it is possible to identify divergent Islamic legal rulings when the *fatwās* issued by the three institutions are compared with each other. To a certain extent, these divergences can be attributed to established cultural practices and social perceptions in Saudi Arabia, Turkey and America.

In Saudi Arabia, it is possible to identify a custom and culture that have been strongly moulded by the Wahhābī religious movement, which consciously seeks to offset the dangers associated with religious innovation. During the eighteenth and nineteenth centuries, the Saudi-Wahhābī alliance helped the dissemination of Wahhābīsm that included intolerant and exclusivist discourses against people who did not follow the Wahhābī understanding in Saudi Arabia.[104] Shahi observes

103 Abdullahi Ahmed an-Na'im, *Toward an Islamic Reformation: Civil Liberties, Human Rights, and International Law* (Syracuse University Press 1990) 185–186.

104 Gwenn Okruhlik, 'State Power, Religious Privilege, and Myths about Political Reform' in

that the enforcement of Wahhābī ideology contributed to the establishment of a Saudi culture that mainly depends upon the tenets and teachings of the Wahhābī movement.[105] The discovery of oil in 1937, a significant moment within Saudi Arabia's history, impacted greatly upon the country's socio-economic development and Wahhābīsation. The steep increase in oil revenues provided the newly established Saudi state with an opportunity to establish administrative and bureaucratic mechanisms (such as the *Muṭawwi'a*) that rigorously enforce and supervise the Wahhābī ideology and policies in the country.[106] This stringent imposition of the Wahhābī ideology led to the emergence of an intolerant and exclusivist Wahhābī-based Saudi culture.

Within the Wahhābī-based Saudi culture, religious minorities endured, and still endure, social discrimination and marginalisation because of their religious convictions and beliefs. The exclusivist attitude that the earlier Wahhābī *'ulamā'* had developed towards other religions later became an entrenched Saudi culture.[107] For a considerable number of decades, non-Muslims, and in particular Westerners, have been portrayed as the enemies of Islam and Saudi society. As Shahi observes, when ideas are repeated for a substantial period of time, they can potentially become socially deep-seated perceptions and values.[108] However, in Saudi Arabia, these ideas and presumptions did not only become established through continual reiteration, but also there is the *Muṭawwi'a*, an enforcement mechanism, put in place by the state to impose the requirements of this religious ideology. The dissemination and entrenchment of this religious movement were complemented by an established enforcement mechanism that has upheld the Wahhābī practices and values through force. Shahi observes that any religious practices and symbolism which contradict the Wahhābī understanding are liable to be harshly repressed by this mechanism.[109]

Despite the fact that there are no official Hindu, Jewish and Christian sanctuaries, the *Muṭawwi'a* does not tolerate even private worship by religious minorities. This entrenched exclusivist attitude finds a fuller expression within state law, as Shashi recognises ("By law, all Saudi nationals are required to be Muslims. This law, which enforces the totality of Islam, justifies the ban on the public practice of any religion other than Islam").[110] Saudi state law establishes that the purpose of the state is not to protect and uphold the rights and liberty of individuals who subscribe to other interpretations of Islam or other religions; rather, it is instead to protect and promulgate the state-supported version of Islam.

Mohammed Ayoop and Hasan Kosabalan (eds), *Religion and Politics in Saudi Arabia: Wahhabism and Saudi Arabia* (Lynne Rienner 2009) 93–95, 96–97, 103.

105 Afshin Shahi, *The Politics of Truth Management in Saudi Arabia* (Routledge 2013) 149.

106 ibid 152.

107 Okruhlik (n 104) 94–95, 98–99.

108 Shahi (n 105) 157.

109 ibid 158.

110 ibid.

Over time, the intolerance that Wahhābīsm demonstrates towards other religions has created a Saudi society that often tries to physically separate itself from non-Muslims; in addition, it has contributed to the emergence of attitudes and social values that condemn any kind of interaction with non-Muslims.[111] In coming of age, Saudi Muslim scholars have no doubt been profoundly influenced by this isolationist mindset. Any kind of interaction or association with non-Muslims is perceived as a corrupting influence on the belief of Muslims and a tempting factor straying Muslims from the pure and true path, Islam. General perceptions and presumptions about non-Muslims that are pervasive within Saudi Arabian society therefore most likely find specific embodiment within the Dār al-Iftā's intolerant and restrictive legal views upon the subject of non-Muslim rights. Wiktorowicz points out the exclusivist attitude which is deeply embedded within the official Wahhābī scholars.[112] The exclusivist tendency, which is dominant amongst the official Saudi-Wahhābī scholars, has potentially led the members of the Dār al-Iftā' to develop an exclusivist and austere view towards non-Muslims.[113] It is possible to find reflections of this exclusivist manner and views in the *fatwās* issued by the Dār al-Iftā'. A number of its *fatwās*, for example, advise Muslims resident in non-Muslim countries to leave the lands of disbelief or to limit their interaction with non-Muslims if they cannot afford to leave these countries.[114]

In contrast to the exclusivist attitudes and austere social perceptions that are directed towards religious minorities in Saudi Arabia, Turkey's attitudes upon this issue are more moderate and tolerant. Throughout its history, the country has hosted a diverse range of cultural, ethnic and religious communities. It is possible to find living traces of all three Abrahamic religions – Judaism, Christianity and Islam – that predate the Ottoman Sultanate.[115] This diverse cultural and religious mosaic was incorporated into and developed by the Sultanate's *millet* system, which defined communities on a religious basis,[116] thus instituting an early arrangement in which religious minorities were recognised and protected. Bayir

111 Thomas W. Lippman, 'A Most Improbable Alliance: Placing Interest over Ideology' in Mohammed Ayoop and Hasan Kosabalan (eds), *Religion and Politics in Saudi Arabia: Wahhabism and Saudi Arabia* (Lynne Rienner 2009) 124–126.

112 Wiktorowicz (n 51) 218.

113 ibid 221.

114 Fatwā No. 2635 in *Fatwas of the Permanent Committee*, 12: 51–54 <http://www.alifta.net/Fatawa/FatawaChapters.aspx?languagename=en&View=Page&PageID=4306&PageNo=1&BookID=7> accessed 07 May 2018; Fatwā No. 19670 in *Fatwas of the Permanent Committee*, 12: 56–58 <http://www.alifta.net/Fatawa/FatawaChapters.aspx?languagename=en&View=Page&PageID=4309&PageNo=1&BookID=7> accessed 07 May 2018; Fatwā No. 19685 in *Fatwas of the Permanent Committee*, 12: 59 <http://www.alifta.net/Fatawa/FatawaChapters.aspx?languagename=en&View=Page&PageID=4310&PageNo=1&BookID=7> accessed 07 May 2018.

115 Mehmet Şeker, *Anadolu'da Bir Arada Yaşama: Turkiye Selçukluları ve Osmanlılar'a Müslim – Gayri-Müslim İlişkileri* (Diyanet İşleri Başkanlığı Yayınları 2012) 13–85.

116 Şeker (n 115) 112–115; Ali Bardakoğlu, *Religion and Society New Perspectives from Turkey* (Diyanet İşleri Başkanlığı 2009) 41, 53–54.

describes the existential dynamics of pluralism during the Ottoman period in more detail. She observes:

> Due to the special administrative configuration of the Ottoman Empire, many non-Turkish groups also kept their linguistic and ethnic characteristic as well as their distinct laws and legal systems.[117]

The multi-cultural, multi-ethnic and multi-religious population of Anatolia and the Ottoman Sultanate developed a civil society in which Muslims and non-Muslims learned how to live together. The diverse cultural, ethnic and religious communities "lived in peace and even mutual respect, in close proximity, and traded, went into partnership, and developed many relationships with each other."[118] At both the level of government and society, flexibility, negotiation and tolerance became ingrained as key components of the Sultanate. However, as time passed, this pluralistic legal and social structure was increasingly supplanted by the modern state and its corollaries (e.g., citizenship, egalitarianism and secularisation).

Contrary to the pluralism that was an attribute of the Ottoman Sultanate, the secularisation project which was initiated by the early Republican government aspired to form a homogenised society. This in turn resulted in excessive state penetration into everyday life which occurred at the expense of ethnic, regional and religious difference.[119] As Kaya observes, the Turkish state extended citizenship to Muslims and non-Muslims alike and restricted any public expression of religion.[120] In contrast to social pressure, this can be designated as a form of state oppression which impacted upon both Muslim and non-Muslim sections of society. This was evidenced by the early Republican government's deliberate policies, which included the closure of religious shrines, the obligatory use of the Turkish language and the prohibition of minority languages – in each of these respects, the Republican government aspired to form a homogenised national culture that rested upon the prior destruction of minority cultures and identities. These restrictions began to be relieved in response to both domestic and international influences. In the first respect, important changes derived from Prime Minister Turgut Özal's neoliberal policies of the 1980s and the AKP's (Justice and Development Party) political agenda, which consolidated in the aftermath of 2002; in the second, globalisation had an important "loosening" impact.[121] The

117 Derya Bayir, *Minorities and Nationalism in Turkish Law* (Routledge 2016) 15.

118 ibid 25.

119 Rifat N. Bali, 'The Politics of Turkification during the Single Party Period' in Hans-Lukas Kieser (ed), *Turkey beyond Nationalism: Towards Post-Nationalist Identities* (I.B. Tauris 2006) 48; Kaya (n 19) 229.

120 Kaya (n 19) 229.

121 Anna Maria Beylunioğlu, 'Freedom of Religion and Non-Muslim Minorities in Turkey' (2015) 13 (4) *Turkish Policy Quarterly* 140–142 <http://turkishpolicy.com/Files/ArticlePDF/freedom-of-religion-and-non-muslim-minorities-in-turkey-winter-2015-en.pdf> accessed 05 May 2018.

AKP's conscious positioning within the Ottoman lineage has been particularly important in this regard. Beylunioğlu observes:

> Along with the dissatisfaction of the past, the AKP's distinctive understanding of the Turkish nation as a continuation of the Ottoman Empire seems to induce the government to take more flexible stance against the non-Muslim citizens of the Republic than previous administrations have done.[122]

However, it is important to make a clear distinction at this point. Although earlier state policies had negated earlier cultural, ethnic and religious diversity within the country, concepts of equality before the law, non-discrimination upon the grounds of ethnicity, language and religion, and state neutrality towards any particular community have been recognised and upheld within legal principles and regulations since the establishment of the Turkish Republic.

In apparent defiance of the earlier Republican government's attempt to form a homogenised society, cultural, ethnic and religious pluralism have continued to be an essential part of Turkey's social structure. Individuals from different religions have lived alongside each other in the country throughout the centuries, and the concept of tolerance is deeply ingrained within Turkish society and is still followed in contemporary Turkey.[123] Although some minorities have been subject to intolerance and mistreatment, the principle of tolerance continues to underpin coexistence within society. Its persistence can be traced back to the Ottoman Sultanate's cultural and legal pluralism. Despite the fact that the material components of the *millet* system that had granted jurisdiction to religious minorities dissolved in the aftermath of the Sultanate's collapse, the tolerance has remained as a core cultural and social antecedent that defines the stance of Turkish society towards non-Muslim residents.

A closer engagement with Turkey's heterogeneous and pluralistic social structure makes it possible to observe recent initiatives that have been spearheaded by the Diyanet with the intention of developing communication and interaction with non-Muslims at the social and theoretical levels. These initiatives resulted in the establishment of "the Directorate of Interreligious Dialogue," which operates within the Diyanet's wider organisational structure.[124] However, these interreligious activities are constrained by law, and this sometimes complicates efforts to engage the needs and requirements of other religious groups.[125] Despite being restricted by these statutory laws, the Diyanet adopts an inclusivist view and seeks to adopt a constructive and unifying language that resonates within a religiously heterogenous society. Bardakoğlu observes:

122 ibid 147.
123 Bardakoğlu (n 116) 40–43.
124 Kaya (n 19) 229.
125 ibid.

> The Diyanet takes positive positions with regard to the protection of religious freedom and liberty for minority faith groups in Turkey. It does not support any acts of violence on the national and international levels, including the targeting members and institutions of religious groups. The Diyanet plants seeds of respect, tolerance and acceptance of religious and cultural diversity, believing that freedoms are the basis of social cohesion. It is due to the historical legacy, constitutional provisions and efforts of the Diyanet, Turkey provides a ground where members of various faith groups can live side-by-side as equal citizens of the same state.[126]

The Diyanet intends to inculcate respect for cultural plurality and religious liberty and therefore seeks to perpetuate the religious approach developed by the Ottoman Sultanate. Bardakoğlu further clarifies that the Diyanet extends the principle of freedom of religion to the Muslim majority, minority faith groups and even atheists (although here it should be acknowledged that the Diyanet's publications include extensive criticism from an Islamic viewpoint with the intention of demonstrating atheism's deficiencies and inconsistencies).[127] The institution also evaluates conversion to other religions within the framework of individual rights and religious freedom.[128]

In America, religious pluralism emerges as a form of culture that represents a culminating point in the understanding of religion. The growing inclusiveness of America towards other religions has resulted in religious diversity being acknowledged as a form of cultural wealth and social capital.[129] Religion and culture emerge as two inextricably linked determinants of American life that have been existed within the scope of American liberal democracy. Many Americans identify themselves as Christian, but even this American Christianity includes a doctrinal variety. Different Christian denominations (e.g., Protestantism, Catholicism, Lutheranism and Anglicanism) coexist, so it is not possible to equate Christianity in America with monotype Christianity.[130] Religious diversity also extends to Judaism, Islam, Hinduism and Buddhism along with an increasing variety of noninstitutional systems (e.g., humanism, scepticism and atheism) – this contributes to a more vibrant religious culture.[131] Religious pluralism therefore constitutes an important component of American cultural and social practices.

126 Bardakoğlu (n 116) 147.

127 ibid.

128 ibid.

129 Gary Laderman and Luis León, *Religion and American Cultures: An Encyclopedia of Traditions, Diversity, and Popular Expressions* vol I (ABC-CLIO 2003) XV.

130 Wade Clark Roof, 'The Pluralist Ideal in American Religion: The Debates Continues' (2007) 612 *The Annals of the American Academy of Political and Social Science* 242; Derek H. Davis, 'Introduction: Religious Pluralism as the Essential Foundation of America's Quest for Unity and Order' in Derek H. Davis (ed), *The Oxford Handbook of Church and State in the United States* (Oxford University Press 2018) 5, 10.

131 Davis (n 130) 11–12.

The ratification of the United States Constitution in 1789 ensured religious freedom to all Americans and proscribed the establishment of a national church.[132] The First Amendment to the Constitution established that all religions were equal before the law – this enabled the development of religious diversity in America.[133] The commitment to pluralism ensures its citizens the right of free exercise in matters of religion, so it is possible to state that the variety in American peoples' religious affiliation reflects values and rights that the American liberal democratic system provides to its citizens. Despite America's commitment to the idea of free exercise of religion, destructive religious uprisings and tensions occasionally occurred within the society as a consequence of religious dissensions.[134] Roof points to the religious conflicts in America during the nineteenth and twentieth centuries. He observes:

> Pluralism in this more encompassing sense has faced considerable resistance as evident in the history of anti-immigrant sentiment toward European, Catholic and Jews, Mormons and others in the nineteenth and early twentieth centuries and toward Latino Catholics, Buddhists, Muslims, Hindus, Sikhs and scores of other faith communities in the late twentieth and early twenty first centuries.[135]

Discrimination and intolerance have been expressed in changing ways. During the nineteenth century, Catholics, Jews and newly emerging religious communities for example were exposed to religious discrimination at the legal level.[136] After the tragic events of September 11, 2001, American Muslims also became "religious others" almost overnight and easily stereotyped as enemies of American secular democracy.[137] The attention of mass media to this gruesome event led to the creation of an impression that Muslims would invade America and impair American democracy – this sometimes resulted in discriminative and exclusivist attitudes being directed against Muslims at the social and psychological levels. Although religious disputes have sometimes resulted in bloody conflicts occurring in American history, the principle of the equality of all faiths before the law has assisted in engraining peaceful dialogue, coexistence and tolerance as social and cultural phenomena within the society.

Despite the predominance of Christianity, there has been an increase in the number of members of other religions. After the mid-1960s, the number of adherents of non-Western religions began to increase as a result of the 1965 Immigration

132 1 Annals of Congress 451 (June 8, 1789); 1 Annals of Congress 757 (August 15, 1789) <https://memory.loc.gov/cgi-bin/ampage> accessed 13 December 2020.

133 Davis (n 130) 8–9.

134 ibid 10.

135 Roof (n 130) 240.

136 Davis (n 130) 10.

137 Jocelyne Cesari, *When Islam and Democracy Meet: Muslims in Europe and in the United States* (Palgrave Macmillan 2004) 2–5; Roof (n 130) 241, 244.

Act, which loosened the restriction upon immigration from the near and far East.[138] The increasing presence of non-Western religions has contributed to the development of a vibrant religious culture, so the religious dynamics of America, that is still Christian in its majority, have started to change. America has turned into a country that rapidly hosts a wide range of diverse religious traditions and that is cognisant and appreciative of its internal religious diversity. The evident increase in the number of different religions has made religious pluralism one of the characteristic features of America – this diversity has constituted a social and cultural praxis that enables American people to live together despite their religious differences.[139] In the late nineteenth century, religious pluralism and its corollaries (dialogue, coexistence and tolerance) began to take shape and root within American society as a consequence of massive immigration, urbanisation and industrialisation.[140] America's long history of religious pluralism has therefore generated a social culture in which Americans respect people's religious orientations and choices as individual rights and personal freedoms.

The founding political principles and large number of immigrants to America have helped to progress and shape a pluralist society since the establishment of the United States.[141] Despite being far from an ideal pluralist society, America is a country in which more adherents of different religions coexist than in any other country across the world. In the first instance, the religious freedom and tolerance that the American legal system established have admittedly played an important role in constructing a multi-religious and multi-cultural country. To put it in other words, religious pluralism is a natural reflection of the liberal secular democratic character of America. Ensuring the individual rights and duties to citizens constitutes the main component of liberal democracy. These rights and freedoms include the right of conscience which encompasses the individual's right to choose his/her own personal religion – this has played a substantial role in enhancing religious pluralism. The equal protection of all faiths before the law has therefore contributed to the peaceful coexistence of different religions and enabled religious discrimination, pressure and conflict to be kept at the minimum.[142] In the second instance, people of various religious persuasions immigrated to America from different countries, and they brought their cultural and religious identities with them, so religious and cultural diversity became an unavoidable reality of American life. Opportunities for individuals to pursue their own personal religious and spiritual choices explain the continuing attraction of America to new ethnic communities and the dissemination of many different religious traditions within the country.[143] The ongoing flow of new ethnic and religious groups has been

138 Roof (n 130) 241–242.
139 Robert Wuthnow, *America and Challenges of Religious Diversity* (Princeton University Press 2007) 4, 94; Cesari (n 137) 80.
140 Roof (n 130) 245; Wuthnow (n 139) 76.
141 Roof (n 130) 245–246.
142 Wuthnow (n 139) 35.
143 Roof (n 130) 245–246.

continuing to shape the American religious and cultural context that includes many diverse religious faith communities.[144] The diversity and pluralism in religion have helped to cultivate a more inclusivist and tolerant attitude amongst members of different faith systems. The liberal democratic values of and the migration of different religious adherents to America therefore have profoundly embedded the concept of religious pluralism into the American consciousness.

Within the liberal democratic secular environment, the majority of American people have developed and espoused a tolerant, inclusivist and interactive attitude towards each other's religious identity rather than discriminative and exclusivist tendencies.[145] The legal scheme regarding religious liberty and the separation of church and state has configured an American society in which a diverse range of religious traditions can live together in peace and with mutual respect. Davis reiterates:

> the separation of church and state has never been understood to exclude religious persons or groups from participating in public debate. This nondiscriminatory right to make genuine contributions toward the public weal, to have bona fide voice in formulating policies that will affect all Americans, is a valuable tradition that forms a solid foundation for unity, respect, and tolerance among Americans in the face of their great diversity.[146]

Even though the majority of Americans acknowledge their particular religions as a true expression related to the religious dimension of human existence, they respect (or at least tolerate) other faith systems apart from their religions.[147] Civil consciousness (or civil religion) in the form of patriotic nationalism has also contributed substantially to the development and dissemination of pluralism – this can be perceived as an abstract concept that refers to the allegiance and affection of Americans towards their country. Civil consciousness therefore emerges as a unifying element that conflates Americans who have different faiths and that alleviates the possible tensions amongst different faith groups.[148] The elevation of national unity through civil consciousness incites all citizens to pledge their allegiance to the American social and political system, and this facilitates the acceptance of citizens who have different religious faiths within the society.

Within the context of American religious pluralism, peaceful coexistence, tolerance, interreligious dialogue and religious freedom have become established as ineradicable social, moral and cultural values. The reality of American religious pluralism and its corollaries exert a tacit influence upon the legal thinking of FCNA members. While evaluating any issue regarding the relationship between

144 ibid.

145 Davis (n 130) 14–15; Wuthnow (n 139) 35.

146 Davis (n 130) 15.

147 Wuthnow (n 139) 35, 75–77.

148 Michael W. McConnell, 'The Origins and Historical Understanding of Free Exercise of Religion' (1990) 103 (7) *Harvard Law Review* 1516–1517.

Muslims and non-Muslims, the FCNA has espoused an inclusivist, tolerant and dialogist approach. The authoritative sources are revaluated and reinterpreted within the religiously pluralist American context in which acceptance of diversity, tolerance and respect have constituted the foundations of its social and cultural values. In engaging with non-Muslims, coexistence, tolerance, religious freedom and dialogue are identified as the general principles derived from the authoritative sources.[149] The questions regarding the relationships between Muslims and non-Muslims have generally been answered in accordance with these general principles that are formulated by FCNA members. It is therefore possible to observe an implicit percolation of American social and cultural values into *fatwās* issued by the FCNA.

Existing cultural practices and social values that have implications for interactions with non-Muslims exert considerable influence upon the intellectual and legal understanding of Muslim scholars within the Dār al-Iftā', the Diyanet and the FCNA. The influence of the Wahhābī-Saudi culture possibly leads the Dār al-Iftā' to adopt an exclusivist and intolerant stance towards non-Muslims when engaging with any issue that relates to interaction with non-Muslims. To take one example, when the attendance at a non-Muslim's funeral was evaluated by the Dār al-Iftā', the Diyanet and the FCNA, they issued diverse *fatwās* upon account of their different considerations that were shaped by their respective social and cultural contexts. In addressing the issues that pertain to the greeting of Christians, the attending of their funerals and offering condolences to them in the aftermath of funerals, the Dār al-Iftā' states:

> If a Kafir (disbeliever) greets a Muslim, the latter should reply by saying "The same to you" as mentioned in the Sahih (sound) Hadith in which the Prophet (peace be upon him) said, {when the people of the Book greet you, you should say, "The same to you."} However, it is not permissible for a Muslim to follow the funeral of a Kafir, for this is considered an act of loyalty to them which is Haram (prohibited). However, consoling them is acceptable if there is a Shar'y (Islamically lawful) probable interest. In this case, they should say, "I offer you my condolences, may your distress be relieved," but they should not say, "May Allah forgive your deceased," for seeking forgiveness for a Mushrik [polytheist or one engaged in the worship of something other than Allah] is not permissible.[150]

The Dār al-Iftā' evaluates the participation of a Muslim in the funeral ceremonies of non-Muslims by referring to the concept of loyalty and disavowal (*al-walā' wal-barā'*). The *fatwā* creates the impression that the mere act of interaction

149 Badawi, 'Muslim/Non-Muslim' (n 1).

150 Fatwā No. 16426 in *Fatwas of the Permanent Committee*, 1: 440 <http://www.alifta.net/Fatawa/FatawaChapters.aspx?languagename=en&View=Page&PageID=10779&PageNo=1&BookID=7> accessed 03 April 2018.

with non-Muslims can cause a Muslim to diverge from the true path of Islam and tempt him/her towards unbelief (*kufr*). Although it is permissible to interact in order to proselytise Islam, the Dār al-Iftā' sees little benefit in dialoguing and communicating with non-Muslims beyond propagating the faith. As the *fatwā* clearly establishes, if a Muslim does not obtain a pragmatic benefit, s/he should desist from such interactions.

In contrast to the exclusivist stance adopted by the Dār al-Iftā', the Diyanet and the FCNA demonstrate quite inclusivist, moderate and tolerant approaches when engaging with issues related to interaction with non-Muslims. Taking into account the tolerant cultural practices and inclusivist social attitudes which are evidenced towards non-Muslims in Turkish society, it appears logical to presuppose that both significantly influence the legal interpretation of Muslim scholars who operate within the Diyanet. A similar question (to the one presented to the Dār al-Iftā') was placed before the Diyanet, but the content of this question was narrower than the question that was posed to the Dār al-Iftā' and focused entirely upon the participation of a Muslim in a non-Muslim's funeral ceremony. The question of whether the attendance at the funeral ceremonies of non-Muslims is in conformity with Islamic law is addressed by the Diyanet. It states:

> Muslims can attend the funeral ceremonies of non-Muslims with humanitarian aims, such as expressing condolence and giving solace to non-Muslims. However, it is forbidden for a Muslim who attends such ceremonies to participate in the rituals and rites that relate to other religions and to plead mercy for a non-Muslim deceased. When Abū Ṭālib, the uncle of the Prophet, was on his deathbed, the Prophet asked him to repeat the testimony of faith (*lā ilāha illallāh*). Upon encountering his disbelief, the Prophet said: "I swear to Allāh, I will pray and plead mercy for you from Allāh as long as it is not prohibited for me." In the aftermath of this event, the Qur'anic verse (Q. 9:113) which precluded [Muslims] from praying and asking mercy for non-Muslims was revealed.[151]

The *fatwā* makes it clear that the Diyanet places communication with non-Muslims under the category of humanitarian dialogue. A Muslim is permitted to console the family of the deceased and attend the funeral ceremonies of non-Muslims upon the condition that s/he does not partake in their funeral rituals. The Diyanet clarifies that interaction with non-Muslims does not negatively impact upon the character and faith of Muslims. For this reason, the institution does not begin from the premise that there is a need for Muslims to distance themselves from their non-Muslim counterparts; however, it does contend that such engagement should only occur upon a humanitarian basis.

In a similar manner to the Diyanet, the FCNA evaluated the questions regarding the relationships between a Muslim convert and his/her family after his/

151 Din İşleri Yüksek Kurulu (n 97) 225.

her conversion to Islam. In addressing the question of whether a Muslim convert can participate in Christmas, marriage and funeral ceremonies organised by their non-Muslim families, the FCNA states:

> one's maintaining the best relations with one's family, in addition to being a part of a Muslim's duty to treat all people in the very best manner, may be considered a subtle form of *da'wah* as well. Therefore, there is nothing wrong with one's maintaining good relations with one's non-Muslim relations, especially one's parents. Indeed, a Muslim should exemplify for his/her family all the characteristic of goodness, kindness and decency.
>
> The answer to this question, therefore, may be prefaced by alluding to the Islamic principle which says that "Islam means to maintain, not to break up, relationships" (*al-Islam yasil wa al-yatqa'*). It is therefore a Muslim convert's duty to remain close to his family. If the Christmas holiday affords such opportunity, there is nothing wrong with a Muslim's meeting with his family at that time and partaking in the family's activities. Obviously, however, as a Muslim, he or she would not participate in Christian religious services (except, where necessary, as an observer).[152]

Even though the Q. 4:1 and 26 are not referred to, the maintenance of family ties is identified as an established principle in accordance with these verses within the scope of Islamic law. The maintenance of family ties is therefore described as a legal duty of new converts towards their family even if they are non-Muslims. Within the boundaries of family relationships, the FCNA evaluates the participation of Muslims in occasions that are arranged by non-Muslims as an opportunity to invite them to Islam, so the concept of invitation (*da'wa*) emerges as one of the legal reasonings upon which the *fatwā* is grounded. It is also accentuated that during these occasions, Muslims should represent Islam in the best way.[153] This emphasis can be acknowledged as the reflection of Muslims' effort to mitigate negative and stereotyped impressions regarding Islam that have been disseminated through media organs in America. In interacting with non-Muslims, exhibiting decent, permissive and attentive attitudes is counselled to Muslims to attract non-Muslims' attention to Islamic teachings.[154] Although interaction with and affection to non-Muslim relatives are permitted within the scope of family relationships, the attendance at non-Muslims' ritual practices, except under necessary conditions, is implicitly accepted as illicit upon the ground that this kind of engagement may erode Muslim identity. Unlike the Dār al-Iftā' that evaluates many issues regarding the relationship between Muslims and non-Muslims within the concept of *al-walā' wal-barā'*, the FCNA prefers to consider

152 DeLorenzo (n 14) 82.
153 ibid.
154 ibid.

similar issues with reference to the concepts of tolerance, respect and coexistence that have been entrenched values in American society.

The three *fatwās* reflect the influence of the social context upon the three institutions. The Dār al-Iftā's *fatwā* creates a legal and social barrier between Muslims and non-Muslims by applying the notion of *al-walā' wal-barā'*. This may be interpreted as reflecting the construction of physical barriers which separate believers and nonbelievers in contemporary Saudi Arabia. In contrast, the Diyanet and the FCNA allude to the possibility of peaceful co-existence with people of other religions when they handle the issue in the context of a more focused engagement with human interactions and social relations within their respective secular democratic environments. This can be seen as one possible illustration of how residence within a multi-cultural, multi-ethnic and multi-religious society can influence the Islamic legal understanding and views of Muslim scholars who serve within the Diyanet and the FCNA. While the Diyanet's *fatwā* explicitly reflects its tendency to preserve the cultural legacy of respect and tolerance inherited from the Ottoman Sultanate, the *fatwā* issued by the FCNA circuitously reflects the influences of the American social values and being a Muslim minority in a non-Muslim country.

A further example can be derived from the *fatwās* issued by both the Dār al-Iftā' and the Diyanet in response to the question of whether it is permissible to give obligatory alms (*zakāt*) to non-Muslims. The Dār al-Iftā' strongly maintains that it is not acceptable for a Muslim to give his *zakāt* to non-Muslims; it is only acceptable for charity, gifts and the meat of sacrificed animals (*uḍhiyya*) to be given to them, and this is upon the condition that the respective parties are not in a state of combat.[155] Although the *fatwā* preferably reiterates that it is not acceptable to provide *zakāt* to disbelievers, it implies that no harm arises when a share is allocated from *zakāt* to *al-mu'allafat al-qulūb* (those whose hearts are inclined to Islam).[156] A separate *fatwā* also states that a Muslim must not participate in non-Muslim celebrations and festivals or extend congratulations during their religious occasions – this is because the Dār al-Iftā' interprets such interactions as assisting disbelievers in their sins and demonstrating content and love to them.[157]

155 Muslims Dealing with Non-Muslims (n 1)

156 ibid.

157 Ruling on celebrating birthdays, in *Fatwas of Ibn Baz*, 4: 286–288 <http://www.alifta.net/Search/ResultDetails.aspx?languagename=en&lang=en&view=result&fatwaNum=&FatwaNumID=&ID=358&searchScope=14&SearchScopeLevels1=&SearchScopeLevels2=&highLight=1&SearchType=exact&SearchMoesar=false&bookID=&LeftVal=0&RightVal=0&simple=&SearchCriteria=allwords&PagePath=&siteSection=1&searchkeyword=112097114116105099105112097116105110103032105110032116104101032099101108101098114097116105111110115032111102032116104101032112101111112108101032111102032116104101032098111111107#firstKeyWordFound> accessed 08 May 2018; Sümeyra Yakar, 'The Consideration of *Bid'a* Concept according to Saudi and Iranian Scholars' (2020) 19 (2) *Mazahib Jurnal Pemikiran Hukum Islam* 237.

In contrast, the Diyanet refers to the possibility of allocating *zakāt* to non-Muslims by drawing upon the Q. 9:60.[158] The *fatwā* refers to the position of the four Sunni *madhhabs*, which draws upon the legal praxis of 'Umar b. al-Khaṭṭāb, the second Caliph, in order to assess whether it is acceptable for a Muslim to provide *zakāt* to non-Muslims. The Diyanet takes the position that the practice of 'Umar does not abrogate the ruling of the Q. 9:60, which had assigned a share for the *al-mu'allafat al-qulūb* in *zakāt*. It therefore observes that 'Umar prevented Muslims from providing *zakāt* to non-Muslims with the intention of preventing those who were not regarded as *al-mu'allafat al-qulūb* from exploiting the prosperity of Muslims.[159] However, it should be remembered that the legal praxis ordered by 'Umar can be held to be a temporary rule that was determined in accordance with the specific circumstances of his period. The Diyanet therefore incorporates non-Muslims who are not hostile to Islam, who do not oppress Muslims or who do not wage war against them – these are preconditions for the inclusion of those who are entitled to take *zakāt* – into the category of *al-mu'allafat al-qulūb*.[160]

Instead of engaging in the allocation of *zakāt* to non-Muslims, the FCNA addresses the issue of utilising donations to mosques that are granted by sinful Muslims and non-Muslims. The *fatwā* alludes to its permissibility upon the condition that the donations should not be used for the places where prayer is performed and equipment that is used in prayer.[161] Nonetheless, it is stated that these donations can be used for either the construction of facilities (e.g., garden, parking lot) or retained in endowment.[162] A similar question was directed to the Dār al-Iftā', but the focus of the question was relevant to the status of a benevolent non-Muslim in the hereafter who donates Muslims to build their mosques.[163] It is stated that the benevolence of non-Muslims towards Muslims is not a reason for them to enter paradise, but they will obtain their reward in this world. Although the Dār al-Iftā' appears more receptive than the FCNA in using the donations granted by non-Muslims, it categorically expulses non-Muslims from paradise through its exclusivist attitude.[164] In contrast to the exclusivist and firm attitude of the Dār al-Iftā', the FCNA espouses a more inclusivist and cordial approach

158 The Q. 9:60 reads: "Zakāh expenditures are only for the poor and for the needy and for those employed for it and bringing hearts together [for Islām] and for freeing captives [or slaves] and for those in debt and for the cause of Allāh and for the [stranded] traveller – an obligation [imposed] by Allāh. And Allāh is Knowing and Wise."

159 Din İşleri Yüksek Kurulu (n 97) 257–258.

160 ibid.

161 DeLorenzo (n 14) 81.

162 ibid.

163 Fatwā No. 13477 in *Fatwas of the Permanent Committee*, <https://www.alifta.gov.sa/En/IftaContents/PermanentCommitee/Pages/FatawaSubjects.aspx?cultStr=en&View=Page&HajjEntryID=0&HajjEntryName=&RamadanEntryID=0&RamadanEntryName=&NodeID=4158&PageID=10109&SectionID=7&SubjectPageTitlesID=10379&MarkIndex=7&0#Istherulingonabenevolentdisbeliever> accessed 18 December 2020.

164 ibid.

towards non-Muslims. When addressing the issue relevant to the exchange of gifts between Muslims and non-Muslims, the FCNA grounds its *fatwā* upon the principle of coexistence and mutual respect. Exchanging gifts is acknowledged as a significant opportunity to establish an interactive relationship between the two sides upon the ground of mutual respect and understanding.[165] A separate *fatwā* also states that a Muslim should indulgently respond to a person who presents Christmas wishes or greetings to him/her – this is because the FCNA interprets such indulgent and cordial interactions as consolidating the existing values (tolerance, coexistence and respect) and alleviating the adverse prejudgements against Muslims in America.[166]

The *fatwās* relating to the construction of non-Muslim worship places within Muslim countries can be taken as another illustrative example that demonstrates how dominant cultural practices and social attitudes within Saudi and Turkish societies influence the juristic understanding of the Dār al-Iftā' and the Diyanet, respectively. At the methodological level, the Dār al-Iftā' draws again upon the concept of *al-walā' wal-barā'*. The *fatwā* states: "it is evident that setting houses for non-Muslim worship, such as churches, or allocating places for them in any Muslim country is of the greatest support for disbelief and endorsement of their faith."[167] It is claimed that a Muslim should not love and support his non-Muslim fellow citizens but should instead disassociate from them and their religion. The Dār al-Iftā' argues that the demonstration of any tolerance to the enemy of God can threaten the individual's belief, as this may in turn result in an acceptance of their customs, faith and tradition.[168] Another *fatwā* related to the naturalisation of non-Muslims in Muslim states expresses:

> It is permissible to grant a non-Muslim the nationality of a Muslim country provided that the danger of Fitnah (sedition) is secured and that his good intentions are sensed. However, he is not allowed to reside in Arabia unless he embraces Islam. This is based on the Prophet's command to expel the non-Muslims from the Arabian Peninsula.[169]

Despite the permissibility of the naturalisation of non-Muslims in Muslim states outside the Arabian Peninsula, the Dār al-Iftā' emphasises the illicitness of the naturalisation of non-Muslims in Muslim countries located in the Arabian Peninsula. The sacrosanct position of the Arabian Peninsula is held as the main

165 DeLorenzo (n 14) 82.
166 ibid 82–83.
167 Fatwā No. 21413 (n 2).
168 ibid.
169 Fatwā No. 6495 in *Fatwas of the Permanent Committee* <https://www.alifta.gov.sa/En/IftaContents/PermanentCommitee/Pages/FatawaSubjects.aspx?cultStr=en&View=Page&HajjEntryID=0&HajjEntryName=&RamadanEntryID=0&RamadanEntryName=&NodeID=4656&PageID=521&SectionID=7&SubjectPageTitlesID=522&MarkIndex=0&0#GrantingthenationalityofaMuslim> accessed 19 December 2020.

ground not to confer citizenship to a non-Muslim in a Muslim country within the land of the Arabian Peninsula. The *ḥadīth* is referred to in which the Prophet states that two religions should not co-exist in the Arabian Peninsula.[170] This *ḥadīth* is literally interpreted as allocating a sacrosanct status to Saudi Arabia in which the exclusivist and intolerance attitudes towards non-Muslims have been predominantly shaped by the Wahhābī religious understanding.

In contrast to the Dār al-Iftā', the Diyanet instead seeks to evaluate the construction of non-Muslim worship places within the scope of the Islamic legal rights of non-Muslims (*ḥuqūq ahl al-dhimma*).[171] Based on the Q. 5:48, Q. 10:99 and Q. 2:256, the *fatwā* primarily refers to the religious freedom that Islam extends to non-Muslims.[172] In the most general sense, these Qur'anic verses can be said to emphasise the general principle which establishes that the freedom to practice any ideology or religion is a gift and right granted by God. In drawing upon these verses, the Diyanet maintains that diversity in culture and religion is the demonstrated reality of the history of humanity, so it would be perverse not to recognise the right to life of religions that extend beyond Islam. The imposition of faith through direct or indirect (e.g., social pressures or inducements of position and/or wealth) means clearly conflicts with the religious freedom ordained by Islam.[173] The *fatwā* proceeds to explain that the faith, life, property and values of non-Muslim residents in a Muslim society must be upheld by the political and legal regulations of Muslim states – this applies because the Prophet and his Companions provided a clear precedent in this respect.[174] In the *fatwā*, there is an explicit indication that the protection of places of worship for other religions (and this extends to the allocation of places of worship and the construction of religious buildings for them) is an obligation that Muslim rulers owe towards their subjects.

In addition, the *fatwā* references the covenants that the Prophet made with the Christians and Jews of his time. The treaties that his Companions concluded with non-Muslims and the historical facts serve to substantiate the proposition that Islam envisages a pluralistic society.[175] The Diyanet also maintains that the relevant Qur'anic injunction provides full protection to the places of worship of non-Muslims. In justification, it directly refers to the Q. 22:40 (which reads: "Did Allah not stop one set of people by means of another, for sure, there have been destroyed monasteries, churches, synagogues, and mosques, where the Name of Allah is praised most often"). In accordance with this verse, it is reiterated that the protection of places of worship of non-Muslims and the respect of their religious relics are religious duties that are designated to both Muslim rulers and residents. Coexistence (*ta'āyush*) therefore emerges as a key concept within the *fatwā*. In drawing upon this concept, the Diyanet establishes that living with non-Muslim

170 ibid.
171 Din İşleri Yüsek Kurulu Kararları (n 1).
172 ibid.
173 ibid.
174 ibid.
175 ibid.

citizens and being part of the same society require positive engagement and a mutual commitment to civic participation from both sides (Muslims and non-Muslims). This is essential to form a healthy and tranquil Muslim nation in which citizenship and equal rights are granted to all members irrespective of their religious belief or practice. In assessing the nature and parameters of normative relationships between Muslims and non-Muslims, the Diyanet mainly grounds its *fatwās* within three important notions (religious freedom, peaceful coexistence and tolerance) which serve to demonstrate that *ḥuqūq ahl al-dhimma* emerges as an influential legal concept often applied. The Diyanet's moderate and tolerant approach towards non-Muslims can be traced back to a democratic and pluralistic (both in culture and religion) Turkish society that has shaped the legal thought and understanding of Muslim scholars to a substantial extent. The interpretation of the textual sources through the lens of this tolerant and pluralistic society potentially leads the Diyanet to engage any issues that relate to non-Muslim citizens within the framework of *ḥuqūq ahl al-dhimma.*

While the Dār al-Iftā' engages in any issue related to the relationship between Muslims and non-Muslims within the concept of *al-walā' wal-barā'*, the Diyanet tackles similar subjects within the framework of *ḥuqūq ahl al-dhimma.* Unlike the Dār al-Iftā' and the Diyanet, the FCNA generally addresses the issues related to the relationship between Muslims and non-Muslims within the concepts of religious freedom, peaceful coexistence and amicable dialogue. In referring to these concepts, the FCNA answers the question regarding the possibility of friendship between Muslims and non-Muslims. In evaluating this issue, the Q. 5:57–58 that ordain not to establish friendship with non-Muslims are connected to the negative situations in which non-Muslims ridicule Muslims when they are called for prayers. The FCNA states that the decontextualisation of these and similar verses invalidates the general principles derived from other verses that impart how peaceful relationships with non-Muslims should be established and developed.[176] The Qur'anic verses that decree Muslims to fight against and dissociate themselves from non-Muslims are restricted to certain specific situations in which non-Muslims persecute and insult Muslims. The permissibility of the marriage of a Muslim man with a Jewish or Christian woman is further alluded to with the intention of consolidating the possibility of establishing friendship with non-Muslims. It is stated:

> According to the Qur'an [5:5], a Muslim man can marry a Jewish and Christian woman. As a wife, her Muslim husband has obligation to her. As revealed in Surah 30, verse 21, he should dwell with her, treat in peace and treat her with love and compassion. Does it make sense that a Muslim would be permitted to marry a non-Muslim, but not befriend her?[177]

176 Badawi, 'Muslim/Non-Muslim' (n 1).
177 ibid.

The generalisation of the meaning of the Q. 5:57–58 that proscribe the befriending of non-Muslims conflicts with the Q. 5:5 that allows Muslim men to marry with believing Jewish and Christian women because the marriage relationship depends on mercy and love, established in the Q. 30:21. With the intention of obviating this conflict, the FCNA restricts the injunction of the Q. 5:57–58 to the specific circumstances in which non-Muslims initiate aggressive and belligerent demeanours against Muslims. The permissibility of marriage between Muslim men and non-Muslim women is therefore interpreted as attesting to the legitimacy of befriending non-Muslims upon the ground of loyalty, affection and compassion.

In contrast to the FCNA, the Dār al-Iftā' and the Diyanet do not lean positively towards the issue of establishing friendship with non-Muslims upon the ground of loyalty and affection. When evaluating the issue of accepting the invitation of a non-Muslim to dinner, the Dār al-Iftā', although the acceptance of the invitation is allowed upon the ground of *da'wa*, states: "There are many types of establishing relationships with other people. Relationship based on mutual affection, love and brotherhood between a Muslim and Kafir [disbeliever] is prohibited. It might render a Muslim as a Kafir."[178] The Dār al-Iftā' references to the Q. 58:22 as evidence for not demonstrating affection and love towards non-Muslims. In a similar manner, the Diyanet also refers to the inappropriateness of establishing a friendship with non-Muslims upon the basis of loyalty, intimacy and benignity – this is consolidated by alluding to the Q. 4:144, 5:51, 5:57 and 9:23.[179] Despite the fact that the necessity of establishing the business and humanitarian relationships with non-Muslims is assented to in accordance with the normative principles of peaceful coexistence, the Diyanet implies the disconformity of enhancing these relationships upon the basis of loyalty, intimacy and benignity with the general principles that regulate the relationship between Muslims and non-Muslims.[180] While the Dār al-Iftā' and the Diyanet converge upon not establishing relationships with non-Muslims that are grounded in loyalty, intimacy and affection, the FCNA explicitly indicates the permissibility of befriending non-Muslims upon the grounds of fidelity, benignity and compassion. In identifying peaceful coexistence as one of the general principles of the normative relationships between Muslims and non-Muslims, the Q. 60:8–9 that regulate the relationship with noncombative non-Muslims are referred to. While explaining the word *birr* in this verse, the FCNA states:

> This verse makes it a Muslim's duty to treat peacefully coexisting persons with equity [Qist] and [Birr]. The term Birr and its derivatives are the same

178 Fatwā No. 4214 in *Fatwas of the Permanent Committee*, 12: 253–254 <https://www.alifta.gov.sa/En/IftaContents/PermanentCommitee/Pages/FatawaSubjects.aspx?cultStr=en&View=Page&HajjEntryID=0&HajjEntryName=&RamadanEntryID=0&RamadanEntryName=&NodeID=4649&PageID=4462&SectionID=7&SubjectPageTitlesID=4513&MarkIndex=17&0#Havingrelationshipswiththem> accessed 20 December 2020.

179 M. Şevki Aydın and others, *Sorularla İslam* (Diyanet İşleri Başkanlığı Yayınları 2015) 165–166.

180 ibid 166–171.

> expressions used in the Qur'an and Hadeeth to refer to one's relationship with his/her parents. Such relationship is more than kindness, since it includes also love and respect.[181]

The incorporation of love and respect into the meaning of *birr* implicitly denotes the possibility of establishing relationships with non-Muslims upon the basis of love, affection and loyalty. It is precisely stated that loving humankind as people and honoured creatures of God does not mean accepting and approving of their different faiths and beliefs.[182] Within the religiously pluralistic American society, the FCNA therefore adopts a more inclusivist and indulgent approach than the Dār al-Iftā' and the Diyanet when addressing any issues regarding relationships with non-Muslims.

Consequently, the practice of *iftā'* is not divorced from societies' cultural practices and social values. The Dār al-Iftā's functioning within a Wahhābī-based Saudi culture that is exclusivist to others may be understood as a major incentive which leads the institution to apply the notion of *al-walā' wa al-barā'* when formulating *fatwās* that relate to interactions with non-Muslims – in this context, this notion is prioritised over other legal concepts and principles. Several *fatwās* categorically affirm that it is illegal to physically harm or inflict injustice upon non-Muslims. However, these specific stipulations offset and at least partially diminish the negative influences of the *fatwās* that endorse psychological discrimination and social suppression and exclusion against non-Muslims. The cultural practices and social perceptions that were constructed by the Wahhābī ideology of enmity and hatred against disbelievers (who can even be Muslims) quite clearly, at least in these instances, permeate deep into the psyche of the Dār al-Iftā's *'ulamā'*. Conversely, the location of the Diyanet within a democratic, heterogenic and secular society can instead be viewed as one of the reasons that lead Muslim scholars within the Diyanet to orientate towards inclusion, moderation and tolerance when engaging with religious issues that relate to non-Muslims. The relevant textual sources associated with the relationships between Muslims and non-Muslims are interpreted through the prism of perceptions and experiences of Muslim scholars who reside within a democratic and heterogenic society. The *fatwās* issued by the institution generally reiterate respect and acceptance of the other – the main exception to this is when textual evidence prevents a Muslim from performing certain practices. In opposition to the Dār al-Iftā's *fatwās*, the Diyanet's *fatwās* clearly envisage coexistence of Muslims and non-Muslims within a Muslim state upon the ground of the concept of *ḥuqūq ahl al-dhimma*. As for the FCNA, its operating within the religiously pluralistic American society that is inclusivist, receptive and indulgent to others may be acknowledged as a principal factor which induces the Council to espouse a more inclusivist, tolerant and civil approach in evaluating issues related to relationships with non-Muslims. Instead

181 Badawi, 'Muslim/Non-Muslim' (n 1).
182 ibid.

of applying the traditionally existing legal concepts (e.g., *al-walā' wa al-barā'* and *ḥuqūq ahl al-dhimma*), the FCNA precisely identifies peaceful coexistence, amicable dialogue, religious freedom and pluralism as the main yardsticks of the holistic hermeneutic reading of the authoritative texts when addressing religious issues that relate to non-Muslims. The consideration of representing Islam in the best way also percolates into almost all *fatwās* issued by the FCNA – this highly likely traces back to the reality of being a representative institution of Muslim minorities within the Christian majority American society. The relevant authoritative texts regarding relationships with non-Muslims are read through the lenses of Muslim minority scholars who reside in a secular liberal democratic society in which peaceful coexistence, tolerance, interreligious dialogue and religious freedom have been established as entrenched social, moral and cultural values. These values therefore have implicitly leached into the FCNA's *fatwās* regarding the relationships between Muslims and non-Muslims. It can be asserted that differences between the *fatwās* are rooted within the perceptions that the Dār al-Iftā', the Diyanet and the FCNA have of the relationships between Muslims and non-Muslims in their respective environments. The wider context, and specifically cultural practices and social values, function as determining and direct factors which closely shape the legal thought of Muslim scholars within the three institutions.

Conclusion

Divergent *fatwās* issued by the Dār al-Iftā', the Diyanet and the FCNA on the same or similar issues are markedly contingent on both the different contextual interpretation of the textual sources and the interaction between Islamic legal methodologies and social environments. The application of selected Islamic legal methodologies, principles and theories to a contemporary issue is, to a certain extent, dependent upon how the three institutions interpret an issue in their surrounding environments. Different understandings make different jurisprudential principles operational in the construction of *fatwās* by the three institutions.

To a certain extent, the *madhhab* affiliation of the three societies has moulded the Islamic legal theories and methodologies followed and espoused by the three institutions. The influence of the Ḥanbalī *madhhab* and the Wahhābī movement can be observed in the *fatwās* issued by the Dār al-Iftā'. The *'ulamā'* in the Dār al-Iftā' still adhere firmly to the authoritative textual sources and transmitted tradition before applying anything else. In complying with the Islamic legal doctrine of the Ḥanbalī *madhhab*, the Dār al-Iftā' generally privileges *naql* (transmitted tradition) over *'aql* (reason). This is manifested in the extensive use of the Qur'an and Sunna and the direct invocation of both by the Dār al-Iftā's *fatwās*. To the same extent, it is possible to observe how the Ḥanafī *madhhab* has exerted influence over the Islamic legal methodologies implemented by the Diyanet within its official decisions and *fatwās*. To some extent, the Diyanet has maintained its scholarly authority by applying the jurisprudential tool of *taqlīd*. For the most part, the Diyanet presents the widely accepted legal views of the Ḥanafī *madhhab* to its audiences. However, it is conceivably the case that operating within a secular democratic society probably leads the Diyanet to develop a more tolerant approach and feature the ethical dimensions and values of Islam during the construction of *fatwās*. This ethic-based approach to Islamic legal issues, on which the Diyanet focuses, in turn probably results in a more flexible predisposition towards the other three Sunni *madhhabs*, Shāfi'īsm, Mālikīsm and Ḥanbalīsm. For a legal judgement to be accurate, the Diyanet generally gives its primary consideration to the compatibility of *fatwās* with the legal principles of *maqāṣid al-sharī'a* and *maṣlaḥa* rather than the legal doctrinal path behind *fatwās*. Although it does not resemble the Diyanet, the Dār al-Iftā' also demonstrates tolerance to other schools. In broad terms, the two institutions insist on recognising and utilising Islamic legal maxims, principles and theories that have been approved by Sunni *madhhabs* – this course of action is preferred to the creation of an entirely new Islamic legal methodology. An inter-*madhhabs* trend, which appears to originate within a desire to confront contemporary challenges, is discernible within the *fatwās* of the two institutions. The two institutions draw upon other *madhhabs* and issue their decisions and *fatwās* in accordance with which of the school's doctrines or opinions is, in their view, the most effective or generally pragmatic: in these instances, it is the matter at hand which is the defining criterion.

The predominant *madhhab* affiliation of the Muslim majority population of Saudi Arabia and Turkey has substantially composed the jurisprudential methodologies that the two institutions, when regulating the day-to-day running of religious affairs in their respective environments, espouse. The diversity in American Muslims' *madhhab* affiliation however emerges as an incentive that orients the FCNA to espouse the concept of *fiqh al-aqalliyyāt* that intends unity amongst Muslim minorities within American society. In not aligning itself with any *madhhab*, the Council aims to address all American Muslims who adhere to different *madhhabs*. The concept of *fiqh al-aqalliyyāt* is a jurisprudence that is specifically designated to provide *fatwās* for Muslim minorities while taking into consideration their particular needs and exigencies. Within the concept of *fiqh al-aqalliyyāt*, the FCNA generally applies the legal principles of *maqāṣid al-sharī'a*, *maṣlaḥa* and *siyāq al-ḍurūf* in the process of issuing *fatwās*. In employing these principles within the borders of *fiqh al-aqalliyyāt*, the FCNA adopts a holistic interpretative approach towards the authoritative sources. After the general principles are identified through the holistic reading, the FCNA superimposes its *fatwās* upon these principles. The general principles are generally linked to social realities through applying to the principles of *maqāṣid al-sharī'a*, *maṣlaḥa* and *siyāq al-ḍurūf*. In the process of establishing links between the general principles and social realities, the FCNA puts divine revelation and reason into play together because they are acknowledged as the complementary sources of law within the scope of *fiqh al-aqalliyyāt*. Functioning within a Christian majority society as a representative institution of American Muslim minorities induces the FCNA to espouse the concept of *fiqh al-aqalliyyāt* during the construction of *fatwās*.

Cultural practices and social values can be also accepted as the wider context which frames and orientates the thought process of individual Muslim scholars. These elements find fuller expression with ideas, outlooks, perceptions and understandings, and directly influence the interpretation of the Qur'an and Sunna, along with the precise legal concepts and methodologies that are deployed during the course of the interpretative process. Even though the authoritative texts are immutable and permanent sources of Islamic law, their interpretation through Islamic legal methodologies and tools is, to a certain extent, linked to pervasive cultural values and social perceptions within a particular society. When Islamic legal decisions, resolutions and *fatwās* issued by the three institutions are subject to closer examination, it can be argued that there is an ongoing relationship between social practices and legal thought that produces those *fatwās*. This relationship is not unilateral but instead cyclical. While *fatwās* can influence aspects of culture and social values, cultural practices and social context can influence the legal understanding of Muslim scholars.

Muslim scholars working in the three institutions are conceivably influenced by the cultural assumptions and social perceptions in their respective environments when evaluating any issue directed to them. As with the *fatwās* that demarcate appropriate relations between Muslims and non-Muslims, the three institutions seek to substantiate their arguments with reference to the authoritative sources, but then deploy different concepts and methodologies in interpreting these authoritative sources. This generally results in the three institutions arriving at divergent conclusions. The Wahhābī-based and generally exclusivist Saudi culture is an important influence that leads the Dār al-Iftā' to draw upon the concept of *al-walā' wa al-barā'* when assessing any issue pertaining to the relationship between Muslims and non-Muslims. However, the Diyanet handles similar issues within the scope of *ḥuqūq ahl al-dhimma* and grounds its *fatwās* within the concepts of peaceful coexistence, religious freedom and respect. Turkey's general atmosphere of tolerance towards its non-Muslim residents has therefore impacted the *fatwas* regarding the relationships with non-Muslims. Unlike the Dār al-Iftā' and the Diyanet, that apply the traditionally existing legal concepts, the FCNA adopts a more inclusivist, tolerant and civil approach in evaluating issues related to the relationships with non-Muslims within the religiously pluralistic American society. America's inclusivist and indulgent approach towards its religiously diverse residents has percolated implicitly into the *fatwās* issued by the FCNA. The concepts of peaceful coexistence, amicable dialogue, religious freedom and pluralism therefore emerge as the general principles upon which the FCNA superimposes its *fatwās* related to interactions with non-Muslims. As a consequence, cultural practices and social values have a kind of energy and potential to influence the legal thought and understanding of Muslim scholars that operate in these institutions.

5 Influence of legal and political systems

The legal and political systems in which the Dār al-Iftā', the Diyanet and the FCNA operate have their own idiosyncratic features. The legal and political systems of each country emerge as the contextual factors that specify the jurisdictions of the three institutions and the functions of their *fatwās* within the countries. The Dār al-Iftā' operates within the borders of an Islamic legal system while the Diyanet and the FCNA function under secular legal systems. Functioning within an Islamic legal system provides the Dār al-Iftā' and its *fatwās* a more influential place in Saudi society when compared to the Diyanet and the FCNA, along with their *fatwās*. The secular legal system and its values generally emerge as implicit elements that restrict the jurisdiction of the Diyanet and the FCNA but probably induce the two institutions to converge upon common ground when they issue *fatwās*. Although the Diyanet and the FCNA operate under secular legal systems, the American secular legal system is quite different from the Turkish secular legal system. The difference between the two also manifests their impact upon the jurisdictions of the Diyanet and the FCNA, along with their *fatwās*.

The political systems of the three countries also demonstrate variations. The Dār al-Iftā' functions under a theocratic monarchy while the Diyanet and the FCNA operate within democratic political systems. This variation especially brings out its influences upon the *fatwās* regarding the polity of each state and the responsibilities of Muslims towards the states in which they live. It can be observed that each institution has developed an Islamic legal thought to legitimate the political systems in which they function. The theocratic monarchy of the Saudi state is legitimised by the Dār al-Iftā' as an Islamic government form while functioning within the secular democratic systems emerges as an incentive that orients the Diyanet and the FCNA to justify democracy as a legitimate polity. It is possible to state that *fatwās* regarding the government form are tailored by the three institutions to their political systems. This chapter specifically addresses the influence of the legal and political systems upon the three institutions and their *fatwās*. In engaging with these two points, this chapter seeks to ascertain the interaction between the politico-legal contexts of each country and the Islamic legal methodologies espoused by the three institutions. Each point is corroborated with *fatwā* samples and their comparative analysis.

DOI: 10.4324/9781003037637-5

The influence of legal systems

The socio-legal dynamics that are adhered to within the wider contexts of the three institutions circuitously influence the issuance of a *fatwā* in their respective environments. The function, influence and role of *fatwās* issued by the three institutions are determined by the legal systems of Saudi Arabia, Turkey and America in which the Dār al-Iftā', the Diyanet and the FCNA respectively operate. The legal systems and associated legal regulations either allocate a wider and more influential authority to *fatwās* or restrict their authoritative functions to Muslim individuals' decisions within the three countries.

It is generally clear that obedience to *fatwās* that derive from the intellectual exertion of Muslim scholars (*ijtihād*) can be said to be morally binding in the most general sense. If an individual questioner (*mustaftī*) is free to follow or obey *fatwās* issued by the three institutions, then it follows that the three legal systems (Saudi Arabia's Islamic system and Turkey's and America's secular systems) do not exert binding force upon individual questioners to comply with the instructions determined in the issued *fatwās*. However, it is possible to detect slight differences with regard to the sanctioning power of *fatwās* which can be traced back to the legal systems in which the three institutions function. Firstly, it should be noted that the official *fatwās* issued by the Dār al-Iftā' are more legally authoritative and influential and command a considerably greater level of respect than those issued by the Diyanet and the FCNA – this is further underlined by the fact that they sometimes even, subject to the approval of the Saudi Arabian King, obtain legally binding status. Secondly, the official *fatwās* issued by the Dār al-Iftā' and the Diyanet may create social norms and normative values because of their functioning within the Muslim majority countries. This can sometimes engender a conflict with secular legal regulations in Turkey. In contrast to the Dār al-Iftā' and the Diyanet, the FCNA operates within a non-Muslim country and issues *fatwās* for Muslim minorities. The fact that American Muslims are in minority status mitigates the possibility of *fatwās* in creating social norms and normative values within American society – this considerably counteracts the possibility of the transformation of *fatwās* into social norms and normative values.

Subsequent to acquiring the approval of the King, the Dār al-Iftā's *fatwās* obtain regulatory and statutory power within Saudi Arabia's Islamic legal system. Islamic legal decisions issued by the BSU, which is the highest religious authority within the Dār al-Iftā's structure and the country more generally, have the potential to become, subject to the King's approval, state laws. To take one example, the legal decision prescribed the death penalty for drug smugglers and traffickers; in addition, the legal decision regarding the issue of *khul'*, many *fatwās* which obliged women to appear in appropriate attire and the recommendation presented to the government to limit the number of students permitted to study abroad were transformed into state regulations through royal decrees.[1] Al-Atawneh observes

1 Muhammad al-Atawneh, *Wahhābī Islam Facing the Challenges of Modernity: Dār al-Iftā in the Modern Saudi State* (Brill 2010) 21, 95, 107; Frank Vogel, *Islamic Law and Legal System: Studies of Saudi Arabia* (Brill 2000) 266.

that the Dār al-Iftā' does not only function as an advisory or consultative body but also takes on the form of a pre-legislative mechanism within the Saudi legal system.[2] In an innovation which can be clearly distinguished from an individual's inner decision to credit a *fatwā*, the King or the Saudi Government formally transforms the non-binding character of a *fatwā* into a binding regulation by exerting discretionary (*ta'zīr*) or legislative power.

Conversely, the Diyanet's *fatwās* do not have any statutory power under the Turkish secular legal system to any extent at all; obedience to Islamic legal decisions and *fatwās* is ultimately subject to the inner decision of individuals who ask questions in order to overcome their inner conflicts or lapses of understanding on matters of Islamic belief and obligation. In addition, it may be observed that the official *fatwās* issued by the Diyanet can generate a normative or social value. Because they operate within a Muslim majority country, the *fatwās* may conceivably obtain a power of social sanction – this would apply despite the fact that they lack a legal or statutory function within the Turkish secular legal system. Given the fact that there is no other entity in Turkey whose religious erudition and services have been institutionalised and systematised to the same extent as the Diyanet, it may be asserted that some religious, social and moral values in Turkish society have been markedly shaped and preserved by the hand of that institution. To take one example, the *fatwās* that concern marriage with milk siblings are obeyed by both religious and secular sections of the society despite the fact that there is no law, regulation or statute within Turkey's secular legal system that prohibits marriage between milk siblings.[3] In the *fatwā* that relates to marriage with milk siblings, the Diyanet states that this kind of marriage is prohibited by Islamic law.[4] This and similar *fatwās* relevant to marriage with milk siblings do not only uphold the Islamic legal prohibition but also give rise to a sanctioning power that operates socially. However, in many cases, this power of *fatwās* only operates within Muslim sections of society, and therefore generally extends to other matters such as abortion, consumption of alcohol and use of interest (*ribā*) in purchase and sale transactions.

Like the Diyanet's *fatwās*, the FCNA's *fatwās* do not have any legally binding authority within the American secular legal system to any extent at all.[5] Despite their non-binding feature, these *fatwās* guide and instruct American Muslims in their religious and social problems. The question of whether the FCNA's Islamic legal resolutions and *fatwās* have the potentiality of forming communal and normative values within the American Muslim community cannot be easily answered because there is not any existing information regarding their acceptability amongst

2 Al-Atawneh (n 1) 21.

3 Emir Kaya, 'Balancing Interlegality through Realist Altruism: Diyanet Mediation in Turkey' (PhD thesis, University of London 2011) 219.

4 Din İşleri Yüksek Kurulu, *Fetvalar* (Diyanet İşleri Başkanlığı Yayınları 2015) 467.

5 Bryan S. Turner and James T. Richardson, 'Islam and the Problems of Liberal Democracy' in Maurits S. Berger (ed), *Applying Shari'a in the West: Facts, Fears and the Future of Islamic Rules on the Family Relations in the West* (Leiden University Press 2013) 52.

American Muslims. It is necessary to have such information in order to determine the potentiality of *fatwās* in creating communal values and norms. However, the ascertainment of to what extent American Muslims adopt the *fatwās* issued by the FCNA is quite difficult on account of the disorderly dispersion of American Muslims over the continent and the diversity of American Muslims' religious inclinations and ethnicities.[6] The admissibility of the *fatwās* is also linked to the acceptance of the authority of the Council's scholars amongst American Muslims. Ayubi reiterates:

> The FCNA's *fatwās* are only binding for those who accept the authority of the scholars on the council and seek an authentic Islamic resolution to religio-legal challenges in America. On a community level, mosque boards, local imāms, and religious elders have also functioned as religious authorities for mediating legal disputes or religious controversies.[7]

Ayubi's statement evinces that American Muslims are selective in seeking *fatwās* for their legal questions and perplexities and that there is no single source of authority for the majority of American Muslims. The FCNA therefore does not have so much authority amongst American Muslims.[8] The *fatwās* related to marriage and divorce issues, for example, seek to establish a congruence between Islamic law and American civil law. The validity of civil marriage performed by a non-Muslim registrar was questioned, and the associated *fatwā* indicated the legality of this kind of marriage in terms of Islamic law.[9] Another *fatwā* regarding divorce states: "[the FCNA] has determined that no Muslim marriage may be terminated unless it is terminated through the court system of the state in which the Muslim is resident."[10] The Council intends to provide a remedy for the abuse and exploitation of Islamic law by lay Muslims, but despite these *fatwās*, many American Muslims perform religious marriages and divorces without obtaining official marriage and divorce certificates from the formal institutions within America.[11] This evidences that the acceptability of the *fatwās* issued by the Council amongst American Muslims is not as authoritative and influential as to form normative values within the American Muslim community.

6 Turner and Richardson (n 5) 57–58; Jocelyne Cesari, *When Islam and Democracy Meet: Muslims in Europe and in the United States* (Palgrave Macmillan 2004) 4, 11.

7 Zahra M. S. Ayubi, 'Negotiating Justice: American Muslim Women Navigating Islamic Divorce and Civil Law' (2010) 30 *Journal for Islamic Studies* 83.

8 Turner and Richardson (n 5) 52.

9 Yusuf Talal DeLorenzo, 'The Fiqh Councilor of North America' in Yvonne Y. Haddad and John L. Esposito (eds), *Muslims on the Americanization Path?* (Oxford University Press 2000) 73.

10 Cited from DeLorenzo (n 9) 73.

11 In conjugal issues, many American Muslims maintain their adherence to classical Islamic law and perform their marriages and divorces in accordance with the regulations identified within the classical Islamic law, without applying the official legal regulations that are specified by civil law in America. For further insight, refer to Ayubi (n 7) 83, 87–89; Cesari (n 6) 59.

The sanctioning power of *fatwās* that have been issued by the religious institutions can be linked to the legal system that prevails within the three countries. If the legal system of the country is Islamic (as in the case of Saudi Arabia), then the *fatwās* issued by the official religious establishment have the potential to become binding legal regulations. However, if the legal system of the country is not Islamic, then *fatwās* can still acquire the power of social sanction, although this is dependent upon the proportion of the Muslim population in a country. The official *fatwās* may sometimes create and formulate a social norm or a moral value acceptable to a large segment of society if the society has a Muslim-majority populace – this is the case within Saudi Arabia and Turkey. What situates the official *fatwās* at the centre of Muslims' practices as the only useful mechanism to deal with Islamic normativity in Turkey is conceivably the disconnection of Islam from the state's legal system. However, the issued *fatwās* do not have any power to legally impose sanctions upon people because they only possess the status of Islamic legal opinions and their implementation depends on the acceptance of the individual who asked the question. If the society has a Muslim minority populace, *fatwās* generally do not produce any social and moral values. As in the case of America, the *fatwās* issued by the FCNA do not have the power to generate social and normative values within the Christian-majority American society and even within the American Muslim minority community. The admissibility of *fatwās* can change in accordance with the ethnicity, culture and *madhhab* affiliation of American Muslims, along with the acceptance of the authority of Council members by American Muslims.

In Saudi Arabia, there is also an enforcement mechanism (the Committee for Encouraging Virtue and Preventing Vice – this is the religious police, more generally known as *Muṭawwi'a*). This mechanism enables the legal rulings of *fatwās* to be implemented in the society and ensures popular obedience to the *fatwās* issued by the Dār al-Iftā'.[12] Shahi has depicted its forceful and repressive character in Saudi Arabia. He states:

> The *Mutawwi'in* are a powerful socio-political force that acts as the vanguards of the Wahhabi state. Its members are portrayed as the "guardians of morality", monitoring public as well as private spheres to standardise collective behaviour in accordance with Wahabi ideology.[13]

The *Muṭawwi'a* has been present since the establishment of the Saudi state.[14] It usually acts in accordance with the *fatwās* issued by the Dār al-Iftā' to ensure that Saudi society obeys and implements Islamic law – the official *fatwās* are not only optional Islamic legal interpretations and rulings but are also compulsory and

12 Al-Atawneh (n 1) 112.
13 Afshin Shahi, *The Politics of Truth Management in Saudi Arabia* (Routledge 2013) 77; Ayman al-Yassini, *Religion and State in the Kingdom of Saudi Arabia* (Westview Press 1985) 143.
14 Shahi (n 13) 157–158.

obligatory norms that exert a considerable influence over Saudi ethical and social values. It is clear that the *Muṭawwi'a* is the main enforcement mechanism that is used to create an ideal Islamic state in which the Wahhābī values and practices are observed. This enforcement mechanism circulated the Wahhābī ideology throughout the newly constructed Saudi Kingdom to the point where it became established as the Saudi national culture and the essential underpinning of core social values.[15]

Turkish citizens are not required to obey *fatwās* that were issued in response to questions asked the Diyanet. There are also no institutionalised mechanisms that enforce declared Islamic legal rulings in the form of *fatwās*. It is entirely permissible for an individual to seek another *fatwā* from a different religious institution or other Muslim scholars within or outside the country. Both lay people and state officials are entitled to seek the Diyanet's view and also benefit from its *fatwās* on religiously sensitive issues. The Diyanet can also provide consultation during the course of legal processes. During the 1980s, in the aftermath of the military coup, the military government asked the Diyanet for its opinions upon state policies, which included banking interest (*ribā*), the headscarf and organ transplantation.[16] In engaging with these issues, the Diyanet's Islamic legal explanations and statements have usually evidenced consistency but have sometimes created the impression that they were issued with the intention of placating the state authorities.

In addressing the issue of banking interest, the Diyanet provided some circumstantial solutions and encouraged the general public and state authorities to conduct themselves with due caution and vigilance.[17] However, the Diyanet's view on this issue was not effective and was not taken into account by the legislative body during the legislative process relating to banking.[18] As to the headscarf issue, the Diyanet maintained that Muslim women are obliged to cover their hair; however, the Constitutional Court disregarded the Diyanet's explanation and ruled against veiling within public buildings, a category which encompassed hospitals, ministries, public schools, the Turkish Parliament building and universities. Although the Diyanet was often presented as the supreme religious authority, its *fatwās* were not sufficiently taken into account by the state legislative body during this period. The headscarf issue brought out the conflict between the *fatwā* issued by the Diyanet and the secular legal regulations within the Turkish Republic, but many Muslim women tended to follow the Diyanet's explanation, as opposed to the state regulations, upon this issue. This created an internal conflict between state departments and also social conflict within the society. Nonetheless, the Diyanet's position on organ transplantation[19] has become a major component of the state's

15 ibid 157–161.
16 Kaya (n 3) 220.
17 ibid.
18 ibid.
19 Din İşleri Yüksek Kurulu (n 4) 535–536.

public engagement on this issue and a key component of related state policies.[20] It has become increasingly clear that even official state bodies, in particular the legislative organs, are free to espouse the Diyanet's Islamic legal decisions and *fatwās* in the legal processes. With regard to this, Kaya argues:

> The Diyanet's view may be sought not only by the public but also by state officials. Its scholarly credibility and freedom of speech are acknowledged by the state. It can contradict the state policies despite working under the government, but its judgement cannot constitute any justification for legislation. This is a feature of Turkish laicism by which the religion's academics and the state's executive liberties are guaranteed against each other. Its reflection on the public is such that the people are presented both religious and secular options, and in case of their conflict, are expected to make their own choices.[21]

The Diyanet is an institution whose services and undertakings are not compulsory or binding in any respect – it does not therefore exert coercive authority over the society.[22] It should nonetheless be observed that the production of *fatwās* is a valuable component of the institution's work which gives it considerable credit and respect.[23] From this perspective, the Diyanet appears as an erudite authority which exerts considerable influence over the public. While the Diyanet may appear at times to embody the state's control over religion, this institution puts in place a reconciliatory approach between religion and secularism. Within the state, the Diyanet presents itself as the main agent of Islamic law and jurisprudence which represents a scholarly tradition that surpasses the legal field and encompasses the entirety of Islam.[24]

Unlike the Dār al-Iftā' and the Diyanet, the FCNA is a fully state-independent 501(c)(3) institution, so it does not have any state support and funding to maintain its existence and continue its operations. Nonetheless, the Council has tax-exempt status and normally receives a substantial part of its income, directly or indirectly, from donations from Muslims in America.[25] The status and jurisdiction boundaries of the FCNA are determined in accordance with the Internal Revenue Code of America, that includes the rules, regulations and procedures with regard

20 Kaya (n 3) 220.

21 ibid 221.

22 M. Hakan Yavuz, 'Tukey: Islam without Shari'a?' in Robert W. Hefner (ed), *Shari'a Politics: Islamic Law and Society in the Modern World* (Indiana University Press 2011) 164.

23 Kaya (n 3) 141.

24 ibid 117.

25 Fiqh Council of North America, 'FCNA Brochure' <http://fiqhcouncil.org/wp-content/uploads/2018/09/FCNABrochure.pdf> accessed 26 December 2020; International Revenue Service (IRS), 'Tax-Exempt Status for Your Organization' (Publication 557 (Rev. January 2020) Cat. No. 46573C) 22, 29.

to 501(c)(3) organisations.[26] Despite the fact that the state-independent character of the FCNA provides it with a more autonomous status, the Council and its *fatwās* are deprived of the authority and notability that the Saudi and Turkish states confer upon the Dār al-Iftā' and the Diyanet, respectively. While the state-dependent character of the Dār al-Iftā' and the Diyanet provides them with the state funding that facilitates their organisational activities and dissemination of their production regarding Islamic knowledge, the maintenance and operation of the FCNA are primarily dependent upon donations that American Muslims have granted. The FCNA therefore has a limited budget to implement its activities and organisations. Nonetheless, the state-dependent character of the Dār al-Iftā' and the Diyanet attests implicitly to the state control of the two institutions while they are operating within their contexts. Especially, it is possible to observe the state pressure and control upon them when these institutions engage with governmental, political, national and international issues. Since its establishment, the FCNA has however functioned as a voluntary organisation to provide Islamic legal solutions to the problems and exigencies that American Muslims face. The Council's voluntary, or state-independent, character emerges as an economically restrictive factor that limits its activities and functions. Some questions directed to the Council have not however been appropriately evaluated and answered on account of its insufficient budget. This can therefore be acknowledged as an implicit factor that restricts the FCNA in reaching a wider audience within the American context.

The secular legal systems of both Turkey and America manifest themselves as restrictive elements that demarcate the jurisdiction of the Diyanet and the FCNA. Cesari observes: "Secularisation, however, represents more than the separation of the religious and the political spheres. It also, and more importantly, stands for the diminished social influence of religion and its institutions in public life."[27] As Cesari states, the secular legal regulations related to religious institutions within Turkey and America have limited the jurisdiction of the Diyanet and the FCNA. In Turkey, the jurisdiction and functions of the Diyanet are explicitly specified by Constitutional regulations. Act 429 and Act 633 designate the Diyanet as a constitutional body that is only responsible for religious affairs while Act 93/4257 establishes that the decisions and *fatwās* issued by the Diyanet merely have an informative and advisory character and are not binding to any extent.[28] The

26 International Revenue Service (IRS) (n 25) 22–40.

27 Cesari (n 6) 43–44.

28 Act no. 429 dated 03 March 1924. See Resmi Gazete (*Official Gazette*), 06. 03. 1924-63 <http://www.resmigazete.gov.tr/main.aspx?home=http://www.resmigazete.gov.tr/arsiv/63.pdf&main=http://www.resmigazete.gov.tr/arsiv/63.pdf> accessed 26 September 2016; Act no. 633 dated 22 July 1965. See Resmi Gazete, 02. 07. 1965-12038 <http://www.resmigazete.gov.tr/main.aspx?home=http://www.resmigazete.gov.tr/arsiv/12038.pdf&main=http://www.resmigazete.gov.tr/arsiv/12038.pdf> accessed 28 September 2016; Act no. 93/4257 dated 19 February 1993. See Resmi Gazete, 30. 04. 1993-21567 <http://www.resmigazete.gov.tr/main.aspx?home=http://www.resmigazete.gov.tr/arsiv/21567.pdf&main=http://www.resmigazete.gov.tr/arsiv/21567.pdf> accessed 06 March 2021.

principle of secularism in Turkey therefore intends to control religion through the Diyanet.

Conversely, the principle of secularism in America is grounded on the total separation of religion and state, so the institutionalisation of any religion depends upon initiatives conducted by its followers. Religious affairs are acknowledged as an aspect of civil society outside the political sphere, and the government merely presents itself as the protector of religious freedom and guarantees equal treatment to all religions and their followers.[29] Nonetheless, the FCNA sometimes assumes the role of arbitration in disagreements that occur between American Muslims.[30] While evaluating predicaments regarding marriage, polygamy and divorce issues that Muslim minorities face in Europe and America, Cesari observes: "A system of arbitration also exists in the United States, where the [FCNA] has sought solutions to cases of conflict between Islamic regulations and prevailing American norms since 1995."[31] This can be accepted as an auxiliary mechanism within the American secular system when it settles the disagreements amongst American Muslims in accordance with the voluntary principle of comity that enables courts to consider religious law in their decisions.[32] However, the secular legal system of Turkey does not strictly allocate such an arbiter role to the Diyanet on account of the infringement of the principle of secularism. It can therefore be asserted that the American secular legal system that depends upon the philosophical principles of tolerance and respect for religious beliefs is more liberal and complaisant towards religious law than the Turkish secular legal system that is grounded on the clear-cut severing of religion from politics and law.

Contrary to the secular legal systems of Turkey and America that disestablish religion from politics, Islam emerges as the foundational element of the Saudi legal system, that provides more authoritative power to the Dār al-Iftā' and its *fatwās* within governmental, political and legal circles. Royal Decree A/137 designates the Dār al-Iftā' as both an advisory body which provides assistance to the King on common law issues and a pre-legislative mechanism which issues Islamic legal decisions that have the potential to become state laws.[33] The Islamic legal system of Saudi Arabia therefore officially allocates a supervisory and pre-legislator role to the Dār al-Iftā' with regard to public affairs and common law issues.

The intricate interaction between Islamic legal theories and contextual environments that arises from the legal systems of the three countries can also be traced through a closer engagement with their laws, statutes and regulations.

29 Cesari (n 6) 70.

30 Fiqh Council of North America (n 25).

31 Cesari (n 6) 60.

32 Sarah M. Fallon, 'Justice for All: American Muslims, Sharia Law, and Maintaining Comity with American Jurisprudence' (2013) 36 (1) *Boston College International and Comparative Law Review* 153, 155; Eugene Volokh, 'Religious Law (Especially Islamic Law) in American Courts' (2014) 66 (2) *Oklahoma Law Review* 431–440.

33 Royal Decree A/137, August 29, 1971, 1–3.

The legal system of Saudi Arabia was structured in accordance with traditional Islamic legal sources, that is, the traditional corpus of Islamic jurisprudence and law has largely contributed to the construction of its legal system. Vogel notes that this grounding within sharīʿa clearly distinguishes the Saudi legal system from its counterparts ("unlike virtually every other country, [Saudi Arabia] has not replaced its legal system with a Western-model constitutional and legal order").[34] The prevailing law was formulated in accordance with the Ḥanbalī *madhhab* and has continually been complemented by royal decrees issued by the King and supplemented by influential developments. Within this sharīʿa-based Saudi legal system, *fatwās* assume a complementary role and function as a secondary source for the Saudi judiciary.

To provide an example, three *fatwā*s on the issue of *ṭalāq* (divorce through the repudiation of the husband) that were provided by the Dār al-Iftā' during the presidency of Ibn Bāz were recognised by the Saudi courts as being legally authoritative sources within the wider context of the legal procedure.[35] The first *fatwā* relates to the issue of divorce by oath, which entails the utterance of words of conditional divorce to fortify vows (for instance, "my wife is divorced if I do this again"). The early *fiqh* authorities established that this type of divorce is valid and operative upon the fulfilment of the condition made through the oath – this classical view was normally applied and upheld within the Saudi courts. The BSU studied this issue, while drawing upon the extensive research that was prepared by the CRLO. At the culmination of this process, two *fatwās* were issued: the first *fatwā* upheld the traditional ruling approved by the majority of the BSU members, while the other *fatwā* was an opposing opinion that was adopted by a minority of the BSU, including Ibn Bāz. The *fatwā* adopted by the minority group clearly establishes that the utterance of words of divorce to fortify vows does not bring about a divorce of spouses; rather, the individual who vowed must be obliged to perform the atonement (*kaffarā*) when the condition is fulfilled.[36] The second *fatwā* is associated with the validity of divorces that are uttered in a state of extreme anger.[37] The Ḥanbalī *madhhab* which is applied within the Saudi courts tends to be too strict on this point. It is generally the case that when the husband utters divorce in a state of anger, the divorce becomes automatically operative.[38] In a manner that closely resembles the first *fatwā*, a minority of the BSU, including Ibn Bāz, decided against accepting the *ṭalāq* uttered in a state of

34 Frank Vogel, 'The Complementarity of Ifta' and Qaḍā': Three Saudi Fatwas on Divorce' in Muhammad Khalid Masud, Brinkley Messick and David S. Powers (eds), *Islamic Legal Interpretation: Muftis and Their Fatwas* (Harvard University Press 1996) 262.

35 Vogel, 'The Complementarity of Ifta'' (n 34) 262.

36 ibid 262–263.

37 ibid 264.

38 Vogel, 'The Complementarity of Ifta'' (n 34) 264–265, 267–268 and Sümeyra Yakar and Emine Enise Yakar, 'A Critical Comparison between the Classical Divorce Types of Ḥanbalī and Ja'arī Schools' (2020) 31 (2) *darulfunun ilahiyat* 281–282.

extreme anger.[39] The last *fatwā* relates to the issuing of three divorces at once. A historical perspective makes it clear that all four of the Sunni *madhhabs* almost unanimously converged upon the view that a triple divorce of this kind has a triple effect. This is the legal regulation which judges apply in the courts. In most likely drawing upon Ibn Taymiyya's view that the triple divorce should be counted as a single divorce, a minority of the BSU, including Ibn Bāz, placed themselves in opposition to the majority view by endorsing three divorces at once as a single divorce.[40] With their authority having been endorsed and reinforced by the president of the Dār al-Iftā', Ibn Bāz's *fatwās* (which evidence a clear leniency towards husbands who seek to offset the consequences of their acts of *ṭalāq*) are taken into consideration by judges before they provide a verdict in the Saudi courts. In some cases, the parties were even advised to benefit from these *fatwās*. As Vogel verifies in his article, the courts provide clear proof that *fatwās* may function as a legal source that the judge may draw upon when issuing their own verdict at the end of the legal process.[41] In Saudi Arabia, a number of judicial arrangements were formulated in accordance with *fatwās*; accordingly, the *fatwā* mechanism can perform a complementary and mediatory role by providing an enhanced level of flexibility to the existing standard of law within the Saudi legal system.

However, the legal system of the country not only influences the function, role and sanctioning power of *fatwās* but also occasionally impinges upon the content and legal ruling of *fatwās* in Turkey and America. A number of *fatwās* issued by the Diyanet are formulated within the context of the state regulations. The early Republican government, which advanced a radical secular agenda, sought to remove the influence of Islamic law upon society and replace it with European codes. In the aftermath of the collapse of the Ottoman Sultanate, the Turkish Republic experienced a process of democratisation, extensive modernisation and secularisation – this radical agenda drew strongly upon the German and Italian Commercial Codes and the Swiss Civil Code in the legal area. These revolutions sought to distance Turkey from the presumed backwardness of the Muslim world and also created a modern society that was more civilised, rational and scientific than its Muslim counterparts.[42] At the conclusion of this process, it was anticipated that "No rules of Sharīʿa were to continue to exist, including such of its features as polygamy and the religious ceremony surrounding marriage."[43] Religion was confined to the private sphere to as great an extent as possible. Despite the state's ongoing attempts to secularise society, Islamic practices and values remained pervasive within Turkish society, with the influence of Islam being evidenced within various spheres of legal and social relations. Hallaq observes:

39 According to the Ḥanbalī school, this kind of divorce is valid, and this position of the Ḥanbalī school is strictly applied by the courts. See Vogel, 'The Complementarity of Ifta'' (n 34) 264.

40 Vogel, 'The Complementarity of Ifta'' (n 34) 265–266.

41 ibid 267–269.

42 Wael B. Hallaq, *Sharīʿa: Theory, Practice, Transformation* (Cambridge University Press 2009) 498.

43 ibid.

> The case of Turkey represents a unique example of a society that has clung to Islamic values despite the structural, even radical, dismantling of the Sharīʿa legal system over nearly a century.[44]

The Diyanet and its *fatwās* have presumably made an essential contribution in supporting the social commitment to Islamic legal values. This assumed role of the Diyanet may be understood better when the *fatwā* that counterpoises official and religious marriage is referred to and examined.

As has already been noted, civil, familial and marital issues within Turkey are legally governed by the Turkish Civil Code, which was imported from the Swiss Civil Code. Act no. 5237 establishes that religious marriage (*nikāḥ*) does not have any official status or legal validity within Turkey's legal system.[45] The couple who performs a religious marriage in the absence of official marriage is held not to be married; therefore, they, as the civil state law establishes, do not have the liabilities, responsibilities and rights that derive from an officially implemented marriage. Amongst many Turks, religious marriage is still a preferred form of marriage that, in contrast to official marriage, makes a marriage legitimate and valid.[46] When explaining the trajectory of Islamic law in Turkey, Hallaq further reiterates this point ("In popular perception, legitimacy of marriage rested solely in the *shar'ī nikāḥ*, and children born within civil marriages were normatively regarded as 'bastards'").[47] Nonetheless, women who perform religious marriage without official marriage do not claim any right before the state's courts subsequent to the nullification of their marriage; meanwhile, children born within religious marriages cannot be registered in the name of their fathers and cannot, by extension, claim any rights from their father's inheritance. In attempting to minimise and resolve potential problems and social disorders that arose from performing only religious marriage, the Diyanet issued several *fatwās* that combined official and religious law. In drawing upon the legal principle of *maṣlaḥa*, the Diyanet guided individuals to fulfil official marriage initially in accordance with the Turkish Civil Code and later to perform *nikāḥ*.[48] However, when the couple performs the official marriage, they must simultaneously fulfil the obligatory conditions and requirements of religious marriage, which include dower (*mahr*).[49] The *fatwās* that relate to civil-religious marriages clearly demonstrate how state laws occasionally infiltrate into Islamic legal decisions and *fatwās* issued by the Diyanet. The institution therefore seeks to offer Islamic legal guidance and solutions with an attempt to resolve the sense of confusion which results when

44 ibid 497.

45 Ihsan Yılmaz, 'Secular Law and the Emergence of Unofficial Turkish Islamic Law' (2002) 56 (1) *Middle East Journal* 121–122.

46 Hallaq (n 42) 498.

47 ibid.

48 Din İşleri Yüksek Kurulu (n 4) 429–432, 439–440.

49 ibid 431–432.

Muslims live under a secular legal system – this is achieved by bridging the gap between Islamic law and official law.

The legal statutes and regulations of America also percolate into the contents of the *fatwās* issued by the FCNA. The minority status of American Muslims induces the FCNA to espouse an approach that is intended to reconcile the legal norms of Islamic law with the legal regulations of America. Conflicts that arise from discord between Islamic legal principles and American legal regulations are therefore generally sought to be resolved through hybridisation. This denotes that the legal prescriptions in *fatwās* are generally reconstructed by taking into account the legal regulations and laws of America. In many *fatwās*, the Council explicitly orients American Muslims to obey the law of the country while at the same time inciting them to pursue Islamic legal values and norms. The FCNA usually intends to obviate the tensions and dilemmas rooted in the dual identity of American Muslims. Their American identity legally obliges American Muslims to obey the secular regulations and laws of the land while being Muslim religiously obliges them to comply with the instructions and regulations that are identified in accordance with Islamic law. The FCNA therefore adopts a reconciliatory approach that temperately seeks to establish a balance between the religious responsibilities and citizenship liabilities of American Muslims and offer creative solutions to the specific problems that confront American Muslims.

The *fatwā* regarding participation in the American military for example engages with the intricate issue that originates in a conflict between the religious and citizenship identities of American Muslims.[50] Here the knotty issue is whether an American Muslim soldier can participate in a war against a Muslim country and whether his loyalty should be to the global Muslim community (*umma*) or his own country, America. In drawing upon the principle of *maṣlaḥa* and *ḍarūra*, the FCNA assents to the participation of American Muslim soldiers in such a war while indicating that the American Muslim soldier must offer his loyalty to America (even if the war is between America and a Muslim country).[51] It is stated that being an American citizen requires American Muslim soldiers to fulfil their responsibilities and obligations towards their country.[52] In ratifying the loyalty of American Muslims to their country, the *fatwā* aspires to reconcile the American legal regulations and Islamic legal norms regarding the allegiance of citizens. An American citizen either by birth or through naturalisation must present allegiance

50 Mohamed Nimer, *The North American Muslim Resource Guide: Muslim Community Life in the United States and Canada* (Routledge 2002) 167–168; Basheer M. Nafi, 'Fatwā and War: On the Allegiance of the American Muslim Soldiers in the Aftermath of September 11' (2004) 11 (1) *Islamic Law and Society* 90–97.

51 The Middle East Media Research Institute (MEMRI), 'Terror in America (23) Muslim Soldiers in the U.S. Armed Forces in Afghanistan: To Fight or Not to Fight?' <https://www.memri.org/reports/terror-america-23-muslim-soldiers-us-armed-forces-afghanistan-fight-or-not-fight> accessed 15 December 2020.

52 ibid.

to America in accordance with the Code of Federal Regulations.[53] 8 U.S.C. 1101 (a)(22) states: "The term 'national of the United States' means (A) a citizen of the United States, or (B) a person, who, though not a citizen of the United States, owes permanent allegiance to the United States."[54] This allegiance requires several promises to be made, including to support and defend the Constitution and the laws of the United States, to bear arms on behalf of the United States when required by the law and to abjure all prior allegiance to any other nation and sovereignty.[55] In considering the legal regulation regarding allegiance, the *fatwā* states:

> The Muslim here is part a whole; if he absconds, his departure will result in a greater harm, not only for him but also for the Muslim community in his country – and here there are many millions of them. Moreover, even if fighting causes him discomfort spiritually or psychologically, this personal hardship must be endured for the greater public good, as the jurisprudence (Fiqh) rule states.[56]

Therefore, allegiance to America is recognised as legitimate upon the grounds of two legal maxims (the choosing of the less harmful of two harms (*aqall al-ḍararayn*) and the principle of intention (*niyya*)). Despite the fact that the participation of American Muslim soldiers in a war against a Muslim country likely causes harm to other Muslims, their renunciation of participation in such a war may engender an adverse influence on the presence and position of the American Muslim community. In the *fatwā*, the emphasis is put on the protection and observance of the welfare of the American Muslim community by narrowing the concept of *umma*.[57] The Council therefore privileges the well-being of the American Muslim community with the intention of accommodating Islamic legal values to American legal regulations.

Gender issues and family matters are the most turbulent domains that conflict with American secular legal regulations. In *fatwās* regarding family issues especially, American Muslims are oriented by the Council to fulfil the requirements of both civil law and Islamic law. The *fatwā* related to alimony (*nafaqa*) for instance indicates that after divorce, the husband should continue to financially support his wife even if he has already paid her dower.[58] The wife does not have the right to claim alimony after the waiting period (*'idda*) in accordance

53 8 CFR ("Aliens and Nationality") <https://ecfr.federalregister.gov/current/title-8/chapter-I/subchapter-C> accessed 17 January 2021.

54 8 U.S.C. 1101 (a) (22) <https://www.govinfo.gov/content/pkg/USCODE-2018-title8/pdf/USCODE-2018-title8-chap12-subchapI-sec1101.pdf> accessed 17 January 2021.

55 8 CFR 337. 1 ('Oath of Allegiance') <https://ecfr.federalregister.gov/current/title-8/chapter-I/subchapter-C/part-337> accessed 17 January 2021.

56 The Middle East Media Research Institute (MEMRI) (n 51).

57 ibid.

58 DeLorenzo (n 9) 73–74.

with the classical Islamic legal regulations, but the Council links this legal ruling to the earlier Muslim scholars' social and cultural context in which the extended family provided necessary supports and services to the divorced woman.[59] Many American Muslim housewives depend financially upon their husbands for their needs, so the Council states that the husband, after his absolute divorce, is responsible for the welfare of the divorced wife until she remarries.[60] This is consolidated through the general principle that is determined in accordance with the Q. 4:34 that renders men to be protectors and maintainers of women. The absence of extended family practice in American society emerges as an influential factor that induces the FCNA to consider American legal regulations regarding alimony. Although the determination of alimony varies from one state to another, each state, except South Carolina, has its own statutes with regard to alimony payments, recovery and penalties.[61] With the intention of dispelling the conflicts relevant to alimony between Islamic legal principles and American legal regulations, the FCNA adopts a reconciliatory approach that syncretises both regulations. Another *fatwā* related to marriage and divorce also states that American Muslims should register their marriages and divorces in accordance with the proper legal formalities of the state in which they are resident, so the FCNA precisely impels American Muslims to fulfil both civil and religious procedures regarding marriage and divorce.[62] These *fatwās* evidence that the Council intends to provide appropriate legal solutions for the conflicts that American Muslims face while also taking into consideration American laws, regulations and statutes. It is therefore possible to observe the percolation of American legal regulations into the *fatwās* issued by the FCNA.

The Islamic character of the Saudi legal system provides a crucial position to the official *fatwās* issued by the Dār al-Iftā' within the Saudi judicial system. They have the potentiality to become state regulations with the approval of the King; in addition, they obtain a recognised place as a legal source that Saudi judges draw upon when issuing a legal verdict. Conversely, *fatwās* issued by the Diyanet can possess the status of ethical norms and moral values within the society while emerging as a form of social sanctioning power. However, they cannot be said to possess an authoritative function and position within the Turkish judicial system. In functioning within a secular legal system, the Diyanet is occasionally forced to take the state law into account so as not to create social disorder and turmoil. A number of *fatwās* issued by the Diyanet evidence a hybrid character which amalgamates religious and state law with the intention of establishing social

59 Zainab Alwani and Celene Ayat Lizzio, 'Religion, Gender and Family Law: Critical Perspectives on Integration for Western Muslims' in Maurits S. Berger (ed), *Applying Shari'a in the West: Facts, Fears and the Future of Islamic Rules on the Family Relations in the West* (Leiden University Press 2013) 232–233; DeLorenzo (n 9) 73–74.

60 DeLorenzo (n 9) 74.

61 Chester G. Vernier and John B. Hurlbut, 'The Historical Background of Alimony Law and Its Present Statutory Structure' (1939) 6 (2) *Law and Contemporary Problems* 201–202.

62 DeLorenzo (n 9) 73, 75–76.

harmony, tranquillity and welfare in the country. Unlike the Dār al-Iftā' and the Diyanet, the FCNA does not have official status and authority in America, so its *fatwās* do not have enough power to form social norms and ethical values within the American Muslim community. The diversity in American Muslims' ethnicities, cultures and religious inclinations manifests as a disincentive factor for the admissibility of the FCNA's *fatwās* for the majority of American Muslims. Like the Diyanet, the FCNA also espouses a reconciliatory approach that combines Islamic legal principles and American legal regulations. It is therefore possible to observe the percolation of American legal regulations into the *fatwās* issued by the Council.

The influence of political systems

The political systems of the three countries have demonstrated their influence over the three institutions, and it is therefore necessary to understand the political systems and the relationship between state and religion. The authority, power and role of official religious scholars within the Dār al-Iftā' and the Diyanet vary in accordance with the political processes and structures that are operative within both contexts. Contrarily, the state-independent character of the FCNA provides more autonomous prerogative to its members when they address the issues relevant to the relationship between politics and religion. In addition, *fatwās* which relate to political forms, religious legitimacy and obedience to political authorities are generally formulated by the three institutions in accordance with the political systems that are specific to Saudi Arabia, Turkey and America.

Since being established, Saudi Arabia has operated as an absolute theocratic monarchy, whose governance has been underpinned by Islamic law. Because there is no separation between religion and state, *fatwās* have a pervasive political influence in Saudi Arabia. Taking into account the fact that the close association between the religious scholars (*'ulamā'*) and the Saud dynasty (*'umarā'*) in the eighteenth century has continued with minor adjustments in contemporary Saudi Arabia, the political role of the official *'ulamā'* has been as important and influential as the ruling dynasty within the state.[63] This interdependence has also been fortified by the doctrine of Wahhābī *siyāsa shar'iyya* which amalgamates politics and religion within doctrinal thought. A number of *fatwās* issued by the Dār al-Iftā' conceive of a complementary relationship between *'ulamā'* and *'umarā'* which is grounded within the doctrine of Wahhābī *siyāsa shar'iyya*, in which both are introduced as authority-holders (*wulāt al-'amr*).

During the twentieth century, Saudi Arabia experienced a modernisation and institutionalisation process which extended to the religious establishment and the practice of *iftā'* regulated by the *'ulamā'*. Although the steep increase in oil revenues during the 1950s produced a series of administrative and institutional reforms, the *'ulamā'*, as the guardians of the Saudi state's religious character,

63 Al-Atawneh (n 1) 35.

were never marginalised as happened in Turkey after the dissolution of the Ottoman Sultanate. Up until the contemporary period, the proposition that the Saudi state is fundamentally Islamic remains central to the efforts of the *'ulamā'* to legitimate the Islamic state's political power. It is perhaps unsurprising that in contemporary Saudi Arabia, the Dār al-Iftā' functions as a closet agency which produces a set of legal and political perspectives that help to sustain and legitimise the political authority of the Saudi dynasty as the *'ulamā'* from the family of Āl al-Shaykh performed from the mid-eighteenth century to the early 1950s. During times of crisis, the Saudi Government resisted and repulsed a considerable number of social and political uprisings and other escalations by strengthening its ties with the religious establishment. During Iraq's 1990 invasion of Kuwait, for example, the Dār al-Iftā' issued a *fatwā* which allowed the US army to be deployed in Saudi Arabia in order to support the policy of the Saudi Government that sought to align itself with the United States.[64] When the repercussions of the Arab Spring began to be felt in Saudi Arabia, the *fatwā* that delegitimises public demonstrations because of their divisive impacts in society was issued by the Dār al-Iftā' to forestall any possible uprising against the Saudi Government.[65] During the Arab-Israel Peace Process, the Dār al-Iftā' issued a *fatwā* that assented to the signing of the truce between Palestine and Israel in accordance with the Saudi Government's foreign policy.[66] These examples clearly demonstrate how the Saudi Government sought to harness the religious authority (the Dār al-Iftā') in order to obtain religious consent that legitimates and supports its political strategy. The official *fatwās* that relate to political issues have been generally used to legitimise the Saudi Government's political policies and curtail the activities of radical movements which seek to challenge the Saudi dynasty. When *fatwās* regarding political issues are analysed, the Dār al-Iftā' generally creates the impression that it is only acting as an agent or office which seeks to legitimate the Saudi Government's political policies. Despite the fact that the Saudi political power compels the official *'ulamā'* to issue *fatwās* that legitimise its policies within the area of politics, their official *fatwās* are effective both within the Saudi political system and Saudi society – this applies irrespective of whether political pressure or repression is an active consideration.

64 'Ulema Council Supports Actions of King Fahd' *Foreign Broadcast Information Service-Near East & South Asia* [*FBIS-NES*] 90–157, August 14, 1990, 26 <http://0-infoweb.newsbank.com.lib.exeter.ac.uk/iw-search/we/HistArchive/?p_product=FBISX&p_theme=fbis&p_nbid=M62Q5CDTMTQ3MTE5NjY1My42NzkyNzg6MToxMjoxNDQuMTczLjYuOTQ&p_action=doc&p_queryname=11&toc=true&p_docref=v2:11C33B0D5F860D98@FBISX-11CAD8A2EEA95BB8@2448118-11CAD8ACEF88AF98@32-11CAD8AD30FFAF98> accessed 15 August 2016; F. Gregory Gause III, 'Official Wahhabism and the Sanctioning of the Saudi-US Relations' in Mohammed Ayoop and Hasan Kosebalaban (eds), *Religion and Politics in Saudi Arabia: Wahhabism and the State* (Lynne Rienner Publishers 2009) 140.

65 Emine Enise Yakar, 'The Influential Role of the Practice of Iftā' in Saudi Politico-Legal Arena' (2020) 16 (1) *Manchester Journal of Transnational Islamic Law and Practice* 47–48.

66 ibid 57–58.

The Dār al-Iftā' and the Saudi Government have an ongoing mutual partnership which institutes an arrangement in which the official members of the religious establishment usually support the government policy, in particular when addressing themselves to politically sensitive issues. The Saudi Government enforces their *fatwās* in return for their sustained support. Mouline observes that there is a strong incessant interdependence between the Saudi rulers and the official *'ulamā'* in the legal and political system within the country.[67] This creates complementary cooperation which divides authority between the official *'ulamā'* and *'umarā'*, which were both defined as possessing authority within the Saudi state.[68] The mutual cooperation has occasionally resulted in harsh and severe criticism being directed towards the Dār al-Iftā' and its official members from different segments of society.[69] These criticisms intermittently undermine the authority and credibility of the institution and compel the official *'ulamā'* to defend themselves. In Turkey, however, the Diyanet has generally chosen to remain silent upon controversial topics, and in particular on issues that are politically sensitive. This has resulted in Turkish Muslims voicing negative views of the institution on various occasions. In contrast to the Dār al-Iftā', which actively endorses government policies, the Diyanet more frequently demonstrates its reluctance or opposing stance against particular aspects of government policies by maintaining its silence.

In operating within Turkey's democratic secular state structure, the Diyanet seeks to balance religion, society and state. In the contemporary period, the Diyanet presents itself as a religious institution that promulgates an inclusive, moderate, tolerant and unifying Islam and denounces its exclusivist, fundamentalist and radical counterparts. Turkey's democratic character should be taken into account as one of the key influences that motivates the Diyanet to espouse a more aggregative, comprehensive and tolerant Islamic understanding. The heterogenous character of Turkey's population is another factor that should also be taken into account. In this respect, it is important to note that the interpretation and understanding of Islam evidence considerable variation in the transition from one Muslim group or sect to another. The Diyanet therefore explicitly intends to unify this diverse Muslim population under the heading of Islam by adopting a constructive and integrative language.

Most of the Diyanet's Islamic legal statements and *fatwās* that relate to the state's secular democratic system reiterate that a democratic political structure does not contradict Islam,[70] but minutely bypass or avoid answering the questions

67 Nabil Mouline, The Clerics of Islam: Religious Authority and Political Power in Saudi Arabia (Ethan S. Rundell (tr) Yale University Press 2014) 11.

68 Obeying rulers and scholars in Ma'rūf to set things right, in *Fatwas of Ibn Baz*, 7:115–119 <http://www.alifta.net/Fatawa/FatawaChapters.aspx?languagename=en&View=Page&PageID=871&PageNo=1&BookID=14> accessed 21 August 2016.

69 Gwenn Okruhlik, 'State Power, Religious Privilege, and Myths about Political Reform' in Mohammed Ayoop and Hasan Kosabalan (eds), *Religion and Politics in Saudi Arabia: Wahhabism and Saudi Arabia* (Lynne Rienner 2009) 92–93.

70 Aydın M. Şevki and others, *Sorularla İslam* (Diyanet İşleri Başkanlığı Yayınları 2015) 153–158.

whose content is associated with secularism. In operating within Turkey's idiosyncratic secular structure, the Diyanet can be interpreted as being considerably freer and more liberal than the Dār al-Iftā', most notably in the production of religious knowledge relating to political issues. If both institutions are assessed with reference to theoretical perspectives that relate to wider political systems, it becomes clear that the secular structure of Turkey conceivably prevents the state from interfering in religious affairs, most noticeably in the production of Islamic knowledge that is subject to the control of the Diyanet. Bardakoğlu states:

> Secularism in Turkey does not mean the exclusion of religion from our lives. It means the separation of the affairs of religion and state. This does not mean the intervention of the state in the interpretation of religion because such an intervention would contradict the very essence of secularism.[71]

However, the divergent policies that different administrative governments have adopted towards religion have partially affected, in both a positive and negative sense, the administrative, functional and jurisdictional role and position of the Diyanet.[72] With the exception of the Diyanet's first period (between 1924 and the late 1940s), it is rare to observe the state's intervention in the area of producing Islamic knowledge and of conveying it to the society that is so seriously and meticulously undertaken by the Diyanet. As Bardakoğlu observes, this freedom and liberality in the production of Islamic knowledge, which extends to Islamic legal decisions and *fatwās*, can conceivably be attributed to the secular structure of the Turkish Republic.

The secular and democratic features of American politics provide the FCNA with a state-independent character. In addressing any issue regarding politics, the Council demonstrates a more autonomous and liberal approach when compared to the Dār al-Iftā' and the Diyanet. Nonetheless, the FCNA displays more enthusiastic inclination towards internalising the liberal democratic norms and values of America. This can be attributed to two main factors. In the first instance, religious freedom, one of the principal foundations of the US Constitution, has been applied by the FCNA to legitimate the permanent residence of Muslims in America. In a number of *fatwās* issued by the FCNA, America is defined as a place where the Muslims can freely and peacefully practice their faith without interference and restrictions by the state, and, by extension, the permanent residence status of American Muslims has been legitimated upon the ground of the religious freedom that has been ensured by American liberal democracy. In the second instance, the freedom of speech and thought emerges as an implicit inducement that directs the FCNA to express more freely certain ideas relevant

71 Ali Bardakoğlu, *Religion and Society New Perspectives from Turkey* (Diyanet İşleri Başkanlığı 2009) 114.

72 Seda Dural, 'The Violence against Woman Policy of the AKP Government and the Diyanet' (MA thesis, Leiden University 2016) 21.

to political participation, allegiance to America, democracy and apostasy. Within the context of American secular democracy, the FCNA conceives of a concept of contractual agreement grounded upon respect for the law of the state with the intention of prompting American Muslims to engage in political life.[73] This concept entails the expression of American Muslims' decisions and free will through their civil and political participation. The liberal and neutral context of America therefore emerges as a legal justification to induce American Muslims to fulfil their citizenship duties that include participating in social and political life, defending their rights, working for the betterment of their society and being loyal to America.

In functioning within a non-Muslim country, the FCNA seeks to integrate American Muslims into American political life while, at the same time, aiming to protect their Muslim identity. The *fatwā* related to the political participation of American Muslims states that it is a necessary obligation for American Muslims. Al-Alwani, the first president of the FCNA, reiterates:

> It is incumbent upon Muslims to actively participate [in the election] for the following reasons: 1) In order to protect our rights as American citizens, we must be involved in politics. 2) Our involvement can facilitate our support of our fellow Muslims around the world. 3) Our interaction with non-Muslims and our involvement will help to spread Islam's message. 4) It helps to convey the universality of Islam ... Our participation is an obligation in Islam, and not merely "a right" that we can choose to forfeit at will. It affords us the opportunity to protect our human rights, guarantee the fulfilment of our needs, and work for the improvement of living conditions for Muslims and non-Muslims in America and abroad ... Whatever helps us to achieve these noble goals becomes Islamically obligatory. This includes: ... Supporting (both politically and financially) those non-Muslim candidates whose beliefs and values are most compatible with ours as Muslims, and who most address and support our issues and causes ... Registering to vote and then voting. Although separate acts, they are both an essential part of the electoral process. Our participation in that process is mandatory.[74]

The political participation of American Muslims is grounded on four premises: the protection of Muslims' rights as American citizens, the maintenance of support to Muslims around the world, the invitation of people to Islam and the declaration

73 Muzammil Siddiqi, 'Being Faithful Muslims and Loyal Americans' <http://fiqhcouncil.org/being-faithful-muslims-and-loyal-americans/> accessed 10 November 2020.

74 Ahmed Bedier, 'What Islamic Scholars Say about Voting'<http://unitedvoices.com/docs/Islamic-perspective-voting1.pdf> accessed 08 November 2020. This is part of the *fatwā* relating to political participation of American Muslims. See Abdullah Saeed, 'Reflections on the Development of the Discourse of *Fiqh* for Minorities and Some of the Challenges It Faces' in Maurits S. Berger (ed), *Applying Shari'a in the West: Facts, Fears and the Future of Islamic Rules on the Family Relations in the West* (Leiden University Press 2013) 242.

of the universality of Islam. These four premises evidence an effort to establish a subtle balance between the responsibilities of American Muslims as being part of both *umma* and American society. The political participation of American Muslims is therefore identified as a religious obligation that opens up a way of putting these premises into practice. Instead of rejecting the engagement in non-Muslim countries' politics, the FCNA encourages American Muslims to actively participate in American politics. It is therefore possible to observe that the FCNA appears unwilling to create religious fissures within the existing framework of the American democracy and politics, in which all American citizens have equal political rights.

In addition, the three institutions have developed and formulated Islamic legal ideas and arguments that function to legitimate the political structures of their countries or render obedience to the states and their prescribed laws obligatory, irrespective of whether they are Islamic, democratic or secular. In Saudi Arabia, the Dār al-Iftā' strongly rejects oppositional or rebellious tendencies upon the grounds that they lead to chaos, division and sedition (*fitna*) in society. They are generally defined as religious innovations (*bid'a*) without precedent in the prophetic model and the practice of the Companions. To take one example, the Saudi Government requested a *fatwā* upon the illegitimacy of public demonstrations from the Dār al-Iftā during the 2011 "Arab Spring" uprisings. When the repercussions of the uprisings began to ripple across the country, the Dār al-Iftā' issued a *fatwā* that strictly warned those who organised and participated in such demonstrations and uprisings against the Saudi Government whose rulers are implicitly portrayed as Muslim by virtue of their recognition of the Qur'an and Sunna as the constitution of the country.[75] It is stated in the *fatwā*:

> Since the Kingdom of Saudi Arabia is based on the Qur'an, sunna, and the oath of allegiance (*bay'a*) along with sticking to the unification of the society and obedience, the reform and advice do not actualize with the [illegitimate] demonstrations, methods and styles which trigger sedition in and divide the society (*jamā'a*). This is the reason why the earlier and present *'ulamā'* of this country have decided to prohibit these kinds of demonstrations and to warn against them.[76]

75 The BSU decision No. 93 of 06 March 2011 <http://www.alifta.net/Search/ResultDetails.aspx?languagename=ar&lang=ar&view=result&fatwaNum=&FatwaNumID=&ID=13350&searchScope=2&SearchScopeLevels1=&SearchScopeLevels2=&highLight=1&SearchType=exact&SearchMoesar=false&bookID=&LeftVal=0&RightVal=0&simple=&SearchCriteria=allwords&PagePath=&siteSection=1&searchkeyword=216167217132217133216184216167217135216177216167216170032217129217138032216167217132216168217132216167216175032217136216170216173216176216177032217133217134032216167217132216167216177216170216168216167216183216167216170032216167217132217129217131216177217138216169032217136216167217132216173216178216168217138216169032216167217132217133217134216173216177216169#firstKeyWordFound> accessed 20 June 2017.

76 ibid.

Within the *fatwā*, the Saudi Kingdom is depicted as an "Islamic" state which requires unconditionally obligatory obedience. Organising demonstrations and protests qualifies as *bid'a* since the Companions of the Prophet never launched demonstrations, revolutions or sit-ins to oppose the rulers. It is accentuated that the Prophet instead recommended that Muslims should provide advice to the rulers in private. The contentious propaganda, mass protests and public demonstrations against government leaders are presented as foreign threats that seek to divide Saudi Arabia's unity. The Dār al-Iftā' states:

> The Kingdom has maintained its Islamic identity as the Kingdom although adopting the means for progress and development by using the legally permissible worldly reasons. It does not and will not permit—by God's will and omnipotence—ideas from the West and the East that aim to detract this identity and disintegrate this society (*jamā'a*).[77]

To a certain degree, the Saudi ruling family derives its authority from religion and, by extension, the Dār al-Iftā', and this is reflected in the Islamic character of the state. The dynasty, in being aware of the extent to which religion is an essential accompaniment of its political power and stability, has generally sought to cultivate a harmonious relationship with the religious establishment.

In operating within the Islamic political structure of Saudi Arabia, the Dār al-Iftā' adopts the doctrine of Wahhābī *siyāsa shar'iyya* with the intention of ensuring the state's political and social stability. This Wahhābī doctrine, which was put in place by the earlier Wahhābī scholars, is built upon the premise that, within Islam, the purpose of the state is to preserve Islamic law and implement its dictates and requirements.[78] The doctrine also establishes that it is not simply the case that a temporal ruler is required to uphold and enforce Islamic law – rather it is instead the case that obedience to him is regarded as an obligatory religious duty. A number of *fatwās* and official statements make it possible to identify clear expressions and indications that the Dār al-Iftā' continues to uphold the views of its predecessors when addressing obligatory obedience to leaders. An example can be found in the following *fatwā*:

> Allah ... says: {O you who believe! Obey Allah and obey the Messenger and those of you (Muslims) who are in authority. (And) if you differ in anything amongst yourselves, refer it to Allah and His Messenger, if you believe in Allah and in the Last Day. That is better and more suitable for final determination.} [the Q. 4: 59] This Qur'anic verse is a Nas on the obligation of obedience to the leaders; the rulers and scholars. The authentic Sunna of the Messenger of Allah explains that this obedience is obligatory, and enjoined duty regarding everything that is looked upon as Ma'ruf (that which

77 ibid.
78 Al-Atawneh (n 1) 38.

> is good, beneficial or fitting by Islamic law and Muslims of sound intellect). The Nas from the Sunna explains the absoluteness of the Ayah to obeying the Muslims in authority in what is judged to be Ma'ruf.[79]

The Dār al-Iftā' contends that the ruler of a country can be defined as the person who has an extensive authority in it. Unless he is an atheist, he can rule the state even if he does not possess a number of the Islamic legal conditions that are required to be a capable and efficient leader.[80] A ruler may, for example, accept the supremacy of God but then promulgate certain laws that transgress the sharī'a in order to advance his personal interests, such as material gain or power. In this instance, the ruler is motivated by his personal self-interest, but this does not entail that he is an apostate or unbeliever.

Some *fatwās* also stress the need for obligatory obedience to regulations issued by the ruler, which include regulations associated with passports, social norms and traffic laws.[81] This obedience is grounded in public welfare because these kinds of regulations benefit Muslims.[82] The only exception to the obligation to obey arises when those who possess authority provide orders that contradict Islamic law. Even in this case, a Muslim should not actively and rebelliously oppose a ruler who does not act in accordance with Islamic law but should instead advise him that he has failed to fulfil his duty. The ruler is only considered an apostate if he rules by something other than the sharī'a and accepts what is forbidden (*ḥarām*) as permissible (*ḥalāl*) or vice-versa.[83] However, in operating in a country such as Saudi Arabia, whose constitution has been declared to be based on the Qur'an and Sunna,[84] the Dār al-Iftā' presumably grounds its argument relating to obligatory obedience on the assumption that the country is an Islamic country and its rulers are still believers because they rule the country in accordance with Islamic law. The doctrine of Wahhābī *siyāsa shar'iyya*, which the Dār al-Iftā' generally upholds, establishes that even if members of the Saudi Government commit a de facto sin (such as gambling, usury, etc.), this does not in itself create a legitimate or valid justification for rebelling against the ruler. Muslims must therefore tolerate and obey the rulers, even if they commit sinful acts, while attempting to rectify their sinful acts through advice.

The fact that the Kingdom's constitution was based on the Qur'an and Sunna provides a sufficiently clear justification for the Dār al-Iftā' to pronounce the state

79 Advice to the Ummah given in the answer to ten important questions, in *Fatwas of Ibn Baz*, 8: 202–209 <https://www.alifta.gov.sa/En/IftaContents/IbnBaz/Pages/default.aspx?cultStr=en&View=Page&PageID=1025&PageNo=1&BookID=14> accessed 27 February 2021.

80 Advice (n 79); Obeying (n 68).

81 Advice (n 79).

82 ibid.

83 ibid.

84 Royal Decree A/90, 1 March 1992. See Basic Law of Governance (Article 1) (Royal Embassy of Saudi Arabia, 1 March 1992) <https://www.saudiembassy.net/basic-law-governance> accessed 08 October 2015.

to be a legitimate authority while rendering obedience to it to be obligatory. It is asserted that other forms of political systems are not regarded as legitimate authorities under Islamic law because any such approval would be interpreted as establishing a situation in which human-made law and institutions are preferred to divine law and governance. A *fatwā* issued by the Dār al-Iftā' clearly establishes this. It states:

> Secularism is the call to separate religion from the affairs of state and to take only the acts of worship and leave the other aspects of religion and recognise what is called "freedom of religion" … Secularism and other corrupted beliefs are immoral and bad calls which people must avoid.[85]

In a separate *fatwā*, the Dār al-Iftā' also states:

> Preferring a secularist state to an Islamic one is tantamount to preferring Kufr (disbelief) to Iman (faith), as Allah (exalted be He) says: {Have you not seen those who were given a portion of the scripture? They believe in Jibt and Tâghût and say to the disbelievers that they are better guided as regards the ways than the believers (Muslims).} (the Q. 4:51) … if someone claims that [the Islamic sharī'a] does not suit this age or that man-made laws are more appropriate, they are considered Kafir, for in so doing, they are disavowing Allah and His Messenger (peace be upon him) with respect to the perfection and applicability of Shari'ah to all times and places.[86]

The rejection of democracy and secularism is presumably based on the assumption that the acceptance of such systems privileges human-made laws and institutions over divine governance. The Dār al-Iftā' maintains that God is the only supreme Legislator and that humans are obliged to obey the sharī'a revealed by God in its entirety. To do otherwise can be taken to imply that human beings should be equipped with the capacity of Legislator, which is a power reserved only for God. This Islamic legal view, which is originally grounded within the concept of the unity and oneness of God (*tawḥīd*) in the Wahhābī ideology,[87] probably leads the

85 Fatwā No. 19351 in *Fatwas of the Permanent Committee*, 22: 238–248 <http://www.alifta.net/Search/ResultDetails.aspx?languagename=en&lang=en&view=result&fatwaNum=&FatwaNumID=&ID=8496&searchScope=7&SearchScopeLevels1=&SearchScopeLevels2=&highLight=1&SearchType=exact&SearchMoesar=false&bookID=&LeftVal=0&RightVal=0&simple=&SearchCriteria=allwords&PagePath=&siteSection=1&searchkeyword=10010110911109911409709912l#firstKeyWordFound> accessed 04 April 2018.

86 Fatwā No. 18396 in *Fatwas of the Permanent Committee*, 2: 142–145 <http://www.alifta.net/Search/ResultDetails.aspx?languagename=en&lang=en&view=result&fatwaNum=&FatwaNumID=&ID=10884&searchScope=7&SearchScopeLevels1=&SearchScopeLevels2=&highLight=1&SearchType=exact&SearchMoesar=false&bookID=&LeftVal=0&RightVal=0&simple=&SearchCriteria=allwords&PagePath=&siteSection=1&searchkeyword=115101099117108097114105115109#firstKeyWordFound> accessed 04 April 2018.

87 Quintan Wiktorowicz, 'Anatomy of the Salafi Movement' (2006) 29 *Studies in Conflict & Terrorism* 207–209.

Dār al-Iftā' to entirely reject secularism, along with other political systems that entail the separation of religion and state in the first instance.

In contradistinction to the Dār al-Iftā', the Diyanet has maintained, in the course of issuing many Islamic legal decisions and *fatwās*, that democracy and democratic values do not conflict with Islam; in addition, it has also upheld that the fundamental principles of a democratic system are in harmony with Islamic legal doctrines associated with politics. One example can be found in the (hypothetical) *fatwā* which the Diyanet issued in response to a question relating to democracy. It states:

> The main sources of Islam, the Qur'an and Sunna, do not suggest any certain political system and government model for the governance of state and society. Their essential aims are to identify the general principles that control the governance of the Muslim states and to draw the general framework that is the most proper for humanity by pointing to the immutable divine laws ... General principles that are prescribed by Islam take, in sum, as the following form:
>
> 1. Ultimate sovereignty belongs to Allāh. That is to say, legislation, execution and judgement must be in accordance with the *shar'ī* rules.
> 2. The consultation (*shūrā*) is the main principle in the process of decision-making.
> 3. Submission to *haqq* (truth and justice) and obedience to law are fundamental. In other words, the state of law must be instituted.
> 4. Fundamental human rights must be preserved.
> 5. Assignment and commission should be made in accordance with justice, capacity and efficiency.
> 6. Social justice should be secured.
> 7. The ideal of the open society should be preserved.
>
> Accordingly, any form of government that complies with these general principles is a legitimate government system in terms of religion, no matter whether it is democratic, monarchical, parliamentary, republican or semi-presidential. The question of which one will be adopted should ultimately be decided in accordance with the exigencies and needs of a society.[88, 89]

Islam and Islamic law do not prescribe any certain political and governmental model for Muslims to follow; as the Diyanet states, these aspects of life are instead subject to human intellect and the developing circumstances of social needs. Even though the political system is grounded in some fundamental Islamic

88 Aydın and others (n 70) 153–154. This quotation is taken from a question-and-answer book that was published by the Diyanet. The quotation can be a *fatwā* issued in response to either a hypothetical or real person.

89 Author's translation.

principles, this should not be understood to imply that politics is an integral component and main focus of religion. The Diyanet maintains that democracy is one of the government systems and that it is compatible with Islam and Islamic law as long as it does not contravene the seven general Islamic principles set out by the institution.

In drawing upon the two Qur'anic verses (Q. 42:38 and Q. 3:159) and the Prophet's Sunna upon consultation (*shūrā*), the Diyanet observes that Islam and Islamic law do not only support democracy and people's participation in the state's affairs but also set out provisions (within the Qur'anic verses) which encourage consultation and counselling. It is stated:

> In the most general sense, democracy means "rule of the people". That is, in electing the ruler and determining legislation, the general preference of the public opinion is regarded as the main determining factor. In populous societies, it is impossible to be ruled by the whole people in and of themselves, so different models are developed to put this system into practice. In the contemporary period, the most well-established democratic system institutes an arrangement in which the established political parties stand for governance and are elected by the people through the exercise of their freewill. Insofar as it does not conflict with any of the aforementioned principles, this system of government cannot be said to conflict with Islam. Indeed, two Qur'anic verses establish that important affairs and matters associated with the society should be mutually decided or resolved through consultation. This is established by the Q. 3:159 ("...consult them in affairs (of moment)") and the Q. 42:38 ("...who (conduct) their affairs by mutual consultation...").[90]

The Diyanet takes the view that the Qur'an and Sunna provide insight into the general ethical and moral principles in the area of *mu'āmalāt* and describe how human beings must conduct their worldly affairs amongst themselves. In setting out the general principles that government systems within Muslim countries should take into account, the Diyanet seeks to support its position with reference to examples drawn from the life of the Prophet. Prior to the Battle of Uhud in 624, the Prophet consulted Muslims in an assembly (*majlis*) which was convened with the intention of identifying how the Meccan enemies could be best repelled.[91] Although the Prophet was instinctively drawn to a defensive war in Medina, he ultimately aligned with the view of the majority which instead favoured countering the Meccan enemies outside Medina.[92] In referring to this, the institution implicitly indicates that even the Prophet consulted his people in worldly matters – by implication Muslims, as the followers of the Prophet, are also required to consult each other with regard to their secular affairs. The

90 Aydın and others (n 70) 154–155.
91 ibid 155.
92 ibid.

Diyanet therefore explicitly asserts a democratic system of government aligned with the general principles as the model of government best suited to the modern world. The (hypothetical) *fatwā* also challenges the views of some scholars who claim that democracy is an alien concept that has been imposed by secular reformers and Westerners upon Muslim societies. The Diyanet maintains that it is fundamentally mistaken to argue that the concept of public sovereignty denies the Islamic affirmation associated with the sovereignty of God and is therefore a form of idolatry.[93] After issues and matters relating to the government and political systems are placed under the heading of *mu'āmalāt*, the argument is then extended to the proposition that, in the contemporary world, democracy can be said to be a requirement of Islam.

Despite functioning within a democratic secular system of government, the Diyanet, in a similar manner to the Dār al-Iftā', asserts that proof of disbelief provides a valid exception to rebelling against a ruler who openly commits an act of disbelief. In the Diyanet's (hypothetical) *fatwā*, it is stated:

> Islam establishes that as long as the source and methods of legislation are legitimate, the laws and regulations enacted by the relevant parliaments and institutions are valid and legitimate. If there are violations in this regard and some laws are enacted without due regard for religious principles, it can be mentioned a sinful act in this situation. It should be noted that the action/deed (*'amal*) is not a part of faith in accordance with the creed of *Ahl al-Sunna*, and a great sin does not make the person who commits it a *kāfir/mushrik* (unbeliever).[94]

In a similar tone, the Dār al-Iftā' states:

> It is obligatory for Muslims to obey those in authority when ordered to do right and good, but not sins. Therefore, if their orders involve any sins, they must not be obeyed, but it is still not permissible to rebel against them due to this, as the Prophet said: {"Mind you! Anyone who has a ruler appointed over them and sees him committing some act of disobedience to Allah, should hate his (the ruler's) act in disobedience to Allah, but must not withdraw the hand from obedience (to the ruler)."} ... The exception is when the Muslims sees clear Kufr, for which there is proof from Allah. In this case, there is nothing wrong in rebelling against these rulers to depose them, if they have power to do so. However, if this is beyond their ability, they should not rebel. Also, if rebelling will result in worse evil, they should not do so to preserve the public interest.[95]

93 ibid 157–158.
94 ibid 157.
95 Advice (n 79).

The distinction between disbelievers (*kāfir*) and sinful Muslims (*mujrim*) provides the fulcrum of the decisions issued by the two institutions. They both concur that committing major sins (e.g., unlawful sexual intercourse (*zinā*), theft (*sāriq*) and drinking alcohol (*shurb al-khamr*)) does not make a Muslim an unbeliever; rather, they are instead an immoral sinner who has weak faith. Both institutions therefore mitigate a possible provocative factor or reason that will be levelled against the political rulers in both countries by referring to the view of *Ahl al-Sunna wal-Jamā'a* – this establishes that a sinner is not a disbeliever as a result of their sin as long as they do not consider it to be lawful.[96]

In addition, fear of anarchy and sedition (*fitna*) indirectly presents itself as a supplementary influence that helps to further strengthen loyalty to the state, with this imperative being reiterated within the Diyanet's decisions and *fatwās*. The Diyanet generally refers to any divisive and provocative actions detrimental to the unity of the state and social order as anarchy and sedition. Society is therefore strongly encouraged not to participate in such actions and incidents.[97] During the 1970s at the height of leftist-socialist activism, for example, the Diyanet promulgated a number of articles that warned the community against the possible divisive, abrasive and perilous effects of this socialist activism upon society.[98] In addressing compliance and deference to the state authority, the Diyanet frequently sought to invoke the authoritative texts that indicate the virtues of obedience to the legitimate authority. The institution has sought to instil loyalty to the state amongst Muslims within Turkey – this is embedded within its claim that the state is "the embodiment and political expression of the organic community of the (Turkish) Muslims."[99,100] The Diyanet's catechism states:

> Islam emphasises the importance of obedience and loyalty to the state, which it understands to be the broadest social institution. The Qur'an states: "O you believe! Obey Allah, and obey the Messenger (Muhammad), and those charged with authority among you…" (the Q. 4:59) The Prophet also stated: "…obey those who are charge of you, you will enter the Paradise of your Lord." (Tirmidhī, No. 616) The *ḥadīth* emphasises the importance and value

96 For more detailed explanation of the view of *Ahl al-Sunna* on that specific issue, see 'Abdullāh ibn 'Abdul-Ḥamīd al-Athari, *Islamic Beliefs: A Brief Introduction to the 'Aqīdah of Ahl as-Sunnah wal-Jamā'ah* (Naṣiruddin al-Khaṭṭab (tr) International Islamic Publishing House 2005) 140–147.

97 Gürpınar Doğan and Ceren Kenar, 'The Nation and its Sermons: Islam, Kemalism and the Presidency of Religious Affairs in Turkey' (2016) 52 (1) *Middle Eastern Studies* 70.

98 ibid.

99 ibid 63.

100 In particular, the sermons delivered in thousands of mosques throughout the country are the main important sources that reflect the Diyanet's stance upon the relationship between the state and its subjects. The ideological component of the Diyanet's sermons presents obedience to the state as a moral and religious requirement. Gürpınar and Kenar analyse sermons authorised and delivered by the Diyanet between 1962 and 2006. They argue that these sermons provide general insight into how this religious institution helped to indoctrinate society into unconditional obedience and deference to the state. Gürpınar and Kenar (n 97) 63–67, 70.

> of obedience to the state authority. The view of *Ahl al-Sunna wal-Jamā'a* maintains that it is necessary to obey the head of state, even if he is sinful (*mujrim*) or debauched (*fāsiq*) ... However, religion does not sufficiently guarantee the safety, tranquillity and welfare of individuals and society, and there is accordingly a need for a state authority to function alongside religion. For this reason, the Prophet sought to construct this structure after migrating from Mecca to Medina...
>
> The respect of the state to religion becomes a reflection of its deference to society and social values. In this manner, executives gain the respect of society ... but it is informed that if there is a case or order encouraging people to rebel against Allāh, [the constituted authority] is not obeyed.[101]

The main argument that the Diyanet uses to legitimise obedience to the state is basically grounded in the proposition that the state maintains social order by preventing anarchy and social disturbances, protecting religion and upholding social unity. It is therefore religiously illegitimate not to obey this authority because it may create anarchy and destroy social order. Social order, public peace and national unity are the main justifications which the Diyanet cites when seeking to substantiate and solidify its Islamic legal stance upon obedience to state authorities. However, Muslims are encouraged not to abide by legal regulations when the rulers order an action which violates Islamic law.[102] In these circumstances, Muslims are counselled to direct a constructive and warning criticism towards the state's authorities rather than actively rebelling against them.[103] In common with the Dār al-Iftā', the Diyanet also encourages Muslims to comply with state laws and regulations associated with social issues and civil duties, which include mandatory military duty, social security and taxation, by citing the legal principle of *maṣlaḥa*.[104]

In a similar vein to the Diyanet's approach regarding democracy and democratic values, the FCNA affirms democracy as a legitimate form of political system from an Islamic legal perspective. Despite the fact that the FCNA has not issued any *fatwā* regarding democracy, its Resolution related to allegiance to America alludes implicitly to the issue of democracy and democratic values. The Resolution expressly qualifies the American democratic system as a legitimate government system in terms of Islamic law. It states:

> Like other faith communities in the US and elsewhere, we see no inherent conflict between the normative values of Islam and the US Constitution and Bill of Rights.

101 Hayrettin Karaman, Ali Bardakoğlu and H. Yunus Apaydın, *İlmihal-II: İslam ve Toplum* (DİB 1998) 550–551.

102 Aydın and others (n 70) 156.

103 Karaman, Bardakoğlu and Apaydın (n 101) 551–552.

104 Aydın and others (n 70) 175–178.

> Contrary to erroneous perceptions and Islamophobic propaganda of political extremists from various backgrounds, the true and authentic teachings of Islam promote the sanctity of human life, dignity of all humans, and respect of human, civil and political rights. Islamic teachings uphold religious freedom and adherence to the same universal values which are accepted by the majority of people of all backgrounds and upon which the US Constitution was established and according to which the Bill of Rights was enunciated.[105]

The Resolution implicitly reflects two tendencies that are adopted by the FCNA in the process of the practice of *iftā'*: didacticism and apologism. Here didacticism alludes to a kind of desire to instil the idea of conformity between Islamic normative values and fundamental principles of democracy in American Muslims. The apological tendency on the other hand refers to the defence of Islam against its widespread negative representation within the American context. Despite the apologist character of FCNA members, they espouse an intricate legal approach that links Islamic legal principles to the US Constitution and the Bill of Rights.

In applying the classical Islamic legal principles and concepts, Council members make a concerted effort to formulate a legal solution appropriate to the American socio-political context. In the first instance, the Council puts its emphasis upon the harmony of Islamic normative values with the foundational democratic principles of America – this is consolidated through the principle of *maqāṣid al-sharī'a*. In the Resolution, it is stated:

> The Qur'an speaks explicitly about the imperative of just and peaceful co-existence, and the rights of self-defence against aggression and oppression that pose threats to freedom and security, provided that, a strict code of behavior is adhered to, including the protection of innocent non-combatants.
>
> The foregoing values and teachings can be amply documented from the two primary sources of Islamic jurisprudence – the Qur'an and authentic Hadith. These values are rooted, not in political correctness or pretense, but on the universally accepted supreme objectives of Islamic Shari'ah, which is to protect religious liberty, life, reason, family and property of all. The Shari'ah, contrary to misrepresentations, is a comprehensive and broad guidance for all aspects of a Muslim's life –spiritual, moral, social and legal. Secular legal systems in Western democracies generally share the same supreme objectives, and are generally compatible with Islamic Shari'ah.[106]

For the FCNA, if a government system provides social justice and respects and promotes human rights, it can be qualified as an Islamic form of political system. The American democratic system is acknowledged as a political system that bears

105 Siddiqi (n 73).
106 ibid.

features pertinent to Islamic norms and values. It is asserted that the US Constitution and the Bill of Rights intend to secure human rights, religious freedom, religious tolerance and equality in citizenship, so all these are roughly norms and values in harmony with the principle of *maqāṣid al-sharī'a* which means to protect people's life, religion, reason, property and progeny. In constructing a profound legal ground to substantiate the moral obligation (or loyalty) of American Muslims to the American political system, the Council attentively adopts a reconciliatory approach that equalises the prevailing American liberal democratic values and the general objectives of Islamic law. The principle of *maqāṣid al-sharī'a* therefore emerges as the main legal methodology applied by the FCNA in legitimating both the American polity and the moral obligation (or loyalty) towards it.

In the second instance, the democratic form of the American political system is precisely legitimated through the concept of *shūrā*. In common with the Diyanet, the FCNA employs the concept of *shūrā* with the intention of verifying the idea of the compatibility of Islamic normative values regarding governance with the American democratic political system. The electoral and voting systems that form the foundations of American democracy are implicitly identified as legitimate mechanisms compatible with Islamic legal principles related to political governance. The Resolution states:

> Likewise, the core modern democratic systems are compatible with the Islamic principles of Shura – mutual consultation and co-determination of all social affairs at all levels and all spheres, family, community, society, state and globally.
>
> As a body of Islamic scholars, we the members of FCNA believe that it is false and misleading to suggest that there is a contradiction between being faithful Muslims committed to God (Allah) and being loyal American citizens. Islamic teachings require respect of the laws of the land where Muslims live as minorities, including the Constitution and the Bill of Rights, so long as there is no conflict with Muslims' obligation for obedience to God. We do not see any such conflict with the US Constitution and Bill of Rights.[107]

The concept of *shūrā* is identified as the fundamental Islamic legal principle in conducting social, political and familial affairs. The Resolution therefore gives the impression that a democratic political system in which Muslims are able to freely participate is more appropriate to Islamic legal principles than authoritarian governments ruled by Muslims.

In the last instance, the belongingness of American Muslims as citizens to their homeland, America, is acknowledged as a social contract that obliges them to obey and respect the law of the land. The FCNA, even though it does not allude explicitly to the Q. 2:177, 5:1 and 17:34, grounds obedience to the requirements,

107 ibid.

regulations and institutions of the American political and legal system on the contractual obligation in these verses that order believers to fulfil their obligations in their contracts. It is stated:

> We believe further that as citizens of a free and democratic society, we have the same obligations and rights of all citizens. We believe that right of dissent can only be exercised in a peaceful and lawful manner to advance the short and long term interests of our country.
>
> [The FCNA] calls on all Muslim Americans and American citizens at large to engage in objective, peaceful and respectful dialogue at all levels and spheres of common social concerns. We call upon all Muslim Americans to be involved in solving pressing social problems, such as the challenge of poverty, discrimination, violence, health care and environmental protection. It is fully compatible with Islam for Muslims to integrate positively in the society of which they are equal citizens, without losing their identity as Muslims (just as Jews and Christians do not lose their religious identity in doing the same).
>
> We believe that emphasis on dialogue and positive collaborative action is a far better approach than following the paths of those who thrive on hate mongering and fear of propaganda. Anti-Islam, anti-Semitism and other similar forms of religious and/or political-based discrimination are all forms of racism unfit for civilized people and are betrayal of the true American as well as Islamic values.[108]

Instead of the isolation and assimilation of American Muslims, the Council intends to promote their positive integration and engagement in the wider socio-political context of America because they have common interests and objectives with other American citizens in promoting their society. The concept of citizenship is therefore identified as "a contractual bond" that includes feelings of allegiance, mutual recognition, tolerance and coexistence amongst the society's members regardless of their ethnic, racial, cultural and religious differences. Nonetheless, the principle of *maṣlaḥa* is applied to consolidate the legitimacy of obeying the secular political system of America and transforming America into a more vibrant and just democratic society together with other citizens. In employing the principle of *maṣlaḥa*, the Council takes into account two factors: preserving the Muslim identity and raising the awareness of responsible citizenship – this evidences that the Council justifies obedience of American Muslims to American authorities through establishing a link between the concept of citizenship and the principle of *maṣlaḥa*.

It is possible to notice clear similarities within the Islamic legal views and *fatwās* issued by the Dār al-Iftā' and the Diyanet upon the subject of obedience to state. However, the form of political authority which the two institutions take to

108 ibid.

be legitimate has been crucially shaped by the political systems which operate in each of the respective countries. In invoking the history of Muslim states, religious scholars within the Dār al-Iftā' and the Diyanet engage with the proposition that the ruler should be obeyed, irrespective of whether s/he is unjust or infringes upon the principles and rulings of Islamic law – this is justified upon the grounds that such a ruler is still better for the community than anarchy, civil strife or social disorder. Taking into account the situation in Syria (a Muslim country), it may be justifiably argued that the main concern of the two institutions is to maintain the public interest, public welfare and social order rather than legitimate their countries' political systems. In 2011, a broad-based uprising sought to overthrow the Syrian regime and put in place a democratic system. Since then, this initial upsurge of popular pressure has produced social disorder, civil strife, severe human rights violations and the widespread loss of innocent life.[109]

Moreover, the Dār al-Iftā' and the Diyanet have sought to root the obligation to obey authority-holders within the doctrine of *siyāsa shar'iyya*, which operates within the Sunni tradition. This is a fundamental legal doctrine related to Islamic governance that establishes the relationship between the state and its subjects. The doctrine was formulated a substantial time ago by prominent scholars, who included Abū Yūsūf (d. 798), Aḥmad b Ḥanbal (d. 855), al-Māwardī (d. 1058) and al-Ghazālī (d. 1111). Each justified obedience to a Muslim ruler even if he is personally impious and oppressive in his rule, with the only exception being if he ordains disobedience to God.[110] Rebellion and insubordination are denounced as acts of instigation and dissension which will drag the Muslim community into civil strife, political disturbance and social chaos.[111] In attempting to prevent potential anarchy and political turmoil, both institutions therefore draw upon the doctrine of *siyāsa shar'iyya* and seek to use it to justify obedience to state authorities within their respective countries. In doing so, they generally refer to the Q. 4:59 and several *ḥadīths* which encourage Muslims to obey the legitimately established authorities. While the Dār al-Iftā' saliently extends a degree of legitimacy to Saudi Arabia's Islamic monarchy, the Diyanet precisely extends a veil of legitimacy over Turkey's secular democratic political system. The two institutions therefore seek to reduce the likelihood of anarchy and social disorder in their society.

Unlike the Dār al-Iftā' and the Diyanet, the FCNA advertently grounds obedience of American Muslims to the American authorities upon the concept

109 Raymond Hinnebusch and Omar Imady, *The Syrian Uprising: Domestic Origins and Early Trajectory* (Routledge 2018) under the title 'Introduction: Origins of the Syrian Uprising: Form Structure to Agency'; Paul Rogers, 'Lost Cause: Consequences and Implications of the War on Terror' in Harmonie Toros and Ioannis Tellidis (eds), *Terrorism, Peace and Conflict Studies: Investigating the Crossroad* (Routledge 2014) 19.

110 Ann K. S. Lambton, *State and Government in Medieval Islam: An Introduction to the Study of Islamic Political Theory: The Jurists* (Oxford University Press 1981) 19–20, 42, 56–57, 86, 114–117; Al-Athari (n 96) 180–185.

111 Al-Athari (n 96) 180–183.

of citizenship and the principle of *maṣlaḥa*. The concept of citizenship generates a moral obligation that incites American Muslims to obey and respect both the constitutional regulations and governmental system of America while the principle of *maṣlaḥa* emerges as a driving factor that induces American Muslims to actively engage in the wider society of America with the intention of contributing to their society's interests. Rather than drawing upon the doctrine of *siyāsa shar'iyya* as the Dār al-Iftā' and the Diyanet do, the FCNA applies more extensively the concept of citizenship and the principle of *maṣlaḥa* with the intention of inducing American Muslims to obey the state authorities. Operating in a non-Muslim country explicitly impels the FCNA to adopt a more flexible and reconciliatory approach in addressing issues regarding obedience to state authorities and participation in American politics. While the participation of American Muslims in political elections is identified as an obligation, they are also counselled to vote for the non-Muslim candidates whose causes and objectives demonstrate similarities with theirs. However, the Dār al-Iftā' and the Diyanet refer to the view of *Ahl al-Sunna wal-Jamā'a* while evaluating the issue relating to rebellion against state authorities. Both of them categorically assert that any rebellious movements and insurrectionary anarchism are illegitimate as long as the ruler is Muslim even if s/he commits sinful and unjust acts – this can be attributed to their functioning within Muslim majority countries. In contrast, the FCNA seeks to integrate American Muslims into all political, social and legal aspects of life upon the ground of the concept of citizenship while also exhorting them to preserve their faith, values and moral system associated with Islam. This can be acknowledged as an equation that includes commitment without isolation and integration without assimilation. Functioning in a non-Muslim context therefore propels the FCNA to consider this equation in addressing any specific issue that confronts American Muslims. In interpreting the authoritative texts regarding governance and obedience to state authorities, the three institutions have espoused different Islamic legal methodologies, concepts and principles to produce Islamic legal views and arguments which are aligned with the government systems and political values of their respective environments. It therefore can be argued that Islamic legal arguments and views developed by the three have the clear imprint of their respective political environments.

Conclusion

The examination of the three institutions and their official *fatwās* from the last two thematic perspectives provides an important insight into how different legal and political contexts have influenced the Islamic legal methodologies deployed by the three institutions and the legal outcomes (*fatwās*) that derive from their legal and intellectual efforts. These two thematic factors are: (1) the legal systems of the three countries and (2) the political structures of the three societies.

The legal systems of the three countries are a further contextual factor that helps to specify the authority, function and role of the *fatwās* issued by the institutions. An Islamic state provides a privileged position to the Dār al-Iftā'. The institution and its official *fatwās* continue to play an important and supplementary role within Saudi Arabia's Islamic legal system. Within this system, official *fatwās* have the potential, subject to the approval of the King, to transform into law as royal decrees. The involvement of the Dār al-Iftā' in the legislative procedure has been evidenced in relation to a substantial number of controversial issues, which include criminal law procedures, ethics and moral issues, family law and social regulations. To a large extent, substantive law is formulated and regulated with full interaction and cooperation between political and religious establishments. In addition, the Dār al-Iftā' possesses a kind of binding coercive authority thanks to *Muṭawwi'a*, that has implemented the legal rulings of official *fatwās* within Saudi society. The Diyanet, in direct contrast, instead presents itself as a persuasive authority that is endowed with the authority of religious erudition by Turkey's secular legal system. Its *fatwās* do not therefore possess a binding or coercive authority within Turkish society. Despite this, *fatwās* issued by the Diyanet probably, because they are applied within a society with a Muslim majority, possess the power of social sanction. Even though they are non-binding, the *fatwās* basically assume two main functions within Turkish society. Firstly, because they are obeyed by a majority of Muslims, they can be said to generate socio-religious norms. As in the case of the marriage of foster siblings, a number of *fatwās* take the form of extra rules that are voluntarily followed by all segments of the society – this applies despite the fact that the Civil Code and the official secular law do not expound regulations upon the issue at hand. Secondly, they can assume a hybrid regulation form – the combination of Islamic legal rulings and secular state laws enables them to simultaneously address the religious priorities of the Muslim population and maintain the public interest and social order. However, the diversity in American Muslims' ethnicity, culture and religious inclinations results in different Islamic legal authorities manifesting within the American context. The multiplicity of authority emerges as a restrictive factor that minimises both the authority of the FCNA amongst and the admissibility of its *fatwās* by the majority of American Muslims. The *fatwās* issued by the FCNA therefore mostly do not generate social and ethical norms within the American Muslim community. Despite the FCNA's lack of recognisability as a persuasive authority amongst American Muslims, the Council adopts a reconciliatory approach that combines Islamic legal norms and American secular legal regulations. FCNA members concur on the idea that obeying the law of America is required of American Muslims because of their civic responsibilities. Within the American legal system, the reconciliatory approach is pursued as an appropriate methodology by the FCNA; hence, the hybridisation of Islamic legal principles and American legal regulations is acknowledged as the most practicable legal methodology. The underlying factor that orients the FCNA to adopt a reconciliatory approach is that the rights of Muslim individuals within family, political and legal structures can be secured. The Council therefore prioritises the prevention of the abuse of legal loopholes that arise from the divergencies between Islamic legal principles and American legal regulations while retaining the basic Islamic legal, moral and normative values. Instead of seeking to develop a parallel legal system grounded upon Islamic law, the civil, legal and social issues are generally resolved through a reconciliatory approach that provides integration between religious and civil requirements. It therefore is possible to assert that the secular legal systems of Turkey and America emerge as influential contextual factors that induce both the Diyanet and the FCNA to develop and adopt a kind of reconciliatory (or hybridisation) approach in their *fatwās*.

Political structures within the three countries also provide further insight into the interaction between Islamic legal methodologies and environmental contexts. In Saudi Arabia, the relationship between religion and state has been configured in accordance with the alliance between the Saudi dynasty and the Wahhābī *'ulamā'* that was established in 1745. This alliance still continues today despite a significant number of institutional and social changes. Islam is the state religion and also functions as a source of constitutional and political legitimacy, thus shaping state activities and policies. The incorporation of the *'ulamā'* into the state administration through the establishment of the Dār al-Iftā' produced changes in the traditional relationship between the Saudi dynasty and the Wahhābī *'ulamā'*. These changes put in place a new *modus operandi* on both sides, with the *'ulamā'* being directly subordinate to the Saudi Government and subject to its control. Despite the fact that the state expanded its jurisdiction to many areas that were formerly regulated and controlled by the *'ulamā'*, the official *'ulamā'* (the Dār al-Iftā') continued to play an important role in legitimating state policies, with this contribution being attributable to the Islamic character of the Kingdom. Both sides developed a mutual partnership within Saudi Arabia's Islamic political system. This can be justified with reference to the Wahhābī *siyāsa shar'iyya*, which institutes both the official *'ulamā'* and the Saudi Government as holders of authority. Within the Islamic monarchical political system, the Dār al-Iftā' performs a central role in legitimating the Saudi Government's political policies, in particular during critical or sensitive situations. To a certain extent, the King or the Saudi Government is obliged to consult the Dār al-Iftā' and to consider its opinions during state affairs. Within Saudi Arabia, official *fatwās* continue to function as instruments that enable the expression of Islamic explanations and views that are associated with major political events and matters. *Fatwās* relevant to political policies which are generally issued at the request of the Saudi Government have the potential to function as the ultimate statements of Islamic law and uphold the general policies of the Saudi Government. It can therefore be ascertained that the monarchy has been built on a fusion of political and religious powers whose harmonious relationship is crucial to the stability of the state. The Saudi Government, by virtue of its Islamic character, continually requires the legitimating power of the Dār al-Iftā' (and generally its *fatwās*) in almost all legal, political, religious and social affairs.

In comparison with Saudi Arabia, the relationship between the state and religion is quite different in Turkey, and this can be attributed to the country's secular democratic character. The establishment of the Turkish Republic in 1923 was a crucial moment in the development of this relationship, as it embodied and upheld the separation of state and religion. The process of state secularisation has sustained this feature in subsequent effect. However, it should be acknowledged that Turkish secularism is distinguished from its counterparts by the existence of the Diyanet, which is a state-dependent religious institution. Its foundation, just one year after the establishment of the Turkish Republic, demonstrates how religion has been incorporated into the sphere of state governance. Like the Dār al-Iftā', the Diyanet can be said to be part of the state machinery. In both countries, the political powers that were ascendant at the time when both religious institutions were founded did not tolerate any autonomous religious domain that might compete with them for the loyalty of citizens. However, the incorporation of the Dār al-Iftā' into the state administration assigns its *fatwās* an influential role in the Islamic state, and its interventions help to legitimate the Saudi Government's political policies. As for the official *fatwās* issued by the Diyanet, they do not have any political effect and legitimating power in the secular democratic state structure – the secular state does not require its approval on any specific political issue. However, the Diyanet has developed its own legal approach which, in engaging with questions of state authority and obedience, extends reassurance to Muslims. The Diyanet's *fatwās* therefore are an important resource that reflects the tangible encounter between Islam and modern/post-modern secularism. Accordingly, many of the Diyanet's decisions and *fatwās* strongly resist attacks upon Turkey's governmental system that are grounded within Islamic arguments. Islam, the Diyanet maintains, establishes general ethical and legal principles and enables human beings to form their own political and governmental systems with reference to these general objectives and principles. The institution also clarifies that a system of democratic government is compatible with Islam and Islamic legal principles, upon the condition that the state authority respects religion. With the intention of further substantiating this proposition, the institution draws deeply upon the Islamic tradition to extract the concept of *shūrā* which is understood to provide an effective foundation for describing and legitimating democracy in Islam. In establishing an analogy between this concept and democratic political systems, the Diyanet makes it clear that democracy and Islam are not incompatible – this impression prevails because the institution's conceptual framing of "democracy" is subject to various limits and qualifications that are regarded as necessary by Islamic law. The concept of *shūrā* presents itself as an operational legal tool that can be used to justify the democratic character of the Turkish state with reference to Islamic ethical values and legal principles. In general terms, it therefore is clear that the Diyanet, in seeking to remain loyal to the scholarly Islamic legal heritage, does not interpret Islam in opposition to the state's democratic system and its secular legal regulations. Turkey's democratic secular structure emerges as one of the potential influences that can cause the institution to adopt a cautious, modest and flexible tone in its *fatwās* concerning political issues.

Although the political systems of Saudi Arabia and Turkey are quite clearly distinct, both institutions embrace the Sunni tradition's doctrine of *siyāsa shar'iyya* in order to promote social stability and encourage obedience to state authorities. The Dār al-Iftā' commands Saudi Muslims to obey an absolute Islamic monarchy, while the Diyanet encourages Turkish Muslims to lend their support to secular democratic authority and its associated regulations. Fear of anarchy and social conflict are the main concerns that lead both institutions to advocate the traditional doctrine of *siyāsa shar'iyya*, which upholds the belief that obedience to state authority is a religious obligation. It is clear that state authorities within both countries have the right to expect, and even demand, obedience – this applies even if they infringe on some Islamic legal regulations. Obedience to state authorities is explicitly rendered obligatory by the two institutions with the intention of preserving social order, unity and welfare. The traditional political doctrine establishes that any act of rebellion or insurgency against state authorities will be considered to be a prohibited act and denounced upon the basis of its anarchical and divisive effects. The two institutions therefore use the doctrine of *siyāsa shar'iyya* in order to justify acquiescence to immoral or oppressive authority. Their application of this doctrine appears as a balancing principle which is grounded within the relationship between their respective countries' governments and their subjects.

As for the FCNA, it functions within the secular democratic context of America. The integration of American Muslims into the American social and political context emerges as one of the main considerations that the FCNA continually underscores in addressing issues regarding governmental form, political participation and loyalty to non-Muslim authorities. With the intention of refracting any objections and confusions of American Muslims, the FCNA applies the principle of *maqāṣid al-sharī'a* to establish a balance between Islamic legal values and American democratic values. The concepts of equality in citizenship, human rights and religious freedom which are embedded in the US Constitution and the Bill of Rights are matched up with the general objectives and principles of Islamic law that intend to protect religion, life, reason, progeny and property. After reconciling Islamic legal principles with the liberal democratic values, the FCNA uses the concept of *shūrā* to legitimate democracy as an appropriate government form that is worthy of obedience and loyalty – this clearly paves way for the FCNA to make sense of the concept of citizenship within the non-Muslim country. The FCNA therefore conceives of the concept of citizenship as a contractual obligation because having American citizenship requires one to fulfil its responsibilities and obligations. The Council seeks to ground the legitimacy of American Muslims' obligations and responsibilities towards the democratic American polity on both the concept of citizenship and the principle of *maṣlaḥa*. The contractual obligation is employed to substantiate American Muslims' obedience to American democratic political authority while the principle of *maṣlaḥa* is applied to facilitate the engagement of American Muslims in American society at both social and political levels. In consolidating the moral and legal grounds of obedience to the non-Muslim authority, the FCNA explicitly argues that a contract that originates in the legal resident status of American Muslims in America obliges them both morally and legally to implement their citizenship duties. The modern concept of citizenship is alluded to generally as the legal and moral equivalent of a tacit contract to base the political obligation of American Muslims to America on an Islamic legal ground in the *fatwās*. The emphasis on the concept of citizenship is not the final legal methodology regarding the issue of civic obligation, so the notion that American Muslims have entered into a form of contract enables FCNA members to assert that these Muslims are under obligation to contribute to the public interests of American society. The principle of *maṣlaḥa* is instead put into play by the FCNA with the intention of inducing American Muslims to engage in American society and contribute to its welfare. The Council therefore explicitly aspires to form an American Muslim community that actively interacts with other citizens in order to contribute to the society and its value system at the political, social and cultural levels.

The Dār al-Iftā' and the Diyanet cursorily acknowledge that the rulers of their states are Muslim. This presupposition facilitates their application to the Sunni tradition's doctrine of *siyāsa shar'iyya* to induce the Muslims in their countries to obedience to state authorities. In contrast, the fact that America is a non-Muslim authority explicitly impels the FCNA to espouse the principle of *maqāṣid al-sharī'a*, the concept of contractual obligation and the principle of *maṣlaḥa* with the intention of orienting American Muslims towards obeying the American state authority. Both the minority and citizenship statuses of American Muslims therefore emerge as contextual factors that incite the FCNA to apply different Islamic legal concepts and principles in evaluating issues regarding the political system, political participation and loyalty to non-Muslim authorities.

Conclusion

The book has provided insight into the organic interaction between contextual elements and Islamic legal methodologies by focusing upon three religious institutions (Saudi Arabia's Dār al-Iftā', Turkey's Diyanet and America's FCNA) and their official *fatwās*. The practice of *iftā'* is an important mechanism that establishes and enhances the ongoing communication between Islamic law and Muslims. This mechanism has assumed a functional and operative role by establishing a vivid connection between Islamic legal methodologies and contextual environments. Until recently, many academics and scholars in the area of Islamic law have specifically focused upon disassociating Islamic law from independent legal reasoning (*ijtihād*) and replacing it with adherence to imitation (*taqlīd*). This may be true, to some extent, when it is examined with reference to the immutable sides and aspects of Islamic law.

However, if Islamic law is instead interpreted as an area of science that is guided by a systematic process of accumulation, it becomes possible to identify particular features that attest to its changing, flexible and mutable character. The practice of *iftā'* can be interpreted as one of these features. The diachronic development of Islamic law renders a process in which the *fatwā* mechanism has adjusted in accordance with circumstances and time. During early periods of Islamic law, the practice was conducted by individual scholars, but this arrangement has been superseded by institutionalisation over time. In the aftermath of the nineteenth century, the practice of *iftā'* became, as a result of initiatives undertaken by Muslim nation-states who sought to control almost every aspect of social relations, subject to an institutionalisation, modernisation and nationalisation process. Through these initiatives, almost every Muslim state established its own national religious institutions that provided a setting in which Muslim scholars could perform the practice of *iftā'* upon a collective rather than an individual basis. More recently, some religious institutions including the FCNA and the ECFR were established with the intention of providing legal guidance to the growing number of Muslims in non-Muslim countries. The contemporary situation reiterates that the practice of *iftā'* has become established as a central institution that brings Islamic legal solutions to contemporary issues, along with the challenges that currently confront Muslims resident in both Muslim and non-Muslim countries.

DOI: 10.4324/9781003037637-102

Meanwhile novel variations of *fatwās*, which included collective, public and state *fatwās*, have begun to appear in the area of Islamic law. In operating within these institutions, scholars have resorted to independent legal reasoning by practicing collective *ijtihād* in order to issue Islamic legal decisions, resolutions and *fatwās* upon a range of contemporary issues, including abortion, autopsy, birth control, democracy and organ donation. The application of *iftā'* as an influential legal instrument underlines the possibilities of adaptability, change and flexibility within Islamic law, providing a clear rebuttal to alternating accounts which contend that Islamic law is disconnected from contemporary issues or that it is, by its very nature, an immutable, fixed and frozen legal system.

Subsequent to the establishment of religious institutions, the practice of *iftā'* began to mostly be implemented by these institutions in their local environments. The book has engaged with the institutions in three specific contexts – the Dār al-Iftā' in Saudi Arabia, the Diyanet in Turkey and the FCNA in America. In considering the three institutions and their official *fatwās* in a comparative framework, the book has provided insight into the interaction between the different contexts and Islamic legal methodologies. The three institutions work in divergent cultural, legal, political and social contexts. The Dār al-Iftā's engagement with the practice of *iftā'* occurs within the wider context of an extremely Islamic state, while the Diyanet issues its *fatwās* in the wider context of an ultra-secular democratic state. Like the Diyanet, the FCNA also functions in the wider context of a secular liberal democratic state, but it issues its *fatwās* for the American Muslim minority community. In seeking to demonstrate how these institutions operate within these diametrically opposed societies, this book incorporated socio-cultural, socio-legal and socio-political perspectives in order to engage with the relationship between religion, society and state. In addition to this, the book sought to answer the question of how the three institutions engage in each of these points while dealing in more detail with the issuance of *fatwās*.

As Chapter 1 illustrates in more detail, Saudi Arabia's Dār al-Iftā' has experienced a long process of centralisation that was completed in 1993 when the office of Grand Muftī was re-established. This official religious body was established in 1951 and was restructured twenty years later with the appointment of a number of senior scholars. In operating under the leadership of the State Grand Muftī, the Dār al-Iftā', which is the highest authority within the state, is responsible for conducting religious research, interpreting Islamic legal sources and issuing *fatwās*. The dramatic increase in oil revenues contributed to a sustained institutionalisation and modernisation process which impacted upon the practice of *iftā'* and the religious establishment. It is clear that the restructuring of the Dār al-Iftā' simultaneously derived from the conscious efforts of the Saudi Government to control the religious establishment and impersonal economic and social changes that ensued from the discovery of petroleum resources in the country. The incorporation of the Dār al-Iftā' into the Saudi state administration made it an official partner of the Saudi Government, or the ruling house, and it accordingly assumed a role in deciding legal, religious and social policies and legitimating the Saudi Government's political agenda. As a consequence, the indigenous structure of cooperative religious power was created by the Saudi Government, and this religious establishment gradually strengthened its official prestige and position by reinforcing the religious character of the Saudi state. However, this religious establishment is not autonomous or independent of the state because the King retains the right to appoint and dismiss members in accordance with his will. This dependence notwithstanding, the Dār al-Iftā' and its official *fatwās* have been simultaneously performing important roles in the legal, religious and social spheres. It might be inferred that this institution has assumed a kind of pre-legislative and pre-consultative mechanism role. It is a pre-legislative mechanism in the sense that the institution's decisions and *fatwās* have always had the potential, subject to the approval of the King, to become law. It can be said to be a consultative mechanism because the institution serves as a consultative body for the King, and his inquiries and questions receive preferential treatment during the issuance of *fatwās* and decisions.

The Diyanet, which is examined in Chapter 2, can be viewed as an extension or remnant of the *Shaykh al-Islām*, the Ottoman Sultanate's religious establishment. During the twentieth century, the newly established Turkish Republic implemented many reforms with the aim of modernising and secularising society. In functioning within the wider context of the state secularisation strategy, the office of *Shaykh al-Islām* was transformed into the Diyanet, which is a bureaucratic religious establishment subject to state control. The reconfiguration of that Ottoman office within the guise of the Diyanet resulted in Muslim scholars losing power because the office was deprived of a number of duties and tasks it had previously executed. The political agenda of the early Republican government and its stance towards religion clearly attest to the intention to establish an "assertive secularism" that would institute religion as a purely personal matter. While the state policy resulted in the short-term marginalisation of Islam and Turkey's Islamic legacy, it fell short of the ultimate aspiration of building a completely secular and unified society. During this period, the Diyanet presented itself as a restricted and inactive religious institution that was established with the aim of diffusing the state's interpretation of Islam within Turkish society. The religious policy of the early Republican government did however produce a social crisis and resulted in the state changing its stance towards the Diyanet and religion more generally. Subsequent to the 1950s, when state policy on religion became more moderate and tolerant, the Diyanet increasingly took on the form of an influential and prestigious religious institution that would exert influence over public life. In the aftermath of the 1980 military coup, the Diyanet became established as one of the foremost state instruments which would contribute to the promulgation of the Turkish-Islamic synthesis within both Turkey and amongst diaspora Turkish communities. Ultimately, the religious institution and the secular state arrived at an agreement of mutual recognition. This agreement is upheld by Articles 2 and 136 of the Constitution, which respectively protect secularism and the Diyanet.

Since its establishment, the Diyanet has focused upon the objectives of social peace and solidarity during times of political and social controversy. In operating within a secular state structure, the Diyanet has strongly emphasised the Sunni tradition's basic doctrine of politics and governance which demands collaboration between scholars and rulers (*'ulamā'-'umarā'*) – this clearly establishes that the Diyanet and its pro-system orientation are not a novelty introduced by the Republic. Instead, this traditional practice can be traced back to the Ottoman and Seljuk Sultanates. The changing ideologies and policies that the state has adopted towards religion indicate alternating phases of the Diyanet's activity and passivity – it is however important to note that the Diyanet was never marginalised by the state except during the first period of its existence (1924 to the mid-1940s). From the 1970s to the 1990s, the Diyanet remained aligned with a state ideology that sought to establish a uniform and monolithic nation by disseminating the ideology of Turkish-Islamic synthesis. Subsequent to the 2000s, the state's political predisposition towards uniformity began to be shaken, and the state has gradually been compelled to adopt a post-modern pluralist social ideology that recognises the threads of pluralism and religious diversity within the society. This change within state ideology has percolated into the Diyanet's activities and publications, and it has encouraged the institution to adopt a new ideal that orientates towards the middle ground between diversity and unity. State ideologies and policies have therefore influenced the Diyanet's religious approaches, discourses and policies.

As Chapter 3 addresses in more detail, the FCNA was established as a fully independent 501(c)(3) non-profit organisation with the intention of providing Islamic legal resolutions and *fatwās* to issues that confront American Muslims. The increasing presence of Muslims in America brought about new intricate issues that exigently needed legal solutions and *fatwās*. The phenomenon of imported *fatwās* therefore became problematic for American Muslims because they were generally produced by Muslim scholars resident in Muslim majority countries and often failed to address the contextual circumstances and conditions of American Muslims. The idea that it was necessary to establish a religious institution that understands and appreciates the contextual circumstances of the American Muslim community induced the Muslim Student Association (MSA) to form the Religious Affairs Committee in the 1970s. The first substructure of the FCNA had been voluntarily set up by the newly formed student association, but the Committee had very limited duties that merely included identifying the dates of the lunar months. When the Islamic Society of North America (ISNA) was established, the Religious Affairs Committee was transformed into the Fiqh Committee of the ISNA in 1982, but the Committee could still not actively engage with the problems of American Muslims on account of the size of its budget and membership. In 1986, the Fiqh Committee was renamed and restructured as the FCNA within the body of the ISNA with the intention of better evaluating the specific needs and problems of the growing American Muslim community. Unlike the Dār al-Iftā' and the Diyanet, the establishment of the FCNA was completely grounded on the voluntary effort of the American Muslim scholars who have integrationist tendencies and who advocate the concept of *fiqh al-aqalliyyāt*. Putting emphasis on the difference between Muslim and non-Muslim contexts, the FCNA has espoused the concept of *fiqh al-aqalliyyāt* as a legal methodology while issuing its *fatwās*. The FCNA therefore was the first translation of *fiqh al-aqalliyyāt* into a concrete institutional structure. In issuing *fatwās*, one of the main objectives of the Council is to accommodate the general principles and values of Islamic law to the contextual circumstances of American Muslims with the intention of facilitating the application of Islamic law in America and integrating American Muslims into their wider society. Nonetheless, the state-independent character of the FCNA has impeded the wide spread of its recognition as an authority within the American Muslim community but has provided it an autonomous character while evaluating issues directed to it.

If the three institutions are compared with reference to their institutionalisation, it is possible to identify differences in the authority, function, influence and power that they exert within their respective societies. The Dār al-Iftā' issues *fatwās* in response to questions that have been submitted to it by the general public, government agencies and the King. Its activities, composition, duties and responsibilities have been specified by royal decrees issued at different points in time – this serves to clarify and reiterate that the institution's authority, modes of operation and organisational structure are generally set out by the King. It is therefore important to acknowledge that the *'ulamā'* in the current Saudi state came to depend upon the Saudi ruling house for their survival and that this dependence became increasingly pronounced after the institutionalisation of the religious domain. Despite the fact that the *'ulamā'* have been transformed into "paid religious civil officials" appointed by the state, the institutionalisation of the *'ulamā'*, as embodied by the establishment of the Dār al-Iftā', potentially increased the formal and official influence of their *fatwās* in governmental circles, the Saudi legal system and Saudi society more generally. However, the religious scholars of the Diyanet, after the transition process of the office of *Shaykh al-Islām*, lost almost all their authority, functional power and prestige within the respective spheres – educational, financial, legislative and political – in which they exerted influence. As the secularisation policy of the early Republican period proceeded apace, the political and religious spheres were separated, and state control expanded over the domains that had been previously controlled by Muslim scholars.

In contrast to the institutionalisation of the *'ulamā'* in Saudi Arabia, the Muslim scholars in Turkey, whose influence was now restricted to the area of religion and religious affairs, lost their authority and power (juridical, legislative and political) which was now subsumed within Turkey's secular legal system. In a similar manner to the Dār al-Iftā', the Diyanet also provides its services within the framework of the Turkish Constitution, laws and regulations – the Diyanet's administrative and organisational structure, jurisdictional power and selection of members (including its president) are therefore subject to the state's regulations. Although the Diyanet, as a state-dependent institution, is administratively and structurally part of the state's bureaucratic system, it enjoys freedom in the intellectual discussion of Islamic issues, the production of religious knowledge and scholarly activities. This originates something of a paradox: while the relationship between the two institutions and their respective state authorities may sometimes detract from their religious authority, in other circumstances this dependence is an attribute or even condition of the same authority.

In contrast to the Dār al-Iftā' and the Diyanet, the FNCA is a state-independent religious institution that consists wholly of volunteer Muslim scholars. The Council issues its Islamic legal resolutions and *fatwās* in response to the questions that have been submitted to it by American Muslims, but its limited budget, originating in the Council's state-independent character, sometimes restricts FCNA members in engaging with all questions. Some questions therefore have been left unanswered. The Council's activities, composition, responsibilities and duties have been identified by the statutes that were determined by the FCNA's Council Executive Committee within the scope of Internal Revenue Code of America. This serves to reiterate that the Council's mode of operation, organisational structure and selection of members (including its president) are set out by the Council Executive Committee while the periphery of its jurisdiction is only specified by the regulations relating to 501(c)(3) organisations. It is therefore significant to acknowledge that the FCNA provides its services within the scope of the American laws and regulations but has a more self-governing character than the Dār al-Iftā' and the Diyanet in conducting its administrative and organisational activities. Nonetheless, the Council explicitly lacks the authority, power and funding that both Saudi and Turkish states provide to the Dār al-Iftā' and the Diyanet, respectively. The FCNA's state-independent character, when compared to the Dār al-Iftā' and the Diyanet, therefore makes it more autonomous but less authoritative.

The Islamic legal methodology espoused by the three institutions also serves to highlight important differences in the practice of *iftā'*. To a substantial extent, the Dār al-Iftā' remains loyal to the doctrines and legal methodologies of the Ḥanbalī *madhhab* when issuing *fatwās*. As the examined *fatwās* demonstrate, the institution's members frequently ground their *fatwās* within the literal meaning of the Qur'an and Sunna, thus offsetting the need to apply reason or rational tools. However, there are indications that the Dār al-Iftā' benefits to some extent from other exegetical tools and legal methods, which include *qiyās*, *maṣlaḥa* and *ḍarūra*, each of which is specific to the Sunni *madhhabs* (Ḥanafīsm, Mālikīsm and Shāfi'īsm). The application of these legal tools, and in particular *maṣlaḥa*, has enabled the institution to approve particularly controversial government policies – the *fatwā* which approved the deployment of US military personnel in Saudi Arabia during the first Gulf War is a particularly striking example. Even though there are signs of changes within their doctrinal and methodological alignment with the Ḥanbalī *madhhab*, these adjustments continue to be very limited and pragmatic in character. Exegetical methods and tools from other Sunni *madhhabs* are generally applied by the Dār al-Iftā' when the relevant issue is controversial and/or multi-faceted – relevant examples include autopsies, internet use, organ transplantation and the political policies at both domestic and international levels.

In issuing *fatwās*, the Diyanet remains faithful to the doctrines, opinions and tenets of the Ḥanafī *madhhab* to a certain extent, especially when the issues posed to the institution are associated with classical legal problems or *'ibādāt*. In answering these questions, the institution does not need to practice collective *ijtihād* if traditional legal rulings put in place by earlier Muslim scholars are appropriate and applicable to given circumstances. Questions are generally answered by prioritising the traditional opinions of the Ḥanafī *madhhab* although the Shāfiʿī *madhhab* features to a lesser extent. As part of an attempt to address contemporary issues, Muslim scholars (predominantly Ḥanafī) have performed the practice of collective *ijtihād* in order to establish the contemporary boundaries of the forbidden and the permissible. In doing so, the Diyanet has sought to identify the fundamental Islamic ethical and legal principles in the light of the Qur'an, with a view to then constructing its *fatwās* upon them. It is even sometimes the case that the classical legal rulings relating to *muʿāmalāt* can be re-examined in order to update specific legal rulings. The Diyanet's legal approach to contemporary issues suggests that Qur'anic principles that are specified by generally using the principles of *maqāṣid al-sharīʿa* and *maṣlaḥa* can provide a basis for the derivation of an Islamic ruling. The Qur'anic text and its established overarching principles are given priority over all other sources of Islamic law, and the *ḥadīth* literature and *fiqhī* texts are subservient to these principles. The heavily contextualised Qur'anic passages and the *ḥadīth* corpus are generally reinterpreted in the light of contemporary contexts through the deployment of analytical reasoning. In common with their Ḥanafī predecessors, the Muslim scholars in the Diyanet also cautiously and critically apply *āḥād ḥadīths* when issuing *fatwās* – these *ḥadīths* are exposed to analytical and moral examination in order to identify their legal validity when establishing a legal ruling on them. Chapter 4 illustrates that when the Diyanet examines the legal position of houses of worship belonging to non-Muslims in Muslim countries, it stresses the fact that the relevant *ḥadīth* (which does not permit a religion other than Islam to be present in the Arabian Peninsula) contradicts the established Qur'anic principles of freedom, free will and tolerance. There are a number of signs which suggest that the Diyanet's legal approach shifts from a focus upon doctrine to ethics or principles when examining contemporary issues.

The establishment of the FCNA is a historical moment that represents the first embodiment of the concept of *fiqh al-aqalliyyāt* in an institutional body. Instead of pursuing the doctrines, opinions and methodology of any specific *madhhab*, the Council predominantly issues *fatwās* within the scope of *fiqh al-aqalliyyāt*. The Council employs all the principles and methodologies of Islamic law and sometimes considers, if it is relevant to the issue, the various opinions of the earlier Muslim scholars who were affiliated with different *madhhabs*. This clearly establishes that the FCNA draws equally upon the legal opinions pertaining to all legal *madhhabs* as legal intellectual sources rather than established immutable rulings in the process of issuing *fatwās*. However, if the question directed to the Council is related to the area of *ʿibādāt*, the Council particularly considers the issue within the scope of the *madhhab* affiliated by the questioner – even in this area, if the question includes new developments and dimensions, the Council evaluates the issue outside the questioner's *madhhab*. As part of an attempt to address contemporary new issues and questions, FCNA members (predominantly advocates of the concept of *fiqh al-aqalliyyāt*) have performed the practice of collective *ijtihād* with the intention of reconciling the rights and duties of American Muslims that originate in their simultaneous belonging to both American and Muslim identities. With the intention of balancing the rights and duties that arise from the dual identity of American Muslims, the Council have sought to accommodate Islamic law to the circumstances of American Muslims through generally employing the principle of *maqāṣid al-sharīʿa* (extended in its volume), the principle of *maṣlaḥa* (specifically focused upon the public interests of the American Muslim community) and the legal maxim of *ḍarūra* (intended to facilitate the lives of American Muslims). In doing so, the FCNA initially identifies the fundamental ethical and legal principles through the holistic reading of the Qur'an and Sunna, with a view to then constructing its *fatwās* upon these principles. The overemphasis upon the different circumstances of America compared to Muslim majority countries is a clear indication that the Council gives an additional consideration to the contextual factors that American Muslims face in their non-Muslim context. In this regard, the *fatwā* which assented to the participation of American Muslims in American military service and the *fatwā* which makes the voting of American Muslims in American presidential elections obligatory are particularly striking examples. There are many signs which reveal that the FCNA gives specific consideration to the evaluation of the circumstances of American Muslims.

The *fatwās* examined in the book can be said to be in large part products of the three institutions' social and temporal contexts. The constituent elements of these textual materials provide considerable insight into the interaction between cultural, legal, political and social contexts and Islamic legal methodologies. These *fatwās* are not merely products of intellectual exertion but can also be said to reflect the environments in which they emerge. As Chapter 4 and Chapter 5 demonstrate in more detail, it is appropriate to situate the thought processes and legal interpretations of scholars who function in the three institutions within the wider context of their socio-cultural and socio-political milieu. When the three institutions issue their official *fatwās*, the wider contextual elements are reproduced in them. These "wider elements" should be theorised as being intrinsic to Muslim scholars' ideas, outlooks and perceptions. Chapter 4 and Chapter 5 have distinguished these surrounding factors into four thematic categories: (1) the *madhhab* affiliation in the three countries; (2) the cultural practices and social presumptions in the three societies; (3) the legal systems of the three countries; and (4) the political structures of the three societies.

With regard to the first category, the Dār al-Iftā' relies mainly on the doctrines and methodologies of the Ḥanbalī *madhhab*, which is adhered to by the majority of the populace in Saudi Arabia, when issuing its *fatwās*. The Ḥanafī *madhhab*, which commands the loyalty of a majority of Turkish Muslims, has a substantial influence upon the Diyanet – the institution does not only follow the methodologies and theories of this school but also adopts its distinctive legal opinions and rulings when issuing *fatwās*. Rather than specifically relying on the doctrines and methodologies of any established *madhhab*, the FCNA applies the concept of *fiqh al-aqalliyyāt* to address all American Muslims who adhere to different *madhhabs*. The diversity of American Muslims' *madhhab* affiliation and their minority status in America explicitly emerge as the main contextual factors that induce the FCNA to espouse the concept of *fiqh al-aqalliyyāt*.

Secondly, cultural practices and social presumptions present themselves as influential implicit elements that encourage Muslim scholars within the three institutions to draw upon particular legal concepts and principles when addressing themselves to identical issues. Chapter 4 suggests that the influence of the exclusivist Wahhābī-based Saudi culture can be interpreted as an effective factor that influences the Dār al-Iftā's application of *al-walā' wal-barā'* to its *fatwās* when it is engaged with relations between Muslims and non-Muslims. Conversely, the influence of a more democratic and tolerant Turkish culture leads scholars within the Diyanet to examine issues pertaining to relations with non-Muslims within the scope of *ḥuqūq ahl al-dhimma*. Contrary to the Dār al-Iftā' and the Diyanet that apply the traditionally existing legal concepts, the FCNA espouses a more inclusivist, tolerant and civil approach when addressing issues related to the relationships between Muslims and non-Muslims. Within the religiously pluralistic American society that is inclusivist, receptive and indulgent to others, the FCNA precisely ascertains peaceful coexistence, amicable dialogue, religious freedom and pluralism as the main principles through the holistic hermeneutic reading of the authoritative sources. The values and norms that have been entrenched within the religiously pluralistic American society emerge as influential contextual factors that implicitly orient FCNA members towards the application of a more embracive and amicable approach.

In addition, the legal systems of the three countries evidence themselves as another influential contextual factor in the practice of *iftā'* that is conducted by the three institutions. The Islamic character of the Saudi legal system provides a practical impetus to the *fatwās* issued by the Dār al-Iftā'. They have the potential to transform into law (although this is subject to the approval of the King) and also have been drawn upon by judges as secondary sources. In this regard, the *fatwā* that relates to drug smugglers is a striking example. In contrast, the *fatwās* issued by the Diyanet do not have any influence within the secular Turkish legal system. Nonetheless, they do have the potential to exert a power of social sanction. Despite the fact that they do not have any legal authority in the Turkish judicial system, they can formulise moral values and social norms. In operating within a secular legal system, the Diyanet is also normally compelled to issue hybrid *fatwās* that combine religious and secular law – the *fatwās* relating to religious marriage are an important example in this regard. Like the Diyanet's *fatwās*, the *fatwās* issued by the FCNA do not have any binding power within the American secular legal system. They are just issued to inform and advise American Muslims with regard to Islamic legal problems and conflicts that they face. However, the FCNA's *fatwās* still do not form moral and normative values within the American Muslim community because of the Council's lack of acceptability as a persuasive authority amongst the ethnically, culturally and religiously diverse American Muslims. Despite this, the Council, like the Diyanet, issues its *fatwās* with the intention of surmounting the legal loopholes between Islamic legal norms and American legal regulations. Functioning in the American legal system induces the FCNA to espouse the reconciliatory, or hybridisation, approach in order to develop the appropriate understanding of the rights and duties – under Islamic law and the American legal system – amongst American Muslims. The *fatwā* regarding paying alimony to the wife after divorce is an influential example.

Finally, the political systems of the three countries, in addition to exerting an important influence over the authority, power and role of the three institutions, can also impact the content of *fatwās* that relate to political issues. In the Saudi theocratic monarchy, there is ongoing cooperation between the *'ulamā'* (the Dār al-Iftā') and the *'umarā'* (the Saudi Government), both of whom are designated as holders of authority by the Wahhābī doctrine of *siyāsa shar'iyya*. While the Dār al-Iftā' helps to legitimise the King's policies, he is also obliged to consult the institution and take its opinion into account when making a decision on any legal, political, religious or social issue. In contrast, within Turkey, the Diyanet and its *fatwās* do not exert any influence within the secular democratic system. With regard to any political issue, the democratic secular government is not in need of the assent of its religious institution on account of the state's secular nature. As for the FCNA, it is a state-independent institution and does not have any influence within the American secular democratic system. The Council just symbolises the religious freedom that American liberal democracy provides to its people. Although the political systems of Saudi Arabia and Turkey diverge in each of the aforementioned respects, it is important to recognise that the Dār al-Iftā' and the Diyanet draw upon the Sunni tradition's doctrine of *siyāsa shar'iyya* with the intention of enhancing social stability within their respective countries by encouraging Muslims' obedience to state authority. While the Dār al-Iftā' pronounces the country's absolute theocratic monarchic system as Islamic by maintaining that the constitution is grounded within the Qur'an and Sunna, the Diyanet seeks to legitimise Turkey's democratic structures by invoking the concept of *shūrā*. In common with the Diyanet, the FCNA also applies the concept of *shūrā* in order to provide legitimacy to democracy as an appropriate government form that is worthy of obedience and loyalty, but it, unlike the Diyanet, uses the concepts of citizenship and contractual obligation with the intention of inciting American Muslims to obey American democratic political authority. In contrast to the Dār al-Iftā' and the Diyanet, which use the Sunni tradition's doctrine of *siyāsa shar'iyya*, operating in a non-Muslim country emerges as an influential factor that induces the FCNA, when addressing issues related to obedience and loyalty to state authority, to apply divergent legal concepts and principles.

The preceding examples serve to establish that the interpretation of textual sources is considerably influenced by the surrounding socio-cultural, socio-legal and socio-political factors. The examination of the official *fatwās* issued by the three institutions does not only highlight the connection between religion, society and state but also brings out the intricate interaction between Islamic legal methodologies and contextual environments. In the context of these insights, it becomes easier for an observer to recognise that the divergences of institutional opinion are only not attributable to the authoritative textual sources of Islamic law but can be attributed to interpretations of these sources. Consequently, the differences can be traced back to the questions of how the three institutions interpret the authoritative sources; which Islamic legal methodologies, principles and maxims are predominantly espoused by the three; and in which cultural, political, legal and social environments these institutions work. In brief, the examined *fatwās* demonstrate that the existing social, political, cultural and legal values, judgements and conceptions should reckon among important tacit factors and parameters in describing Muslims scholars' legal thinking in the practice of *iftā'*.

Bibliography

Abdalla Mohammad, 'Do Australian Muslims Need a Mufti? Analyzing the Institution of *Ifta* in the Australian Context' in Nadirsyah Hossen and Richard Mohr (eds), *Law and Religion in Public Life the Contemporary Debate* (Rutledge 2011).

Abdul Rahman, Noor Naemah, Asmak Abd Rahman and Abdul Karim Ali, 'A Study on Students' Research related to Fatwa Summited at Malaysian Public Universities' (2012) 2 (18) *International Journal of Humanities and Social Science* 129.

Abou El Fadl Khaled, 'Striking a Balance: Islamic Legal Discourse on Muslim Minorities' in Yvonne Y. Haddad and John L. Esposito (eds), *Muslims on the Americanization Path?* (Oxford University Press 2000).

Abu Zahra Muhammad, *The Four Imams: The Lives and Teachings of Their Founders* (Aisha Bewley (tr) Dar Al Taqwa 2001).

Act no. 429 dated 03 March 1924.

Act no. 430 dated 03 March 1924.

Act no. 1222 dated 10 April 1928.

Act no. 1452 dated 30 June 1929.

Act no. 1827 dated 8 June 1931.

Act no. 2800 dated 14 June 1935.

Act no. 3115 dated 05 February 1937.

Act no. 5634 dated 23 March 1950.

Act no. 633 dated 22 July 1965.

Act no. 2820 dated 22 April 1983.

Act no. 93/4257 dated 19 February1993.

Act no. 98/11479 dated 24 July 1998.

Act no. 5237 dated 26 September 2004.

Act no. 6002 dated 01 July 2010.

Act no. 8044 dated 19 August 2015.

Adanalı Ahmet Hamdi, 'The Presidency of Religious Affairs and the Principle of Secularism in Turkey' (2008) 98 (2–3) *The Muslim World* 228.

Advice to the Ummah given in the answer to ten important questions, in *Fatwas of Ibn Baz*, 8: 202–209 <https://www.alifta.gov.sa/En/IftaContents/IbnBaz/Pages/default.aspx?cultStr=en&View=Page&PageID=1025&PageNo=1&BookID=14> accessed 27 February 2021.

Afsaruddin Asma, 'Shari'a and Fiqh in the United States' in Yvonne Y. Haddad and Jane I. Smith (eds), *The Oxford Handbook of American Islam* (Oxford University Press 2014)

Agrama Hussein Ali, 'Ethics, Tradition, Authority: Toward an Anthropology of the Fatwa' (2010) 37 (1) *American Ethnologist* 2.

Ahmad Imad-ad-Dean, 'Shuratic Iftā': The Challenge of Fatwa Collectivization' in Zulfiqar Ali Shah (ed), *Iftā and Fatwa in the Muslim World and the West* (The International Institute of Islamic Thought 2014).

Ahmed Akgunduz, *Islamic Law in Theory and Practice* (IUR Press 2010).

Aksanyar Necati, 'Demokrat Partinin Din Politikalarının Türk Basınına Yansımaları (1950–1954)' (2007) 11 *Akademik Bakış* 1.

Al-Alawi Irfan, 'Top Saudi Cleric: Ban Christian Churches in Arabia: Let Girls Marry at 10' (Gatestone Institute International Policy Council, 23 May 2012) <https://www.gatestoneinstitute.org/3073/saudi-fatwa-ban-christian-churches> accessed 20 November 2017.

Al-Alwani Taha Jabir, *Source Methodology in Islamic Jurisprudence: Usul al-Fiqh al-Islami* (The International Institute of Islamic Thought 2003).

———, *Towards a Fiqh for Muslim Minorities: Some Basic Reflections* (Ashur A. Shamis (tr) The International Institute of Islamic Thought 2003).

———, 'Muslims' Participation in the US Political Life' <https://archive.islamonline.net/?p=6367> accessed 13 September 2017.

Alwani Zainab and Celene Ayat Lizzio, 'Relgion, Gender and Family Law: Critical Perspectives on Integration for Western Muslims' in Maurits S. Berger (ed), *Applying Shari'a in the West: Facts, Fears and the Future of Islamic Rules on the Family Relations in the West* (Leiden University Press 2013).

Alwani Zainab, 'The Quranic Concepts on Gender Relations' <http://www.fiqhcouncil.org/node/12 > accessed 13 May 2017.

Al-Atawneh Muhammad, *Wahhābī Islam Facing the Challenges of Modernity: Dār al-Iftā in the Modern Saudi State* (Brill 2010).

———, 'Wahhābī Legal Theory as Reflected in Modern Official Saudi *Fatwās*: Ijtihād. Taqlid, Sources, and Methodology' (2011) 18 (3/4) *Islamic Law and Society* 327.

Al-Athari 'Abdullāh ibn 'Abdul-Ḥamīd, *Islamic Beliefs: A Brief Introduction to the 'Aqīdah of Ahl as-Sunnah wal-Jamā'ah* (Naṣiruddin al-Khaṭṭab (tr) International Islamic Publishing House 2005.

Al-Bukhārī Abū 'Abdullah Muhammad ibn Ismāī'īl, *Ṣaḥīḥ al-Bukharī* (Muhammad Muhsin Khan (tr) Darussalam 1997).

Al– Dawīs Ahmad b. 'Abd al-Rāziq, *Fatawā al-Lajna al-Dā'ima li al-Buḥūth al-'Ilmiyya wa al-Iftā wa al-Da'wā wa al-Irshād* (Maktabad al-'Ibīkān 2000).

Al-Fahad Abdulaziz, 'Commentary: From Exclusivism to Accommodation: Doctrinal and Legal Evolution of Wahhabim' (2004) 79 (2) *New York University Law Review* 485.

Al-Gharyānī Aḥmad Selāmat, 'Fatāwā al-'Ulamā' fī Ḥukm al-Tawsi'at al-Jadīda lil-Mas'ā wa 'Ademu Jawāzi al-Sa'ī fihā' <http://www.ahlalhdeeth.com/vb/showthread.php?t=199230 > accessed 05 August 2016.

Al-Huda University, 'Dr. Mohamad Adam El-Sheikh' <http://alhudauniversity.org/dr-mohamad-adam-el-sheikh > accessed 01 July 2017.

Al-Ḥanbalī Abd al-Rahmān ibn 'Abd Allāh al-Ba'lī, *Kashf al-Mukhaddarāt wal-Riyāḍ al-Muzhirāt lil-Sharḥ Skhṣar al-Mukhtasarāt* vol II (Dār al-Bashaer al-Islāmiyya 2001).

Al-JawziyyaIbn Qayyim, *I'lām al-Muwaqqi'īn 'an Rabb al-'Ālamīn*, vol I (Dār al-Jīl 1973).

Al-Matroudi Abdul Hakim I., *The Ḥanbalī School of Law and Ibn Taymiyya* (Routledge 2006).

Al-Nawawī Abū Zakriyyā Yaḥyā ibn Sharaf, *Al-Majmū' Sharḥ al-Madhhab (Irshād)*, vol XI (Maktabat al-Irshād 2008).

Al-Qaraḍāwī Yusuf, *Al-Ijtihād al-Mu'āṣir bayna al-Indibāṭ wal- Infirāṭ* (Al-Maktab al-Islāmī 1998).

Al-Qarāfī Aḥmad ibn Idrīs *Al-Iḥkām fī Tamyīz al-Fatāwā 'an al-Aḥkām wa-Taṣarrufāt al-Qāḍī wa al-Imām* (Maktab al-Maṭbū'āt al-Islāmiyya bi-Ḥalab 1995).

Al-Qāsimī Zafer, *Nizam al-Hukm Fi Al-Shari'ah Wal-Tareek* (Dar Anafa'is 1974).

Al-Rasheed Madawi, *A Most Masculine State: Gender, Politics, and Religion in Saudi Arabia* (Cambridge University Press 2013).

———, *Contesting the Saudi State: Islamic Voices from a New Generation* (Cambridge University Press 2007).

Al-Shalhūb 'Abd al-Raḥmān, *Al-Niẓām al-Dustūrī fi al-Mamlaka al-'Arabiyya al-Sa'ūdiyya bayna al-Sharī'a al-Islāmiyya wal-Qānūn al-Muqāran* (Maktabat Fahd al-Waṭaniyya 1999).

Al-Shāshī Nidhām al-Dīn, *Introduction to Usul Ul-Fiqh: According to the Hanafi School* (Abdul Aleem (tr) Cordoba Academy 2015).

Al-Shuway'ir Muḥammad b. Sa'd *Majmū' Fatāwā wa-Maqālāt Mutanawwi'a* (Dār al-Qāsim 2000) <https://ia800308.us.archive.org/30/items/mfmmmfmm/mfmm07.pdf > accessed 23 July 2016.

Al-Ṭabarī, 'The Battle of al-Qādisiyyah and the Conquest of Syria and Palestine' in Ehsan Yar-Shater (ed), *The History of al- Ṭabarī*, vol XII, XVI (Yohanan Friedmann (tr) State University of New York Press 1997).

Al-Taḥdhīru min al-Safar ilā Bilād al-Kafara wa Khaṭarahu 'alā al-'Aqīda wal-Akhlāq, in Majallat al-Buḥūth al-Islāmiyya, 16:7–10 <http://www.alifta.net/Fatawa/FatawaChapters.aspx?languagename=ar&View=Page&PageID=2283&PageNo=1&BookID=2> accessed 18 November 2017.

'Al-Tamdīd li-Arba'a A'ḍāi' fil-Lajna al-Ḍā'ima lil-Fatwā wa Amrun Malikiyyun: I'āda Takwīn Hay'at Kibār al-'Ulamā' bi-Ri'āsa Āl al-Shaykh wa 20 'Ul-Tam *Al-Jazīra* (Riyadh, 3 December 2016) <http://www.al-jazirah.com/2016/20161203/ln39.htm> accessed 24 October 2017.

Al-Turki Abdullah, 'Interfaith Dialogue: From Makkah to New York' in Muhammed al-Bishr (ed), *Interfaith Dialogue: Cross-Cultural Views* (1st edn, Ghainaa Publications 2010).

Al-Yassini Ayman, *Religion and State in the Kingdom of Saudi Arabia* (Westview Press 1985).

American Learning Institute for Muslims, 'Dr. Zainab Alwani' <https://www.alimprogram.org/scholars/dr-zainab/> accessed 01 July 2017.

An-Na'im Abdullahi Ahmed, *Toward an Islamic Reformation: Civil Liberties, Human Rights, and International Law* (Syracuse University Press 1990).

Arslan Berna Zengin, 'State and Turkish Secularism: The Case of the Diyanet' in Bryan S. Turner (ed), *The Religious and the Political: A Comparative Sociology of Religion* (Cambridge University Press 2013).

Auda Jasser, 'Should Muslim in the North Fast 23 Hours a Day?' <http://www.fiqhcouncil.org/node/82> accessed 22 August 2017.

Ayar Talip, *Osmanlı Devletinde Fetvâ Eminliği (1892–1922)* (Diyanet İşleri Başkanlığı Yayınları 2014).

Aydar Hidayet, 'The Issue of Chanting the Adhan in Languages Other than Arabic and related Social Reactions in Turkey' (2006) 13 *İstanbul Üniversitesi İlahiyat Fakültesi Dergisi* 45.

———, 'Türklerde Anadilde İbadet Meselesi -Cumhuriyet Dönemi-' (2007) 15 *İstanbul Üniversitesi İlahiyat Fakültesi Dergisi* 72.

Aydın M. Şevki and others, *Sorularla İslam* (Diyanet İşleri Başkanlığı Yayınları 2015).

Ayubi Zahra M. S., 'Negotiating Justice: American Muslim Women Navigating Islamic Divorce and Civil Law' (2010) 30 *Journal for Islamic Studies* 78.

Badawi Jamal, *Gender Equity in Islam: Basic Principles* (American Trust Publications 1999).

———, 'Gender Equity in Islam' <http://www.fiqhcouncil.org/node/26> accessed 20 September 2015.

———, 'Muslim/Non-Muslim Relations' <http://fiqhcouncil.org/muslim-non-muslim-relations/> accessed 23 November 2020.

Bakırtaş Turgay, 'Din ve Devlet Birlikteliği Bu Ülkenin Kaderidir' (Gerçek Hayat, 25 February 2016) <http://www.gercekhayat.com.tr/gundem/1050/> accessed 05 December 2016.

Bali Rifat N., 'The Politics of Turkification during the Single Party Period' in Hans-Lukas Kieser (ed), *Turkey beyond Nationalism: Towards Post-Nationalist Identities* (I.B.Tauris 2006).

Bardakoğlu Ali, *Religion and Society New Perspectives from Turkey* (Diyanet İşleri Başkanlığı 2009).

'Basic Law of Governance' (Royal Embassy of Saudi Arabia, 1 March 1992) <https://www.saudiembassy.net/basic-law-governance> accessed 08 October 2015.

Bayir Derya, *Minorities and Nationalism in Turkish Law* (Routledge 2016).

Bedier Ahmed, 'What Islamic Scholars Say about Voting' <http://unitedvoices.com/docs/Islamic-perspective-voting1.pdf> accessed 08 November 2020.

Beylunioğlu Anna Maria, 'Freedom of Religion and Non-Muslim Minorities in Turkey' (2015) 13 (4) *Turkish Policy Quarterly* 139.

Boucek Chritopher, 'Saudi Fatwa Restrictions and the State-Clerical Relationship' (Carnegie Endowment for International Peace, 27 October 2010) <https://carnegieendowment.org/2010/10/27/saudi-fatwa-restrictions-and-state-clerical-relationship/6b81 > accessed 23 September 2017.

Brachman Jarret M., *Global Jihadism: Theory and Practice* (Routledge 2009).

Büyükkara Mehmet Ali, *İhvan'dan Cüheyman'a Suudi Arabistan ve Vehhabilik* (Rağbet Yayınları 2016).

Caeiro Alexandre, 'The Shifting Moral Universes of the Islamic Tradition of *Iftā*': A Diachronic Study of Four *Adab al-Fatwā* Manuals' (2006) 96 (4) *The Muslim World* 661.

———, 'Transnational Ulama, European Fatwas, and Islamic Authority: A Case Study of the European Council for Fatwa and Research' in Martin van Bruinessen and Stefano Allievi (eds), *Producing Islamic Knowledge: Transmission and Dissemination in Western Europe* (Routledge 2011).

Calder Norman, 'Friday Prayer and the Juristic Theory of Government: Sarakhsī, Shīraāzī, Māwardī' (1986) 49 (1) *Bulletin of the School of Oriental and African Studies* 35.

Carmon Yigal and Y. Admon, 'Reforms in Saudi Arabia under King 'Abdallah' (*The Middle East Research Institute (MEMRI)*, 04 June 2009) <https://www.memri.org/reports/reforms-saudi-arabia-under-king-abdallah> accessed 22 November 2017.

Cesari Jocelyne, *When Islam and Democracy Meet: Muslims in Europe and in the United States* (Palgrave Macmillan 2004).

———, 'Islamic Organisations in the United States' in Yvonne Y. Haddad and Jane I. Smith (eds), *The Oxford Handbook of American Islam* (Oxford University Press 2014).

Considine Craig, 'Religious Pluralism and Civic Rights in a "Muslim Nation": An Analysis of Prophet Muhammad's Covenants with Christians' (2016) 7 (15) *Religions* 1.

Coulson N. J., 'The State and the Individual in Islamic Law' (1957) 6 (1) *The International and Comparative Law Quarterly* 49.

Crawford M. J., 'Civil War Foreign Intervention, and the Question of Political Legitimacy: A Nineteenth-Century Sa'ūd ī Qāḍī's Dilemma' (1982) 14 (3) *International Journal of Middle East Studies* 227.

Çakır Ruşen and İrfan Bozan, *Sivil Şeffaf ve Demokratik Bir Diyanet İşleri Başkanlığı Mümkün mü?* (TESEV Yayinlari 2005).

Çalışkan İlker, Hasan Mollaoğllu and Muhammed Acar, *Aileye İlişkin Sorunlar: İstişare Toplantısı* (Diyanet İşleri Başkanlığı Yayınları 2009).

Çelik Mehmet, 'Islamic Scholars Agree on a Shared Lunar Calendar for Muslim World' (*Daily Sabah Turkey*, 31 May 31 2016) <http://www.dailysabah.com/nation/2016/05/31/islamic-scholars-agree-on-a-shared-lunar-calendar-for-muslim-world> accessed 20 November 2016.

Dadaş Mustafa Bülent, 'Kuruluşundan Günümüze Din İşleri Yüksek Kurulunun Fetva Siyaseti' (2015) 13 (25–26) *Türkiye Araştırmaları Literatür Dergisi* 37.

Dağcı Şamil, 'Din İşleri Yüsek Kurulu Karalarına Fetva Konseptinde Bir Yaklaşım' (2002) 38 (4) *Diyanet İlmi Dergi* 5

Danger of women joining men in their workplace, in *Fatwas of Ibn Baz*, 1:418–427 <http://www.alifta.net/Search/ResultDetails.aspx?languagename=en&lang=en&view=result&fatwaNum=&FatwaNumID=&ID=75&searchScope=14&SearchScopeLevels1=&SearchScopeLevels2=&highLight=1&SearchType=exact&SearchMoesar=false&bookID=&LeftVal=0&RightVal=0&simple=&SearchCriteria=allwords&PagePath=&siteSection=1&searchkeyword=119111109101110039115032119111114107\lfirstKeyWordFound> accessed 29 November 2017.

Davis Derek H., 'Introduction: Religious Pluralism as the Essential Foundation of America's Quest for Unity and Order' in Derek H. Davis (ed), *The Oxford Handbook of Church and State in the United States* (Oxford University Press 2018).

Declaration and warning against world conference on women, Beijing, in *Fatwas of Ibn Baz*, 9:203–204 <http://www.alifta.net/Fatawa/FatawaDetails.aspx?languagename=en&lang=en&IndexItemID=42704&SecItemHitID=46014&ind=20&Type=Index&View=Page&PageID=1209&PageNo=1&BookID=14&Title=DisplayIndexAlpha.aspx accessed 01 November 2017>.

DeLorenzo Yusuf Talal, 'Fiqh and the Fiqh Council of North America' (1998) 3 (2) *Journal of Islamic Law* 193.

———, 'The Fiqh Councilor of North America' in Yvonne Y. Haddad and John L. Esposito (eds), *Muslims on the Americanization Path?* (Oxford University Press 2000).

Din İşleri Yüksek Kurulu, *Kuruluşundan Günümüz Din İşleri Başkanlığı (Tarihçe-Teşkilat ve Faaliyetleri) (1924–1997)* (Diyanet İşleri Başkanlığı Yayınları 1999).

———, *Türkiye'de Dini Hayat Araştırması* (Diyanet İşleri Başkanlığı Yayınları 2014).

———, *Fetvalar* (Diyanet İşleri Başkanlığı Yayınları 2015).

Din İşleri Yüksek Kurulu Başkanlığı, 'Din Şuraları' <http://www2.diyanet.gov.tr/dinisleriyuksekkurulu/Sayfalar/DinSuralarison.aspx> accessed 20 November 2016.

———, 'İlkeler ve Hedefler' <http://www2.diyanet.gov.tr/dinisleriyuksekkurulu/Sayfalar/IlkelerVeHedefler.aspx> accessed 12 December 2016.

———, 'Uluslararası Hicri Takvim Birliği Kongresi Sonuç Bildirgesi' <http://www2.diyanet.gov.tr/dinisleriyuksekkurulu/Sayfalar/HaberDetay.aspx?rid=64&lst=HaberlerListesi&csn=/dinisleriyuksekkurulu> accessed 20 November 2016.

———, 'Kurul Üyeleri: Muhlis Akar' <http://www2.diyanet.gov.tr/dinisleriyuksekkurulu/Sayfalar/uyeler/MuhlisAkar.aspx> accessed 14 November 2016.

———, 'Kurul Üyeleri: Rifat Oral' <http://www2.diyanet.gov.tr/dinisleriyuksekkurulu/Sayfalar/uyeler/RifatOral.aspx> accessed 14 November 2016.
———, 'Kurul Üyeleri: Zekeriya Güler' <http://www2.diyanet.gov.tr/dinisleriyuksekkurulu/Sayfalar/uyeler/ZekeriyaGuler.aspx> accessed 14 November 2016.
———, 'Kurul Üyeleri: Zeki Sayar' <http://www2.diyanet.gov.tr/dinisleriyuksekkurulu/Sayfalar/uyeler/ZekiSayar.aspx> accessed 14 November 2016.
Din İşleri Yüsek Kurulu Kararları, 'İslam Geleneğinde Gayr-ı Müslim Mabetlerin Dini ve Hukuki Durumu' <https://kurul.diyanet.gov.tr/Karar-Mutalaa-Cevap/4373/islam-geleneginde-gayr-i-muslim-mabetlerinin-dini-ve-hukuki-durumu> accessed 03 April 2018.
———, 'Kadınların İş Hayatında ve Siyasette Yer Almaları' <https://fetva.diyanet.gov.tr/Karar-Mutalaa-Cevap/2913/kadinlarin-is-hayatinda-ve-yonetimde-yer-almalari> accessed 27 August 2015.
———, 'Kadınların Cuma, Bayram ve Cenaze Namazı Kılıp Kılamayacağı ve Bunların Saflardaki Durumu' <https://kurul.diyanet.gov.tr/Cevap-Ara/2747/medyada-tartismasi-yapilan-bazi-konular?enc=QisAbR4bAkZg1HImMxXRn2t8ij%2beDtMkJdRGirgyeb8%3d> accessed 28 November 2020.
———, 'Uluslararası Hicri Takvim Birliği Kongresi Sonuç Bildirgesi' <http://www2.diyanet.gov.tr/dinisleriyuksekkurulu/Sayfalar/HaberDetay.aspx?rid=64&lst=HaberlerListesi&csn=/dinisleriyuksekkurulu> accessed 20 November 2016.
Din İşleri Yüsek Kurulu Dini Bilgilendirme Platformu, 'Fetva Yöntemimiz' <https://fetva.diyanet.gov.tr/FetvaYontem> accessed 12 September 2020.
Diouf Slyviane A., 'The First Stirrings of Islam in America' in Yvonne Y. Haddad and Jane I. Smith (eds), *The Oxford Handbook of American Islam* (Oxford University Press 2014).
Doğan Recep, *Usūl al-Fiqh: Methodology of Islamic Jurisprudence* (Tughra Books 2013).
Doi Abdur Rahman I., *Non-Muslims under Shari'ah (Islamic Law)* (Kazi Publications 1981).
Dr. Jamal Badawi, 'About Dr. Jamal Badawi' <http://jamalbadawi.org/index.php?option=com_content&view=category&layout=blog&id=2&Itemid=2> accessed 01 July 2017.
———, 'A Guide to Political Left' <http://www.discoverthenetworks.org/individualProfile.asp?indid=1009> accessed 01 July 2017.
Dural Seda, 'The Violence against Woman Policy of the AKP Government and the Diyanet' (MA thesis, Leiden University 2016).
Duran Khalid, 'Demographic Characteristics of the American Muslim Community' (1997) 36 (1) *Islamic Studies* 57.
Erdem Gazi, 'Religious Services in Turkey: From the Office of Şeyhülislām to the Diyanet,' (2008) 98 (2–3) *The Muslim World* 199.
Esposito John L., 'Introduction: Muslims in America or American Muslims?' in Yvonne Yazbeck Haddad and John L. Esposito (eds), *Muslims on the Americanization Path?* (Oxford University Press 2000).
———, 'Exclusivist Muslims and the Threat to the Religious Reform' (*Religion and Ethics*, 15 May 2012) <http://www.abc.net.au/religion/articles/2012/05/15/3503503.htm> accessed 20 November 2017.
Fallon Sarah M., 'Justice for All: American Muslims, Sharia Law, and Maintaining Comity with American Jurisprudence' (2013) 36 (1) *Boston College International and Comparative Law Review* 153.
Farḥāt Muṣṭafā, 'Akbar Tawsi'at lil-Ḥaramayn Tuthīru bayna al-'Ulamā' fī al-Sa'ūdiyya' <http://www.djazairess.com/echorouk/25380> accessed 06 August 2016.

Farquhar Mike, 'The Islamic University of Medina since 1961: The Politics of Religious Mission and the Making of a Modern Salafi Pedagogy' in Masooda Bano and Keiko Sakurai (eds), *Shaping Global Islamic Discourses: The Role of al-Azhar, al-Medina and al-Mustafa* (Edinburgh University Press 2015).

'Fatwa' in the Oxford Dictionary of Islam, John L. Esposito (eds), Oxford Islamic Studies Online <http://www.oxfordislamicstudies.com/article/opr/t125/e646> 16 March 2018.

Fatwā No. [Absent] in *Fatwas of the Permanent Committee*, 17: 53–54 <https://www.alifta.gov.sa/En/IftaContents/PermanentCommitee/Pages/FatawaSubjects.aspx?cultStr=en&View=Page&HajjEntryID=0&HajjEntryName=&RamadanEntryID=0&RamadanEntryName=&NodeID=682&PageID=6330&SectionID=7&SubjectPageTitlesID=6382&MarkIndex=16&0#Isitpermissibleforwomento> accessed 27 November 2020.

Fatwā No. 2061 in *Fatwas of the Permanent Committee*, 5: 42–43 <http://www.alifta.net/Fatawa/FatawaChapters.aspx?languagename=en&View=Page&PageID=1377&PageNo=1&BookID=7> accessed 27 November 27, 2017.

Fatwā No. 2573 in *Fatwas of the Permanent Committee*, 5: 36–38 <http://www.alifta.net/Fatawa/FatawaChapters.aspx?languagename=en&View=Page&PageID=1368&PageNo=1&BookID=7> accessed 27 November 2017.

Fatwā No. 2635 in *Fatwas of the Permanent Committee*, 12: 51–54 <http://www.alifta.net/Fatawa/FatawaChapters.aspx?languagename=en&View=Page&PageID=4306&PageNo=1&BookID=7> accessed 07 May 2018.

Fatwā No. 2768 in *Fatwas of the Permanent Committee*, 17: 233–237 <http://www.alifta.net/Search/ResultDetails.aspx?languagename=en&lang=en&view=result&fatwaNum=&FatwaNumID=&ID=6509&searchScope=7&SearchScopeLevels1=&SearchScopeLevels2=&highLight=1&SearchType=exact&SearchMoesar=false&bookID=&LeftVal=0&RightVal=0&simple=&SearchCriteria=allwords&PagePath=&siteSection=1&searchkeyword=105110116101114109105110103108105110103032109101110032097110100032119111109101110#firstKeyWordFound> accessed 29 November 2017.

Fatwā No. 2815 in *Fatwas of the Permanent Committee*, 5: 34–35 <http://www.alifta.net/Fatawa/FatawaChapters.aspx?languagename=en&View=Page&PageID=1368&PageNo=1&BookID=7> accessed 27 November 2017.

Fatwā No. 2847 in *Fatwas of the Permanent Committee*, 17: 281–284 <http://www.alifta.net/Search/ResultDetails.aspx?languagename=en&lang=en&view=result&fatwaNum=&FatwaNumID=&ID=6540&searchScope=7&SearchScopeLevels1=&SearchScopeLevels2=&highLight=1&SearchType=exact&SearchMoesar=false&bookID=&LeftVal=0&RightVal=0&simple=&SearchCriteria=allwords&PagePath=&siteSection=1&searchkeyword=087111109101110032104105106097098#firstKeyWordFound> accessed 02 December 2017.

Fatwā No. 2872 in *Fatwas of the Permanent Committee*, 5: 44–45 <http://www.alifta.net/Fatawa/FatawaChapters.aspx?languagename=en&View=Page&PageID=1368&PageNo=1&BookID=7> accessed 27 November 2017.

Fatwā No. 2961 in *Fatwas of the Permanent Committee*, 5: 42–43 <http://www.alifta.net/Fatawa/FatawaChapters.aspx?languagename=en&View=Page&PageID=1368&PageNo=1&BookID=7> accessed 27 November 2017.

Fatwā No. 3323in *Fatwas of the Permanent Committee*, 5: 41 <http://www.alifta.net/Fatawa/FatawaChapters.aspx?languagename=en&View=Page&PageID=1368&PageNo=1&BookID=7> accessed 27 November 2017.

Fatwā No. 4172 in *Fatwas of the Permanent Committee*, 5: 28–29 <http://www.alifta.net/Fatawa/FatawaChapters.aspx?languagename=en&View=Page&PageID=1368&PageNo=1&BookID=7> accessed 27 November 2017.

Fatwā No. 4214 in *Fatwas of the Permanent Committee*,12: 253–254 <https://www.alifta.gov.sa/En/IftaContents/PermanentCommitee/Pages/FatawaSubjects.aspx?cultStr=en&View=Page&HajjEntryID=0&HajjEntryName=&RamadanEntryID=0&RamadanEntryName=&NodeID=4649&PageID=4462&SectionID=7&SubjectPageTitlesID=4513&MarkIndex=17&0#Havingrelationshipswiththem> accessed 20 December 2020.

Fatwā No. 4522 in *Fatwas of the Permanent Committee*, 5: 43–44 <http://www.alifta.net/Fatawa/FatawaChapters.aspx?languagename=en&View=Page&PageID=1368&PageNo=1&BookID=7> accessed 27 November 2017.

Fatwā No. 4671 in *Fatwas of the Permanent Committee*, 17: 17 <http://www.alifta.net/Search/ResultDetails.aspx?languagename=en&lang=en&view=result&fatwaNum=&FatwaNumID=&ID=6301&searchScope=7&SearchScopeLevels1=&SearchScopeLevels2=&highLight=1&SearchType=exact&SearchMoesar=false&bookID=&LeftVal=0&RightVal=0&simple=&SearchCriteria=allwords&PagePath=&siteSection=1&searchkeyword=105110116101114109105110103108105110103032109101110032097110100032119111109101110#firstKeyWordFound> accessed 29 November 2017.

Fatwā No. 4945 in *Fatwas of the Permanent Committee*, 17: 54–55 <http://www.alifta.net/Search/ResultDetails.aspx?languagename=en&lang=en&view=result&fatwaNum=&FatwaNumID=&ID=6509&searchScope=7&SearchScopeLevels1=&SearchScopeLevels2=&highLight=1&SearchType=exact&SearchMoesar=false&bookID=&LeftVal=0&RightVal=0&simple=&SearchCriteria=allwords&PagePath=&siteSection=1&searchkeyword=119111109101110039115032109105120105110103032119105116104032109101110#firstKeyWordFound> accessed 29 November 2017.

Fatwā No. 5082 in *Fatwas of the Permanent Committee*, 17: 81–85 <http://www.alifta.net/Search/ResultDetails.aspx?languagename=en&lang=en&view=result&fatwaNum=&FatwaNumID=&ID=6368&searchScope=7&SearchScopeLevels1=&SearchScopeLevels2=&highLight=1&SearchType=exact&SearchMoesar=false&bookID=&LeftVal=0&RightVal=0&simple=&SearchCriteria=allwords&PagePath=&siteSection=1&searchkeyword=105110116101114109105110103108105110103032109101110032097110100032119111109101110#firstKeyWordFound> accessed 29 November 2017.

Fatwā No. 5089 in *Fatwas of the Permanent Committee*, 17: 108–109 <http://www.alifta.net/Fatawa/FatawaChapters.aspx?languagename=en&View=Page&PageID=6392&PageNo=1&BookID=7> accessed 02 December 2017.

Fatwā No. 5166 in *Fatwas of the Permanent Committee*, 5: 38–41 <http://www.alifta.net/Fatawa/FatawaChapters.aspx?languagename=en&View=Page&PageID=1368&PageNo=1&BookID=7> accessed 27 November 2017.

Fatwā No. 5363, in *Fatwas of the Permanent Committee*, 17: 109 <http://www.alifta.net/Fatawa/FatawaChapters.aspx?languagename=en&View=Page&PageID=6394&PageNo=1&BookID=7> accessed 02 December 2017.

Fatwā No. 5512 in *Fatwas of the Permanent Committee*, 17: 54–55 <http://www.alifta.net/Search/ResultDetails.aspx?languagename=en&lang=en&view=result&fatwaNum=&FatwaNumID=&ID=6509&searchScope=7&SearchScopeLevels1=&SearchScopeLevels2=&highLight=1&SearchType=exact&SearchMoesar=false

&bookID=&LeftVal=0&RightVal=0&simple=&SearchCriteria=allwords&PagePath=&siteSection=1&searchkeyword=11911110910111003911503210910512010511010303211910511610403210910111O#firstKeyWordFound> accessed 29 November 2017.

Fatwā No. 6341 in *Fatwas of the Permanent Committee*, 26: 162–163 <http://www.alifta.net/Fatawa/FatawaChapters.aspx?languagename=en&View=Page&PageNo=1&FromMoeasrID=26068&PageID=10212&BookID=7> accessed 08 April 2018.

Fatwā No. 6495 in *Fatwas of the Permanent Committee* <https://www.alifta.gov.sa/En/IftaContents/PermanentCommitee/Pages/FatawaSubjects.aspx?cultStr=en&View=Page&HajjEntryID=0&HajjEntryName=&RamadanEntryID=0&RamadanEntryName=&NodeID=4656&PageID=521&SectionID=7&SubjectPageTitlesID=522&MarkIndex=0&0#GrantingthenationalityofaMuslim>, accessed 19 December 2020.

Fatwā No. 7484 in *Fatwas of the Permanent Committee*, 17: 232–233 <http://www.alifta.net/Search/ResultDetails.aspx?languagename=en&lang=en&view=result&fatwaNum=&FatwaNumID=&ID=6509&searchScope=7&SearchScopeLevels1=&SearchScopeLevels2=&highLight=1&SearchType=exact&SearchMoesar=false&bookID=&LeftVal=0&RightVal=0&simple=&SearchCriteria=allwords&PagePath=&siteSection=1&searchkeyword=105110116101114109105110103108105110103032109101110032097110100032119111109101110#firstKeyWordFound> accessed 29 November 2017.

Fatwā No. 7523 in *Fatwas of the Permanent Committee*, 17: 109–110 <http://www.alifta.net/Fatawa/FatawaChapters.aspx?languagename=en&View=Page&PageID=6392&PageNo=1&BookID=7> accessed 02 December 2017.

Fatwā No. 9783 in *Fatwas of the Permanent Committee*, 5: 35–36 <http://www.alifta.net/Fatawa/FatawaChapters.aspx?languagename=en&View=Page&PageID=1368&PageNo=1&BookID=7> accessed 27 November 2017.

Fatwā No. 11296 in *Fatwas of the Permanent Committee*, 5: 29–32 <http://www.alifta.net/Fatawa/FatawaChapters.aspx?languagename=en&View=Page&PageID=1368&PageNo=1&BookID=7> accessed 27 November 2017.

Fatwā No. 11780 in *Fatwas of the Permanent Committee*, 17: 13–16 <http://www.alifta.net/Fatawa/fatawacoeval.aspx?languagename=en&View=Page&HajjEntryID=0&HajjEntryName=&RamadanEntryID=0&RamadanEntryName=&NodeID=4660&PageID=6300&SectionID=7&SubjectPageTitlesID=6352&MarkIndex=19&0#Inwhichwomenareprohibitedto> accessed 25 August 2015.

Fatwā No. 13477 in *Fatwas of the Permanent Committee*, <https://www.alifta.gov.sa/En/IftaContents/PermanentCommitee/Pages/FatawaSubjects.aspx?cultStr=en&View=Page&HajjEntryID=0&HajjEntryName=&RamadanEntryID=0&RamadanEntryName=&NodeID=4158&PageID=10109&SectionID=7&SubjectPageTitlesID=10379&MarkIndex=7&0#Istherulingonabenevolentdisbeliever> accessed 18 December 2020.

Fatwā No. 15631 in *Fatwas of the Permanent Committee*, 23: 401 <http://www.alifta.net/Search/ResultDetails.aspx?languagename=en&lang=en&view=result&fatwaNum=&FatwaNumID=&ID=3&searchScope=15&SearchScopeLevels1=&SearchScopeLevels2=&highLight=1&SearchType=exact&SearchMoesar=false&bookID=&LeftVal=0&RightVal=0&simple=&SearchCriteria=allwords&PagePath=&siteSection=1&searchkeyword=111098101100105101110099101032116111032114117108101114#firstKeyWordFound> accessed 06 September 2016.

Fatwā No. 15885 in *Fatwas of the Permanent Committee*, 11: 317–319 <http://www.alifta.net/Fatawa/FatawaChapters.aspx?languagename=en&View=Page&PageID=14645&PageNo=1&BookID=7> accessed 02 December 2017.

Fatwā No. 16426 in *Fatwas of the Permanent Committee*, 1: 440 <http://www.alifta.net/Fatawa/FatawaChapters.aspx?languagename=en&View=Page&PageID=10779&PageNo=1&BookID=7> accessed 03 April 2018.

Fatwā No. 17831 in *Fatwas of the Permanent Committee*, 2: 168–172 http://www.alifta.net/Fatawa/FatawaSubjects.aspx?languagename=en&View=Page&HajjEntryID=0&HajjEntryName=&RamadanEntryID=0&RamadanEntryName=&NodeID=4100&PageID=10898&SectionID=7&SubjectPageTitlesID=11293&MarkIndex=8&0#ImitatingtheFourMadh-habs(Hanafi> accessed 20 April 2018.

Fatwā No. 18396 in *Fatwas of the Permanent Committee*, 2: 142–145 <http://www.alifta.net/Search/ResultDetails.aspx?languagename=en&lang=en&view=result&fatwaNum=&FatwaNumID=&ID=10884&searchScope=7&SearchScopeLevels1=&SearchScopeLevels2=&highLight=1&SearchType=exact&SearchMoesar=false&bookID=&LeftVal=0&RightVal=0&simple=&SearchCriteria=allwords&PagePath=&siteSection=1&searchkeyword=115101099117108097114105115109#firstKeyWordFound> accessed 04 April 2018.

Fatwā No. 19351 in *Fatwas of the Permanent Committee*, 22: 238–248 <http://www.alifta.net/Search/ResultDetails.aspx?languagename=en&lang=en&view=result&fatwaNum=&FatwaNumID=&ID=8496&searchScope=7&SearchScopeLevels1=&SearchScopeLevels2=&highLight=1&SearchType=exact&SearchMoesar=false&bookID=&LeftVal=0&RightVal=0&simple=&SearchCriteria=allwords&PagePath=&siteSection=1&searchkeyword=100101109111099114097099121#firstKeyWordFound> accessed 04 April 2018.

Fatwā No. 19359 in *Fatwas of the Permanent Committee*, 17: 54–55 <http://www.alifta.net/Search/ResultDetails.aspx?languagename=en&lang=en&view=result&fatwaNum=&FatwaNumID=&ID=6509&searchScope=7&SearchScopeLevels1=&SearchScopeLevels2=&highLight=1&SearchType=exact&SearchMoesar=false&bookID=&LeftVal=0&RightVal=0&simple=&SearchCriteria=allwords&PagePath=&siteSection=1&searchkeyword=119111109101110039115032109105120105110103032119105116104032109101110#firstKeyWordFound> accessed 29 November 2017.

Fatwā No. 19670 in *Fatwas of the Permanent Committee*, 12: 56–58 <http://www.alifta.net/Fatawa/FatawaChapters.aspx?languagename=en&View=Page&PageID=4309&PageNo=1&BookID=7> accessed 07 May 2018.

Fatwā No. 19685 in *Fatwas of the Permanent Committee*, 12: 59 <http://www.alifta.net/Fatawa/FatawaChapters.aspx?languagename=en&View=Page&PageID=4310&PageNo=1&BookID=7> accessed 07 May 2018.

Fatwā No. 20397 in *Fatwas of the Permanent Committee*, 24: 398–399 <http://www.alifta.net/Search/ResultDetails.aspx?languagename=en&lang=en&view=result&fatwaNum=&FatwaNumID=&ID=9660&searchScope=7&SearchScopeLevels1=&SearchScopeLevels2=&highLight=1&SearchType=exact&SearchMoesar=false&bookID=&LeftVal=0&RightVal=0&simple=&SearchCriteria=allwords&PagePath=&siteSection=1&searchkeyword=105110116101114109105110103108105110103032109101110032097110100032119111109101110#firstKeyWordFound> accessed 29 November 2017.

Fatwā No. 20836 in *Fatwas of the Permanent Committee*, 17: 226–227 <https://www.alifta.gov.sa/En/IftaContents/PermanentCommitee/Pages/FatawaSubjects.aspx?cultStr=en&View=Page&HajjEntryID=0&HajjEntryName=&RamadanEntryID

=0&RamadanEntryName=&NodeID=682&PageID=6492&SectionID=7&SubjectPageTitlesID=6544&MarkIndex=17&0#Isitpermissibleforwomento> accessed 27 November 2020.

Fatwā No. 20968 in *Fatwas of the Permanent Committee*, 26: 93–96 <http://www.alifta.net/Search/ResultDetails.aspx?languagename=en&lang=en&view=result&fatwaNum=&FatwaNumID=&ID=10135&searchScope=7&SearchScopeLevels1=&SearchScopeLevels2=&highLight=1&SearchType=exact&SearchMoesar=false&bookID=&LeftVal=0&RightVal=0&simple=&SearchCriteria=allwords&PagePath=&siteSection=1&searchkeyword=115116117100121105110103032097098114111097100#firstKeyWordFound> accessed 29 November 2017.

Fatwā No. 21413 in *Fatwas of the Permanent Committee*, 1: 468–471 <http://www.alifta.net/Search/ResultDetails.aspx?languagename=en&lang=en&view=result&fatwaNum=&FatwaNumID=&ID=10807&searchScope=7&SearchScopeLevels1=&SearchScopeLevels2=&highLight=1&SearchType=exact&SearchMoesar=false&bookID=&LeftVal=0&RightVal=0&simple=&SearchCriteria=allwords&PagePath=&siteSection=1&searchkeyword=067104117114099104101115032105110032065114097098105097110032080101110105110115117108097#firstKeyWordFound> accessed 12 November 2017.

Fatwa, 'The Inclusion of Women in Masjid' <http://fiqhcouncil.org/the-inclusion-of-women-in-masjids/> accessed 26 November 2020.

Fiqh Council of North America, 'About FCNA' <http://fiqhcouncil.org/about-fcna/> accessed 13 September 2020.

———, 'FCNA Brochure' <http://www.fiqhcouncil.org/sites/default/files/FCNABrochure.pdf> accessed 23 April 2017.

———,'History of the Fiqh Council' <http://fiqhcouncil.org/wp-content/uploads/2018/09/FCNABrochure.pdf> accessed 21 February 2021.

———, 'Meet Our Council's Executive Members' <http://www.fiqhcouncil.org/node/13> accessed 13 September 2020.

———, 'Moon Sighting Calculations-1' <http://www.fiqhcouncil.org/node/31> accessed 01 May 2017.

———, 'Ramadan & Shawwal 1438 (2017)' <http://www.fiqhcouncil.org/node/83> accessed 01 May 2017.

Fishman Shammai, 'Fiqh al-Aqalliyyat: A Legal Theory for Muslim Minorities' (2006) 1 (2) *Center on Islam, Democracy, and the Future of the Muslim World* 1.

Gause III F. Gregory, 'Official Wahhabism and the Sanctioning of the Saudi-US Relations' in Mohammed Ayoop and Hasan Kosebalaban (eds), *Religion and Politics in Saudi Arabia: Wahhabism and the State* (Lynne Rienner Publishers 2009).

Glaberson William, 'Interpreting Islamic Law For American Muslims' (*The New York Times*, 21 October 2001) <http://www.nytimes.com/2001/10/21/us/interpreting-islamic-law-for-american-muslims.html> accessed 04 June 2017.

Graduate Theological Foundation, 'Mohammad Qatanani' <http://www.gtfeducation.org/faculty-staff/mohammad-qatanani.cfm> accessed 31 May 2017.

Görmez Mehmet, 'The Status of the Presidency of Religious Affairs in Turkish Constitution and Its Execution' (2008) 98 (2–3) *The Muslim World* 244.

Gözaydın İştar, *Religion, Politics and the Politics of Religion in Turkey* (Friedrich-Naumann-Stiftung für die Freiheit 2013).

———, 'Management of Religion in Turkey: The *Diyanet* and Beyond' in Özgür Heval Çınar and Mine Yıldırım (eds), *Freedom of Religion and Belief in Turkey* (Cambridge Scholars Publishing 2014).

Gürpınar Doğan and Ceren Kenar, 'The Nation and its Sermons: Islam, Kemalism and the Presidency of Religious Affairs in Turkey' (2016) 52 (1) *Middle Eastern Studies* 60.

Habib John S., 'Wahhabi Origins of Contemporary Saudi State' in Mohammed Ayoop and Hasan Kosebalaban (eds) *Religion and Politics in Saudi Arabia: Wahhabism and the State* (Lynne Rienner Publishers 2009).

Haddad Yvonne Yazbeck, 'The Dynamics of Islamic Identity in North America' in Yvonne Yazbeck Haddad and John L. Esposito (eds), *Muslims on the Americanization Path?* (Oxford University Press 2000).

Haddad Yvonne Y. and Jane I. Smith, *The Oxford Handbook of American Islam* (Oxford University Press 2014).

Hallaq Wael B., 'From Fatwās to Furū': Growth and Change in Islamic Substantive Law' (1994) 1 (1) *Islamic Law and Society* 25.

———, 'Ifta' and Ijtihād in Sunni Legal Theory: A Development Account' in Muhammad Khalid Masud, Brinkley Messick and David S. Powers (eds), *Islamic Legal Interpretation Muftis and Their Fatwas* (Harvard University Press 1996).

———, *Sharī'a: Theory, Practice, Transformation* (Cambridge University Press 2009).

Hasan Aznan, 'An Introduction to Collective Ijtihad (Ijtihad Jama'i): Concept and Applications' (2003) 20 (2) *The American Journal of Islamic Sciences* 26.

Haseki Dini Yüksek İhtisas Merkeziniin Tarihçesi, 'Merkezimiz' <http://www.hasekidiyanet.gov.tr/?pnum=122&pt=M%C3%BCd%C3%BCr%C3%BCm%C3%BCz%C3%BCn%20Kaleminden%20Merkezimizin%20Tarih%C3%A7esi> accessed 09 November 2016.

Hassan Said, 'Law-Abiding Citizen: Recent Fatwas on Muslim Minorities'g Loyalty to Western Nations' (2015) 105 (4) *The Muslim World* 516.

Hassan Salih Fares, *Fiqh al-Aqalliyāt: History, Development and Progress* (Palgrave Macmillan 2013).

Henderson Simoon, *After King Abdullah Succession in Saudi Arabia* (The Washington Institute for Near East Policy 2009).

Hinnebusch Raymond and Omar Imady, *The Syrian Uprising: Domestic Origins and Early Trajectory* (Rutledge 2018).

Member Scholars of the Permanent Committee for Ifta', 'His Eminence Shaykh 'Abdul-'Aziz ibn 'Abdullah ibn Muhammad Al Al-Shaykh' <http://www.alifta.com/Fatawa/MoftyDetails.aspx?languagename=en&Type=Mofty&section=tafseer&ID=8> accessed 11 November 2017.

———, 'His Eminence Shayhkh 'Abdullah ibn Mani'' <http://www.alifta.com/Fatawa/MoftyDetails.aspx?languagename=en&Type=Mofty&section=tafseer&ID=6> accessed 05 November 2016.

———,'His Eminence Shaykh Salih ibn Fawzan Al-Fawzan' <http://www.alifta.net/Fatawa/MoftyDetails.aspx?languagename=en&ID=7> accessed 03 June 2016.

———, 'Ibn Baz: Concise Biography' <http://www.alifta.net/Search/ResultDetails.aspx?languagename=en&lang=en&view=result&fatwaNum=&FatwaNumID=&ID=3&searchScope=14&SearchScopeLevels1=&SearchScopeLevels2=&highLight=1&SearchType=exact&SearchMoesar=false&bookID=&LeftVal=0&RightVal=0&simple=&SearchCriteria=allwords&PagePath=&siteSection=1&searchkeyword=1050981100320980971 22#firstKeyWordFound> accessed 11 November 2017.

Hukm al-Awrāq al-Naqdiyya, in *Majallat al-Buḥūth al-Islāmiyya*, 1: 51–54 <http://www.alifta.net/Fatawa/FatawaChapters.aspx?languagename=ar&View=Page&PageID=18&PageNo=1&BookID=1> accessed 02 November 2017.

Hukm al-Tashrīḥ Jathat al-Muslim, in *Majallat al-Buḥūth al-Islāmiyya*, 2: 8–10 <http://www.alifta.net/Fatawa/FatawaChapters.aspx?languagename=ar&View=Page&PageID=126&PageNo=1&BookID=1> accessed 02 November 2017.

Ibn Qudāma'Abdullah ibn Aḥmad ibn Muḥammad, *al-Kāfī fī Fiqh Ahmad Ibn Ḥanbal*, vol I (Dār al-Kutub al-'Ilmiyya 1994).

Ibn Rushd Abū al-Walīd Muḥammad Ibn Aḥmad, *al-Bayān wa al-Taḥṣīl wa al-Sharḥ wa al-Tawjīh al-Ta'līl fī Masāil al-Mustakhraj* vol XVII (Dār al-Gharb al-Islāmī 1988).

Ibn Taymiyya Ahmad Ibn 'Abd al-Ḥalīm, *Majmū' al-Fatāwā*, vol XII, XIII (Majmu' al-Malik Fahd 2004).

———, *Fatwas of Muslim Women* (Sayed Gad (tr) Dar al-Manrah 2000).

Ibrahim B, M. Arifin and S. Z. Abd Rashid, 'The Role of *Fatwa* and *Mufti* in Contemporary Muslim Society' (2015) 23 *Pertanika Social Sciences & Humanities* 322.

Ibrahim Ahmed Fekry, 'Talfīq/Takhayyur', The Oxford Encyclopedia of Islamic Law (2013) <http://www.oxfordislamicstudies.com/article/opr/t349/e0082> accessed 11 June 2017.

Imam al-Qazwini Sayid Hassan, 'Biography' <http://alqazwini.org/qazwini_org/biography.htm> accessed 01 July 2017.

Imber Colin, *Ebu's-su'ud: Islamic Legal Tradition* (Edinburgh University Press 1997).

International Revenue Service (IRS), 'Tax-Exempt Status for Your Organization' (Publication 557 (Rev. January 2020) Cat. No. 46573C).

Islam Online Archive, 'Astronomical Calculations for Islamic Dates Position of the Fiqh Council of North America' <https://archive.islamonline.net/?p=15065> accessed 25 August 2017.

———, 'Fiqh Council of North America: Regarding the Adoption' <https://archive.islamonline.net/?p=15065> accessed 25 August 2017.

Islamic Society of North America, 'Islamic Horizons Magazine' <http://www.isna.net/islamic-horizons-magazine/> accessed 06 June 2017.

———, 'Vision and Mission' <http://www.isna.net/mission-and-vision/> accessed 06 June 2017.

Islamic Society of Orange Country, 'Islamic Director's Biography Dr. Muzammil Siddiqi' <https://web.archive.org/web/20070218010407/ http://www.isocmasjid.com/Administration/dbio.htm> accessed 01 July 2017.

Ismail Raihan, *Saudi Clerics and Shī'a Islam* (Oxford University Press 2016).

İstatistikler, 'İstatiksel Tablolar (31.12.2015 tarihi itibariyle): Personel' <http://www.diyanet.gov.tr/tr/kategori/istatistikler/136> accessed 10 October 2016.

Jaques R. Kevin, 'Islamic Organisations in America' in Gary Laderman and Luis León (eds), *Religion and American Cultures: An Encyclopaedia of Traditions, Diversity* Gary Laderman and Luis León, vol I (ABC-CLIO 2003).

Jones Tobi Craig, 'Religious Revivalism and Its Challenge to the Saudi Regime' in Mohammed Ayoop and Hasan Kosebalaban (eds), *Religion and politics in Saudi Arabia: Wahhabism and the State* (Lynne Rienner Publishers 2009).

Kamali Mohammad Hashim, *Principles of Islamic Jurisprudence* (St Edmundsbury Press 1991).

Kaptein Nico J. G., 'The Voice of the '*Ulamā*': *Fatwas* and Religious Authority' (2004) 49 (125) *Archives de Sciences Sociales des Religions* 115.

Kara İsmail, 'Din ile Devlet Arasına Sıkışmış Bir Kurum: Diyanet İşleri Başkanlığı' (2000) 18 *Marmara Üniversitesi İlahiyat Fakültesi Dergisi* 29.

Karaman Hayrettin, *İslam'in Işıginda Günün Meseleleri* (İz Yayınçılık 2012).

Karaman Hayrettin, Ali Bardakoğlu and H. Yunus Apaydın, *İlmihal-I İman ve İbadetler* (DİB 1998)

———, İlmihal-II: *İslam ve Toplum* (DİB 1998).
Karaman Fikret, 'The Status and Function of the PRA in the Turkish Republic' (2008) 98 (2–3) *The Muslim World* 282.
Kaya Emir, 'Balancing Interlegality Through Realist Altruism: Diyanet Mediation in Turkey' (PhD thesis, University of London 2011).
Kazemipu Abdolmohammad, 'Reckoning with the Minority Status: On Fiqh al-aqalliyyat al-Muslema (Jurispurdence of Muslim Minorities)' in Mario Peucker and Rauf Ceylan (eds), *Muslim Communiity Organizations in the West: History, Developments and Future Perspectives* (Springer 2017).
Kechichian Joseph A., 'The Role of Ulama in the Politics of an Islamic State: The Case of Saudi Arabia' (1996) 18 (1) *International Journal of Middle East Studies* 53.
Kenar Ceren and Doğan Gürpınar, 'Cold War in the Pulpit: The Presidency of Religious Affairs and Sermons during the Time of Anarchy and Communist Threat' in Cangül Örnek and Çağdaş Üngör (eds), *Turkey in Cold War Ideology and Culture* (Palgrave Macmillan 2013).
Koca Bayram, 'Diyanet İşleri Başkanlığı ve Aleviler Arasındaki Meseleye Liberal Bir Bakış' (2014) 19 (73–74) *Liberal Düşünce Yıl* 39.
Koçak Mustafa, 'Islam and National Law in Turkey' in Jan Michiel Otto (ed), *Sharia and National Law: Comparing the Legal Systems of Twleve Islamic Countries* (The American University in Cairo Press 2010).
Kuruluş ve Tarihi Gelişim, 'Türkiye Cumhuriyeti Başkanlık Diyanet İiyeti Başka.com?' <http://www.diyanet.gov.tr/tr/icerik/kurulus-ve-tarihce/8> accessed 26 September 2016.
Kutlu Sönmez, 'Diyanet İşleri Başkanlığı ve İslamiçi Dini Gruplarla (Mezhep ve Tatikatlar) İlişkileri' (2009) 12 (33) *Dini Araştırmalar* 107.
———., 'The Presidency of Religious Affairs' Relationship with Religious Groups (Sects/ Sufi Orders) in Turkey' (2008) 98 (2–3) *The Muslim World* 249.
Kutty Faisal, ''Sharia' Courts in Canada: A Delayed Opportunity for the Indigenization of Islamic Legal Rulings' in Anna C. Korteweg and Jennifer A. Selby (eds), *Debating Sharia: Islam, Gender Politics, and Family Law Arbitration* (University Toronto Press 2012).
Küçükcan Talip, 'Are Muslim Democrats a Threat to Secularism and Freedom of Religion? The Turkish Case' in Allen D. Hertzke (ed), *The Future of Religious Freedom: Global Challenges* (Oxford University Press 2013).
Laderman Gary and Luis León, *Religion and American Cultures: An Encyclopedia of Traditions, Diversity, and Popular Expressions* vol I (ABC-CLIO 2003).
Lambton Ann K. S., *State and Government in Medieval Islam: An Introduction to the Study of Islamic Political Theory: The Jurists* (Oxford University Press 1981).
Lawrence Bruce B., 'Islam in America' in Gary Laderman and Luis León (eds) *Religion and American Cultures: An Encyclopedia of Traditions, Diversity*, vol I (ABC-CLIO 2003).
Leonard Karen Isaksen, *Muslims in the United States* (Russell Sage Foundation 2003).
———, 'American Muslims and Authority: Competing Discourses in a Non-Muslim State' (2005) 25 (1) *Journal of American Ethnic History* 5.
Lippman Thomas W., 'A Most Improbable Alliance: Placing Interest over Ideology' in Mohammed Ayoop and Hasan Kosabalan (eds), *Religion and Politics in Saudi Arabia: Wahhabism and Saudi Arabia* (Lynne Rienner 2009).
Masud Muhammad Khalid, 'The Doctrine of *Siyāsa* in Islamic Law' (2001) 18 *Recht van de Islam* 1.

———, 'The Significance of *Istiftā'* in the *Fatwā* Discourse' (2009) 48 (3) *Islamic Studies* 358.

Masud Muhammad Khalid, Brinkley Messick and David S. Powers, *Islamic Legal Interpretation: Muftis and Their Fatwas* (Harvard University Press 1996).

March Andrew F., 'Are Secularism and Neutrality Attractive to Religious Minorities? Islamic Discussions of Western Secularism in the "Jurisprudence of Muslim Minorities" (*Fiqh al-Aqalliyyat*) Discourse' (2009) 30 (16) *Cardozo Law Review* 2821.

McConnell Michael W., 'The Origins and Historical Understanding of Free Exercise of Religion' (1990) 103 (7) *Harvard Law Review* 1416.

Ménoret Pascal, 'Fighting for the Holy Mosque: The Mecca Insurgency' in C. Christine Fair and Sumit Ganguly (eds), *Treading on Hallowed Ground: Counterinsurgency in Sacred Spaces* (Oxford University Press 2008).

Mert Hamdi, 'Gündem: Alevilik ve Başörtüsü' (1992) 12 *Diyanet Aylık Dergisi* 6.

'Ministerial Statement of 6 November 1962 by Prime Minister Amir Faysal of Saudi Arabia' (1963) 17 (1/2) *Middle East Journal* 161 <http://0-www.jstor.org.lib.exeter.ac.uk/stable/pdf/4323561.pdf?_=1468274273021> accessed 03 June 2016.

Mohammed Amjad M., *Muslims in Non-Muslims Lands: A Legal Study with Applications* (The Islamic Text Society 2013).

Mouline Nabil, *The Clerics of Islam: Religious Authority and Political Power in Saudi Arabia* (Ethan S. Rundell (tr) Yale University Press 2014).

———, 'Enforcing and Reinforcing the State's Islam: The Functioning of the Committee of Senior Scholars' in Bernard Haykel, Thomas Hegghammer and Stéphane Lacroix (eds), *Saudi Arabia in Transition: Insights of Social, Political, Economic and Religious Change* (Cambridge University Press 2015).

Mubarak Haida, 'A Man of His Times: A Pioneer of Islamic Reform' (2016) 45 (3) *Islamic Horizons* 9.

Muhamad Nazlida, '*Fatwa* Rulings in Islam: A Malaysian Perspective on Their Role in Muslim Consumer Behaviour' in Özlem Sandıkcı and Gillian Rice (eds), *Handbook of Islamic Marketing* (Edward Elgar Publishing 2011).

Muslims Dealing with Non-Muslims, in *Fatwas of Ibn Baz*, 6: 283–285 <http://www.alifta.net/Search/ResultDetails.aspx?languagename=en&lang=en&view=result&fatwaNum=&FatwaNumID=&ID=735&searchScope=14&SearchScopeLevels1=&SearchScopeLevels2=&highLight=1&SearchType=exact&SearchMoesar=false&bookID=&LeftVal=0&RightVal=0&simple=&SearchCriteria=allwords&PagePath=&siteSection=1&searchkeyword=116104101032112101111112108101032111102032116104101032098111111107#firstKeyWordFound> accessed 03 April 2018.

Mustapha Nadira, 'Islamic Legal Tehory and Practiice in the North American Context: An Epistemological and Methodological Analysis of the Fiqh Council of North America' (PhD thesis, McGill University 2013).

Nafi Basheer M., 'Fatwā and War: On the Allegiance of the American Muslim Soldiers in the Aftermath of September 11' (2004) 11 (1) *Islamic Law and Society* 78.

Nimer Mohamed, *The North American Muslim Resource Guide: Muslim Community Life in the United States and Canada* (Routledge 2002).

Obeying rulers and scholars in Ma'rūf to set things right, in *Fatwas of Ibn Baz*, 7:115–119 <http://www.alifta.net/Fatawa/FatawaChapters.aspx?languagename=en&View=Page&PageID=871&PageNo=1&BookID=14> accessed 21 August 2016.

Okruhlik Gwenn, 'State Power, Religious Privilege, and Myths about Political Reform' in Mohammed Ayoop and Hasan Kosabalan (eds), *Religion and Politics in Saudi Arabia: Wahhabism and Saudi Arabia* (Lynne Rienner 2009).

Okumuş Ejder, 'Turkey-Religiosity and the PRA' (2008) 98 (2–3) *The Muslim World* 354.

Organizing Fatwas, in *Fatwas of the Permanent Committee*, 5: 1 <http://www.alifta.net/Fatawa/FatawaSubjects.aspx?languagename=en&View=Page&HajjEntryID=0&HajjEntryName=&RamadanEntryID=0&RamadanEntryName=&NodeID=4106&PageID=1345&SectionID=7&SubjectPageTitlesID=1364&MarkIndex=0&0#OrganizingFatwas> accessed 26 November 26, 2017.

Öcal Sami, 'From "the Fetwa" to "Religious Questions": Main Characteristic of Fetwas of the Diyanet' (2008) 98 (3) *The Muslim World* 324.

Öktem Kerem, 'Global Diyanet and Multiple Networks: Turkey's New Presence in the Balkans' (2012) 1 *Journal of Muslims in Europe* 27.

Parray Tauseef Ahmad, 'The Legal Methodology of "Fiqh al-Aqalliyyat" and its Critics: An Analytical Study' (2012) 32 (1) *Journal of Muslim Minority Affairs* 88.

Peters Rudolph, *Crime and Punishment in Islamic Law: Theory and Practice from the Sixteenth to the Twenty-first Century* (Cambridge University Press 2005).

Powell Russel, 'Evolving Views of Islamic Law in Turkey' (2013) 28 (2) *Journal of Law and Religion* 467.

Powers David S., *Law, Society, and Culture in the Maghrib, 1300–1500* (Cambridge University Press 2002).

Public Health Service, Centers for Disease Control and National Center for Health Statistics, *Handbook on Divorce Registration* (U.S. Department of Health and Human Services 1988).

Public Health Service, Centers for Disease Control and National Center for Health Statistics, *Handbook on Marriage Registration* (U.S. Department of Health and Human Services 1988).

Questions and Answers on 'Aqīdah, in *Fatwas of Ibn Baz*, 5: 298–299 <http://www.alifta.net/Fatawa/FatawaDetails.aspx?languagename=en&View=Page&PageID=531&PageNo=1&BookID=14 \l "P298" > accessed 02 December 2017.

RAQABA: Shari'a Audit and Islamic Financial Advisory, 'Our Senior Professionals' <https://raqaba.co/en/> accessed 13 September 2020.

Abdul Rahman Noor Naemah, Asmak Ab Rahman and Abdul Karim Ali, 'A Study on Students' Research related to Fatwa Summited at Malaysian Public Universities' (2012) 2 (18) *International Journal of Humanities and Social Science* 129.

Republic of Turkey's Presidency of Religious Affairs, 'High Board of Religious Affairs' <http://diyanet.gov.tr/en/icerik/high-board-of-religious-affairs/12598.lmaz> accessed 05 November 2016.

Resmi Gazete (*Official Gazette*) <http://www.resmigazete.gov.tr/default.aspx> accessed 26 September 2016.

Resolution, 'Statement of Fiqh Council of North America on Fossil Fuel Divestment' <http://www.crescentsofbrisbane.org/00%20Files%20&%20Images/CCN783/FIQH%20Climate%20Change.pdf> accessed 28 November 2020.

Rogers Paul, 'Lost Cause: Consequences and Implications of the War on Terror' in Harmonie Toros and Ioannis Tellidis (eds), *Terrorism, Peace and Conflict Studies: Investigating the Crossroad* (Routledge 2014).

Roof Wade Clark, 'The Pluralist Ideal in American Religion: The Debates Continues' (2007) 612 *The Annals of the American Academy of Political and Social Science* 240.

Royal Decree A/137, 29 August 1971.

Royal Decree A/90, 1 March 1992.

Royal Decree, A/4, 9 July 1993.

Royal Degree A/88, 29 May 2001.

Royal Decree A/48, 15 January 2013.

Ruling on celebrating birthdays, in *Fatwas of Ibn Baz*, 4: 286–288 <http://www.alifta.net/Search/ResultDetails.aspx?languagename=en&lang=en&view=result&fatwaNum=&FatwaNumID=&ID=358&searchScope=14&SearchScopeLevels1=&SearchScopeLevels2=&highLight=1&SearchType=exact&SearchMoesar=false&bookID=&LeftVal=0&RightVal=0&simple=&SearchCriteria=allwords&PagePath=&siteSection=1&searchkeyword=112097114116105099105112097116105110103032105110032116104101032099101108101098114097116105111110115032111102032116104101032112101111112108101032111102032116104101032098111111107#firstKeyWordFound> accessed 08 May 2018.

Saeed Abdullah, 'Reflections on the Development of the Discourse of *Fiqh* for Minorities and Some of the Challenges It Faces' in Maurits S. Berger (ed), *Applying Shari'a in the West: Facts, Fears and the Future of Islamic Rules on the Family Relations in the West* (Leiden University Press 2013).

Sa'id Āmin, *Fayṣal al-'Azim: Nashātuhu – Sīratuhu – Akhlāquhu - Bay'ahu - Iṣlaḥātuhu - Khaṭbuhu* (Maṭābi' Najd al-Tijārīyah 1970).

Salafi Asghar Ali Imam Mahadi and Abul Hayat Ashraf, 'Expansion of the Mataaf," "Aiming High" and "Welcome Change,"' (2011) 5 (4) *The Simple Truth* 13.

Salman Yüksel, 'Diyanet İşleri Başkanlığının Kuruluşunun 81. Yıl Dönümü Üzerine' (2005) 171 *Diyanet Aylık Dergisi* 34.

Samuel Mark L., *John's Assignment: A Satire on the Human Condition* (Author House 2013).

Schacht Joseph, *An Introduction to Islamic Law* (The Clarendon Press 1964).

Serhan Randa B., 'Muslim Immigration to America' in Yvonne Y. Haddad and Jane I. Smith (eds), *The Oxford Handbook of American Islam* (Oxford University Press 2014).

Shah Zulfiqar Ali, *Iftā and Fatwa in the Muslim World and the West* (The International Institute of Islamic Thought 2014).

Shahi Afshin, *The Politics of Truth Management in Saudi Arabia* (Routledge 2013).

Shavit Uriya, 'The Wasaṭī and Salafī Approaches to the Religious Law of Muslim Minorities' (2012) 19 (4) *Islamic Law and Society* 416.

———, '"The Lesser of Two Evils": Islamic Law and the Emergence of a Broad Agreement on Muslim Participation in Western Political Systems' (2020) 8 *Contemporary Islam* 239.

Siddiqi Muzammil, 'Being Faithful Muslims and Loyal Americans' <http://fiqhcouncil.org/being-faithful-muslims-and-loyal-americans/> accessed 10 November 2020.

Skovgaard-Petersen Jakob, *Defining Islam for the Egyptian State: Muftis and Fatwas of the Dār al-Iftā* (Brill 1997).

———, 'A Typology of Fatwas' (2015) 55 (3–4) *Die Welt Des Islams* 278.

Steinberg Guido, 'The Wahhabiya, Saudi Arabia and the Salafist Movement' in Frank Peter and Rafael Ortega (eds), *Islamic Movements of Europe: Public Religion and Islamophobia in the Modern World* (I.B. Tauris & Co. Ltd 2014).

Steinberg Guido, 'The Wahhabiyya and Shi'ism, from 1744/5 to 2008' in Ofra Bengio and Meir Litvak (eds), *The Sunna and Shi'a in History: Division in the Muslim Middle East* (Palgrave Macmillan 2011).

Sunier Thijl and others, *Diyanet: The Turkish Directorate for Religious Affairs in a Changing Enviroment*, (VU University of Amsterdam and Utrecht University 2011).

Ṣaḥeeḥ International (tr), *The Qur'an English Meanings* (al-Muntada al-Islami 2010).

Şeker Mehmet, *Anadolu'da Bir Arada Yaşama: Turkiye Selçukluları ve Osmanlılar'a Müslim - Gayri-Müslim İlişkileri* (Diyanet İşleri Başkanlığı Yayınları 2012).

Taha Dina, 'Muslim Minorities in the West: Between Fiqh Minorities and Integration' (2013) 1 *Electronic Journal of Islamic and Middle Eastern Law* 1.

Taḥdīd al-Nasl, in *Majallat al-Buḥūth al-Islāmiyya*, 2: 525–527 <http://www.alifta.net/Fatawa/FatawaChapters.aspx?languagename=ar&View=Page&PageID=207&PageNo=1&BookID=1> accessed 02 November 2017.

Takim Liyakatali, 'Shi'ite Movements' in Gary Laderman and Luis León (eds) *Religion and American Cultures: An Encyclopedia of Traditions, Diversity*, vol I (ABC-CLIO 2003).

Tarhanlı İştar B., *Müslüman Toplum, "Laik" Devlet: Türkiye'de Diyanet İşleri Başkanlığı* (Afa Yayınları 1993).

Taş Kemaleddin, *Türk Halkının Gözüyle Diyanet* (İz Yayıncılık 2002).

Teitelbaum Joshua, *Holier Than Thou: Saudi Arabia's Islamic Opposition* (The Washington Institute for Near East Policy 2000).

The BSU decision No. 85 of 10 September 1981 <http://www.alifta.net/Search/ResultDetails.aspx?languagename=ar&lang=ar&view=result&fatwaNum=&FatwaNumID=&ID=1676&searchScope=2&SearchScopeLevels1=&SearchScopeLevels2=&highLight=1&SearchType=exact&SearchMoesar=false&bookID=&LeftVal=0&RightVal=0&simple=&SearchCriteria=allwords&PagePath=&siteSection=1&searchkeyword=217130216177216167216177032217135217138216166216169032217131216168216167216177032216167217132216185217132217133216167216161#firstKeyWordFound> accessed 10 December 2017.

The BSU decision No. 93 of 06 March 2011 <http://www.alifta.net/Search/ResultDetails.aspx?languagename=ar&lang=ar&view=result&fatwaNum=&FatwaNumID=&ID=13350&searchScope=2&SearchScopeLevels1=&SearchScopeLevels2=&highLight=1&SearchType=exact&SearchMoesar=false&bookID=&LeftVal=0&RightVal=0&simple=&SearchCriteria=allwords&PagePath=&siteSection=1&searchkeyword=216167217132217133216184216167217135216177216167216170032217129217138032216167217132216168217132216167216175032217136216170216173216176216177032217133217134032216167217132216167216177216170216168216167216183216161672161700322161672171322171292171312161772171382161690322171362161672171322161732161782161682171382161690322161672171322171332171342161732161772171292161 69#firstKeyWordFound> accessed 20 June 2017.

The BSU decision No. 138 of 02 February 1987 <"http://ar.islamway.net/article/17711/%D8%AD%D9%83%D9%85-%D9%85%D9%87%D8%B1%D8%A8-%D9%88%D9%85%D8%B1%D9%88%D8%AC-%D8%A7%D9%84%D9%85%D8%AE%D8%AF%D8%B1%D8%A7%D8%AA" http://ar.islamway.net/article/17711/%D8%AD%D9%83%D9%85-%D9%85%D9%87%D8%B1%D8%A8-%D9%88%D9%85%D8%B1%D9%88%D8%AC-%D8%A7%D9%84%D9%85%D8%AE%D8%AF%D8%B1%D8%A7%D8%AA> accessed 30 June 2016.

The BSU decision No. 148 of 25 August 1988, <http://www.alifta.net/Search/ResultDetails.aspx?languagename=ar&lang=ar&view=result&fatwaNum=&FatwaNumID=&ID=3505&searchScope=2&SearchScopeLevels1=&SearchScopeLevels2=&highLight=1&SearchType=exact&SearchMoesar=false&bookID=&LeftVal=0&RightVal=0&simple=&SearchCriteria=allwords&PagePath=&siteSection=1&searchkeyword=217130216177216167216177032217135217138216166216169032217131216168216167216177032216167217132216185217132217133216167216161032216177217130217130216130217133#firstKeyWordFound> accessed 31 December 2017.

The Constitution of Republic of Turkey, 1924 <http://www.anayasa.gen.tr/1924tek.htm> accessed 25 September 2016.

The Constitution of Republic of Turkey, 1982 <https://global.tbmm.gov.tr/docs/constitution_en.pdf> accessed 16 September 2016.

The Constitution of the United States, 'First Amendment' <https://constitution.congress.gov/constitution/amendment-1/> accessed 15 February 2021.

The interview of Okaz newspaper with His Eminence Shaykh 'Abdul- 'Aziz ibn Baz, in *Fatwas of Ibn Baz*, 5: 259–261 <http://www.alifta.net/Search/ResultDetails.aspx?languagename=en&lang=en&view=result&fatwaNum=&FatwaNumID=&ID=513&searchScope=14&SearchScopeLevels1=&SearchScopeLevels2=&highLight=1&SearchType=exact&SearchMoesar=false&bookID=&LeftVal=0&RightVal=0&simple=&SearchCriteria=allwords&PagePath=&siteSection=1&searchkeyword=115116117100121105110103032097098114111097100\lfirstKeyWordFound> accessed 29 November 2017.

The Islamic Center of Boston, 'Fiqh Council of North America: Regarding the Adoption of an Astronomically Calculated Islamic Calendar' <http://www.icbwayland.org/include/moonsightingdecisionweb.pdf> accessed 04 June 2017.

The Middle East Media Research Institute (MEMRI), 'Terror in America (23) Muslim Soldiers in the U.S. Armed Forces in Afghanistan: To Fight or Not to Fight?' <https://www.memri.org/reports/terror-america-23-muslim-soldiers-us-armed-forces-afghanistan-fight-or-not-fight> accessed 15 September 2017.

The Shura Council, 'Shaykh 'Abd Allāh b. Mu/example. Ibrāhīm Āl al-Shaykh' <https://www.shura.gov.sa/wps/wcm/connect/ShuraEn/internet/CV/Abdullah+Bin+Mohammed+Bin+Ibrahim+Al-Sheikh/> accessed 01 November 2017.

Turner Bryan S. and Berna Zengin Arslan, 'State and Turkish Secularism: The Case of the Diyanet' in Bryan S. Turner (ed), *The Religious and the Political: A Comparative Sociology of Religion* (Cambridge University Press 2013).

Turner Bryan S. and James T. Richardson, 'Islam and the Problems of Liberal Democracy' in Maurits S. Berger (ed), *Applying Shari'a in the West: Facts, Fears and the Future of Islamic Rules on the Family Relations in the West* (Leiden University Press 2013).

Türkisch Islamische Union de Anstalt für Religion e.V./ Diyanet İşleri Türk-İslam Birliği, 'Kuruluş ve Teşkilat Yapısı' <http://www.ditib.de/default1.php?id=5&sid=8&lang=en> accessed 08 March 2017.

Türkiye Cumhuriyeti Başkanlık Diyanet İşleri Başkanlığı, 'Basın Açıklaması' <http://www.diyanet.gov.tr/tr/icerik/basin-aciklamasi/6123> accessed 05 December 2016.

———, 'Başkan Görmez Kürtçe Ezan Konusunda TRT'ye Konuştu' <http://www.diyanet.gov.tr/tr/icerik/baskan-gormez-kurtce-ezan-konusunda-trt%E2%80%99ye-konustu-%E2%80%9Cezanin-herhangi-bir-dile-ve-lehceye-cevrilmesinin-ezan-olarak-kabul-edilmesi-asla-mumkun-degildir/6836> accessed 10 October 2016.

———, 'Din, Yenileşme ve Modern Hayat' <http://www3.diyanet.gov.tr/tr/icerik/din-yenilesme-ve-modern-hayat-prof-dr-ali-bardakoglu-diyanet-isleri-baskani-istanbul/6217> accessed 25 February 2017.

———, *Güncel Dini Meseleler Istişare Toplantısı-I* (Diyanet İşleri Başkanlığı Yayınları 2004).

———, 'Tanıtım' <http://www2.diyanet.gov.tr/DisIliskilerGenelMudurlugu/Sayfalar/Tanitim.aspx> accessed 08 March 2017.

Türkiye İstatistik Kurumu, 'İstatistiklerle Aile' 2012' <http://www.tuik.gov.tr/PreHaberBultenleri.do?id=13662> accessed 03 November 2016.

'Ulema Council Supports Actions of King Fahd' Foreign Broadcast Information Service-Near East & South Asia [*FBIS-NES*] 90–157, August 14, 1990 <http://0-infoweb.newsbank.com.lib.exeter.ac.uk/iw-search/we/HistArchive/?p_product=FBISX&p_theme=fbis&p_nbid=M62Q5CDTMTQ3MTE5NjY1My42NzkyNzg6MToxMjoxNDQ

uMTczLjYuOTQ&p_action=doc&p_queryname=11&toc=true&p_docref=v2:11C33B0D5F860D98@FBISX-11CAD8A2EEA95BB8@2448118-11CAD8ACEF88AF98@32-11CAD8AD30FFAF98> accessed 15 August 2016.

Ulutas Ufuk, 'Religion and Secularism in Turkey: The Dilemma of the Directorate of Religious Affairs' (2010) 46 (3) *Middle Eastern Studies* 389.

Umm al-Qurā (Mecca 4 April 1971) 2387.

United States Commission on International Religious Freedom (USCRIF), *United States Commission on International Religious Freedom: Annual Report 2010* (U. S. Commission on International Religious Freedom 2010).

Ünlücayaklı Emre, 'The Official Discourse in Religion in post-1980 Turkey: The Official Boundaries of the Religious Field, National Belonging and Heritage' (PhD thesis, McGill University 2012).

Vernier Chester G. and John B. Hurlbut, 'The. Historical Background of Alimony Law and Its Present Statutory Structure' (1939) 6 (2) *Law and Contemporary* 197.

Vickar Syed Ahamed (tr), *English Translation of the Message of the Qur'an* (Books of Signs Foundation 2007).

Vogel Frank, *Islamic Law and Legal System: Studies of Saudi Arabia* (Brill 2000).

———, 'The Complementarity of Ifta' and Qaḍā': Three Saudi Fatwas on Divorce' in Muhammad Khalid Masud, Brinkley Messick and David S. Powers (eds), *Islamic Legal Interpretation: Muftis and Their Fatwas* (Harvard University Press 1996).

Volokh Eugene, 'Religious Law (Especially Islamic Law) in American Courts' (2014) 66 (2) *Oklahoma Law Review* 431.

Wazāra al-Awqāf wa al-Shu'ūn al-Islāmiyya-Kuwait, *al-Mawsū'a al-Fiqhiyya vol XIX* (Wazāra al-Awqāf wa al-Shuūn al-Islāmiyya 1983).

Wehr Hans, Arabic-*English Dictionary* (Milton Cowan, 4th edn, Otto Harrassowitz 1994).

Wiktorowicz Quintan, 'Anatomy of the Salafi Movement' (2006) 29 *Studies in Conflict &Terrorism* 207.

Wilcke Christoph, *Looser Rein, Uncertain Gain: A Human Rights Assessment of Five Years of King Abdullah's Reforms in Saudi Arabia* (Human Rights Watch 2010).

Wuthnow Robert, *America and Challenges of Religious Diversity* (Princeton University Press 2007).

Yakar Emine Enise, 'The Concept of *Maṣlaḥa* in the Thought of Hayrettin Karaman' (MA thesis, University of Exeter 2014).

———, 'A Critical Comparison between the Presidency of Religious Affairs (Diyanet İşleri Başkanlığı) and the Office of Shaykh al-Islâm' (2019) 6 (11) *Kilis 7 Aralık Üniversitesi İlahiyat Fakültesi Dergisi* 421.

———., 'The Influential Role of the Practice of Iftā' in *Saudi Politico-Legal Arena* (2020) 16 (1) *Manchester Journal of Transnational Islamic Law & Practice* 35.

Yakar Emine Enise and Sümeyra Yakar, *The Transformational Process of the Presidency of Religious Affairs in Turkey* (King Faisal Center for Research and Islamic Studies 2017).

———, 'A Critical Comparison between the Classical Divorce Types of Ḥanbalī and Ja'arī Schools' (2020) 31 (2) *darulfunun ilahiyat* 275.

———, 'The Symbolic Relationship between '*Ulamā*' and '*Umarā*' in Contemporary Saudi Arabia' (2021) 13 (1) *Ortadoğu Etütleri* 23.

Yakar Sümeyra, 'The Usage of Custom in the Contemporary Legal System of Saudi Arabia: Divorce on Trial' (2009) 6 (11) *Kilis 7 Aralık Üniversitesi* 395.

———, 'The Consideration of *Bid'a* Concept according to Saudi and Iranian Scholars' (2020) 19 (2) *Mazahib Jurnal Pemikiran Hukum Islam* 219.

Yavuz M. Hakan, 'Tukey: Islam without Shari'a?' in Robert W. Hefner (ed), *Shari'a Politics: Islamic Law and Society in the Modern World* (Indiana University Press 2011).
Yılmaz Ihsan, 'Secular Law and the Emergence of Unofficial Turkish Islamic Law' (2002) 56 (1) *Middle East Journal* 113.
Yiğit Yaşar, İbrahim Ural and Mehmet Bulut, *Diyanet İşleri Başkanlığı: Din İşleri Yüksek Kurulu* (Türkiye Diyanet Vakfı Yayınları 2009).
———, *Religious Affairs Presidency: High Religious Affairs Committee* (Türkiye Diyanet Vakfı Yayınları 2010).
Zakariyah Luqman, *Legal Maxims in Islamic Criminal Law: Theory and Applications* (Brill 2015).
Zaman Muhammad Qasim, *Modern Islamic Thought in a Radical Age: Religious Authority and Internal Criticism* (Cambridge University Press 2012).
———, ''Ulama'' in Gerhard Bowering (ed), *Islamic Political Thought: An Introduction* (Princeton University Press 2015).
Zāda Abd al-Raḥmān ibn Muḥammad ibn Sulaymān al-Mad'ū Bashī, *Majmū' al-Anhir fī Sharḥ Multaqā al-Abḥar* vol IV (Dār al-Kutub al-'Ilmiyya 1997).
Zuhur Sherifa, *Middle East in Focus: Saudi Arabia* (ABC-CLIO 2011).
1 Annals of Congress 451 (June 8, 1789) <https://memory.loc.gov/cgi-bin/ampage> accessed 13 December 2020.
1 Annals of Congress 757 (August 15, 1789) <https://memory.loc.gov/cgi-bin/ampage> accessed 13 December 2020.
8 CFR ("Aliens and Nationality") <https://ecfr.federalregister.gov/current/title-8/chapter-I/subchapter-C> accessed 17 January 2021.
8 U.S.C. 1101 (a)(22) <https://www.govinfo.gov/content/pkg/USCODE-2018-title8/pdf/USCODE-2018-title8-chap12-subchapI-sec1101.pdf accessed 17 January 2021.
8 CFR 337. 1 ("Oath of Allegiance") <https://ecfr.federalregister.gov/current/title-8/chapter-I/subchapter-C/part-337> accessed 17 January 2021.

Websites

The Dār al-Iftā'

http://www.alifta.net
https://www.saudiembassy.net/basic-law-governance

The Diyanet

http://www.anayasa.gen.tr
http://www.diyanet.gov.tr
http://www.mevzuat.gov.tr
http://www.resmigazete.gov.tr
https://www.tbmm.gov.tr

The FCNA

http://fiqhcouncil.org

Index

Page numbers in **bold reference tables.